T0181548

Communications
in Computer and Information Science 1757

More information about this series at https://link.springer.com/bookseries/7899

Miguel Botto-Tobar ·
Marcelo Zambrano Vizuete ·
Sergio Montes León · Pablo Torres-Carrión ·
Benjamin Durakovic (Eds.)

Applied Technologies

4th International Conference, ICAT 2022
Quito, Ecuador, November 23–25, 2022
Revised Selected Papers, Part III

 Springer

Editors
Miguel Botto-Tobar 🆔
Eindhoven University of Technology
Eindhoven, The Netherlands

Sergio Montes León 🆔
Universidad Rey Juan Carlos
Madrid, Spain

Benjamin Durakovic 🆔
International University of Sarajevo
Sarajevo, Bosnia and Herzegovina

Marcelo Zambrano Vizuete 🆔
Universidad Técnica del Norte
Ibarra, Ecuador

Pablo Torres-Carrión 🆔
Universidad Técnica Particular de Loja
Loja, Ecuador

ISSN 1865-0929   ISSN 1865-0937 (electronic)
Communications in Computer and Information Science
ISBN 978-3-031-24977-8   ISBN 978-3-031-24978-5 (eBook)
https://doi.org/10.1007/978-3-031-24978-5

This Springer imprint is published by the registered company Springer Nature Switzerland AG
The registered company address is: Gewerbestrasse 11, 6330 Cham, Switzerland

Preface

The Universidad de las Fuerzas Armadas ESPE in its 100th anniversary organized the International XVII Congress on Science and Technology and co-hosted the 4th International Conference on Applied Technologies (ICAT) in the main campus in Quito, Ecuador during November 23–25, 2022 and was organized in collaboration with GDEON. The ICAT series aims to bring together top researchers and practitioners working in different domains in the field of computer science to exchange their expertise and to discuss the perspectives of development and collaboration. The content of this volume is related to the following subjects:

- Human Computing and Information Science
- IT Financial and Business Management

ICAT 2022 received 415 submissions written in English by 1245 authors coming from 12 different countries. All these papers were peer-reviewed by the ICAT 2022 Program Committee consisting of 185 high-quality researchers. To ensure a high-quality and thoughtful review process, we assigned each paper at least three reviewers. Based on the peer reviews, 114 full papers were accepted, resulting in an 27% acceptance rate, which was within our goal of less than 40%.

We would like to express our sincere gratitude to the invited speakers for their inspirational talks, to the authors for submitting their work to this conference, and to the reviewers for sharing their experience during the selection process.

November 2022

Miguel Botto-Tobar
Marcelo Zambrano Vizuete
Sergio Montes León
Pablo Torres-Carrión
Benjamin Durakovic

Organization

General Chair

Miguel Botto-Tobar   Eindhoven University of Technology,
The Netherlands

Program Committee Chairs

Miguel Botto-Tobar   Eindhoven University of Technology,
The Netherlands

Marcelo Zambrano Vizuete   Universidad Técnica del Norte, Ecuador

Sergio Montes León   Universidad Rey Juan Carlos, Spain

Pablo Torres-Carrión   Universidad Técnica Particular de Loja, Ecuador

Benjamin Durakovic   International University of Sarajevo,
Bosnia and Herzegovina

Organizing Chairs

Miguel Botto-Tobar   Eindhoven University of Technology,
The Netherlands

Marcelo Zambrano Vizuete   Universidad Técnica del Norte, Ecuador

Sergio Montes León   Universidad Rey Juan Carlos, Spain

Pablo Torres-Carrión   Universidad Técnica Particular de Loja, Ecuador

Benjamin Durakovic   International University of Sarajevo,
Bosnia and Herzegovina

Steering Committee

Miguel Botto-Tobar   Eindhoven University of Technology,
The Netherlands

Angela Díaz Cadena   Universitat de Valencia, Spain

Program Committee

Andrea Bonci   Marche Polytechnic University, Italy

Ahmed Lateef Khalaf   Al-Mamoun University College, Iraq

Aiko Yamashita   Oslo Metropolitan University, Norway

Alejandro Donaire   Queensland University of Technology, Australia

Alejandro Ramos Nolazco	Instituto Tecnólogico y de Estudios Superiores Monterrey, Mexico
Alex Cazañas	The University of Queensland, Australia
Alex Santamaria Philco	Universitat Politècnica de València, Spain
Alfonso Guijarro Rodriguez	University of Guayaquil, Ecuador
Allan Avendaño Sudario	Escuela Superior Politécnica del Litoral (ESPOL), Ecuador
Alexandra González Eras	Universidad Politécnica de Madrid, Spain
Ana Núñez Ávila	Universitat Politècnica de València, Spain
Ana Zambrano	Escuela Politécnica Nacional (EPN), Ecuador
Andres Carrera Rivera	University of Melbourne, Australia
Andres Cueva Costales	University of Melbourne, Australia
Andrés Robles Durazno	Edinburgh Napier University, UK
Andrés Vargas Gonzalez	Syracuse University, USA
Angel Cuenca Ortega	Universitat Politècnica de València, Spain
Ángela Díaz Cadena	Universitat de València, Spain
Angelo Trotta	University of Bologna, Italy
Antonio Gómez Exposito	University of Sevilla, Spain
Aras Can Onal	Tobb University Economics and Technology, Turkey
Arian Bahrami	University of Tehran, Iran
Benoît Macq	Université catholique de Louvain, Belgium
Benjamin Durakovic	International University of Sarajevo, Bosnia and Herzegovina
Bernhard Hitpass	Universidad Federico Santa María, Chile
Bin Lin	Università della Svizzera italiana (USI), Switzerland
Carlos Saavedra	Escuela Superior Politécnica del Litoral (ESPOL), Ecuador
Catriona Kennedy	University of Manchester, UK
César Ayabaca Sarria	Escuela Politécnica Nacional (EPN), Ecuador
Cesar Azurdia Meza	University of Chile, Chile
Christian León Paliz	Université de Neuchâtel, Switzerland
Chrysovalantou Ziogou	Chemical Process and Energy Resources Institute, Greece
Cristian Zambrano Vega	Universidad de Málaga, Spain, and Universidad Técnica Estatal de Quevedo, Ecuador
Cristiano Premebida	Loughborough University, ISR-UC, UK
Daniel Magües Martinez	Universidad Autónoma de Madrid, Spain
Danilo Jaramillo Hurtado	Universidad Politécnica de Madrid, Spain
Darío Piccirilli	Universidad Nacional de La Plata, Argentina
Darsana Josyula	Bowie State University, USA
David Benavides Cuevas	Universidad de Sevilla, Spain

David Blanes	Universitat Politècnica de València, Spain
David Ojeda	Universidad Técnica del Norte, Ecuador
David Rivera Espín	University of Melbourne, Australia
Denis Efimov	Inria, France
Diego Barragán Guerrero	Universidad Técnica Particular de Loja (UTPL), Ecuador
Diego Peluffo-Ordoñez	Yachay Tech, Ecuador
Dimitris Chrysostomou	Aalborg University, Denmark
Domingo Biel	Universitat Politècnica de Catalunya, Spain
Doris Macías Mendoza	Universitat Politècnica de València, Spain
Edison Espinoza	Universidad de las Fuerzas Armadas (ESPE), Ecuador
Edwin Rivas	Universidad Distrital de Colombia, Colombia
Ehsan Arabi	University of Michigan, USA
Emanuele Frontoni	Università Politecnica delle Marche, Italy
Emil Pricop	Petroleum-Gas University of Ploiesti, Romania
Erick Cuenca	Université catholique de Louvain, Belgium
Fabian Calero	University of Waterloo, Canada
Fan Yang	Tsinghua University, China
Fariza Nasaruddin	University of Malaya, Malaysia
Felipe Ebert	Universidade Federal de Pernambuco (UFPE), Brazil
Fernanda Molina Miranda	Universidad Politécnica de Madrid, Spain
Fernando Almeida	University of Campinas, Brazil
Fernando Flores Pulgar	Université de Lyon, France
Firas Raheem	University of Technology, Iraq
Francisco Calvente	Universitat Rovira i Virgili, Spain
Francisco Obando	Universidad del Cauca, Colombia
Franklin Parrales	University of Guayaquil, Ecuador
Freddy Flores Bahamonde	Universidad Técnica Federico Santa María, Chile
Gabriel Barros Gavilanes	INP Toulouse, France
Gabriel López Fonseca	Sheffield Hallam University, UK
Gema Rodriguez-Perez	LibreSoft, and Universidad Rey Juan Carlos, Spain
Ginger Saltos Bernal	Escuela Superior Politécnica del Litoral (ESPOL), Ecuador
Giovanni Pau	Kore University of Enna, Italy
Guilherme Avelino	Universidade Federal do Piauí (UFP), Brazil
Guilherme Pereira	Universidade Federal de Minas Gerais (UFMG), Brazil
Guillermo Pizarro Vásquez	Universidad Politécnica de Madrid, Spain
Gustavo Andrade Miranda	Universidad Politécnica de Madrid, Spain

Hernán Montes León	Universidad Rey Juan Carlos, Spain
Ibraheem Kasim	University of Baghdad, Iraq
Ilya Afanasyev	Innopolis University, Russia
Israel Pineda Arias	Chonbuk National University, South Korea
Jaime Meza	Université de Fribourg, Switzerland
Janneth Chicaiza Espinosa	Universidad Técnica Particular de Loja (UTPL), Ecuador
Javier Gonzalez-Huerta	Blekinge Institute of Technology, Sweden
Javier Monroy	University of Malaga, Spain
Javier Sebastian	University of Oviedo, Spain
Jawad K. Ali	University of Technology, Iraq
Jefferson Ribadeneira Ramírez	Escuela Superior Politécnica de Chimborazo, Ecuador
Jerwin Prabu	BRS, India
Jong Hyuk Park	Korea Institute of Science and Technology, South Korea
Jorge Charco Aguirre	Universitat Politècnica de València, Spain
Jorge Eterovic	Universidad Nacional de La Matanza, Argentina
Jorge Gómez Gómez	Universidad de Córdoba, Colombia
Juan Corrales	Institut Universitaire de France et SIGMA Clermont, France
Juan Romero Arguello	University of Manchester, UK
Julián Andrés Galindo	Université Grenoble Alpes, France
Julian Galindo	Inria, France
Julio Albuja Sánchez	James Cook University, Australia
Kelly Garces	Universidad de Los Andes, Colombia
Kester Quist-Aphetsi	Center for Research, Information, Technology and Advanced Computing, Ghana
Korkut Bekiroglu	SUNY Polytechnic Institute, USA
Kunde Yang	Northwestern Polytechnic University, China
Lina Ochoa	CWI, The Netherlands
Lohana Lema Moreira	Universidad de Especialidades Espíritu Santo (UEES), Ecuador
Lorena Guachi Guachi	Yachay Tech, Ecuador
Lorena Montoya Freire	Aalto University, Finland
Lorenzo Cevallos Torres	Universidad de Guayaquil, Ecuador
Luis Galárraga	Inria, France
Luis Martinez	Universitat Rovira i Virgili, Spain
Luis Urquiza-Aguiar	Escuela Politécnica Nacional (EPN), Ecuador
Maikel Leyva Vazquez	Universidad de Guayaquil, Ecuador
Manuel Sucunuta	Universidad Técnica Particular de Loja (UTPL), Ecuador
Marcela Ruiz	Utrecht University, The Netherlands

Marcelo Zambrano Vizuete	Universidad Técnica del Norte, Ecuador
María José Escalante Guevara	University of Michigan, USA
María Reátegui Rojas	University of Quebec, Canada
Mariela Tapia-Leon	University of Guayaquil, Ecuador
Marija Seder	University of Zagreb, Croatia
Marisa Daniela Panizzi	Universidad Tecnológica Nacional – Regional Buenos Aires, Argentina
Marius Giergiel	KRiM AGH, Poland
Markus Schuckert	Hong Kong Polytechnic University, Hong Kong, China
Matus Pleva	Technical University of Kosice, Slovakia
Mauricio Verano Merino	Technische Universiteit Eindhoven, The Netherlands
Mayken Espinoza-Andaluz	Escuela Superior Politécnica del Litoral (ESPOL), Ecuador
Miguel Botto-Tobar	Eindhoven University of Technology, The Netherlands
Miguel Fornell	Escuela Superior Politécnica del Litoral (ESPOL), Ecuador
Miguel Gonzalez Cagigal	Universidad de Sevilla, Spain
Miguel Murillo	Universidad Autónoma de Baja California, Mexico
Miguel Zuñiga Prieto	Universidad de Cuenca, Ecuador
Mohamed Kamel	Military Technical College, Egypt
Mohammad Al-Mashhadani	Al-Maarif University College, Iraq
Mohammad Amin	Illinois Institute of Technology, USA
Monica Baquerizo Anastacio	Universidad de Guayaquil, Ecuador
Muneeb Ul Hassan	Swinburne University of Technology, Australia
Nam Yang	Technische Universiteit Eindhoven, The Netherlands
Nathalie Mitton	Inria, France
Nayeth Solórzano Alcívar	Escuela Superior Politécnica del Litoral (ESPOL), Ecuador and Griffith University, Australia
Noor Zaman	King Faisal University, Saudi Arabia
Omar S. Gómez	Escuela Superior Politécnica del Chimborazo (ESPOCH), Ecuador
Óscar León Granizo	Universidad de Guayaquil, Ecuador
Oswaldo Lopez Santos	Universidad de Ibagué, Colombia
Pablo Lupera	Escuela Politécnica Nacional, Ecuador
Pablo Ordoñez Ordoñez	Universidad Politécnica de Madrid, Spain
Pablo Palacios	Universidad de Chile, Chile
Pablo Torres-Carrión	Universidad Técnica Particular de Loja (UTPL), Ecuador

Patricia Ludeña González	Universidad Técnica Particular de Loja (UTPL), Ecuador
Paulo Batista	CIDEHUS.UÉ-Interdisciplinary Center for History, Cultures, and Societies of the University of Évora, Portugal
Paulo Chiliguano	Queen Mary University of London, UK
Pedro Neto	University of Coimbra, Portugal
Praveen Damacharla	Purdue University Northwest, USA
Priscila Cedillo	Universidad de Cuenca, Ecuador
Radu-Emil Precup	Politehnica University of Timisoara, Romania
Ramin Yousefi	Islamic Azad University, Iran
René Guamán Quinche	Universidad de los Paises Vascos, Spain
Ricardo Martins	University of Coimbra, Portugal
Richard Ramirez Anormaliza	Universitat Politècnica de Catalunya, Spain
Richard Rivera	IMDEA Software Institute, Spain
Richard Stern	Carnegie Mellon University, USA
Rijo Jackson Tom	SRM University, India
Roberto Murphy	University of Colorado Denver, USA
Roberto Sabatini	RMIT University, Australia
Rodolfo Alfredo Bertone	Universidad Nacional de La Plata, Argentina
Rodrigo Barba	Universidad Técnica Particular de Loja (UTPL), Ecuador
Rodrigo Saraguro Bravo	Universitat Politècnica de València, Spain
Ronald Barriga Díaz	Universidad de Guayaquil, Ecuador
Ronnie Guerra	Pontificia Universidad Católica del Perú, Perú
Ruben Rumipamba-Zambrano	Universitat Politecnica de Catalanya, Spain
Saeed Rafee Nekoo	Universidad de Sevilla, Spain
Saleh Mobayen	University of Zanjan, Iran
Samiha Fadloun	Université de Montpellier, France
Sergio Montes León	Universidad de las Fuerzas Armadas (ESPE), Ecuador
Stefanos Gritzalis	University of the Aegean, Greece
Syed Manzoor Qasim	King Abdulaziz City for Science and Technology, Saudi Arabia
Tatiana Mayorga	Universidad de las Fuerzas Armadas (ESPE), Ecuador
Tenreiro Machado	Polytechnic of Porto, Portugal
Thomas Sjögren	Swedish Defence Research Agency (FOI), Sweden
Tiago Curi	Federal University of Santa Catarina, Brazil
Tony T. Luo	A*STAR, Singapore
Trung Duong	Queen's University Belfast, UK
Vanessa Jurado Vite	Universidad Politécnica Salesiana, Ecuador

Waldo Orellana	Universitat de València, Spain
Washington Velasquez Vargas	Universidad Politécnica de Madrid, Spain
Wayne Staats	Sandia National Labs, USA
Willian Zamora	Universidad Laíca Eloy Alfaro de Manabí, Ecuador
Yessenia Cabrera Maldonado	University of Cuenca, Ecuador
Yerferson Torres Berru	Universidad de Salamanca, Spain and Instituto Tecnológico Loja, Ecuador
Zhanyu Ma	Beijing University of Posts and Telecommunications, China

Organizing Institutions

Sponsoring Institutions

Collaborators

Contents – Part III

Human Computing and Information Science

"A Single Mother's Perspective on Her 5-Year-Old Child's Self-esteem": A Case Study in Early Childhood Education

Miluska Minaya-Llerena and Ivan Iraola-Real[✉] [iD]

Universidad de Ciencias y Humanidades, Lima 15314, Perú
miluskaminaya16@gmail.com, ivanir701@hotmail.com

Abstract. Self-esteem at preschool age can be influenced by various aspects, with separation from parents being a determining factor that can affect the infant's development socially, affectively and at school. Therefore, the objective of this study is to analyze the perspective of a single mother on the self-esteem of her five-year-old preschool child in a school in the district of Los Olivos (Lima-Peru). Likewise, the methodology corresponds to the qualitative approach of descriptive type and case study. A semi-structured interview of nine questions was applied to two single mothers. At the conclusion, the results showed that in the social perspective, the child is accessible and relates to older children. In addition, in the affective perspective the child showed feelings of sadness and fear. In addition, in the scholastic perspective the child had difficulties in his studies maintaining low grades.

Keywords: Self-esteem · Childcare · Single mother

1 Introduction

Numerous scientific findings in the field of psychology define self-esteem, for example, in the past self-esteem was defined in a positive and negative way. So, high self-esteem where the subject had satisfaction and success in life. In addition, low self-esteem where there were accumulated consequences related to failure, depression and social problems (Van der Cruijsen and Boyer 2021). Today that definition is still valid, but in summary, self-esteem refers to the attitude that a person has about his or her own life (Kärchner et al. 2021). For example, the case of single mothers is a problem that is related to generating low self-esteem, especially those who are young and are internationally known as teenage mothers; according to a report by the Economic Commission for Latin America and the Caribbean (ECLAC) almost 30% of them did not reach the age of 20 to become mothers (ECLAC 2014). Faced with this problem, the Peruvian context has not been left behind, since according to the National Institute of Statistics and Informatics (INEI 2019), the 2017 census found 410,834 single mothers.

1.1 Influence of Being a Single Mother

In this way, these women are affected by the imminent changes of marital separation, where they must assume a dual role, facing criticism from society and depriving themselves of continuing their studies (Hanson 2020; Harkness et al. 2020). Therefore, the self-esteem of single mothers will begin to have an impact on their lives and subsequently on that of their children, since, the attitudes of parents will influence the personality of their children. That is, if the child's proxies maintain a healthy self-esteem, their children will build an adequate social welfare and therefore a good performance at school (Şahan and Kahtali 2021; Kinga et al. 2014; Lewis et al. 2020). Well, in the educational field there is a relationship between self-esteem and school performance, where students who do not have adequate self-esteem tend to manifest poor educational performance (Ugwuanyi et al. 2020).

1.2 About the Types of Self-esteem

In this way, it has been considered to analyze three characteristics, which will be called social, affective and scholastic categories (Haeussler and Milicic 2014). First, social self-esteem is related to feeling rejected or accepted within a certain social group, having the feeling of belonging and the intrapersonal strength of feeling capable of facing any type of conflict, solving problems that are generated in their context, taking personal initiatives and relating to other people (Seon 2021; Grady 2020; Saklz et al. 2021). In the opposite of this category, having low self-esteem will prevent achieving social integration, i.e., it will prevent relating to other people, creating barriers due to fear and insecurity, losing confidence in others (Nichols et al. 2021). Children, on the other hand, capture the emotions of their parents and reflect it in their social behavior; when they feel that something is wrong in their context, they choose to isolate themselves, keep quiet and repress their guilt, damaging their personality, as well as their competencies and performance at school (Lunkenheimer et al. 2020).

On the other hand, the affective category is usually the most difficult to face in a family separation, seeing how love turns to hate affects not only the mother but also the children, since households that go through this situation change their behaviors, affection and the security of feeling protected (Bozan et al. 2021). As a consequence, children in schools are fearful to participate in activities, feel insecure, lower their grades and are often taken to psychology to be treated for physical and verbal aggressions they receive at home (Davies and Berger 2019).

Finally, the school category is related to the ability to successfully face the academic stage, however, when a child's self-esteem is not good, the interest in achieving participation in school begins to decrease, children do not comply with homework, do not attend, do not obey, do not want to study and by not having the reinforcement at home the process of their learning does not develop normally (Unamba et al. 2020; Kgomotlokoa 2020). Therefore, self-esteem is constituted as an important factor for the development of the infant's personality and educational performance. The school is well aware of the importance of parental involvement; therefore, it is currently implementing workshops, lectures, schools for parents and family counseling in order to strengthen the self-esteem of parents and their children, ensuring the social and educational welfare of students (Proctor et al. 2020).

1.3 Research Objectives

Thus, the following general objective has been set to analyze the perspective that a single mother has on the self-esteem of her five-year-old preschool child in a school in the district of Los Olivos (Lima-Peru). Specifically, to identify the perspective of a single mother on the social self-esteem, affective self-esteem and academic self-esteem.

2 Methodology

The research approach corresponds to the qualitative descriptive approach, through which a direct analysis is made of the object of study (Cecilia and Lévano 2007). Likewise, a case study is proposed that will allow the understanding of the phenomenon within its real context (Arzaluz 2005).

2.1 Participants

The sample is constituted by two single mothers belonging to an educational institution of initial level in the district of Los Olivos, Lima-Peru. The selection process was given through a convenience sampling procedure (Otzen and Manterola 2017) with the help of one of the teachers, who has identified two single mothers in the classroom.

2.2 Instruments

The research technique to be used corresponds to the semi-structured interview (Burgos et al. 2019), thus the instrument to be applied is an interview script (Cecilia and Lévano 2007), which will include the elaboration of nine open questions which were drafted based on the specific objectives. For example, in specific objective one, the following question was considered: How has the social relationship of your youngest child been with other people in the same environment? In the second specific objective, the following question was considered: How would you describe the personality of your youngest child? Finally, in the third specific objective, the following question was considered: Do you think that being a single mother would affect the school performance of your youngest child? In this way, we will proceed with the discussion and results analysis.

3 Discussion Analysis and Results

For the presentation of the discussion and results analysis, the following order will be followed: First, identify a single mother's perspective on social self-esteem. Second, to analyze a single mother's perspective on affective self-esteem. Third, to describe a single mother's perspective on school self-esteem, these data were processed and coded through the triangulation matrix.

3.1 Social Self-esteem Perspective

Social self-esteem is closely linked to the interaction with the group, it refers to how people feel accepted or not by others; if this happens, the feeling of belonging could be reinforced and at the same time the self-strength that generates the ability to face difficulties by personal initiative (Saklz et al. 2021). Considering this, the mothers interviewed made reference to the fact that the social self-esteem of their children implies a process of adaptation by relating with other children, participating in family meetings and interacting with their classmates and teachers; as can be evidenced in the emergent categories:

A. He is socially adaptable, a bit shy but approachable

Social development in early childhood can be affected in different ways, one of which is the absence of the father of the family, which has resulted in children having difficulty socializing with others who are not from their environment, opting for a shy and unapproachable posture (Grady 2020). Thus, one of the mothers interviewed mentioned the following testimony.

> Well, socially he adapts, he is a little shy but accessible. As I can explain, my son gets along very well with those who live in my house and we don't have access to other family members other than my dad who is his grandfather and my brother who is his uncle (...) [MS-1] [MS-1].

One of the characteristics of social self-esteem is the interaction with other people such as family members (Saklz et al. 2021). However, the lack of self-esteem in infants is given by the lack of paternal attachment in some male family member (Seon 2021). As pointed out by the single mother in her comment by stating that the child has more access to his grandfather and uncle with whom he lives at home; which contributes to the development of social self-esteem, in addition to socialization with the children, as analyzed in the following emerging category.

B. Interacts with other children older than him/her

Similarly, identifying with whom the child relates most could help to understand his or her social development, since group participation can influence his or her personality (Kärchner et al. 2021). In this way, one of the mothers interviewed noted in her commentary.

> (...) I have not had any problem with my child, he is a normal child and interacts with other children older than him (...) with older children who are his little cousins, he is a sociable and participative child, in that area I have not had any problem [MS-2].

Similar to the previous category the child adapts and relates to older people who are his cousins, which demonstrates an interest in engaging in social relationships with positive attitudes (Seon 2021), as analyzed in the following emerging category.

III.   **He is friendly, cheerful and playful**

Now, the attitudes of being friendly, cheerful and playful are important characteristics of socialization, which will allow the child to have a better performance that will lead to better relationships (Grady 2020). As can be seen in the following commentary.

He is friendly and has a lot of affinity with certain companions and if he is cheerful, playful. He has always been like that with the children, at the beginning when he first meets new children he approaches them little by little, because he is a little shy at the beginning, but after he gets to know them he enters the game and he is very much included in the group [MS-1].

On the other hand, it is known that children with low self-esteem are afraid of being hurt or feeling rejected, therefore, they opt for a distant posture (Nichols et al. 2021). Which is not evident in this child, since at the beginning, he shows shyness, but once he is included in the group he is completely participative, as analyzed in the following emergent category.

IV.   **Is participative when there are meetings at home**

The social development of every child begins first at home where he/she can interact with other members of his/her family (Seon 2021), so that when there is a good relationship at home, the child's behavior will be positive, as one of the mothers interviewed pointed out.

He is a child, as I said, he participates when there are meetings at home and with his family, he is a child who shares with his cousins and uncles, he is not shy or shy, on the contrary, he is a child who participates, dances, plays and talks. As I said he, shares with his older cousins and his uncles and aunts at home (...) [MS-2].

However, children who do not enjoy a good family relationship face an emotional conflict that will result in distancing, poor participation and learning problems (Lunkenheimer et al. 2020). This makes social development difficult at certain times, as evidenced in the following emerging category.

E.   **Gets along well with those with whom he/she has affinity**

Here, the meaning of affinity is to coincide with other people who share the same interests; this behavior can often generate rejection (Nichols et al. 2021), as pointed out by one of the mothers interviewed when commenting that her son does not approach certain groups.

(...) I think that like every child, he has his own little group, but he hangs out more with certain children and has a lot of affinity; as I said, there are other children that he does not get very close to [MS-1].

Interviewer: And, with those children do you establish communication?

(...) he does not talk to them, for the same reason, as I said, he is a little shy and when they start talking to him or when they talk to him and he answers them and feels that affinity, he groups with them. Nevertheless, I see those who suddenly do not pay attention to him, he does not insist, but he gets along well with those with whom he has affinity [MS-1].

The behavior presented by the child is part of the distrust and rejection little communication is evident, which indicates that the child initially doubts whether he/she will be included, as he/she will seek a sense of belonging with other people he/she feels comfortable with (Saklz et al. 2021). Finally, the last emerging category of social self-esteem will be reflected upon.

F.   **Interacts with peers and teacher**

Social self-esteem at school plays a fundamental role, since children learn to coexist and relate to other children (Lapshova et al. 2021). In this regard, one of the mothers made the following comment.

In the classroom now that it is virtual, he knows that he has to get up and be in his class and participate with his classmates; he greets, turns on his microphone and camera, greets everyone and interacts with his classmates and his teacher. When they ask him questions, he answers in that part, well I do not have a problem, of course, I would like it to be in that face-to-face form so that he has contact with the children and can play, but unfortunately because of the pandemic, we are all isolated [MS-2].

Regarding the relationship that the child has with his teacher and other classmates, it can be seen that he maintains a participatory social rhythm (Grady 2020). However, as these are virtual classes, social interactions are completely different, since the mother prefers that the interaction be face-to-face.

3.2 Affective Self-esteem Perspective

Affective self-esteem due to its intrapersonal nature is considered a difficult situation to face (Bozan et al. 2021), as it is closely linked to feelings, love and emotions both personal and social. With this in mind, the mothers interviewed made reference to the following emerging categories.

A.   **He was somewhat apprehensive and introverted**

Apprehensive and introverted behavior is associated with fear and difficulty in expressing feelings, which, being an internal problem is often not easy to control and is one of the causes of low self-esteem (Bozan et al. 2021). In this way, the mothers interviewed stated the following.

At the beginning, he was shocked, he was a little nervous, his behavior changed a little, he was a little apprehensive and introverted, but he was able to cope with it, I think like every child he knew how to mature his feelings and understand the situation [MS-1].

In his self-esteem I think it might have affected him a little bit, I feel that I am working a lot with him on that part and with my other little one as well [MS-2].

Now, recognizing that affective self-esteem is the most sensitive, it can be understood that many children do not overcome the separation from their parents easily and carry sadness and fear for many years (Nichols et al. 2021), as evidenced in the following emerging category.

B. I had feelings of sadness and fear

Affective self-esteem in the home is strengthened through living together; children develop feelings of love, affection and security when their parents stay together. (Page 2021). However, when this relationship is broken, it generates negative emotions in the personality, as one of the mothers interviewed pointed out in the following commentary.

I noticed that he did have feelings of sadness and fear; sadness for the situation and fear of being alone, because he felt that he was missing a person in his family, such as his father, mother and son, and he was afraid of being alone [MS-1].

In this way, the child's greatest concern is the fear of being alone; therefore, they repress their feelings reflecting insecurity in affective self-esteem (Grimaldo and Merino 2020) as evidenced in the following emerging category.

III. He does not know how to show his emotions

Repressing emotions can be understood as a characteristic of resentment, where people, after being hurt by those they love, choose not to express themselves affectively again (Puertas et al. 2020), even hiding their emotions, as pointed out by one of the mothers interviewed.

(…) he does not know how to show his emotions very well, he is a little confused about what he feels and what emotion he feels now, he gets a little confused [MS-1].

Therefore, the mother must act immediately on her child's affective self-esteem, must fill the empty spaces with positive feelings of love and affection and give her the necessary time so that she can understand the situation of separation from her parents (Bozan et al. 2021), as evidenced in the following emerging category.

IV. I focus on giving you more time

Single mothers go through various realities. In some of the cases, many of them do not know how to overcome the pain and let their personal problems influence their children's self-esteem (Kinga et al. 2014). Therefore, one of the mothers interviewed advises the following comment.

I think that like every mother, suddenly at some point we think we are not doing things right, but if you separate the other part of the relationship, you not only focus on your problem but also on your children, that's why I give them affection and love to my children. I do not have to worry about my personal problems, I have to worry more about my children and I focus on giving them more time, I always work hard to give them a good example [MS-2].

This positive attitude is important to value, since love towards children is more important, therefore, they deserve to be listened to, to have time alone and to be reciprocated, in this way self-esteem and behavior can be strengthened (Page 2021), as evidenced in the following emergent category.

E. We have strengthened their behavior

With respect to this category, it should be remembered that the self-esteem shown by the mother will have an impact on her youngest child (Sahan and Kahtali 2021), therefore, she should know how to regulate her intrapersonal attitudes and emotions in order to teach by example, as one of the mothers interviewed stated in the following testimony.

He is not a spoiled or ill-mannered child; on the contrary, he is a child with values that I have been teaching him and good values that he sees in his older brother [MS-2].

In this way, the mother's effort to strengthen her child's self-esteem and behavior can be noted, which demonstrates good commitment as a guardian (Proctor et al. 2020). Next, it will be analyzed in the following emerging category.

F. His strength is being sociable, cheerful, friendly and curious

On the other hand, if the mother educates by example and commitment she will be able to strengthen the affective self-esteem of her children, since feelings and emotions are developed in an intrapersonal way and it requires a lot of love, affection, attention and education to make the infant cheerful, friendly, affectionate, curious and playful (Mata et al. 2018), as shown by both mothers interviewed in the following comments.

(...) His strength is to be sociable and cheerful; he is friendly and curious, because that is why he learns a lot [MS-1].

He is a playful child, he is very affectionate I would say, he likes to talk, he is also very affectionate as I repeat, he likes to do research like YouTube, Google. In his personality he is very affectionate, shows what he feels, and says very nice words as if I love you. [MS-2].

According to the above, the child, despite the difficulties, has managed to show himself as an affectively sociable person, his attitudes are the product of the effort of a mother who only wants her child to show affection in his self-esteem (Morrison 2020), thus achieving that the child can express words of love, as evidenced in the last emerging category.

A.   He is a very demonstrative child and says words like I love you

With respect to the child's feelings, it has been possible to get him to overcome his weaknesses affectively, since it is not easy to grow up without the presence of a father figure (Hanson 2020), however, the mother has managed to get her son to be a demonstrative person, as one of the mothers points out in the following commentary.

(...) in the case of feelings he is a very demonstrative child he says words like I love you, I love you in his feelings now that he is a little boy he says what he feels he is a happy child [MS-2].

Thus, the child's self-esteem does not manifest any problems demonstrating that in this category the mother has succeeded in making her child a person with feelings (Palmer 2018). Which leads us to reflect on the following general category.

3.3   School Self-esteem Perspective

Thus, School self-esteem is related to the educational performance that the child manifests during the school stage (Ugwuanyi et al. 2020). Taking this into account, the mothers interviewed referred to the following emerging categories.

A.   **It was an emotional shock**

The relationship between school performance and low self-esteem is a topic of study that continues to be investigated to this day, where it is pointed out that if the child shows poor grades and disinterest in school, it is a sign that something is happening with his or her self-esteem (Lewis et al. 2020). In this way, the mothers interviewed commented on their children's experience at school.

At the beginning he was shocked and I could understand him, I talked a lot with the teacher and he understood the situation, the conversation we have had with him has helped him and he has understood what we are going through and how things are going to be done. So at the time it was an emotional shock, of course his grades also went down, but with time, with conversations and with the help of his classmates and family he has been coping and he is already improving [MS-1].

At the beginning, he was a little shocked, but little by little, you start talking and conversing with him and with that he has been improving [MS-2].

Consequently, the separation of the parents affected the child who at first began to have no interest in studies (Gilchrist-Petty 2018), but with the help of his mother, classmates, teacher and family members through communication he managed to improve in his studies, as evidenced in the following emerging category.

B. Currently a child who has very good grades

One of the characteristics of low self-esteem in school is the absence of interest, poor grades and even undesired behaviors that end up keeping the child away from school (Kgomotlokoa 2020). In this case, they were able to overcome their weaknesses, as pointed out by one of the mothers in the following commentary.

At present, he is a child whose grades are really good, at the beginning, he was shocked, but after that everything went smoothly, as I said, he is a child who likes to learn, sometimes he finishes his classes earlier and wants to do more things, but I tell him to wait because sometimes he gets desperate to do [MS-2].

Now, it can be noted that the mother's participation through communication has managed to strengthen her child's school self-esteem (Neeleman 2019), which leads to the assumption that parental involvement in the school stage helps to improve their school performance, as evidenced by the following emerging category.

III. Depends a lot on parents and adults

Each child in his or her educational stage will have different characteristics, the school should know how to identify through teachers how students learn and at the same time what personal problems they present, thus being able to better guide them (Proctor et al. 2020). Therefore, it can be said that it will depend on adults and parents to help children during school, as pointed out by one of the interviewed mothers.

(...) but I think that all of this also depends on the parents, on how much we talk to them, that the child is well received, and also how the situation is, and well, it depends a lot on us as parents and adults. So that they also have peace of mind and can cope with the situation and it does not affect their studies and their emotions [MS-1].

Therefore, parents as well as teachers must be willing to contribute to the welfare of children (Rahill 2018), because for the family the child must be their main priority, as evidenced in the last emerging category.

IV. For me, my children are my priority

By showing, that children are a top priority in the family is demonstrating how valuable they are and that will help them to trust themselves so that they can overcome any obstacles they may have in school (Drake 2019). In this way, one of the mothers makes an emotional reflection, as evidenced by the commentary.

I think that, if you don't separate things, if you don't put your children first you wouldn't be a mother, for me, my children are my priority my center my everything

I try to work a lot on their self-esteem and give them the best (...). I do not know if I am doing my job well or badly as a mother, but I try to give everything of myself and I always give the best to them to my children [MS-2].

Finally, the priority of putting children first is a great step in demonstrating that despite the problems there are courageous mothers who never give up and who will do everything possible to ensure a healthy self-esteem for their children.

4 Conclusions and Future Works

Thus, it is concluded that the perspective that single mothers have on the social, affective and scholastic self-esteem of their children is adequate, since in spite of the inconveniences that a marital separation can cause, the children have shown a good attitude and have been able to overcome the obstacles, which demonstrates a good self-esteem. Likewise, it is specifically concluded that, within the first category of social self-esteem, the child adapts socially, is accessible, relates with children older than him, shows friendly behavior, is cheerful, playful, and participatory, has affinity with other children and interacts with his classmates and teacher. Additionally, in the second category of affective self-esteem it is concluded that at the beginning the child was apprehensive and introverted, had feelings of sadness and fear, which led the mother to give him more attention, strengthening his behavior, thus the child was sociable, cheerful, friendly, curious and demonstrative in his affective feelings. Then, in the third school category, it is concluded that the separation of his parents caused an emotional shock in his studies. However, those later thanks to his mother he was able to overcome it by having good grades, so that the influence of parents and adults at school play a satisfactory role, because from the mother's perspective her child is her main priority.

Finally, this study leaves open the possibility that other researchers can go deeper into the subject, expanding the sample and considering related problems such as the case of student mothers, professional single mothers, dependent mothers, adoptive mothers, and adolescent single mothers, being social phenomena that are related to self-esteem and emotions. Likewise, this study leaves a small theoretical framework on self-esteem, which can be updated from new categories such as: physical, ethical, cognitive and psychological through updated national and international sources.

Acknowledgment. I want to thank God for allowing me to achieve so many things in my life. I also thank my parents for their unconditional support and my son for always being with me in every moment of my life.

References

Arzaluz, S.: La utilización del estudio de caso en el análisis local. Región y Sociedad **17**(32), 108–142 (2005)

Bozan, K., Evgin, D., Gördeles, N.: Relatıonship bullying in adolescent period with family functionalities and child behaviors. Psychol. Sch. **58**(8), 1451–1473 (2021)

Burgos, N., Amaiquema, F., Beltrán, G.: Métodos y técnicas en la investigación cualitativa. Algunas precisiones necesarias. Conrado **15**(70), 455–459 (2019)

Cecilia, A., Lévano, S.: Investigación cualitativa: diseños, evaluación del rigor metodológico y retos **13**(13), 71–78 (2007)

Comisión Económica para América Latina y el Caribe: Casi 30 % de las jóvenes latinoamericanas ha sido madre adolescente (2014). https://www.cepal.org/es/comunicados/casi-30-de-las-jovenes-latinoamericanas-ha-sido-madre-adolescente. Accessed 21 Nov 2021

Davies, S., Berger, E.: Teachers' experiences in responding to students' exposure to domestic violence. Aust. J. Teach. Educ. **44**(11), 96–109 (2019)

Drake, G., et al.: Is there a place for children as emotional beings in child protection policy and practice? Int. J. Emotional Educ. **11**(1), 115–134 (2019)

Grady, J.: Parents' reactions to toddlers' emotions: relations with toddler shyness and gender. Early Child Dev. Care **190**(12), 1855–1862 (2020)

Gilchrist-Petty, E.: Taking interest in students' disinterest: best practices for mitigating amotivation in the basic course. J. Commun. Pedagogy **1**(1), 101–108 (2018)

Hanson, A.: Career killer survival kit: centering single mom perspectives in composition and rhetoric. Compos. Stud. **48**(1), 34–52 (2020)

Haeussler, I., Milicic, N.: Confiar en uno mismo: programa de desarrollo de la autoestima. Santiago de Chile: Catalonia (2014)

Harkness, S., Gregg, P., Fernández, M.: The rise in single-mother families and children's cognitive development: evidence from three British birth cohorts. Child Dev. **91**(5), 1762–1785 (2020)

Instituto Nacional de Estadística e Informática: Características de los hogares de madres y padres solos con hijos/as menores de 18 años de edad (2019). www.inei.gob.pe2021/08/14

Kärchner, H., Schöne, C., Schwinger, M.: Beyond level of self-esteem: exploring the interplay of level, stability, and contingency of self-esteem, mediating factors, and academic achievement. Soc. Psychol. Educ. **24**(2), 319–341 (2021). https://doi.org/10.1007/s11218-021-09610-5

Kgomotlokoa, L.: The influence of educational provision on teacher performance and learner outcomes among Limpopo primary schools. S. Afr. J. Educ. **40**(4), 1–10 (2020)

Kinga, T., Mwaura, J., Muriithi, W.: Comparative study of levels of self esteem among students of single and dual parent families. The Case of Students in Selected Secondary Schools in Nakuru Municipality, Kenya. Res. Hum. Soc. Sci. **4**(1), 55–58 (2014)

Lapshova, A., Bystrova, N., Smirnova, Z., Bulaeva, M.: Organization of virtual interaction in the context of the coronavirus pandemic Organización de la interacción virtual en el contexto de la pandemia de coronavirus. Propósitos y Representaciones **9**(1), 1–8 (2021)

Lewis, E., Hooley, C., Feely, M., Lanier, P., Korff, S., Kohl, P.: Engaging child welfare-involved families in evidence-based interventions to address child disruptive behavior disorders. J. Emot. Behav. Disord. **28**(1), 43–51 (2020)

Lunkenheimer, E., Hamby, C., Lobo, F., Cole, P., Olson, S.: The role of dynamic, dyadic parent-child processes in parental socialization of emotion. Dev. Psychol. **56**(3), 566–577 (2020)

Mata, L., Pedro, I., Peixoto, F.: Parental support, student motivational orientation and achievement: the impact of emotions. Int. J. Emotional Educ. **10**(2), 77–92 (2018)

Morrison, G.: The affectivity of good teaching: towards the transformative practice of possessing a 'thinking heart.' Int. Stud. Cathol. Educ. **12**(1), 35–50 (2020)

Muchotrigo, M., Merino, C.: Efectos de un Programa de Intervención sobre las habilidades emocionales en niños preescolares. Revista Española de Orientación y Psicopedagogía **31**(1), 62–80 (2020)

Neeleman, A.: The scope of school autonomy in practice: an empirically based classification of school interventions. J. Educ. Change **20**(1), 31–55 (2019)

Nichols, L., Mueller, S., Donisthorpe, K.: School refusal in a multi-tiered system of supports model: cognitive-behavioral and mindfulness interventions. J. Sch. Couns. **19**(2), 1–30 (2021)

Otzen, T., Manterola, C.: Técnicas de Muestreo sobre una Población a Estudio. Int. J. Morphol. **35**(1), 227–232 (2017)

Page, D.: Family engagement in alternative provision. Br. Edu. Res. J. **47**(1), 65–84 (2021)

Golomski, C.: Empathy. Acad. Psychiatry **41**(6), 760 (2017). https://doi.org/10.1007/s40596-017-0695-3

Puertas, P., Zurita, F., Chacóns, R., Castro, M., Ramírezo, I., González, G.L.: inteligencia emocional en el ámbito educativo: un meta-análisis. Anales de Psicología / Annals of Psychology **36**(1), 84–91 (2020)

Proctor, H., Roch, A., Breidenstein, G., Forsey, M.: Parents, schools and the twenty-first-century state: comparative perspectives. Comp. Educ. **56**(3), 317–330 (2020)

Rahill, S.: Parent and teacher satisfaction with school-based psychological reports. Psychol. Sch. **55**(6), 693–706 (2018)

Şahan, B., Kahtali, D.: The role of parental attitudes, irrational beliefs, need for social approval and self-esteem in speech anxiet. Eur. J. Altern. Educ. Stud. **6**(1), 96–115 (2021)

Saklz, H., Mert, A., Sarlçam, H.: Self-esteem and perceived social competence protect adolescent students against ostracism and loneliness. J. Psychol. Counsellors Sch. **31**(1), 94–109 (2021)

Seon, Y.: Self-esteem as a mediator of parental attachment security and social anxiety. Psychol. Sch. **58**(8), 1545–1556 (2021)

Unamba, E., Okwara, C., Georgeline, I.: Comparative study of levels of academic self esteem and academic achievement in mathematics among pupils of two and single parent families. Malikussaleh J. Math. Learn. (MJML) **3**(2), 2620–6323 (2020)

Kinga, T., Mwaura, J., Muriithi, W.: Comparative study of levels of self esteem among students of single and dual parent families. The Case of Students in Selected Secondary Schools in Nakuru Municipality, Kenya. Res. Hum. Soc. Sci. **4**(1), 55–58 (2014)

Ugwuanyi, C., Okeke, C., Asomugha, C.: Prediction of learners' mathematics performance by their emotional intelligence, self-esteem and self-efficacy. Cypriot J. Educ. Sci. **15**(3), 492–501 (2020)

Van der Cruijsen, R., y Boyer, B.: Explicit and implicit self-esteem in youth with autism spectrum disorders. Autism Int. J. Res. Pract. **25**(2), 349–360 (2021)

Didactic Strategies in the Face of Disruptive Behavior at the School Stage

Mirella Cabanillas-Ricaldi, Ariana Diaz-Medina, Rosa Villa-Rojas, and Ivan Iraola-Real(✉) 🄳

Universidad de Ciencias y Humanidades, Lima 15314, Perú
mirella.c1998@gmail.com, ivanir701@hotmail.com

Abstract. The research study consists of proposing didactic strategies to confront the different disruptive behaviors that are generated during the school stage in fourth grade elementary students and for this, we established two higher priority studies. Using a mixed methodology, the study was organized into: In study 1, the quantitative method with the Likert Scale was applied to 28 students, 14 of them were female (50%) and 14 males (50%). The age range was between 9 and 10 years old (Mean = 9.36), in order to measure the level of behavior of each one of them during the classes, being men with high percentages of indiscipline with respect to women. In study 2, the qualitative method was applied in which a female teacher participated. Finally, the results showed the teacher used the strategy of dialogue, tutorial support and social staff area in order to reduce the disruptive behavior of each one of the students .

Keywords: Educational strategies · Disruptive behavior · Elementary education

1 Introduction

Today, the various types of behaviors that primary school students manifest are increasingly relevant and complex, generating uncontrollable situations that the teacher has to face; being Disruptive behavior the main cause of educational conflicts that generate disorder, rebellion, defiant attitude and aggressiveness [1] which, on average, are more common in boys than girls. In the studies conducted by Olweus (1993), the presence of aggressive behaviors in the classroom is estimated, in general, at 15%. However, this percentage varies between studies by Craig and others (2009) in Northern European countries and Baltic countries, where discrepancies are found ranging from 8.6% to 45.2% in the case of men and from 4.8% to 35.8% in the case of women. These results show us that boys are the most aggressive, with girls being the victims in school [2].

For this reason, teachers recognize that in the face of disruptive student behaviors, the students themselves are at risk of being rejected, failing at the school stage and being opposed to the authority [3]. Consequently, each teacher will determine different strategies looking for students to work in a harmonious and healthy way in the classroom.

Faced with this challenge, teachers must first identify the existence of various types of disruptive behaviors such as taunts towards tasks, not presenting the requested material,

M. Botto-Tobar et al. (Eds.): ICAT 2022, CCIS 1757, pp. 16–24, 2023.
https://doi.org/10.1007/978-3-031-24978-5_2

breaking the rules of coexistence, generating disorders in the classroom, challenging the teacher without listening and interrupt his class, followed by aggressions and teasing towards his classmates [4]. Likewise, this type of behavior includes attention deficit disorder that not only affects children but also adolescents making it difficult for the school stage and subsequently their social life [5].

Among the strategies that the teacher can use to regulate disruptive behaviors is a variety of resources used such as collective work with parents, since the family has an important role and it depends on them to overcome the conflicts that generate antisocial behaviors, being a psychological influence in the raising of the infant; providing security [6]. Thus, in the face of oppositional behavior, one of the solutions would be to apply social integration strategies as an important element; in this way positive behaviors would be stimulated and fed back [7].

Each child in turn represents different contexts and not always, the strategies employed by teachers will have the same results, which is why in order to regulate disruptive behaviors teachers must develop various strategies and identify which of them achieves favorable results. Therefore, working in a group or individual way will be able to stop conflicts, reduce them and prevent school violence; because by listening or observing what students want, teachers can be more successful in their strategies leaving behind the old school educational practices [8].

1.1 Research Objectives

Regarding the above about the didactic strategies used by teachers in the face of disruptive behavior of students [1], there are diverse resources that can be used by classroom teachers [7]. For this reason, the present study is oriented under the general objective: To determine the didactic strategies that teachers use to face the disruptive behavior of students of 4th grade of a primary school in Comas. (Lima-Peru). Also, the specific objectives:

- Identify the various problems of disruptive behavior of students of 4th grade of a primary school in Comas. (Lima-Peru).
- Explain the didactic strategies that teachers know to improve the disruptive behavior of students of 4th grade of a primary school in Comas.
- Describe the difference in appropriate didactic strategies by teachers according to the disruptive behaviors presented by fourth graders at a school in Comas (Lima-Peru).

2 Methodology

In this study it corresponds to the mixed approach due to its greater depth to be able to use various methodologies to respond to the problems, thus verifying the validity of hypotheses [9] and achieving better results was oriented according to the mixed type explanatory (see Fig. 1) [10] and descriptive to detail relevant events [11].

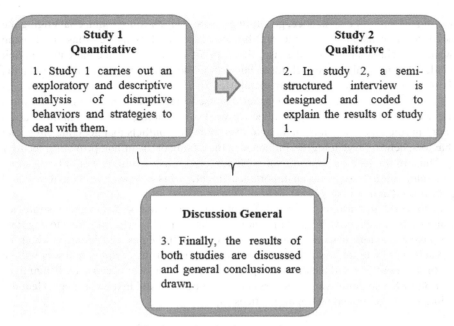

Fig. 1. Study mixed type explanatory.

3 Study 1

It is in a quantitative study to obtain the necessary information and answer each of the questions [12].

3.1 Participants

Through an intentional non-probabilistic sampling procedure, 28 students were selected, 14 of them were female (50%) and 14 male (50%). The age range was between 9 and 10 years old (Mean = 9.36). All students correspond to the primary level of an educational institution in Lima-Peru.

3.2 Instruments

The instrument used in the present study was a Likert scale that measures personal attitudes in different social contexts and which in turn can act in various ways on the object of study [13]. This scale assesses students' disruptive behavior problems and what strategies teachers use to counteract disruptive behavior. It is made up of nine items with options of answers in Likert scale with five dimensions. (e.g.: 2.- I have attacked and struck the classmates of my school, 3.- "they made fun of me in class and did me some kind of harm.").

3.3 Results

After the implementation of the instruments, the results were analyzed.

3.3.1 Descriptive Statistics

Table 1 shows the minimum and maximum ranges, means and standard deviation according to each item analyzed.

Table 1. Relationship between variables

Items	Dimensions	Minimum	Maximum	Mean	SD
Item 1	Various problems of Disruptive Behaviors	1	3	1.14	.448
Item 2		1	5	1.61	1.031
Item 3		1	5	1.86	1.177
Item 4		1	1	1.00	.000
Item 5	Strategies used to deal with disruptive behaviors in students	3	5	4.86	.448
Item 6		1	5	3.63	1.497
Item 7		1	5	2.54	1.644
Item 8		1	5	3.39	1.423
Item 9		1	5	4.50	1.000

In Table 1, when analyzing the means of the dimension "Various problems of Disruptive Behaviors" of the students (from item 1 to 4), it can be seen that among the response ranges from 1 to 5, in which 1 equals never and 5 equals always; the students responded with averages of 1.86 or less. This indicates that according to their own perception of their actions, they never or almost never engaged in disruptive behaviors such as deceiving, insulting, attacking, mocking or breaking the work of their classmates.

Regarding the dimension "Strategies used to deal with disruptive behaviors in students" (from item 5 to 9), it can be seen that among the response ranges from 1 to 5, in which 1 equals never and 5 equals to always; the students responded with averages of 3.39 or more (for items 5, 6, 8 and 9). The highest average was that of item 5 ("The teacher talks to us to control discipline in the classroom") with a value of 4.86. These results show that the teacher sometimes and always applies strategies to improve disruptive behaviors. However, in item 7 the average was 2.54, showing that the teacher almost never "performs activities such as games, singing and other activities when there is a problem in the classroom".

3.3.2 Box Plot Analysis

The analysis of boxes [14] (see Fig. 2) indicates that girls tend to be teased and did some kind of harm to them. It is evident that between the 25th to 75th percentile (1st to 3rd of the Tukey hinge) boys and girls are on equal terms, but in the case of girls it is perceived that the greatest value (not atypical) indicates that they have always been victims of taunts and some kind of harm.

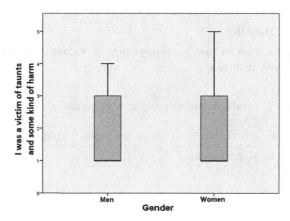

Fig. 2. Students who are victims of taunts and some of harm.

The analysis of boxes [14] (see Fig. 3) shows that girls and boys have a smaller value that does not become atypical. This means that students have not insulted, or purposely deceived teachers. It is also evident that children have two extreme cases: values far more than 3 box lengths of the 75th percentile (13, 15), that is, in several times these two students insulted or attacked their teacher. Likewise, girls have an extreme case: values far more than 3 box lengths from the 75th percentile (7). This means that only one girl has rarely insulted or deceived her teacher on purpose.

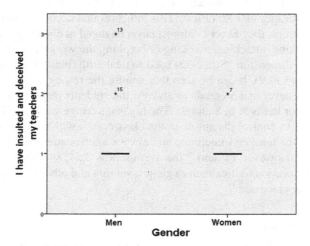

Fig. 3. Students who purposely insult or deceive teachers.

The analysis of boxes [14] (see Fig. 4) shows that boys tend to attack and strike classmates unlike girls. It is observed that between the 25th to 75th percentiles (1st to 3rd of the Tukey hinge) the males have a higher value, which means that they perform acts of physical aggression. As for girls, there are three extreme cases with values far more than 3 box lengths from the 75th percentile (these cases are 4, 8 and 10), in which the girl 4 with the girl 8 and the girls 10 perceive that they have also incurred acts of physical violence. However, the most distant extreme case of girls reached the average level of physical violence on the scale, but it is significantly lower than that of boys.

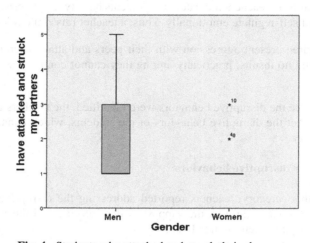

Fig. 4. Students who attacked and struck their classmates.

4   Study 2

This qualitative study offers the opportunity to focus on finding answers to questions that focus on the social experience [12].

4.1   Participants

This study involved a fourth grade female teacher (one teacher) in primary education from a school in Lima-Peru.

4.2   Instrument

The instrument used was a semi-structured interview that has great flexibility in asking planned questions with the possibility of encouraging the free expression of the intervie-wee [15] (eg: "1.- What kind of behavioral problems are observed in 4th grade primary students? Could you explain it?, 4.- According to your experience, do these applied strategies help improve the behavior of your students? Could you mention the changes you observe?").

4.3   Results

For this study, an analysis was carried out using coding and data triangulation processes that were organized according to the pre-established categories.

Below, the first category will be analyzed:

A.   Type of disruptive behavior problems

In this category, it was intended to identify what are the types of disruptive behaviors that students manifest. Teachers indicated that students have types of verbal aggressions [3] and could not self-regulate emotionally. Thus, a teacher raised the following:

> [...] the children present aggression with their peers and attack each other with foul words and no insults, practically among they cannot control their emotions (D: 4-5).

Moreover, once the disruptive behaviors were identified, the teachers tried to apply strategies to correct the disruptive behaviors of the students; which is analyzed in the following category.

B.   Strategies for disruptive behaviors

Regarding this category, teachers reported addressing the disruptive behavior of emotional lack of control through the support of the Tutoring and the Social Studies Area. Thus, one of the teachers stated that:

> [...] Well, we have worked with the control of emotions, with the traffic light in tutoring, also with the traffic light in (the Area) of Social Studies so that they can make a comparison and be able to calm down, control their emotions and improve those behaviors that they have (D: 8-10).

In addition, additionally, in the present study it had been proposed to identify the strategies of frequent use in the face of disruptive behaviors; category analyzed below:

III.   Strategies that you use frequently

In this category, the teacher usually uses dialogue strategies to control students' emotions. For example, the following testimony states that:

> [...] talk a lot with them letting them know that it is very important that they can control their emotions. Also, guide them that in school we should practice a good treatment with all their classmates and not only in school, also at home and on the street. That is what we are practicing now (D: 12-15).

Likewise, the teacher guides students to practice good treatment inside and outside the school to improve society. In addition, this study also sought to identify if the applied strategies generated changes in the students; which is analyzed below.

IV. **Based on the strategies applied, what changes you have observed in your students**

Regarding this category, the experiences that the teacher had towards the students showed that they have to take a deep breath, calm down to dialogue and to be able to listen to them. Therefore, aggressions are observed at recess, where they get their emotions and impulses out of control. To confirm this, a teacher indicated that:

> [...] Well, according to how we are making progress is that they remember and when they act, they take a deep breath, observe their classmates and try to calm down. We try to talk to them a lot so that they can listen and be listened by their classmates.

> In the classroom, we still control it; the aggressions are seen at recess. In the classroom, they try to control their emotions, their impulses, but at recess, they leave and begin to forget practically what they did. In the classroom, they return with many complaints: they have been pushed and insulted. So to improve that we try to talk with them and guide them so that does not happen again (D: 18-25).

It is appreciated that teachers work the dialogue and provide guidance to eradicate all types of violence and promote good treatment, improve their behaviors and establish a harmonious school life within the classroom.

5   Discussion

The purpose of this study was to determine the didactic strategies used by teachers to deal with the disruptive behavior of students of 4th grade of a primary school in Comas.

In Study 2 (qualitative), through the coding and triangulation analysis, it was possible to identify in the first category that the most frequent disruptive behaviors were verbal aggression [4] and emotional self-control problems. However, in the analysis of the descriptive statistics of Study 1 (quantitative), a low average was observed regarding the self-perception of disruptive behaviors on the part of the students; that is, they indicated that they did not engage in disruptive behaviors. This result was contradictory in the analysis of boxes, in which it was observed that girls were more likely to be victims of verbal and physical aggression. For example, in Fig. 3, it was observed that two boys and one girl repeatedly insulted or attacked their teacher. Regarding Study 1, in the analysis of the Box plots [14], it was possible to identify that men are more likely to engage in acts of physical violence unlike women [2].

Moreover, regarding the use of strategies in the face of disruptive behaviors, in Study 1 a high average was identified in terms of the dialogue strategy to control discipline in the classroom. This coincided with Study 2, in which, according to the second category, it was concluded that the teacher attended to such disruptive behaviors based on the Tutoring and the Social Studies Area. Additionally, in the third category, the teacher expressed the use of constant dialogue with students; which had changes in the behavior of students who learned self-control techniques (category 4).

References

1. Alegre, M.: Mejoran los programas conductuales las actitudes y resultados de los alumnos? Iválua, 2–29 (2018)
2. Olweus, D.: Violencia escolar, un problemaque aumenta en la escuela primaria costarricense 13(2), 1–20 (2013)
3. Cruz, Y., Bonillo, A., Claustre, M.: Parents' executive functions, parenting styles, and oppositional defiant disorder symptoms: a relational model. Universitas Psychologica 17(2), 1–10 (2018)
4. Romero, V., Gómez, M., Ricarte, A.: Juegos educativos y cooperativos: como mejorar el aprendizaje de la Biología y Geología en grupos disruptivos de 1° de la ESO. Iberoamericana, Noviembre (2018)
5. Karimy, M., et al.: Disruptive behavior scale for adolescents (DISBA): development and psychometric properties. Child Adolesc. Psychiatry Ment. Health 12(17), 1–7 (2018)
6. Rivera, R., Cahuana, M.: Influencia de la familia sobre las conductas antisociales en adolescentes de Arequipa-Perú. Actualidades en Psicología 30(120), 85–95 (2016)
7. Monsalve, A., Mora, L., Ramírez, L., Roso, V., Puerto, D.: Estrategias de intervención dirigidas a niños con trastorno negativista desafiante, una revisión de la literatura. Cienc. Salud. 15(1), 105–127 (2017)
8. Pavlovic, D., Stanisavljevic, Z., Injac, M.: Teachers' characteristics and development of students' attitudes towards school. J. Educ. Teach. 8(1), 239–252 (2017)
9. Pereira, Z.: Los diseños de método mixto en la investigación en educación: Una experiencia concreta. Revista Electrónica Educare 15(1), 15–29 (2011)
10. Creswell, W., Plano Clark, L., Gutmann, L., Hanson, E.: Advanced mixed methods research designs. In: Tashakkori, A., Teddlie, C. (eds.) Handbook of Mixed Methods in Social and Behavioral Research, pp. 209–240. Sage, Thousand Oaks (2003)
11. Valdi, D., Driessnack, M., Costa, I.: Revisión de diseños de investigación. Rev Latino-am Enfermagem 15(3) (2007)
12. Cadena, P., Rendon, R., Aguilar, J., Silinas, E., De La Cruz, F., Sangerman, D.: Métodos cuantitativos, métodos cualitativos o su combinación en la investigación: un acercamiento en las ciencias sociales. Remexca 8(7), 1603–1617 (2017)
13. García, J., Aguilera, J., Castillo, A.: Guía técnica para la construcción de escalas de actitud. Odiseo 8(16), 1–13 (2011)
14. Helsel, D.: Statistics for Consored Environmental Data Using Minitab and R, 2nd edn. Wiley, Denver (2011)
15. Díaz, L., Torruco, U., Martínez, M., Varela, M.: La entrevista, recurso flexible y dinámico. Investigación en Educación Médica 2(7), 162–167 (2013)

Demystifying EFL Teachers' Experiences During the Pandemic: A Study of the Psychosocial Risks Resulting from COVID-19

Evelyn Almeida[1,2]([envelope]) [iD], Diego Cajas[3] [iD], Jorge Bernal[4] [iD], and Andres Baldassari[2] [iD]

[1] Universidad de Las Fuerzas Armadas ESPE, Sangolquí, Ecuador
evalmeida@espe.edu.ec
[2] Universidad Central del Ecuador, Quito, Ecuador
[3] Universidad Nacional de Educación, Azogues, Ecuador
[4] Universidad Técnica Estatal de Quevedo, Quevedo, Ecuador

Abstract. This study aims to identify the main psychosocial risks that COVID-19 has caused in Ecuadorian EFL teachers and determine the factors associated with developing these risks. This study employed a quantitative approach and a non-experimental cross-sectional design, with a sample of 980 teachers from different educational levels from Ecuador. The data analysis was done using Stata 16 statistical program and a multivariate binary logistic regression (LR). The results showed that teachers are emotionally drained, isolated, frustrated with teaching, and exhausted because of teaching during the pandemic, being the women the most affected. The main factors that increased the probability of suffering these psychosocial effects were extra activities beyond working hours, status in the teacher's institutions, and gender.

Keywords: Psychosocial risks · Factors · COVID-19 · Ecuador · Online teaching

1 Introduction

In the last two years, humanity has experienced unthinkable changes which resulted from COVID-19. These changes affected every aspect of our lives, such as work, social interactions, the economy, and health. Concerning work, people, in some cases, could maintain their jobs and continue their activities from their houses. Opposite to a significant number of people who lost their jobs due to the confinement mandated by different governments aiming to control the pandemic. Many companies and businesses closed, leaving their workers jobless from one day to another. Isolation reduced social interactions to the minimum or, in some cases, interactions with other people outside their homes were nonexistent. This negatively impacted the mental health of the world population. To worsen things, the global economy was affected, and, as usual, developing countries were the ones that were severely hit. Their impoverished economies rapidly slumped, resulting in a dramatic cut of social services budgets, particularly health, when it was the most needed because of COVID-19.

M. Botto-Tobar et al. (Eds.): ICAT 2022, CCIS 1757, pp. 25–36, 2023.
https://doi.org/10.1007/978-3-031-24978-5_3

Fortunately, education did not stop during these tumultuous times but completely moved to a virtual environment. A new reality that teachers, who were unprepared to face, had to adapt rapidly. Most teachers had to overcome their struggles, sufferings, and fears and adjust to the new demands to provide their students with an appropriate education and had to use digital tools when teaching and learning [1]. In addition, teachers had to develop a curriculum that helps students think critically about the situations around them [2] using the existing resources.

Considering that education is one of the foundations of society, much attention was given to this aspect. Media turned their attention to how governments were dealing with the educational systems in their countries, and - as expected - teachers were in the spotlight. Teachers were the target of positive and negative criticisms about their practices [3]. Teachers who could quickly adapt to virtual education were admired and praised, unlike teachers who could not cope with these fast changes received negative comments. People did not understand that changes do not happen overnight and that the cultural background does not evolve as fast as society's expectations, as mentioned in [4].

These changes and pressure to perform under challenging times affected teachers. Some of them experienced psychological or health problems [5]. However, most of the studies happening during the pandemic time focused more on teaching methodology rather than teachers. Thus, it is essential to identify the main psychosocial risks that COVID - 19 has caused in Ecuadorian EFL teachers and determine the factors associated with developing these risks.

2   Literature Review

2.1   Psychosocial Risks

When the confinement started in Ecuador, teachers had to teach from their houses. This situation forced educators to juggle between their home and teaching responsibilities, raising their psychosocial risks as their stress levels increased. In most cases, this led to cardiovascular problems and loss of concentration [4]. The EU-OSHA [6] found that the [p]sychosocial risks and work-related stress are among the most challenging occupational safety and health issues. Hernandez et al. [7] mention that Karasek indicated that job demands (work rate, availability, time pressure, difficulty, and effort) and job decision latitude (potential to control daily tasks) are also factors that increase the psychosocial risks.

How people respond to work and working conditions depends on the psychosocial environment they are part of [8]. Depending on the characteristics of the environment, workers' mental, physical, and social health can be negatively affected. For example, a working environment with no regular schedules, unpredictable activities, and extra online work increases exponentially the possibility of suffering psychosocial risk among workers [9].

It is essential to consider that work is a fundamental part of the person's identity, and the labor relationships can carry psychic aftermath [10] in the form of psychosocial risks. Thus, the importance of promoting a healthy job environment. However, as [4] and [10] mention, administrators generally focus more on economic and administrative issues rather than the workers' welfare, and to perpetuate these practices, they promote these statements:

1. Stress depends on the person; some people are predisposed to experience high-stress levels, unlike others.
2. Lack of information about the adverse effects derived from psychosocial risks.
3. Cultural background that associates stress only with certain kinds of jobs.
4. Disbelief and skepticism about mechanisms that can reduce the level of stress [10, p. 57]

These misconceptions are more evident in education, where all attention is given to students and not to teachers. Media, parents, and authorities judge the teachers' work superficially without considering that they are also humans and, like the rest of the workers, are exposed to the same job pressure, stress, and risks. ILO [11, p. 7] defines *risks* as environment, job content, organizational conditions, workers' capacities, needs, culture, and personal extra-job interaction with each other. These interactions do not always occur harmonically. The environment where these interactions occur and the tasks given by the institution can also result in psychosocial risks [10], creating discomfort affecting their personal lives and reducing their levels of job satisfaction to the minimum.

3   Methodology

3.1   Approach, Design, and Scope of the Research

This study employed a quantitative approach and a non-experimental cross-sectional design to identify the main psychosocial risks that COVID - 19 has caused in Ecuadorian EFL teachers and determine the factors associated with developing these risks. It also sought to validate the following hypothesis: *factors related to teachers' gender, age, school location, qualifications, types of contracts, working space, and mode of instruction increase the probability of developing psychosocial risks.*

To achieve this objective, 980 teachers from private and public primary, secondary and higher education institutions participated in this study. The institutions were located in 23 provinces from the three regions of the country, namely, Highlands, Coast, and Amazonia. The scope of this research was descriptive, exploratory, and explanatory.

The data for this study was collected through a questionnaire that contained eleven closed-ended items. For the statistical analysis, this instrument comprised variables such as age, gender, ethnicity, marital status, level of education, institution location, type of institution, time spent in class preparation, and other factors related to psychosocial risks.

3.2 Data collection Procedure

The data collection process was carried out using a probabilistic sampling where all Ecuadorian EFL teachers working in all levels of education in the three regions of the country had the same probability of being surveyed. Following this methodology, a sample of 980 teachers participated in this study.

Once the questionnaire was validated and piloted, it was uploaded on the Google Forms platform. The link to respond to the instrument was sent to the sample through email, WhatsApp, and Facebook. The researchers opted to use this mode of data collection to increase the response rate and widen its reach to all country regions. Furthermore, the respondents' anonymity and confidentiality were highlighted to increase participation and obtain objective and consistent information. The questionnaire was administered online during January, February, and March 2021, and respondents needed 7 to 10 min to complete it.

3.3 Data Analysis

Following the study's focus and its scope to achieve its objective and validate the general hypothesis, a multivariate logistic regression analysis was used. After refining and organizing the data, the Stata 16 statistical program was used to carry out the numerical procedure.

3.4 Econometric Methodology

Given the nature of the distribution of the dependent variable and the objective of the study, a multivariate binary logistic regression (LR) was used. Through this model, it is possible to determine the relationship between a dichotomous qualitative dependent variable (dependence) and multiple independent or explanatory variables, either qualitative with various categories and/or quantitative.

To obtain an adjusted estimate of the occurrence probability of an event from the independent variables vector, whose main characteristic is the relationship between the obtained coefficients in the quantification of the effect through the Odds Ratio (OR). When the coefficient of the variable is positive, we get an OR > 1; conversely, if the coefficient is negative, the OR < 1 [12, pp. 553–556] $\Pr(Y = 1|X_1, X_2, ..., X_k) = F(\beta_0 + \beta_1 X_1 + \beta_2 X_2 + ... + \beta_k X_k)$ [13, p. 283].

Based on this model, the researchers were able to explain the probability of the occurrence of psychosocial risks among EFL teachers. As is shown below in the general equation that represents the econometric model employed in this study:

$$\text{excessivework} = \beta_0 + \beta_1 \text{ gender} + \beta_2 \text{ age} + \beta_3 \text{ instlocation} + \beta_4 \text{ acadegree}$$
$$+ \beta_5 \text{edulevelwork} + \beta_6 \text{dedicationtime} + \beta_7 \text{typecontract} + \beta_8 \text{workplace}$$
$$+ \beta_9 \text{extractivities} + \beta_{10} \text{synchclasshours} + u_i$$

The variables used in the specification of the econometric model are presented in Table 1:

Table 1. Description of variables

Type of variable	Variables	Description	Values
Dependent	Psychosocial Risks (excessivework)	It is the proxy variable that represents psychosocial risks. Indicates if the EFL teachers consider that they work excessively in virtual teaching	1 = Yes 0 = No
Independent	Gender (Gender)	Represents the teacher's gender	1 = Male 0 = Female
	Age (age)	Represents the teacher's age	Years
	Location of the institution (instlocated)	Indicates the location of the institution where EFL teachers work	1 = Urban 0 = Rural
	Academic degree (acadegree)	Indicates the highest academic degree achieved by teachers	1 = Higher education, undergrad 2 = Higher education, post-grad 3 = Superior technical and / or technological 4 = High school
	Education level work (edulevelwork)	Indicate the level of education that teachers work with	1 = Higher education 2 = Secondary 3 = Primary and preschool 4 = Superior technical and / or technological
	Hiring scheme (dedicationtime)	Indicates the time teacher works in the institution	1 = Full – time 2 = Part- time 3 = Hourly
	Status (labrelationship)	Indicates the type of contract teachers have with their institutions	1 = Non-permanent 2 = Permanent or tenure 3 = Probationary status 4 = Professional services

(*continued*)

Table 1. (*continued*)

Type of variable	Variables	Description	Values
	Workplace (workergonomic)	Indicates whether the teacher's workstation (chair, desk, shelves) is ergonomically adjusted to their needs	1 = Yes 0 = No
	Extra activities (extractivities)	Indicate whether the teachers have been assigned extra activities to those that they regularly carried out	1 = Yes 0 = No
	Synchrounous classes hours (synchclasshours)	Represents the average number of hours per day that the teacher dedicates to teaching synchronous classes	Hours
	Random error (Randomerror)	Represents all the independent variables that can affect the dependent variable and have not been explicitly considered in the model specifications	ui

4 Discussion

During the pandemic caused by the COVID − 19, teachers never stopped teaching. They had to change their lives abruptly and turn their homes, personal and sacred spaces, into classrooms exposing their private lives [5]. This phenomenon may have created an unhealthy job environment and, therefore, increased teachers' stress levels. Unfortunately, little was said about this by educational authorities and the media.

The lack of public awareness about the teachers' struggles may result from the fake job statements that administrators aim to perpetuate [4, 10] to minimize the psychosocial risks that EFL teachers experience. The media started advertising and praising teachers' extra activities, such as traveling to their students' houses to deliver their assignments or providing in-person tutorials at the high of the pandemic. Besides, additional activities such as posting ELT videos online or giving online tutorials outside working hours became the norm in online teaching.

Ecuadorian society started to relate the number of the teachers' activities done outside their class time with their vocation and commitment. Teachers who did not work extra hours or were not available for students and parents outside the class schedule were considered irresponsible and insensitive to the health situation. This may have resulted from the country's shared cultural background, which reduces the role of teachers as mere providers of teaching services and care at the expense of their own welfare.

According to the survey results (Table. 2), approximately 40 out of 100 teachers sometimes felt emotionally more exhausted as consequence of online work, and 32 out of 100 said they felt frequently exhausted. Likewise, 20 out of 100 teachers always felt more tired at the end of the virtual day than the face-to-face day, and 37 out of 100 only sometimes. On the other hand, around 34 out of 100 teachers sometimes felt socially isolated due to the pandemic. In addition, 40 out of 100 teachers said they sometimes feel frustrated at work due to this new type of study. Finally, 39 out of 100 teachers sometimes felt fatigued in the face of the online workday.

Table 2. Main Psychosoical risks

	Emotionally more exhausted	More tired at the end of the day	Socially isolated	Frustrated at my job	Fatigued
Sometimes	40,5% 397	37,3% 366	33,7% 330	39,9% 391	39,2% 384
Usually	7,1% 70	7,5% 73	16,1% 158	18,8% 184	23,9% 234
Rarely	31,7% 311	30,5% 299	26,9% 264	16% 157	12,8% 125
Never	3,8% 37	4,2% 41	10,3% 101	18,4% 180	19,3% 189
Always	16,8% 165	20,5% 201	13% 127	6,9% 68	4,9% 48
Total	100% 980	100% 980	100% 980	100% 980	100% 980

To bring to the fore teachers' struggles and their probability of suffering psychosocial risks, data in Table. 3. Shows the magnitude of the effect (increase or decrease in terms of probability) that each independent variable has on the binomial dependent variable (psychosocial risk). The results in Table. 3. Show that the probability of experiencing psychosocial risks increased 2.4 times when EFL teachers engaged in additional activities beyond their working hours and responsibilities ($\alpha = 0.01$). Furthermore, each extra synchronous teaching hour added to their usual timetables ($\alpha = 0.05$) increased 1 more time this probability.

In the educational system in the country, EFL teachers can be classified according to their status as tenured and non-tenured. Depending on their hiring scheme, teachers are classified as full-time (40 h per week), part-time (20 h per week), and hourly (less than 20 h per week) teachers. Apart from teaching, institutions usually assign managing or administrative responsibilities to tenured-full-time teachers. During the pandemic, these responsibilities rose 1.9 times the probability of facing psychosocial risks compared to non-tenured teachers ($\alpha = 0.01$). With EFL teachers' status, the teacher's hiring scheme also played a fundamental role. The lesser hours their contract included, the lesser the probability of experiencing psychosocial risks. Table. 3. Shows that part-time teachers ($\alpha = 0.01$) had 0.3 fewer possibilities of encountering psychosocial risks and hourly teachers 0.8.

Concerning gender (male or female) with a statistically significant effect of $\alpha = 0.05$, data reveals that female teachers had 1.161 more probabilities of suffering psychosocial risks than male teachers. This could be the result of the archaic idea about the role that women are expected to perform in our society (managing the family and their homes) [5], which, combined with the job demands and job decision latitude [7], must have led to high levels of stress. Thus, the need to promote gender equality and equity in our society.

Another factor that influenced the psychosocial risks was the age ($\alpha = 0.01$) and the experience that goes with it. More experienced EFL teachers showed 0.9 less probability to have psychosocial risks. How EFL teachers arranged their physical space in an ergonomic-adapted working station that facilitated ELT online, also depended on their experience. Data shows that having a proper teaching space ($\alpha = 0.01$) reduced 0,4 times the probabilities of psychosocial risk. This debunks the common perception that young teachers deal better with virtual education since they are more familiar with the technology. Results in Table. 3. Also confirm that effective virtual education goes beyond technological tools and is a holistic practice that starts with having an adequate teacher's space to deliver their classes.

Table 3. Results of the calculation of mulivariate regression approach (OLS)

Dependent Variable: PSYCHOSOCIAL RISK (Overload of work)

Variables	Variable Categories	N	Omitted Category	Coefficient	Standard Error	P> |z|	Odds Ratio	dy/dx	IC 95%
Gender	Male	301	X						
	Female	679		0.149	0.206	0.046**	1.161	.0189	.775 - 1.739
Age	-	980		-0.025	0.009	0.011***	.975	-.003	.957 - 0.994
Institution located	Urban	830	X						
	Rural	150		0.270	0.244	0.268	1.310	.034	.812 - 2.114
Academic degree	Higher education third level	491	X						
	Higher education fourth level	448		-0.159	0.243	0.051*	.853	-.019	.529 - 1.373
	Superior technical and / or technological	21		-0.817	0.530	0.123	.442	-.121	.156 - 1.248
	High school	20		-0.291	0.569	0.609	.747	-.038	.245 - 2.279
Education level work	University higher education	265	X						
	Secondary	288		-0.534	0.291	0.067*	.586	-.071	.331 - 1.037
	Primary y preschool	348		0.048	0.314	0.880	105	.005	.566 - 1.941
	Superior technical and / or technological	79		-0.400	0.392	0.308	.670	-.052	.310 - 1.446
Dedication time	Full - time	881	X						
	Part-time	50		-1.048	0.353	0.003***	.351	-.166	.175 - 0.700
	Hourly- time	49		-0.132	0.396	0.047**	.876	-.017	.402 - 1.905
Labor relationship	Hired Staff (Contrato occasional)	254	X						
	Permanent status or tenure (nombramiento permanente)	597		0.678	0.227	0.003***	1.969	.087	1.262 - 3.072
	Probationary status (Nombramiento provisional)	98		-0.276	0.305	0.367	.759	-.045	.417 - 1.381
	Professional services	31		-0.328	0.461	0.477	.720	-.054	.292 - 1.778

(continued)

Table 3. (*continued*)

Ergonomic Workplace	Yes	X	
	No		-0.891
Extra activities	Yes	X	
	No		0.882
Synchronous class time	-		0.071
Constant			1.993

Observations:	980
Pseudo R²:	0,114
Prob > chi²:	0.000
Prob > chi² (Hosmer-Lemeshow):	0.3941
Correctly classified :	83.06%
Area under ROC curve:	0,736

Statistic Significance : *** p<0.01, ** p<0.05, * p<0.1
Coefficients without asteriscs = non-significant parameter at any level

5 Conclusions

Teaching is a profession that requires dedication and vocation to help students. Unfortunately, this intrinsic aspect of teaching seems to hide the adverse effects teachers can have in their lives due to their job. For example, this pandemic praised teachers for exceeding their responsibilities and working hours. In contrast, those who did not engage in such activities were heavily criticized. The inadequate understanding of the teaching profession, which labels teachers as good or bad depending on their extra work, has prevented open debates about the risk of suffering psychosocial effects.

This study shows that many teachers are emotionally drained, isolated, frustrated with teaching, and exhausted because of teaching during the pandemic, being women the most affected. The factors that increased the probability of suffering these psychosocial effects were: first, extra activities beyond the working hours; second, teachers' status; third, gender; fourth, type of contract (full-time teachers suffered more); fifth, age (young teachers were not that able to manage their stress level) and finally the adequate working spaces teachers created in their houses.

Regrettably, there have not been any debates or references about this aspect in the media or by the authorities. The lack of understanding of the teaching profession has reduced teachers' role to a mere provider of services without much consideration for them as people with emotions and susceptible to psychosocial effects. Hence, recognizing the risks existing in teaching could provide non-academic support to teachers during their professional practice.

References

1. Lederman, D.: Will shift to remote teaching be boon or bane for inline learning? 2020 March 2020. https://www.insidehighered.com/digital-learning/article/2020/03/18/most-tea ching-going-remote-will-help-or-hurt-online-learning. Accessed 13 Mar 2021
2. Martinez, J.: Take this pandemic moment to improve education, 22 June 2020. https://edsource.org/2020/take-this-pandemic-moment-to-improve-education/633500. Accessed 14 Marzo 2021
3. Almeida, E., Baldassari, A., Cajas, D., Sanguña, S.: Teachers' practices in language online courses in higher education during the COVID-19 health emergency, 6 June 2020. https://journal.espe.edu.ec/ojs/index.php/vinculos/article/view/1722. Accessed 13 Mar 2021
4. Prado-Gasco, V., Gomez, M., Soto, A., Rodriguez, L., Navarro, D.: Frontiers in psychology, 30 septiembre 2020. https://www.frontiersin.org/journals/psychology. Accessed 27 Feb 2021
5. Almeida, E., Baldassari, A., Bernal, J., Rosero, A., Zapata, A.: Factors that contribute to teachers' burnout during the COVID 19 pandemic in Ecuador, Quito (2022)
6. OSHA: European Agency for SAfety and Work, n/a n/a 2021. https://osha.europa.eu/en/themes/psychosocial-risks-and-stress. Accessed 1 Marzo 2021
7. Hernández, M., Salanova, P., Peiro, M.: Redalyc, 11 Mayo 2007. https://www.redalyc.org/pdf/727/72719413.pdf. Accessed 25 Febrero 2021
8. HSE: Health and safety executive, 1 Abril 2022. https://www.hse.gov.uk/msd/mac/psychosocial.htm
9. Rubinni, N.: Los riesgos psicosociales en el trabajo, Memoria Académica, pp. 1–17 (2012)
10. Freire, J., Corrales, N.: Riesgos psicosociales y su influencia en el desempeño laboral de los docentes universitarios, Didacsc@lia **IX**(4), 53–68 (2018)

11. ILO: Psychological risks, stress and violence in the world of work. Int. J. Labour Res. **8**(1–2), 12–80 (2016)
12. Gujarati, D., Porter, D.: Econometría, 5 edn. Mc Graw Hill Educación, Mexico (2010)
13. Stock, J.H., Watson, M.W.: Introducción a la Econometría. Pearson Educación SA, Madrid (2012)

Parents Participation at the Initial Level in Virtual Education: A Case Study in a Peruvian School

Manuelitha Bances Castro, Maydu Cantaro Ugaz, Brigitte Villafuerte Pardu, and Ivan Iraola-Real[✉] [iD]

Universidad de Ciencias y Humanidades, Lima 15314, Perú
stephanyugaz25@gmail.com, ivanir701@hotmail.com

Abstract. Currently, parental participation is being developed through the virtual modality, being the only means of educational accompaniment that favors children's learning. Therefore, the purpose of this research was to analyze the participation of preschool parents during virtual classes. To achieve this, a qualitative, ethnographic approach was used, in which a semi-structured interview with a preschool teacher and two self-interviews were applied to collect important information based on their experiences. In conclusion, it was obtained as a result that parents do have a constant and active participation during the remote classes, in addition, it is demonstrated that through their daily involvement and cooperation during the pedagogical activities, children improve their school performance; thus, parents are now the first formative pillars in the education of their children.

Keywords: Paternal involvement · Distance education · Early childhood · Virtual education

1 Introduction

Education is a fundamental element in the full development of the human being, being this a process in which the person acquires a series of competencies, capacities and skills that allow them to develop in their daily lives. In this sense, education is considered an inherent right of the individual, which is described in the framework of the General Education Law No. 28044, Article 3, which guarantees the quality and universalization of education in its three levels: initial, primary and secondary (Ministry of Education [MINEDU] 2003). So that it can respond to the needs, desires and full realization of the subject allowing him/her to build his/her personal identity; especially in children, who are vulnerable and need greater support in the teaching-learning process by their parents to achieve such development (Palomino 2020).

Therefore, in order to train capable and competent people, educational institutions were created, whose responsible are the teachers, who are responsible for imparting knowledge, knowledge, experiences and above all provide tools that will allow them to face everyday situations of life (Tocora and García 2018). On the other hand, parents are the first educators of their children, who spend more time in their homes acquiring values

© The Author(s), under exclusive license to Springer Nature Switzerland AG 2023
M. Botto-Tobar et al. (Eds.): ICAT 2022, CCIS 1757, pp. 37–44, 2023.
https://doi.org/10.1007/978-3-031-24978-5_4

and principles that will serve as a basis for social coexistence. Therefore, the family and the school are the main teaching entity. For this reason both parents and school must collaborate, act and walk hand in hand articulately having the same vision to enhance their comprehensive education (Pedraza et al. 2017).

1.1 About Parents Participation

It is important that parents intervene and participate in the school process of their children, since only in this way they will achieve the goals and objectives. In addition, they will become solid and competent professionals who respond to a demanding society in knowledge. Therefore, this participation of both agents must be dynamic, flexible and harmonious, in order to generate trust thus strengthening the links between them; all this will allow the infant to have a single model that favors their learning (Lastre et al. 2018).

Despite this, the methodology used in educational institutions has become more complex, causing disinterest on the part of parents, since most of them do not have a high degree of academic instruction, thus generating a rupture between both entities, where parents think that all educational responsibility falls on the school. This distancing would cause a higher level of disinterest and little participation of parents in school activities (Hurtado 2020; Lastre, et al. 2018).

As mentioned in previous lines, the importance of caregivers' participation is essential to achieve the required learning in the child, which would imply a greater involvement in the child's educational development aiming at his or her integral formation. In this sense, three levels of parental involvement are described. First, there is the informative level, in which parents have limited participation, since they only receive information about their children's school process, but do not get involved in them (Calvo et al. 2016). Secondly, the collaborative level, which implies two fundamental points, one of them refers to the contribution of parents in school activities and the other to the cooperation of parents who contribute from home. Moreover, thirdly, the control level comprises monitoring school progress by parents towards their children, in addition to encouraging them to fulfill their educational roles (Gonzales 2017). It is evident that these types of involvement demand the commitment of both agents to guarantee meaningful and quality learning.

However, the sudden appearance of SARS-Cov2 currently known as COVID-19 in the last two years not only caused a series of diseases, but also caused a radical change in education, causing countries to temporarily prohibit access to educational centers in order to lessen the consequences of the pandemic, thus harming 94% of the world's students (United Nations Educational, Scientific and Cultural Organization [UNESCO] 2020). Due to this problem, countries had to quickly devise a strategic plan so that students would not miss the school year. Thus, at present, homes have been transformed into high schools for students to continue acquiring knowledge and values; therefore, the family has become a fundamental link to continue with the process of their education (Hurtado 2020). Unfortunately, the implementation of distance education has to overcome some challenges. One of them is the lack of skills and lack of knowledge of pedagogical tools on the part of parents to respond to the demands of the teaching-learning process at home (Santos et al. 2020; United Nations International Children's Emergency Fund [UNICEF] 2020).

This research alludes that the absence of communication and collaboration on the part of parents in the formal education of their children in the face-to-face context has generated insufficient support in the learning process in the virtual modality (Vásquez et al. 2020). In addition, parents do not have adequate preparation to accompany their children in the distance education process (Kurnia and Maningtyas 2020; Narváez and Yépez 2021). Unfortunately, no evidence has been found on the participation of parents in distance education at the preschool level. This is a knowledge gap in the aforementioned study, which aims to answer the following question: How is the participation of parents at the preschool level during virtual classes?

1.2 Research Objectives

Taking into account the gaps, the general objective of this research is to analyze the participation of preschool parents during virtual classes and the specific objectives are to describe the informative participation of preschool parents in the educational process in the virtual modality. Also, to describe the collaborative participation of preschool parents during virtual classes in the face of technology and finally, to describe the control participation of preschool parents in the educational process in the virtual modality.

In order to achieve these objectives, the methodology to be used is explained below:

2 Methodology

According to the particularities of the investigated reality, it was decided to approach the research according to the qualitative approach, thus being able to apply an interpretive analysis of a phenomenological type (Leavy 2017). In addition, because it is a specific context and space, the research corresponds to a case study.

2.1 Participants

The sample was selected through a non-probabilistic procedure by convenience (Otzen and Manterola 2017) and consisted of 1 preschool teacher and 2 interns from the Educational Institution.

2.2 Instruments

As for the data collection techniques, the semi-structured interview was used, which has greater flexibility, allowing the interviewee to respond more freely (Lopezosa 2020); also, the autobiographical interview was used, where the researcher himself investigates himself in a reflexive manner (Hernández and Rifá 2011).

In addition, the interview guide was used as an instrument for the collection of information, which allows the collection of information from the interviewee through questions (Arias 2020) and is composed of three categories: informative participation, collaborative participation and parental control participation. This instrument has 6 open-ended questions. For example, *"Do parents constantly monitor the performance of their job? Could you explain your answer?"*.

3 Analysis and Discussion of Results

After the theoretical introduction and the methodology, we proceed to analyze and discuss the findings of the interviews, following a structure based on categories and subcategories. In this way, we proceed to analyze the first category called.

3.1 Informative Parental Participative

Regarding this type of participation, parents are only recipients of information about their children learning (Calvo et al. 2016). In addition, in relation to this, the following subcategory was established:

A. They require information from the learning process

Parents are often only recipients of information and participate occasionally and sporadically (Calvo et al. 2016). Therefore, it is observed that sometimes parents consult about what is happening with their children and other times they do not, as shown in the following responses of the interviewees:

– No, they do not ask for it, we give them, as I said, every two or three months, bimonthly or semiannually, and then they find out about their children (Teacher 1).
– Parents do not request information about their children learning process, but they are aware of the day the teacher hands out their progress report (Teacher 2).
– At the beginning of the literary activity workshop, a mom asked about her child's progress and the miss mentioned that it was going well and that she would contact her at the end of the workshop to give her more details (Teacher 3).

It can be seen that two teachers indicate that parents do not request information about their children learning process and it is the teacher who has to provide them with the information. Nevertheless, one particular case refers to the fact that a mother did consult about her child's progress, but especially in a workshop in which her collaborative participation was required.

3.2 Collaborative Parent Participation

In particular, in this type of participation, parents cooperate in their children's school activities, and get involved both at school and at home (Gonzales 2017). Moreover, in the context of virtuality, collaboration from home has increased the frequency of parental participation in learning sessions, as can be seen in the following subcategory:

A. Accompanying parents with their children in virtual classes

As part of the formative work, parents accompany their children in the process of solving tasks in order to achieve their integral development (Palomino 2020). Thus, the teachers interviewed mentioned that:

– Yes, they accompany them, guiding them in the learning that one sends them in their banners [...] Most of them are with their mothers who support them every day, no, others are with their little sisters, brothers or grandparents (Teacher 1).
– Yes, parents accompany their children from the beginning of the class session until it ends, in case the child's mother or father is not present, a family member accompanies them (Teacher 2).
– Yes, it could be observed that the accompaniment of the parents is continuous, constant and permanent [...]. Every day the great majority of parents accompanied and supported their children from the beginning to the end of the workshop. It could even be seen that 70% of the parents collaborated in the psychomotor activity workshop by carrying out the motor activity together with their children (Teacher 3).

In the teachers' testimonies, we can see that there is a constant participation of parents or family members during the virtual classes; in addition, the support they provide is active, carrying out activities together with them.

B. Parent attendance at school meetings

School meetings allow parents to acquire more information regarding their child's development at school as long as they attend frequently (Uriol and Tapia 2021). In this regard, the teachers interviewed mentioned that:

– Yes, few are those who enter. A group of 15 or so. Of which 5 or 6 participate by asking questions that are not concise and precise, and one must give them answers so that they are satisfied and can participate and follow the sequence and theme of the work (Teacher 1).
– Yes, some parents leave messages on WhatsApp asking for the link to the meeting so they can enter [...]. There are parents who sometimes do not attend and try to get information from the teacher before the workshop starts, or they tell the teacher that they will call her later (Teacher 2).
– Yes, the attendance of parents could be evidenced through WhatsApp, since the teacher sent the list of parents who attended through the Google Meet application and sent an audio to the group mentioning that those parents who could not participate in the meeting should communicate with her privately to give some information about the progress of their children (Teacher 3).

The responses obtained by the teachers show that few parents attend the virtual school meetings; however, parents who do not attend usually communicate with them at other times to find out what has happened. On the other hand, there is a peculiar case, where it is the teacher who asks the parent to communicate with her to inform her about the progress of her child. In this aspect, it can be seen that not all parents are aware of the work that teachers do with their children, so it can be deduced that they have a controlling participation, as described in the following lines.

3.3 Paternal Involvement

In relation to this type of participation, parents give constant follow-up to the educational process of their children (as) and in turn supervise the teaching work (Gonzales 2017). Therefore, the following subcategories were established:

A. Parents consult with the teacher about their child's performance

Mostly parents ask about their children's school activities when teachers provide feedback (Vásquez et al. 2020). Given this, the following is demonstrated:

- Yes, either WhatsApp or video call or calls always connect us. They give me information about learning, how they are doing with their children, they have a lot, that is, they know how their children are doing (Teacher 1).
- Yes. During the virtual class session, they ask the teacher if what their child is doing is okay, or how they should do it (Teacher 2).
- No, since communication or any information about the children was discussed directly with the classroom teacher (Teacher 3).

Teacher 1 refers that the most communication she has with the parent to know about her child's progress is through video calls or phone calls since this is the only informative means; while teacher 2 mentions that parents ask about their child's performance during class. On the other hand, teacher 3 mentions that she was not able to visualize this fact because parents talked directly to the teacher in charge.

B. Frequency with which parents communicate with the teacher to know the progress of their child

Lack of constant interaction of parents in the schooled education of their children, has evidenced the little capacity to support them in their learning process in the context of the pandemic (Rigo and Donolo 2019). Next, the teachers expose us the following:

- The frequency of the parents, mostly during the week, some ask twice and others ask sometimes (Teacher 1).
- Once a week, before starting the workshop, some parents ask if their child is doing well or what is missing; sometimes they tell the teacher that their child cannot or does not want to do certain tasks (Teacher 2).
- The communication of the parents was directly with the teacher […] that is to say, we did not have any communication with the parents (Teacher 3).

In this regard, both teachers (1 and 2) show that parents are interested in knowing how their children are progressing. However, teacher 3 is not able to demonstrate this, since the teacher in charge is the one who dialogues with the parents personally.

III. **Parents monitor compliance with the work of teachers**

Parents collaborate in school activities, as they tend to take a vigilant attitude because they distrust the work and actions of the teacher at school (Gubbins et al. 2020). In this regard, the teachers mention:

- No, I will tell you that they don't try to watch because I have my banners, I show them well, the learning is specified, the videos, I clarify so much in audio, sometimes I send them messages in writing [...] (Teacher 1).
- No Parents receive in time the information of what is going to be worked on during the day through banners, videos, audios or WhatsApp messages [...] (Teacher 2).
- No, but the parents used WhatsApp to ask what time the workshops would be held and what materials would be used so that they could have it in advance [...] (Teacher 3).

It is evident from the teachers' testimonies that the parents do not have a vigilant attitude towards the teacher's work; on the contrary, they keep an eye on the material that the teacher offers.

4   Conclusions and Future Works

In conclusion, it was observed that parents have an informative participation since they expect teachers to inform them about their children's progress, but they do not have the initiative to ask questions. In terms of collaborative participation, it was found that parents are very willing to participate in school activities. Finally, in terms of control participation, parents do not assume a vigilant attitude; on the contrary, they value the work done by teachers in daily activities. For future research, it is suggested to conduct it in person, using a larger sample of participants, in which it is possible to work directly with the parents, since they are the basis of the study, as well as to make use of other instruments for data collection, since it will allow obtaining an in-depth analysis.

References

Arias, J.: Técnicas e instrumentos de investigación científica (2020). http://repositorio.concytec.gob.pe/handle/20.500.12390/2238. Accessed 21 Nov 2021

Calvo, M., Verdugo, M., Amor, A.: La Participación Familiar es un Requisito Imprescindible Para una Escuela Inclusiva. Revista Latinoamericana de Educación Inclusiva **10**(1), 99–113 (2016)

Gonzales, L.: Nivel de apoyo de los padres de familia y su influencia en el logro de aprendizaje de los niños y niñas de 5 años de la institución educativa inicial n° 1327 Echarati en el año 2016 (tesis de maestría) (2017). http://repositorio.unap.edu.pe/bitstream/handle/UNAP/8839/Luzmila_Gonzales_Segovia.pdf?sequence=1&isAllowed=y. Accessed 7 Sept 2021

Gubbins, V., Ugarte, E., Cárcamo, H.: Estilos comunicativos docentes y su incidencia en los modos de participación de los padres desde la mirada de madres de grupos vulnerables. Propósitos y Representaciones **8**(2) (2020)

Hernández, F., Rifá, M.: Investigación autobiográfica y cambio social. Octaedro, Barcelona (2011)

Hurtado, F.: La educación en tiempos de pandemia: Los desafíos de la escuela del siglo XXI. Revista Arbitrada del Centro de Investigación y Estudios Gerenciales **44**, 176–187 (2020)

Kurnia, D., Maningtyas, R.: Parents' involvement in distance learning during the Covid-19 pandemi. Adv. Soc. Sci. Educ. Hum. Res. **487**, 94–97 (2020)

Lastre, K., López, L., Alcázar, C.: Relación entre apoyo familiar y el rendimiento académico en estudiantes colombianos de educación primaria. Psicogente **39**(21), 102–115 (2018)

Leavy, P.: Research Design: Quantitative, Qualitative, Mixed Methods, Arts-Based, and Community-Based Participatory Research Approaches. The Guilford Press, London (2017)

Lopezosa, C.: Entrevistas semiestructuradas con NVivo: pasos para un análisis cualitativo eficaz. Anuario de Métodos de Investigación en Comunicación Social **1**, 88–97 (2020)

Ministerio de Educación: Ley N° 28044. Ley General de Educación (2003). http://www.minedu. gob.pe/p/ley_general_de_educacion_28044.pdf. Accessed 7 Sept 2021

Narváez, D., Yépez, J.: Tiempos de pandemia y el papel de la familia en la educación. Revista Huellas **1**(13), 10–16 (2021)

Otzen, T., Manterola, C.: Técnicas de Muestreo sobre una Población a Estudio. Int. J. Morphol. **35**(1), 227–232 (2017)

Palomino, A.: Acompañamiento de los padres de familia en el desarrollo de las tareas de sus hijos. Revista Universitaria de Informática RUNIN **10**, 42–46 (2020)

Pedraza, A., Salazar, C., Robayo, A., Moreno, E.: Familia y escuela: dos contextos comprometidos con la formación en el ciclo III de la educación básica. Análisis **49**(91), 301–314 (2017)

Rigo, D., Donolo, D.: Implicación familiar y compromiso escolar: El desafío de crear puentes. Psicologia da Educação **48**, 25–34 (2019)

Santos, V., Villanueva, I., Rivera, E., Vega, E.: Percepción docente sobre la educación a distancia en tiempos de covid-19. Ciencia América **9**(3) (2020)

Tocora, S., García, I.: La importancia de la escuela, el profesor y el trabajo educativo en la atención a la deserción escolar. Revista Científico-Metodológica **66**, 1–9 (2018)

United Nations Educational, Scientific and Cultural Organization.: El Secretario General de las Naciones Unidas advierte de que se avecina una catástrofe en la educación y cita la previsión de la UNESCO de que 24 millones de alumnos podrían abandonar los estudios (2020). https://es.unesco.org/news/secretario-general-naciones-unidas-advierte-que-se-avecina-catastrofe-educacion-y-cita. Accessed 26 Sept 2021

United Nations International Children's Emergency Fund.: Mamás y papás deben apoyar el aprendizaje de las y los adolescentes en el hogar (2020). https://www.unicef.org/bolivia/histor ias/mam%C3%A1s-y-pap%C3%A1s-deben-apoyar-el-aprendizaje-de-las-y-los-adolescentes-en-el-hogar. Accessed 2 Oct 2021

Uriol, G., Tapia, M.: Acompañamiento familiar y proceso de aprendizaje en estudiantes del nivel primario. Rev Hacedor **5**(1), 68–79 (2021)

Vásquez, M., Bonilla, W., Acosta, L.: La educación fuera de la escuela en época de pandemia por COVID 19. Experiencias de alumnos y padres de familia. Revista Electrónica sobre Cuerpos Académicos y Grupos de Investigación **7**(14) (2020)

Teaching Experience on Virtual Dramatization in the Development of Social Skills in Preschoolers

Stephany Gomez-García, Rosario Marín-Flores, Keyla Vallejos-Poma, and Ivan Iraola-Real(✉)

Universidad de Ciencias y Humanidades, 15314 Lima, Perú
stephany.gg22@gmail.com, ivanir701@hotmail.com

Abstract. Dramatization is a resource that is used in the classroom by some preschool teachers, allowing them to address the development of social skills. Therefore, the purpose of this research was to analyze the teaching experience of virtual dramatization in the development of social skills in preschool children. This research objective oriented the study through the qualitative approach and biographical study method in which our sample is non-probabilistic, selecting a teacher specializing in dramatization with preschool children. A semi-structured interview was applied, analyzing the answers and discussing them with the support of the reviewed bibliography. In conclusion, it was obtained as a result that the application of dramatization in the virtual modality is a resource that provides the child with several benefits; also a direct contact is required for better results in the development of social skills in preschool children.

Keywords: Dramatization · Socialization · Corporal expression · Preschool education

1 Introduction

Throughout their training, teachers begin to build their professional knowledge; they establish their pedagogical and disciplinary knowledge through the various experiences that are developed in the classroom (Pérez, Baigorria, De la Torre, and Pérez, 2019). However, because of the pandemic, most students are affected by the closure of schools (United Nations Educational, Scientific and Cultural Organization [UNESCO], 2020). So many educational institutions, both private and public, have had to remotely start their synchronous classes in order not to lose contact with their students (Peredo, 2020), because the preschool stage is essential, which seeks to develop adequate preparation of the infant, which will be essential for a later educational level (Pekdogan and Akgul, 2016). Demonstrating that the role of each teacher is paramount, because they have the responsibility to promote situations where the student is the protagonist of their learning; in addition, they can interact with their environment, taking into account the interests and needs of each student, in order to achieve a satisfactory education (Gómez, Muriel and Londoño, 2019).

That is why dramatization has become an essential complement in the formation of the student, it promotes enthusiasm, generates new stimuli, allows them to be able to communicate, express themselves, dialogue and form bonds of friendship with others. Knowing this, it is important that the teacher in early education uses dramatization as an instrument (Sotil, 2020), therefore it is necessary to bet and implement dramatic projects that encourage the revaluation of the true essence of this artistic genre (Llamazares and Selfa, 2016). All activities based on drama and expressive arts are used in spaces where children can express their thoughts and emotions (Solis, Monsivais and Huber, 2021). Among the benefits, it helps the child to be able to communicate their feelings, develop memory and creativity (Polevikova and Shvets, 2019). In addition, it contributes to the development of body expression, recognition of his body in space, also allows the development of imagination, originality and creativity, through musical and plastic expression, generating in the infant security, confidence and self-regulation of their emotions (Armesto, 2019). As a result, students build cooperative learning through the strategies developed by using dramatization (Medrano, 2016). Symbolic representation is part of theatrical activities, which allows groups to explore real and imaginary situations using language to express their ideas, feelings and creativity (Muszynska, Urpí and Galazka, 2017).

1.1   Influence of Dramatization in CHIldren's Learning

Dramatization has advantages, which are strengthening interpersonal relationships, motivates linguistic expression, generates self-confidence, helps to express what is difficult to verbalize and promotes empathy (Álvarez and Martín, 2016). In addition, it allows the child to be able to find himself and heal any event he has suffered during his childhood; making use of theatrical arts he can develop and acquire therapeutic skills that help him to face different situations of his daily life (Schnyder, Wico and Huber, 2021). In such a way, the practice of dramatization seeks to generate new communication links between people, and thus eradicate the fear of expressing oneself before others (Yataco, Fuster, Guillen, Nieto, and Luy, 2021). On the other hand, one of the main disadvantages that a teacher encounters when putting dramatization into practice is the lack of time that occurs within schools, since to carry it out requires more execution time and dedication (Casanova and Couto, 2019). It also becomes challenging to perform it virtually, since one is used to working physically with others, so factors such as space and not being able to observe each other face to face, limit dramatic work (Gorman, Kanninen and Syrjä, 2020).

Dramatization can be employed in several ways. First, drama is developed in an experiential way, contributing to a comprehensive education for the student to develop his skills with the aim of enabling him to improve his relationships with his environment (Pavlou, Anagnou, and Fragkoulis, 2021). Secondly, the use of puppets allows the development within the classroom of a positive climate, in turn, communication is established, allowing a pleasant atmosphere to be created when interacting (Kröger, 2019), thus generating more possibilities for trust and the development of positive attitudes, helping them to be able to develop teamwork (Ocal, Karademir, Saatcioglu, and Demirel, 2021). Similarly, it provides children with a meaningful experience, where it stimulates their creativity by making fun puppets having the opportunity to tell stories and get involved in the character (Maharani, 2016). Thirdly, role-playing helps the student to learn naturally from various meaningful experiences, which promote their learning and attitudes towards others; it also gives them the opportunity to enjoy through play (Rashid and Qaisar, 2017). Fourth, dramatic play is important because it allows peer interaction, favoring collective work using expressive language and thought, by performing various games (Khomais, Al-Khalidi, and Alotai, 2019). Fifth, improvisation is considered as an art, where theatrical performances are created spontaneously, and allowing group work during the creation of scenes without the use of a script and without any previous rehearsal, with the aim of creating a space for social play (Tanner and Miller, 2018).

Therefore, dramatization is considered as an alternative in the improvement for social skills, demonstrating that it provides a space for entertainment and socialization, favoring their self-esteem and the denotation of their emotions (Togia, Charitaki and Soulis, 2017). In addition, it allows to have a dynamic contact during the live process, where children develop their autonomy and various skills (Lirola, Ruiz, Hernández, and Prados, 2020), including the achievement of communication skills (Altun, 2019).

1.2 Dramatization in Preschool

In the preschool stage, the development of social skills is sought, this allows children to relate to others and thus adapt to their educational environment (Maleki, Mardani, Mitra, Dianatinasab, and Vaismoradi, 2019). Also, it is considered that social skills allow guiding and giving meaning to the infant's life, especially for the development of their personality (Özbey and Köycegiz, 2019), thus achieving greater success in their social life and especially in the educational environment (Tersi and Matsouka, 2020).

Therefore, it is essential that social skills are acquired in the preschool stage (Ergin and Özkan, 2021) where the school plays a fundamental role, so it should stimulate in the child the skills to positively enhance their personality, self-respect and behavior towards others; likewise, within the classroom different methods should be worked (Gemechu, 2020). Which allow the infant to have an active participation, an integral development, and above all to reach positive results of their achievements and objectives (Aguilar and Baltazar, 2019), thus seeking to consolidate assertive social behaviors (Aksoy, 2020), such as good social interaction, empathy, cooperation and appropriate conflict resolution (Wu, Mak, Hu, He and Fan, 2018). That is why; dramatization has a positive impact on the social skills of those who apply it, developing socialization among peers and leading them to find their hidden talents (Batdi and Elaldi, 2020). In addition, an arts education promotes activities related to the branches of art, including dramatization, also integrating itself to various activities, employing methods or techniques based on play and aligned to learning (Yazici, 2017). Therefore, students in various ways perform practices of this art through the virtual modality, using creativity, exploring their feelings and expressing their emotions (Lima, 2021).

1.3 Research Objectives

In accordance with the above, the purpose of this research is to analyze the teaching experience of virtual dramatization in the development of social skills in preschool children. Specifically, it is desired to know the benefits of dramatization for the development of social skills and to analyze the way in which it is used in preschool children through the virtual modality.

2 Methodology

The present article is of qualitative approach, which are characterized by being inductive and present flexibility in their research design (Cadena et al., 2017). It was conducted using the biographical study method, since it allows capturing the lived experiences of a subject through research that can generate new contributions (Landín and Sánchez, 2019).

2.1 Participants

The sample is non-probabilistic, since it takes into account the researcher's criteria, which are faster and less complex (Arispe et al., 2020). For this reason, in this research, a 40-year-old teacher of the initial level was selected as a participant, who studied at the National Pedagogical Institute of Monterrico (Lima - Peru), and also studied a Master's degree in Education through Art and is currently pursuing a doctorate in Humanities with a mention in Cultural Studies. Since 2004, she has been working as a teacher and that same year, she started her project on dramatization. Currently, she is carrying out a project for children called "Rinconcito Infantil" and develops training workshops for adults in certain opportunities.

2.2 Instruments

The interview was used as a technique (Cruz, 2018). Therefore, the instrument is the semi-structured interview guide, which allows the researcher to explore and collect information based on the interviewee's experience (Evans and Lewis, 2018). To conduct the interview, 6 questions were considered, in relation to the two categories, where the first three questions correspond to the category of benefits of dramatization; for example, question 1 asks the following: "Explain, in what way do you consider that dramatization is beneficial for preschool children?". Moreover, the last three questions belong to the second category of dramatization use, e.g., question 5 asks the following, "How do you use dramatization techniques to develop social skills? Mention which ones do you use? Why?" The present instrument was validated by an expert judgment procedure. Which allows validating the content to obtain appropriate instruments that can be replicated (Suhaini, Ahmad and Mohd, 2021).

3 Discussion Analysis and Results

After explaining the methodology, the sample and the instruments, the following is the analysis of the interviewee's answers and their discussion with the support of the reviewed bibliography.

3.1 Benefits of Dramatization

Among the benefits of dramatization, it can be said that it has become a key element in the formation of the learner, generating new stimuli, enthusiasm, making the individual capable of communicating, dialoguing, expressing him/herself and forming affective bonds with others. Therefore, the early education teacher should use dramatization as an instrument (Sotil, 2020). In relation to this, the teacher interviewed refers that dramatization in preschool children favors the development of social skills, presenting advantages as well as disadvantages, which can be observed in the analysis of the following subcategories:

3.1.1 Benefits of Dramatization in Preschool Children

Within it, children can express their feelings, develop their memory and enhance their creative side (Polevikova and Shvets, 2019). Likewise, it favors the development of their body expression, the location of their body in space, stimulates their imagination by making use of plastic and musical expression, originating the infant to build their confidence, security and manage the self-regulation of their emotions (Armesto, 2019). Thus, the teacher interviewed stated that the benefits of dramatization in preschool children are as follows:

[Dramatization...] enables children's capacities such as socioemotional development, creativity, imagination, integral development and the approach to emotions.

This testimony confirms that the practice of dramatization favors the integral (Pavlou, et al. 2021), emotional (Togia, et al. 2017) and creative (Armesto, 2019) development of children; demonstrating that dramatization is beneficial as discussed below in the following subcategory.

3.1.2 Dramatization for the Improvement of Social Skills

It is considered that dramatization is a useful means for the development of social skills, because it provides a playful environment, generating peer relationships, which promotes the improvement of self-esteem and the manifestation of their emotions (Togia, et al. 2017). Regarding this, the teacher interviewed mentioned the way in which dramatization improves social skills, indicating the following:

[Dramatization allows the improvement of social skills] through symbolic play, it allows children to socialize based on their characters, as I think it is through dialogue. With this imaginary game, the creative aspect is developed.

The teacher's response states that dramatization helps to improve social skills (Batdi and Elaldi, 2020). Moreover, using symbolic representation, it allows them to work in groups exploring and imagining, using language and their creativity at all times (Muszynska, et al. 2017). Which will be observed when analyzing the advantages and disadvantages in the following subcategory.

3.1.3   Advantages and Disadvantages of Dramatization

The advantages include the consolidation of the interpersonal relationship, good linguistic expression, and self-confidence, allows verbalizing what is difficult to express and develops empathy (Álvarez and Martín, 2016). The main disadvantage that a teacher finds is the lack of time when employing dramatization within the classroom, because it requires more time of dedication. (Casanova and Couto, 2019). Therefore, the interviewee mentioned the following regarding the advantages and disadvantages of dramatization when employing it in the virtual modality:

> I think they are all advantages; the disadvantage I feel is the fact that it is virtual, since it will not allow you to have the freedom. In addition, you will not be able to observe the facial expression of their emotions, besides we cannot get closer in that way we do not develop the close body field with the other. [The main advantages that are given] thanks to dramatization is that they can develop very well, feel good about themselves, because dramatization and any type of art is also therapeutic, that is, it heals you; it also has a very important power which is the work of resilience, it makes us very strong and they develop the language thought.

Through the response provided by the teacher, it can be identified that the main disadvantage is to perform the dramatization virtually, because it is not possible to work physically with the participants, there is no direct contact and the space is smaller, making it a challenge (Gorman, et al., 2020). However, among the advantages of dramatization, it is emphasized that it is a therapeutic medium, which helps the child to face and overcome various childhood situations (Schnyder, et al. 2021). In this way, communication links are generated, eradicating the fear of being able to express oneself to others (Yataco, et al., 2021). Therefore, the following subcategory will show how dramatization is used in virtual mode .

3.2   Use of Dramatization

Activities focused on expressive and dramatic arts are used in spaces that help children to express their ideas and feelings (Solis, et al. 2021). In this regard, the teacher interviewed states that using dramatization virtually has led her to use some techniques that fit her reality in order to demonstrate the children's social skills; which will be observed in the following analysis of the subcategories:

3.2.1   Application of Dramatization in the Virtual Modality

Students perform the dramatization in the virtual modality making use of their creativity, where they explore their feelings and express their emotions (Lima, 2021). Therefore, the teacher interviewed mentions the way she applies dramatization in the virtual modality, expressing the following:

> In my case, I like to start with a playful activity of a game or a song, then with a story represented by the characters, and finally, what the children often make are their puppets, their characters or their little theater. [The children in the virtual modality apply dramatization] not only as spectators, but also as dramatization.

The teacher comments that she uses various strategies (music, games, etc.) that allow her to apply dramatization in a virtual way, in this way the child has the opportunity to have meaningful experiences that allow the stimulation of his creativity by being himself the creator and protagonist of some puppet character (Maharani, 2016). Thus, it is shown that it is necessary to employ the use of dramatization techniques as pointed out in the following subcategory.

3.2.2 Use of Dramatization Techniques

It can be used in several ways. First, theater contributes to a holistic education (Pavlou, et al. 2021). Secondly, the use of puppets favors a positive climate (Kröger, 2019). Third, role play provides the opportunity for meaningful experiences (Rashid and Qaisar, 2017). Fourth, dramatic play is conducive to collective work (Khomais, et al., 2019). Fifth, improvisation allows performances to be created spontaneously (Tanner and Miller, 2018). In view of this, the teacher manifests the use of the techniques she uses in dramatization:

The puppet has a component that to me personally leads to a personal transformation, there is a very rich work where the child works the imagination and we have to know how to use it. [Likewise], we have to try to make the children play and represent everything that comes to their minds and there we also discover the values, from the positive to the negative.

This testimony affirms that the use of puppets generates confidence and allows the development of positive attitudes in children, thus helping them to work collaboratively (Ocal, et al. 2021), demonstrating that dramatization is favorable for social skills and that it is evident when applied in the virtual modality, as analyzed in the following subcategory.

3.2.3 Evidence of Social Skills After Applying Dramatization

Therefore, dramatization also generates a positive effect on the social skills of the subjects who use this dramatic technique, allowing them to socialize and generate self-knowledge, while discovering their talents (Batdi and Elaldi, 2020). From her point of view, the teacher interviewed comments on the different social skills she observes in her students after applying dramatization:

The children are not in direct contact, but they do socialize, since we have the opportunity to meet with a child from Piura, the other is in Chaclacayo and from other districts or different places. [Other skills that are evident is when] communication flows easily, I think it is precisely because of the play component, in this way the children have the facility to communicate, to express what they feel and to be autonomous.

The teacher's testimony certifies that socialization is evident and communication flows through the virtual modality. Since, dramatization allows a dynamic contact to be maintained, along with the development of autonomy and other skills (Lirola, et al. 2020), such as the achievement of verbal skills (Altun, 2019).

4 Conclusions and Future Works

It is concluded that dramatization has multiple benefits, such as socioemotional development, creativity, integral development, language skills, socialization and therapeutic; however, the only disadvantage is that it is given virtually because there is no direct contact, making the application of dramatization a challenge. Likewise, in the use of dramatization, the teacher worked with puppets, because it allows personal transformation and the discovery of both positive and negative values. For future research work, it is intended to develop in person, not only interviewing a teacher but also several teachers, parents and children, as well as applying other methodologies such as the quantitative correlational method in order to obtain better results.

Acknowledgment. First, we thank God for giving us wisdom and perseverance to achieve our goals. We also thank each of our families for the moral support they gave us at all times. Likewise, a special thanks to the teachers who supported us and collaborated with us during the course of the research.

References

Aguilar, R., Baltazar, S.: Habilidades sociales en los estudiantes de educación inicial de la Universidad Nacional de Huancavelica. Apuntes de Ciencia y Sociedad **09**(01), 7–14 (2019)

Altun, M.: Drama: a neglected source in language teaching to improve communication. Int. J. English Linguist. **9**(5), 242–248 (2019)

Álvarez, P., Martín, A.: Theater as a Pedagogical Tool to Teach History of Contemporary Education. Revista Digital de Investigación en Docencia Universitaria, 10(1), 41–51 (2016). https://revistas.upc.edu.pe/index.php/docencia/article/view/459/435

Arispe, C., Yangali, J., Guerrero, M., Rivera, O., Acuña, L., Arellano, C.: Investigación científica una aproximación para los estudios de posgrado. Universidad Internacional del Ecuador (2020). Homepage, https://repositorio.uide.edu.ec/bitstream/37000/4310/1/LA%20INVESTI GACI%C3%93N%20CIENT%C3%8DFICA.pdf, (Accessed 02 Oct 2021)

Armesto, M.: Dramatización y literatura infantil: un binomio innovador para el desarrollo de la expresión oral y corporal en Educación Infantil Padres Y Maestros. J. Parents Teach. **379**, 24–28 (2019)

Aksoy, P.: Metaphoric perceptions on the concept of "social skills" of preschool teachers. Int. J. Progress. Educ. **16**(5), 176–198 (2020)

Batdi, V., Elaldi, S.: Effects of drama method on social communication skills: A comparative analysis. Int. J. Res. Educ. Sci. (IJRES) **6**(3), 435–457 (2020)

Cadena, P., Rendón, R., Aguilar, J., Salinas, E., De la Cruz, F., Sangerman, D.: Quantitative methods, qualitative methods or combination of research: an approach in the social sciences. Revista Mexicana de Ciencias Agrícolas **8**(7), 1603–1617 (2017)

Casanova, A., Couto, P.: English language in the classroom: A text dramatization experience in Galicia. DIGILEC: Revista Internacional de Lenguas Y Culturas **5**, 52–69 (2019)

Cruz, M.: Cosmovisión andina e interculturalidad: una mirada al desarrollo sostenible desde el sumak kawsay. Revista chakiñan,(5), 119–132 (2018) http://scielo.senescyt.gob.ec/pdf/rchakin/n5/2550-6722-rchakin-05-00119.pdf

Ergin, G., Özkan, B.: Examining the effect of merakli minik activities on preschool children's social skills. Southeast Asia Early Childhood J. **10**(1), 28–36 (2021)

Evans, C., Lewis, J.: Analysing Semi-Structured Interviews Using Thematic Analysis: Exploring Voluntary Civic Participation Among Adults. SAGE Publications, pp. 2–6 (2018)

Gemechu, G.: Problems of social skills in early childhood education program in ethiopia. IOJPE **9**(2), 156–170 (2020)

Gómez, L., Muriel, L., Londoño, D.: El papel del docente para el logro de un aprendizaje significativo apoyado en las TIC. Encuentros **17**(02), 118–131 (2019)

Gorman, T., Kanninen, M., Syrjä, T.: Immersive telepresence in theatre: performing arts education in digital spaces. Designing and implementing virtual exchange – a collection of case studies, pp. 23–35 (2020)

Khomais, S., Al-Khalidi, N., Alotaibi, D.: Dramatic play in relation to self- regulation in preschool age. Contemporary Issues Educ. Res. (CIER) **12**(4), 103–112 (2019)

Kröger, T.: Puppet as a Pedagogical Tool: A Literature Review. Int. Elect. J. Elementary Educ. **11**(4), 393–401 (2019)

Landín, R., Sánchez, I.: El método biográfico-narrativo: una herramienta para la investigación educativa. Educación **28**(54), 227–242 (2019)

Lima, A.: El teatro desde el aula virtual: una herramienta para generar seres resilientes. Ibero puebla, (12) (2021). Homepage, https://repositorio.iberopuebla.mx/bitstream/handle/20.500.11777/4938/PIT_LIMA_AnaLaura_FH.pdf?sequence=1&isAllowed=y, (Accessed 01 Aug 2021)

Lirola, M., Ruiz, G., Hernández, A., Prados, M.: Body expression-based intervention programs for persons with intellectual disabilities: a systematic review. Int. J. Eviron. Res. Public Health **17**(20), 1–13 (2020)

Llamazares, M., Selfa, M.: La dramatización de poemas infantiles: algunos ejemplos de trabajo para el aula de Educación Infantil y Primaria. Álabe **14**, 1–22 (2016)

Maleki, M., Mardani, A., Mitra, M., Dianatinasab, M., Vaismoradi, M.: Social Skills in Children at Home and in Preschool. Behav. Sci. **9**(7), 74 (2019)

Maharani, S.: The use of puppet: Shifting speaking skill from the perspective of students' self-esteem. Register J. **9**(2), 101–126 (2016)

Medrano, R.: The use of dramatization as a cooperative teaching-learning strategy. Revista Torreón Universitario **5**(2), 80–90 (2016)

Muszynska, A., Urpí, C., Galazka, A.: Teacher Education through Drama. CLIL Practice in the Spanish Context: Formación del profesorado a través de la dramatización: Práctica en el Aprendizaje Integrado de Lengua y Contenido en el contexto español. Estudios sobre educación **32**, 179–195 (2017)

Ocal, E., Karademir, A., Saatcioglu, O., Demirel, B.: Preschool teachers' preparation programs: The use of puppetry for early childhood science education. Int. J. Educ. Methodol. **7**(2), 305–318 (2021)

Özbey, S., Köycegiz, M.: Investigation of the effect of social skills training on the motivation levels of preschool children. Int. Electr. J. Elementary Educ. **11**(5), 477–486 (2019)

Pavlou, V., Anagnou, E., Fragkoulis, I.: Towards professional development: training needs assessment of primary school theater teachers in greece. Educ. Quart. Rev. **4**(1), 49–60 (2021)

Pekdogan, S., Akgul, E.: Preschool Children's School Readiness. Int. Educ. Stud. **10**(1), 144 (2016)

Peredo, R.: Volvemos a clases? Análisis desde la Psicología Educativa ante los efectos de la pandemia por Covid-19. Revista de Investigación Psicológica, (ESPECIAL) 55–66 (2020)

Pérez, C., Baigorria, H., De la Torre, Y., Pérez, C.: Experiencias de la práctica docente: Las Primeras Prácticas Docentes en la escuela rural. En O. Echevarria. Reflexión Academica en Diseño & Comunicación. 174–178. Universidad de Palermo (2019). Homepage, https://fido.palermo.edu/servicios_dyc/publicacionesdc/archivos/746_libro.pdf, (Accessed 07 Sep 2021)

Polevikova, O., Shvets, T.: Organization of different kinds of play with preschoolers – Perspectives of science and education, pp. 1–9 (2019)

Rashid, S., Qaisar, S.: Role play: a productive teaching strategy to promote critical thinking. Bull. Educ. Res. **39**(2), 197–213 (2017)

Schnyder, S., Wico, D., Huber, T.: Theater arts as a beneficial and educational venue in identifying and providing therapeutic coping skills for early childhood adversities: a systematic review of the literature. Inte. Electron. J. Elementary Educ. **13**(4), 457–467 (2021)

Solis, S., Monsivais, D., Huber, T.: Theater arts as a beneficial and educational venue in identifying and providing therapeutic coping skills for early childhood adversities: a systematic review of the literature. Int. Electron. J. Elementary Educ. **13**(4), 457–467 (2021)

Sotil, W.: Dramatización de cuentos para la práctica de valores morales en el nivel inicial, Chaglla – 2019. Revista Identidad **6**(2), 125–128 (2020)

Suhaini, M., Ahmad, A., Mohd, N.: Assessments on vocational knowledge and skills: a content validity analysis. Euro. J. Educ. Res. **10**(3), 1529–1540 (2021)

Tanner, S., Miller, E.: Some strange magic: the disruption of the whiteness of castle play through improvisation. Critical Questions Educ. **9**(2), 84–99 (2018)

Tersi, M., Matsouka, O.: Improving social skills through structured playfulness program in preschool children. Int. J. Instr. **13**(3), 259–274 (2020)

Togia, G., Charitaki, G., Soulis, S.: Special educators' perceptions about learning fundamental social skills through theatrical play: the case of children with special educational needs. Asian J. Appli. Sci. Technol. (AJAST) **1**(6), 95–100 (2017)

United Nations Educational, Scientific and Cultural Organization.: Interrupción y respuesta educativa (2020). Homepage, https://es.unesco.org/covid19/educationresponse, (Accessed 23 Sep2021)

Yataco, J., Fuster, D., Guillen, S., Nieto, J., Luy, C.: Educational Dramatization: A Fundamental Piece in Literature. Revista Gestão Inovação E Tecnologias **11**(3), 661–678 (2021)

Yazici, E.: The impact of art education program on the social skills of preschool children. J. Educ. Train. Stud. **5**(5), 17–26 (2017)

Wu, Z., Mak, M., Hu, Y., He, J., Fan, X.: A validation of the social skills domain of the social skills improvement system-rating scales with chinese preschoolers. Psychol. Sch. **56**(1), 126–147 (2018)

Assessing Digital Competence Through Teacher Training in Early Education Teachers

Geovanna Guallichico[1(✉)], Mauro Ocaña[1,2(✉)] (iD), Cristhian Tejada[3],
and Cuauhtémoc Bautista[4]

[1] Universidad de Las Fuerzas Armadas ESPE, Sangolquí, Ecuador
{gkguallichico,mhocana}@espe.edu.ec
[2] Departamento de Pedagogía, Facultad de Filosofía, Letras y Ciencias de la Educación,
Universidad Técnica de Manabí, Portoviejo, Ecuador
[3] Ayllu Academia, Caledon, Canada
[4] Agile Thought, Ciudad de México, Mexico

Abstract. Training programs on digital competences for teachers are often carried out without a thorough diagnosis, so it is difficult to accurately identify which digital competences need to be developed in teachers. Best-case scenario, questionnaires are proposed as the only diagnostic tool, and the answers are often based on the subjectivity of respondents which inevitably led to contradictions as revealed by the literature. In this study, a machine learning algorithm has been used to determine the teachers' needs in terms of detecting which and how much they need to improve their digital competences. 181 teachers took a 4-week-virtual course containing two modules (Content Creation and School Management) to assess specific teacher competences.

Results showed that the type of question used in the evaluations influences the academic performance of the participants. Data were analyzed based on 1) three types of questions (matching, multiple choice and true/false) and 2) scores obtained by the participants at the end of the course.

Firstly, matching questions reflect a greater distribution in the results, which indicates that this type of question may be more challenging, followed by the multiple-choice questions. While true or false questions should not be included as they leave too much room for chance.

Secondly, performance level reflects that demographic information (e.g. age, type of institution, and level at which they teach) is associated with final performance of digital competences. This type of analytics can provide a much more detailed overview in terms of detecting strengths and weaknesses in the development of digital competences of teachers.

Keywords: Learning analytics · Teacher training · Online course · Assessment · Digital skills

1 Introduction

It is widely acknowledged that digital literacy is a must in current times. Yet, this field has received scant attention despite that teachers must constantly be upgrading their

M. Botto-Tobar et al. (Eds.): ICAT 2022, CCIS 1757, pp. 55–68, 2023.
https://doi.org/10.1007/978-3-031-24978-5_6

competences to meet the evolving demands of digital education systems [1]. Among all professions, training of digital competences for preservice teachers is considered the lowest of all [2]. Consequently, it is becoming increasingly difficult to ignore that teachers need the necessary set of skills to integrate technology in their daily practices, mainly when students are developing their own digital expertise and learning from early ages, see e.g. [3–5]. Trends show us an increasing number of technologies which are waiting for well-trained teachers to be implemented in the 21st century classroom [6]. In the coming section, a review of the literature is presented to scope what has been done in the field of teachers' digital competences.

1.1 Digital Competence

The term digital competence is as elusive as evolving due to, among others, the rapid social and technological changes. Apart from some confusion about its conceptualization (competence, competency and competencies) [7], no one can deny that they are relevant to the educational field nowadays. Thus, Oberländer et al. [8] refer to digital competencies as "a set of basic knowledge, skills, abilities, and other characteristics that enable people…to efficiently and successfully accomplish their job tasks regarding digital media at work" whereas Ferrari [9] conceptualized digital competence as 'the set of knowledge, skills, attitudes, abilities, strategies and awareness that are required when using ICT [information and communication technologies] and digital media to perform tasks; solve problems; communicate; manage information; collaborate; create and share content; and build knowledge effectively, efficiently, appropriately, critically, creatively, autonomously, flexibly, ethically, reflectively for work, leisure, participation, learning and socialising' (p. 30).

Yet, there are few mechanisms to differentiate which digital competences teachers need to focus on. The most common tools are perception surveys and some frameworks intended to capture the nature of indicators in the complex field of digital competences. Although useful, both mechanisms heavily rely on personal opinions and, as such, perceptions regarding one's own competencies might be prone to subjectivity. Moreover, respondents may be confronted to choose between what they want instead of what they need to develop around their digital competences. In consequence, there are divergent results in early and primary education teachers who are the focus of the current study. Betancourt-Odio et al. [10] reported that 427 teachers from 15 Ibero-american countries found their digital competences ineffective to cope with changing situations (such as those of the Covid-19 pandemic). Even more, when digital competences are compared between levels, early childhood educators seem to have a better performance than their counterparts in primary education [11]. Sometimes student teachers attribute digital skills deficiency to their professors [12] or the outdated university programs [13]. That judgement may be because, in some contexts, teaching the basics of a program (e.g. a word processor) is considered to be enough, denying thus the utilization of other interactive resources that may help in the teaching tasks [14].

Even if digital competencies were identified, teachers usually use them inconsistently throughout the teaching process or with more emphasis in some subjects than others [15] which, again, widen the existing gaps in the field of teachers' digital competencies. In this regard, some local attempts, e.g. in Slovakia, to improve curricula are usually made, but again, they are based on subjectiveness [16].

On the other hand, there are several frameworks which have tried to standardize digital competences of teachers. Of the most seven used, the European framework for the digital competence of educators or DigCompEdu [17] has been considered the most favored by specialists which, of course, does not disregard the usefulness of other frameworks [18]. In addition to the obvious bias of self-perception, a common disadvantage is that each framework do not always point to the same indicators which has led researchers to take their own pathway through scale validations, see [19].

When applying DigCompEdu, it is usually the case that early childhood educators obtain the lowest scores [20] which contradicts what other studies found, e.g. [2, 7]. But this is not the only contradiction. There are more inconsistencies regarding the digital competences of early childhood educators. Despite acknowledging the importance of digital competences, student teachers in early childhood education believe that little these competences can help to their career and, although they recognize that ICTs may have a motivator effect on children, they do not always want to be trained in digital competences [21]. This perception is similar when other types of surveys are applied to early childhood education students [22]. However, in countries such as Portugal, the level of digital competences in teachers at primary and secondary level seems to be moderate while the pedagogic and student management competences are considered to be low [23, 24].

Another less frequent framework is the Common Framework for Teachers' Digital Competence (MCCDD, acronym in Spanish) which is supported by the Spain's National Institute of Educational Technologies and Teacher Training (INTEF). Supporters of this framework assure that it improves the digital competences in teachers mainly when it is combined with active methods [25]. Nevertheless, regardless which framework is taken into account, they all either use self-reporting instruments or are not adapted to countries in Latin America but the specific European contexts.

An additional oversighted component of every training program is the type of assessment used to evaluate digital literacy in early childhood educators. The next section deals with the type of assessment questions used in training programs for digital competences in education.

1.2 Types of Assessment Questions

The type of assessment may play a significant role in the teacher training of digital competences. Given the wide variety of questions to be used during a training program, stakeholders need to choose the best options. Some argue that formative assessment guided by a system can help trainees to better learn [26] as it has a positive influence on students due to its engaging nature [27]. Likewise, Draskovic et al. [28] calls our attention to the fact that students benefit from a more efficient method of performing tasks when using digital assessment items compared to pen and paper. Although, teachers may initially feel a little overloaded, the authors assert that teachers found this type of items easier to administrate and score than those of pen and paper. While there is some discussion about the fact that the type of question does not greatly affect the learning outcomes [29] others give special importance to certain types of questions. In this way, contemporary pedagogical models and their implementation in ICT mediating tools show a tendency towards quantitative and summative evaluation [30]. These researchers found that commonly used learning management systems (LMS) include a variety of quantitative assessment questions, with multiple choice questions being the most common.

On this subject, Mafinejad et al. [31] found that scores for multiple choice questions are significantly related to total skill scores while others, e.g. [32], see that multiple choice questions have the drawback that the student can choose the correct answer by guessing, without following the proper procedure to solve a problem. Where most research seems to agree is on the fact that there is practically no difference between text-based questions and multiple choice questions [33].

As described above, this section has outlined the importance of digital competences in teachers and how these competences are assessed. The evidence presented thus far suggests that discrepancies found among studies in the field of teachers' digital competences may emerge from the subjective nature of the instruments to assess. As a way to find another alternative outside the realm of self-reporting instruments, we launched a training course to assess digital competences in the very field through learning analytics. Based on the literature review, we hypothesized that assessment of digital competences is also threatened by the type of questions used to assess those digital competences. Accordingly, this study set out to apply a highly reliable algorithm 1) to identify how the type of question affected assessment of digital competences. Then, 2) to determine digital competences of teachers based on their performance.

2 Methodology

2.1 Research Design

This study adopted a quantitative non-experimental cross-sectional design without any manipulation of the variables which were measured at a given time [34]. Based on this, our research followed four differentiated and sequential stages: (a) introduction, which aimed at analyzing previous gaps; (b) methodological design, in which we selected research tools and techniques, study sample, and the data analysis method; (c) results, which showcased figures and tables of findings; finally (d) discussion, to compare and contrast our findings with previous studies.

2.2 Participants

181 early childhood educators from different provinces in Ecuador were enrolled in our course. Their age ranged from 22–59 years old. Of them, the largest subgroup (59%) was made of teachers between 22–38 years old followed by a smaller subgroup (36%) with ages between 39–53 years and finally the smallest subgroup (3%) with an age between 54 -59 years old.

They all came from 12 out of the 24 provinces of Ecuador, being Pichincha the most representative (94%), followed by Azuay, Loja, Santo Domingo (3%) and finally the other provinces (1%). Concerning the type of institution, 32% reported to work in public schools, 29% in private institutions, 34% were not working at that time and 5% worked in charter schools.

Regarding the educational level in which they taught, 36% worked with children from 5–6 years old, 24% with children from 4–5 years old, 22% with children from 3–4 years old, 11% with children from 7 -8 years and 6% work with children between 5–6 years. For this study, the results of the first 59 teachers who finished the course were taken to avoid noise in the results.

2.3 Instruments and Procedures

For data collection, a virtual training course was planned, designed and implemented in an institutional Learning Management System (LMS). This course was called *How to teach children through the Internet* (in Spanish), and aimed at early childhood education teachers. The course was made of 3 blocks whose contents are detailed below (Table 1):

Table 1. Blocks of the course How to teach children through the Internet.

No	Block's name	Goal	Skill to develop
1	Working online classes with children	Show playful strategies to attract the attention of children in the virtual environment	Identification of playful strategies that can be used in virtual learning environments
2	Digital content creation	Design digital technological materials	Production of images, audios and videos
3	School Management	Provide teachers with digital school management tools	Management of digital tools, management of evidence, institutional communication and collaborative teaching

For the purposes of this study, only blocks 2 and 3 were taken into account since block 1 was introductory and focused on capturing the attention of the participants rather than evaluating their technological skills. Hereafter, block 2 will be named Module 1 (Digital Content Creation) and block 3 will be named Module 2 (School Management).

Advertising of the virtual course was carried out through the institutional Facebook and registrations were open for two weeks during the height of the Covid-19 pandemic in 2021. At the end of the registrations, 181 teachers from different provinces of Ecuador were enrolled. Once the course was finished, the records of the grades of each student were retrieved from the online platform database.

2.4 Data Analysis

For data analysis we used a data mining approach. Data mining combines several technologies and theories (e.g. artificial intelligence, mathematical statistics, data visualization) to extract and link useful information to make scientific decisions more efficient [35].

Therefore, analyses were carried out in Python 3 [36] along with Pandas [37] (for tabular data management), numpy [38] (for array management), seaborn [39] (to make graphics) and scikit-learn [40] (for clusterization). Data were cleaned prior to descriptive and multivariate analyses by removing non-relevant information. Additionally, demographic data were coded according to province, city, institution in which teachers worked and the educational level in which they taught.

Data Analysis 1: How the Type of Question Affected Assessment

Data related to assessment were classified according to the type of question (multiple choice, true/false, matching). To determine which questions were easy or difficult for teachers, an analysis was carried out regarding the type of questions. To this end, the average for each participant grouped according to the type of question was obtained by following these steps: 1) data preprocessing, words were all turned to lowercase, spaces were changed to hyphens, special characters and accents were removed. 2) All scores were scaled to avoid extreme values. One of the main purposes of scaling is to make all datapoints be comparable, so we used the MaxAbsScaler method. 3) In order to compare the impact of the three types of questions: MC (multiple choice), T/F (True/False) and M (matching), the mean of the scores grouped by question type was obtained, to create three variables: MC_score, T/F_score and M_score (See Table 2).

Data Analysis 2: Digital Competences of Teachers

To determine the teachers' academic performance in terms of their digital competences, we applied k-means clustering which is an unsupervised classification method that groups individuals into subgroups based on their characteristics [41]. Additionally, the "k-means clustering algorithm is considered one of the most powerful and popular data mining algorithms in the research community" [42] (p. 1) and it has proven its value in grouping large amounts of data in virtual courses [43]. The value of k is fundamental in carrying out an adequate clustering, so the elbow method was used to determine the value of k. To get k-number of groups, it was necessary to compute the square of the distance between the sample points in each group and the center of the cluster to give a series of k values [41] (p. 2). Thus, the optimal number of groups was 3. In addition, the XGBoost regression model was used to determine the attributes that contributed the most to the final score of participants. i.e. we used XGBoost to make a feature selection of the most important characteristics of individuals.

3   Results

3.1   How the Type of Question Affected Assessment

The first reported results are based on the scores grouped by question type: MC (mul-tiple choice), T/F (True/False) and M (matching).

Table 2. Scores grouped by question type

	Count	Mean	Std	Min	25%	50%	75%	Max
MC_score	59.0	1.991	1.505	2.000	2.0	2.0	2.0	2.0
T/F score	59.0	2.000	2.000	2.000	2.0	2.0	2.0	2.0
M_score	59.0	1.873	0.218	1.725	2.0	2.0	2.0	2.0

Table 2 shows the mean of the scores obtained by the participants with respect to the type of question. It can be seen that each score is slightly different, with TF_score being the highest, followed by MC_score and M_score.

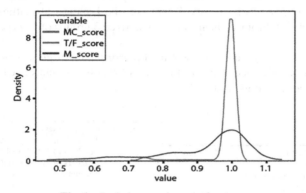

Fig. 1. Scaled scores by question type.

Figure 1 and Table 2 show that matching questions have a greater distribution of scores, which tells us that, for students, this type of question could be a little more complicated or that, by having a greater rating range, the information is more variable.

Additionally, the Pearson correlation coefficient was used to determine a linear relationship between age, module 1, module 2, final score, MC score and M_score.

Table 3. Relationship between attributes of the scores grouped by type of question

	Age	Module_1	Module_2	Score	MC_score	M_score
Age	1	−0.2063	0.1711	−0.0140	−0.0457	−0.0408
Module_1	−0.2063	1	0.3042	0.7930	0.2047	0.3672
Module_2	0.1711	0.3042	1	0.8215	0.2795	0.4528
Score	−0.0140	0.7930	0.8215	1	0.3013	0.5093
MC_score	−0.0457	0.2047	0.2795	0.3013	1	0.1228
M_score	−0.0408	0.3672	0.4528	0.5093	0.1228	1.0000

Table 3 indicates that there is a slight negative correlation (-0.2063) between age and module 1 (Digital Content Creation), which suggests that the older the age the lower the score in module 1 (Digital Content Creation). Conversely, a slight positive correlation (0.1711) between age and module 2 (School Management) which makes sense as the older the age the higher the score in module 2 (School Management). Likewise, a marginal positive correlation between module 1 (Creation of Digital Content) and module 2 (School Management) (0.3042) meaning that the higher the score in module 1 (Creation of Digital Content), the higher the score in module 2 (School Management).

3.2 Digital Competences of Teachers

As there were multiple digital competences assessed throughout the two modules of the course, a rigorous procedure that objectively grouped teachers according to the mastery of those competences was necessary. Therefore, the k-means algorithm was used as explained in Sect. 2.4. From such analyses, we derived 3 groups of teachers with similar characteristics.

Henceforth, these 3 groups will be called *performance groups*, which present the following characteristics according to the type of institution and educational level to which teachers belong (Figs. 2 and 3).

group	institution	frequency
0	public	7
	currently not working	5
	private	2
1	currently not working	8
	public	8
	private	7
	charter school	2
2	private	8
	currently not working	7
	public	4
	charter school	1

Fig. 2. Teacher groups according to the type of institution.

group	education level	frequency
0	Teachers of 5-6 year-old	6
	Teachers of 3-4 year-old	4
	Teachers of 7-8 year-old	2
	Teachers of 6-7 year-old	1
	Teachers of 4-5 year-old	1
1	Teachers of 5-6 year-old	9
	Teachers of 4-5 year-old	7
	Teachers of 7-8 year-old	5
	Teachers of 6-7 year-old	2
	Teachers of 3-4 year-old	2
2	Teachers of 3-4 year-old	7
	Teachers of 4-5 year-old	6
	Teachers of 5-6 year-old	6
	Teachers of 6-7 year-old	1

Fig. 3. Teacher groups according to the educational level where they teach.

Group 0: It is mostly made of teachers who work in public institutions and teach at first grade level (children 5–6 years old).

Group 1: It is mostly made of teachers who are not currently working but teach at first grade level (children 5–6 years old).

Group 2: It is mostly made of teachers who work in private institutions and teach at early level 1 (children 3–4 years old).

Performance Groups According to Their Final Scores

Table 4 shows that group 0 (public teachers-teaching children 5–6 years old) obtained the lowest mean (51.08 points) and approximately 50% of the participants obtained a score of 52.00 points out of 60. Group 1 (teachers who are not currently working - teach

Table 4. Final scores (module 1 + module 2)

group	count	mean	std	min	25%	50%	75%	max
0	20	51.087	2.371	45.33	50.670	52.000	52.340	50.0
1	25	56.988	1.498	54.00	56.010	56.670	56.000	59.0
2	14	52.159	1.542	49.55	50.865	52.335	53.612	56.0

children 5–6 years old) obtained the highest mean (56.98 points) and approximately 50% of them obtained a score of 56.67 points out of 60. Group 2 (private teachers - teaching children 3–4 years old) obtained an average of 52.15 and approximately 50% of the participants obtained a score of 52.33 points out of 60.

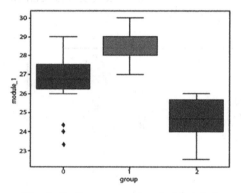   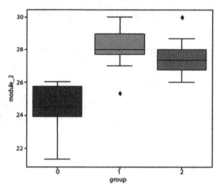

Fig. 4. Performance groups in Module 1   **Fig. 5.** Performance groups in Module 2

The maximum score for each module was 30 points. So, Fig. 4 shows that, in Module 1 (Digital Content Creation), the scores of group 0 (public teachers- teaching children of 5–6 years) are more dispersed compared to group 1 (teachers who are not working-teach to children aged 5–6 years) which are more compact. This means that the level of knowledge/proficiency in group 0 is more heterogeneous which could imply a wider variety in terms of training in contrast to group 1 which has a more homogeneous level of digital competences.

On the other hand, Fig. 5 shows that, in Module 2 (School Management), the grades of group 0 (public teachers- teaching children of 5–6 years) are more scattered than those of group 2 (private teachers - teaching children 3–4 years old). This means that group 0 showed greater heterogeneity in terms of mastering the school management skills, which implies that this group may need a wider variety of training courses in the near future.

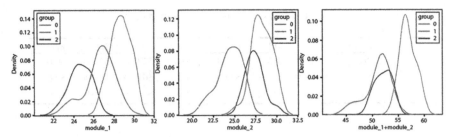

Fig. 6. Graphical comparison of the 3 groups regarding final score and modules 1 and 2

Figure 6 reveals that group 1 (teachers who are not currently working and teach children aged 5–6 years) in green performed better academically than the other groups in both module 1 (Digital Content Creation, left) and module 2 (School Management, center) as well as in the final result of the course (right).

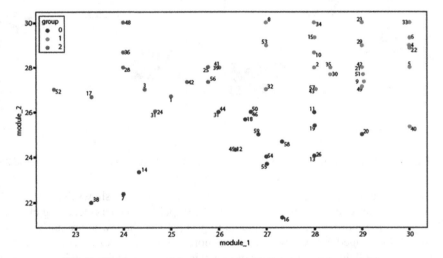

Fig. 7. Final scores of the 3 groups in relation to modules 1 and 2

Figure 7 shows comparatively, in greater detail, the academic performance in both modules (Digital Content Creation and School Management). Group 0 (in blue) had a higher score in module 1 (Digital Content Creation) but their performance is low in module 2 (School Management) whereas group 1 (in orange) obtained the highest grade in the two modules and group 2 (in green) obtained a low grade in module 1 (Digital Content Creation) but their score went up in module 2 (School Management).

4 Discussion and Conclusion

Assessment of digital competences in teachers is often carried out through self-reporting instruments which may usually induce biased or contradictory outcomes as reported by the literature (see Sect. 1.1). However, our study set out a different approach by applying machine learning techniques on the digital competence behaviors of early childhood educators who took an online training course about how to teach children through the Internet. The course in itself was intended to develop and assess digital competencies in participants at the end of it. Yet we used learning analytics to unveil further details.

The results of this study have shown that groups of teachers sharing similar characteristics also share some common digital competences. The k-means algorithm grouped all participating teachers in three clusters: group 0 (public teachers-teaching children of 5–6 years), group 1 (teachers who are not working-teach to children aged 5–6 years) and group 2 (private teachers - teaching children 3–4 years old). Of all these three groups of teachers, group 1 showed the highest performance in the competences of the two modules of the course: Module 1 (Digital Content Creation) and Module 2 (School Management). While group 0 scored second place in Module 1 (Digital Content Creation) and group 2 obtained second place in Module 2 (School Management). That a group of teachers who are not currently working had obtained the highest performance may indicate that teacher training should not take place during periods of high workload.

It was also found that age seems to be associated with digital competencies i.e. the younger the teachers the higher their digital competencies which, in turn, support those initiatives to include such skills in the curricula of pre-service teachers. Comparing these findings with those of other studies, e.g. [44–47], confirm age as predictor of the mastery of digital competences. Regarding the level where teachers work (which seems to be another predictor of teacher competencies), our research showed consistency with past studies, e.g. [48, 49].

The second major finding was that the type of question does influence the outcome of assessment, in this case, of teacher digital competences. Matching questions are the ones with the greatest dispersion in their data, followed by the Multiple Choice and T/F questions, which shows that the Matching questions and Multiple-Choice questions are more complex. The max and min score in the T/F questions do not have any variation, which reveals that these questions have much less complexity. This indicates that matching and multiple choice questions seem to be most suitable as they can cover a wider range of knowledge in terms of content as stated by previous studies, e.g. [50, 51], and can discourage students to guess the correct answer as contrarily stated by [32].

In conclusion, teacher training should be organized according to diagnoses that reveal the most important variables to be intervened. This research shows that the type of question used in training courses is key, as well as the level of education to which it is directed and, to a lesser degree, the age of the teachers. In other words, teacher training on technological teacher competencies must be adjusted to the type of institution and educational level in which teachers have worked recently, considering the existing weaknesses. An implication of this is the possibility for institutions to design digital literacy training programs for their teachers according to these specifics.

Taken together, these results suggest that there are much more objective ways to assess teacher digital competences than sole self-reporting instruments. As with all such studies, there are limitations that offer opportunities for further research. Further work containing a larger sample size is required in order to reach more generalizable results.

References

1. Davydenko, V., Kuznetsova, A., Chichik, N.: Impact of digitalization trends on the development of the Russian system of advanced training and methodological support for teachers (2021)
2. Senkbeil, M., Ihme, J.M., Schöber, C.: Dissemination of media literacy at school in a digital world: are teacher candidates digitally competent? Psychol. Erzieh. Unterr. **68**(1), 4–22 (2021)
3. Quinga, Y., Pilataxi, N., Carvajal, V., Ocaña, M.: Virtual activities to strengthen basic math skills in children. In: Botto-Tobar, M., Cruz, H., Díaz Cadena, A., Durakovic, B. (eds.) Emerging Research in Intelligent Systems. CIT 2021. Lecture Notes in Networks and Systems, vol. 406. Springer, Cham (2022). https://doi.org/10.1007/978-3-030-96046-9_13
4. Vega, B., Velasco, M., Ocaña, M., Rebeca, M. (2022). Scratchjr visual programming language for early math skills development in 4–7 years old children. In: Botto-Tobar, M., Cruz, H., Díaz Cadena, A., Durakovic, B. (eds.) Emerging Research in Intelligent Systems. CIT 2021. Lecture Notes in Networks and Systems, vol. 406. Springer, Cham. https://doi.org/10.1007/978-3-030-96046-9_19
5. Albán Bedoya, I. and M. Ocaña-Garzón. *Educational Programming as a Strategy for the Development of Logical-Mathematical Thinking*. 2022. Cham: Springer International Publishing
6. Alexander, B., et al., *Educause Horizon report: 2019 Higher Education edition*. 2019
7. Moore, D.R., Cheng, M.I., Dainty, A.R.J.: Competence, competency and competencies: performance assessment in organisations. Work Study **51**(6), 314–319 (2002)
8. Oberländer, M., Beinicke, A., Bipp, T.: Digital competencies: a review of the literature and applications in the workplace. Comput. Educ. **146**, 103752 (2020)
9. Ferrari, A., *Digital competence in practice: An analysis of frameworks*, in *JRC IPTS*. 2012, Joint Research Centre of the European Commission: Sevilla. p. 82116
10. Betancourt-Odio, M.A., et al.: Self-perceptions on digital competences for M-learning and education sustainability: a study with teachers from different countries. Sustainability (Switzerland) **13**(1), 1–12 (2021)
11. Urrea-Solano, M., et al.: The learning of e-sustainability competences: A comparative study between future early childhood and primary school teachers. Educ. Sci. **11**(10), 644 (2021)
12. Gómez-Trigueros, I.M., de Atalaya, S.P.L., Ros, R.D.: Towards an insertion of technologies: the need to train in digital teaching competence. Int. Multi. J. Soc. Sci. **10**(3), 64–87 (2021)
13. Záhorec, J., Hašková, A., Munk, M.: Teachers' professional digital literacy skills and their upgrade. Eur. J. Contemp. Educ. **8**(2), 378–393 (2019)
14. Záhorec, J., Hašková, A., Munk, M.: Integration of Digital Technology Applications into the Pre-gradual Teacher Training, pp. 892–901 (2020)
15. Záhorec, J., Nagyová, A., Hašková, A.: Teachers' attitudes to incorporation digital means in teaching process in relation to the subjects they teach. Int. J. Eng. Pedagogy **9**(4), 100–120 (2019)
16. Záhorec, J., Hašková, A., Munk, M.: Curricula design of teacher training in the area of didactic technological competences. In: Auer, M.E., Guralnick, D., Simonics, I. (eds.) ICL 2017. AISC, vol. 716, pp. 383–393. Springer, Cham (2017). https://doi.org/10.1007/978-3-319-73204-6_43
17. Redecker, C.: European framework for the digital competence of educators: DigCompEdu., Joint Research Centre (Seville, Spain) (2017)

18. Cabero-Almenara, J., Romero-Tena, R., Palacios-Rodríguez, A.: Evaluation of teacher digital competence frameworks through expert judgement: the use of the expert competence coefficient **9**(2), 19 (2020)
19. Barragán-Sánchez, R., et al.: Teaching digital competence and eco-responsible use of technologies: development and validation of a scale. Sustainability (Switzerland) **12**(18), 7721 (2020)
20. García-Vandewalle García, J.M., et al.: Analysis of digital competence of educators (DigCompEdu) in teacher trainees: the context of Melilla, Spain. Technology, Knowledge and Learning (2021)
21. Pérez-Jorge, D., et al.: Training in digital skills in early childhood: education teachers the case of the university of la laguna. Int. J. Interact. Mob. Technol. **14**(20), 35–49 (2020)
22. Romero-Tena, R., et al.: The challenge of initial training for early childhood teachers. A cross sectional study of their digital competences. Sustainability (Switzerland) **12**(11), 4782 (2020)
23. Dias-Trindade, S., Moreira, J.A.: Assessment of high school teachers on their digital competences. Magis **13**, 01–21 (2020)
24. Dias-Trindade, S., Moreira, J.A., Ferreira, A.G.: Evaluation of the teachers' digital competences in primary and secondary education in Portugal with digcompedu checkin in pandemic times. Acta Scientiarum - Technology **43**, e56383–e56383 (2021)
25. Romero-García, C., Buzón-García, O., de Paz-Lugo, P.: Improving future teachers' digital competence using active methodologies. Sustainability (Switzerland) **12**(18), 7798 2020
26. Hettiarachchi, E., Huertas, M.A., Mor, E.: E-assessment system for skill and knowledge assessment in computer engineering education. Int. J. Eng. Educ. **31**(2), 529–540 (2015)
27. Hettiarachchi, E., et al.: Improving student performance in high cognitive level courses by using formative e-assessment. Int. J. Technol. Enhanced Learn. **7**(2), 116–133 (2015)
28. Draskovic, D., Misic, M., Stanisavljevic, Z.: Transition from traditional to LMS supported examining: a case study in computer engineering. Comput. Appl. Eng. Educ. **24**(5), 775–786 (2016)
29. Tetteh, G.A., Sarpong, F.A.A.: Infuence of type of assessment and stress on the learning outcome. J. Int. Educ. Bus. **8**(2), 125–144 (2015)
30. Torres-Madroñero, E.M., Torres-Madroñero, M.C., Botero, L.D.R.: Challenges and possibilities of ICT-mediated assessment in virtual teaching and learning processes. Future Internet **12**(12), 1–20 (2020)
31. Mafinejad, M.K., et al.: Use of Multi-Response format test in the assessment of medical students' critical thinking ability. J. Clin. Diagn. Res. **11**(9), LC10-LC13 (2017)
32. Jaquez, J., et al.: TecEval: an on-line dynamic evaluation system for engineering courses available for web browsers and tablets (2015)
33. Jahn, G.: Smooth transition from text-based exams to multiple-choice, pp. 448–453 (2022)
34. Hernández-Sampieri, R., Torres, C.P.M.: Metodología de la investigación, vol. 4 (2018). McGraw-Hill Interamericana México^ eD. F DF
35. Pan, L.: A big data-based data mining tool for physical education and technical and tactical analysis. Int. J. Emerg. Technol. Learn. **14**(22), 220–231 (2019)
36. Van Rossum, G., Drake, F.L.: Python 3 reference manual (2007). CreateSpace
37. McKinney, W.: Data structures for statistical computing in python. In: Proceedings of the 9th Python in Science Conference, Austin, TX (2010)
38. Harris, C.R., et al.: Array programming with NumPy. Nature **585**(7825), 357–362 (2020)
39. Waskom, M.L.: Seaborn: statistical data visualization. J. Open Source Softw. **6**(60), 3021 (2021)
40. Pedregosa, F., et al.: Scikit-learn: machine learning in Python. J. Mach. Learn. Res. **12**, 2825–2830 (2011)
41. Yuan, C., Yang, H.: Research on k-value selection method of k-means clustering algorithm. J **2**(2), 226–235 (2019)

42. Ahmed, M., Seraj, R., Islam, S.M.S.: The k-means algorithm: a comprehensive survey and performance evaluation. Electronics **9**(8), 1295 (2020)
43. Ocaña, M., Khosravi, H., Bakharia, A.: Profiling language learners in the big data era. In: ASCILITE 2019 - 36th International Conference of Innovation, Practice and Research in the Use of Educational Technologies in Tertiary Education: Personalised Learning. Diverse Goals. One Heart, pp. 237–245 (2019)
44. Claro, M., et al.: Teaching in a digital environment (TIDE): defining and measuring teachers' capacity to develop students' digital information and communication skills. Comput. Educ. **121**, 162–174 (2018)
45. Ertl, B., Csanadi, A., Tarnai, C.: Getting closer to the digital divide: an analysis of impacts on digital competencies based on the German PIAAC sample. Int. J. Educ. Dev. **78**, 102259 (2020)
46. Nguyen, M.H., Hunsaker, A., Hargittai, E.: Older adults' online social engagement and social capital: the moderating role of Internet skills. Inf. Commun. Soc. **25**, 1–17 (2020)
47. Saikkonen, L., Kaarakainen, M.-T.: Multivariate analysis of teachers' digital information skills - the importance of available resources. Comput. Educ. **168**, 104206 (2021)
48. Cabero-Almenara, J., et al.: Classification models in the digital competence of higher education teachers based on the DigCompEdu framework: logistic regression and segment tree. J. E-Learn. Knowl. Soc. **17**(1), 49–61 (2021)
49. Záhorec, J., Hašková, A., Munk, M.: First results of a research focused on teachers' didactic technological competences development. In: Auer, M.E., Tsiatsos, T. (eds.) ICL 2018. AISC, vol. 917, pp. 461–472. Springer, Cham (2018). https://doi.org/10.1007/978-3-030-11935-5_44
50. Siddiqui, N.I., et al.: Contemplation on marking scheme for Type X multiple choice questions, and an illustration of a practically applicable scheme. Indian J. Pharmacol. **48**(2), 114–121 (2016)
51. Tangianu, F., et al.: Are multiple-choice questions a good tool for the assessment of clinical competence in internal medicine? Italian J. Med. **12**(2), 88–96 (2018)

Social Networks, Sustainable, Satisfaction and Loyalty in Tourist Business

Giovanni Herrera-Enríquez[1]([⊠]), Eddy Castillo-Montesdeoca[1],
Juan Gabriel Martínez-Navalón[2], and Vera Gelashvili[2]

[1] Citur, Universidad de las Fuerzas Armadas – ESPE, Sangolquí, Ecuador
gpherrera@espe.edu.ec
[2] Departament of Business Economics, Rey Juan Carlos University, 28032 Madrid, Spain

Abstract. This research analyses the impact of social networks with environmentally friendly content on the levels of trust and satisfaction of customers of tourism companies in Ecuador. The study uses a questionnaire applied to a sample of 2800 people. The results are analyzed through the partial least squares method and allow us to accept the hypotheses on the positive impact of environmentally friendly content in social networks on the satisfaction levels of customers of tourism services, as well as the positive impact of satisfaction on their loyalty.

1 Introduction

Social networks allow consumers to achieve real contact with specific people within the organization, and good customer service achieves numerous objectives, including increasing customer satisfaction and, therefore, customer loyalty. In this context, satisfaction is a causal factor for recommending and repeating the use or consumption of a product or service. Ribbink, van Riel, Liljander, and Streokens (2004) consider that social networks can complement customers' perception of satisfaction and motivate them to communicate their experiences to others, which determines an opportunity for companies that wish to use this medium to improve satisfaction and strengthen loyalty.

It has been identified that companies make use of social networks not only to promote their products and/or services or to position their image but also for sustainability (Du, Yalcinkaya, Bstieler, 2016), whose meaning has been developed from different approaches (Brown, Hanson, Liverman, and Merideth, 1987), within the business context, sustainability is understood as environmentally friendly policies and actions in which economic development takes place in an environment of social balance (Martínez-Navalón, Gelashvili, and Saura, 2020), from this perspective the promotion of sustainability has nowadays become an important objective for companies in different sectors.

Sustainability is vital for business and society. Nevertheless, the evidence of its study is limited in developing countries such as Ecuador, a country that, like many others in the region, is highly dependent on the tourism sector for its income and which, in recent years, has been affected by unprecedented crises, such as the SARS-CoV2 pandemic and the consequences of the armed conflict between Russia and Ukraine. Tourism development has generally been considered a positive contribution to economic growth (Che Chou, 2013), so its analysis is always a topical issue.

Tourism activity in Ecuador is essential; during 2015–2018, an increasing influx of foreign tourists was reported, with 2.43 million foreigners visiting the country in 2018. At the end of 2019, this influx was reduced by 16% compared to the previous year (Ministry of Tourism, 2022). Most foreign tourists entering the country in 2019 came from Colombia (38%), the United States (20%), and Peru (15%). Tourism revenues reached USD 2.4 billion at the end of 2018 and represent the third-largest source of non-oil revenues (Ministry of Tourism, 2022). Data for 2020, 2021, and 2022 are atypical due to the consequences of the global impact crises.

Tourism companies materialize their activity in the satisfactory or unsatisfactory experience of their customers, which is why the relationship between the use of social networks and this economic sector is of particular interest (Martínez-Navalón, Gelashvili, Saura, 2020). For tourism, social networks are a fast and powerful way to connect with current and potential customers. Improving customer perception is also vital for developing the localities where tourism activity occurs and where social media's role is relevant (Zhang and Zhang, 2018).

2 Literature Review

2.1 Social Networking, Tourism, Satisfaction, and Loyalty

Companies have started to use social media to interact, facilitate information search, promote, and improve customer buying behaviors (Zeng and Gerritsen, 2014). By the end of 2019, its use accelerated exponentially in response to the SARS-CoV2 confinement, leaving many questions about its harms and benefits (Yul Lee, Soo Yang, Ghauri, and Park, 2022).

Interactivity is one of the most relevant factors determining customer engagement in social media communities. Social media, in turn, has been shown to increase revenue, business efficiency, and the impact of promotions and advertising (Alalwan, Rana, Dwivedi, Yogesh, and Algharabat, 2017). The use of social media is directly linked to relationship marketing strategies, which seek to create a collaborative relationship with the customer and a greater sense of belonging to the company's brand. Relationship marketing aims to achieve customer loyalty, which occurs when the individual is a favorable attitude toward the company when buying its products or services (Campón, Baptista, and Hernández, 2009). In the tourism sector, consumers have a higher degree of uncertainty due to the nature of the services and the consequences on their satisfaction and loyalty, which tends to be greater in comparison with other sectors, which is why the relationship marketing approach in tourism companies is particularly appropriate.

Trust has a positive effect on relationship commitment; if customers maintain a good relationship with the company in the long term, the trust they have in the company will generate or be a strong driver of loyalty, commitment, and loyalty in the customer relationship (Kassim and Abdullah, 2010). Therefore, it can be stated that customer satisfaction is strongly and positively related to the trust they have in a company, even more so in the case of tourism services.

2.2 Social Media Marketing and Sustainability in the Tourism Sector

Sustainability in the business world starts its evolutionary path from corporate social responsibility initiatives focused on marketing, being an integral part of the strategic planning system (Fuxman, Mohr, Mahmoud, and Grigoriou, 2022). However, it has several edges. One of these is environmental sustainability, which is related to the protection and preservation of natural resources and the development of renewable energy sources, and a balanced consumption with the environment and human development (Gelashvili, Martínez-Navalón, and Herrera-Enríquez, 2021). Signitzer and Prexl (2008) argue that sustainability relates to environmentally responsible products, social justice, and sustainable awareness.

By integrating the concepts of sustainability and marketing, it can be understood that price, product, place, and promotion actions will be oriented to satisfy three criteria: customer needs, company objectives, and the compatibility of processes with the ecosystem (Lee, 2016), consequently relationship marketing focused on sustainability can make use of social networks as a mechanism to reach its customers and establish it as an effective strategy to strengthen its positioning around the concept of sustainable business (Kotler, Kartajaya, and Setiawan, 2010), however, to achieve this it must achieve customer satisfaction that will materialize in consumer loyalty.

Tourism is representative of many developing countries because it generates wealth and distributes it more equitably (Chica, Hernández, and Perc, 2022). Tourism has a direct relationship with the environment, society, and the economy, so the balance of these three components is essential; consequently, consumers of these products and services are aware that this integral and harmonious relationship must be part of the offer (Zhang, Zhong, and Yu, 2022). Evidencing the sustainable exercise of tourism is a challenge for companies dedicated to this sector, so communication through social networks is presented as an alternative to strengthen satisfaction and generate consumer loyalty.

3 Hypothesis Development

The development of the hypotheses considers the different studies that evidence relationships between marketing and environmental sustainability that is achieved through the development of innovative and competitive products and services that generate customer satisfaction and trust (Walch and Dodds, 2017). It would be expected that the results in the case raised confirm these statements. The variables of environmental sustainability and consumer satisfaction allow the following hypothesis to be put forward:

Hypothesis H1. Publications on social networks related to environmental sustainability directly and positively influence user satisfaction. According to Martínez-Navalón, Gelashvili, and Saura (2020), the relationship between the satisfaction of users of social networks related to tourism companies in Spain has a positive effect on the trust of companies, so it would be expected that this relationship is present in the case raised, so the following hypothesis is proposed:

Hypothesis H2. The satisfaction of social network users with tourism companies directly and positively influences their trust in these companies. The literature on environmental sustainability, satisfaction, and loyalty was carried out. The following study model (See Fig. 1) is proposed, as well as the hypotheses proposed (See Fig. 1).

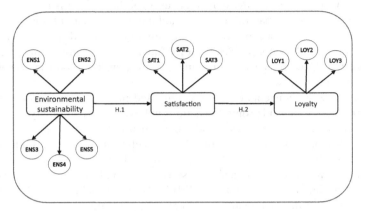

Fig. 1. Research model

4 Methodology

4.1 Data

The study uses a questionnaire that has been developed based on the literature review related to the subject. The questionnaire was carried out in person at different points in Quito (Ecuador). The specialized nature of the data collection made it possible to analyze users directly after the pandemic and to gather their evaluations more accurately.

The questionnaire was applied to 2850 people; 50 were discarded because the information was incomplete. It should be noted that the data collection is completely anonymous, and it is impossible to identify the respondents' origin a posteriori, which allows us to preserve their anonymity and comply with the different data protection regulations.

For the collection of the sample of 2800 valid questionnaires, a questionnaire was used, which is divided into two parts. Firstly, questions were asked to classify the individual, these being classificatory questions. Secondly, individuals are asked questions about the three variables analyzed and which allows us to measure the level of sentiment in each of them.

A questionnaire is used to measure the sentiment in the questions and therefore be able to carry out a complete analysis (Gelashvili, Martínez-Navalón, and Herrera-Enríquez, 2021) used, whose questions are on a Likert scale. This scale is structured with a measurement where five is "strongly agree," and 0 is "strongly disagree." This scale is considered one of the most reliable and valuable in Social Sciences (Alismail and Zhang, 2020).

The variables analyzed in the questionnaire were environmental sustainability, satisfaction, and loyalty. For each of the variables, different questions were asked to allow the measurement of each variable. The questions were obtained from a thorough literature review.

Table 1. Sample characteristics (n = 345)

Classification variable	Variable	Frequency	Percentage
Gender	Female	1410	50.36%
	Male	1382	49.36%
	Others	8	0.29%
Population of the place of residence	< 5.000 people	132	4.71%
	5000–20.000 people	500	17.86%
	20.000–100.000 people	843	30.11%
	> 100.000 people	1325	47.32%
Employment situation	Housewife/man	161	5.75%
	Unemployed	476	17.00%
	Self-employed	1130	40.36%
	Employee	1004	35.86%
	Retired	28	1.00%
Level of education	Without studies	4	0.14%
	Basic studies	109	3.89%
	High school	738	26.36%
	Vocational training	944	33.71%
	University studies	1005	35.89%
Minutes devoted to social medias per day	< 30	170	6.07%
	30–60	415	14.82%
	60–90	554	19.79%
	90–120	709	25.32%
	> 120	952	34.00%

Table 1 shows the characteristics of the respondents. These characteristics are obtained by classificatory questions that allow us to classify the respondents as a posteriori. Firstly, the sample is very even in terms of the sex of the respondents. Slightly more women than men (50.36% and 43.36%, respectively). Secondly, it is worth noting that most of the users surveyed reside in a population of over 100,000 inhabitants (43.37%), followed by 30.11% of the individuals who have their habitual residence in a population of between 20,000 and 100,000 inhabitants. It can be deduced that most respondents reside in large towns. Thirdly, the sample comprises mainly self-employed individuals

(40.36% of the sample), followed by employees (35.86%). Fourthly, the level of education of the sample, in general, is high, with 35.89% having a university education. Lastly, an important data point in this study is the number of minutes individuals spend each day on social networks. Most respondents spend more than 2 hours a day on social networks.

4.2 Method of Data Analysis

In analyzing the variables proposed in the model (Fig. 1) and after having carried out the theoretical approach, we proceed to analyze both the variables and the relationships between them. For these analyses, the partial least squares (PLS) technique is used in this study. Using structural equations based on variances is one of social science studies most widely used techniques.

It should also be noted that it is one of the most widely used techniques in studies where the measurement of the respondents' feelings is carried out using a Likert scale for data collection (Del-Castillo-Feito, Blanco-González, and González-Vázquez, The relationship between image and reputation in the Spanish public university. 2019). The software used in this case is SmartPLS, which allows us to assess the reliability and validity of the different measurement scales and test the structural model (Henseler, Ringle, and Sarstedt, 2015). Its choice is based on its capacity for the graphical resolution of the study and the set of possible statistical methods that can be applied during the research (Cachon Rodriguez, Blanco-González, Prado-Román, and Diez-Martin, 2021).

This study evaluation technique allows measuring the simultaneous behavior of the relationships proposed as a dependent. It also allows for very comprehensive multiple regression and factor analysis studies. Relationships can be studied without having to fix the relationships of the influences in the hypotheses, allowing for a more complex and varied study (Liengaard et al. 2021).

5 Analysis of the Results

5.1 Measurement Model

Once the study sample has been analyzed, we proceed to analyze the proposed model. Before starting, this analysis is divided into two processes. In the first process, the study of the scale of measurement proposed must be carried out. In this analysis, the questions used to measure the variables are checked to ensure that they are correct and, therefore, valid for the analysis (Gelashvili, Vera, Martínez-Navalón, and Saura, 2021). In the second process, once the scale has been validated, the hypotheses set out in the model are analyzed (Fig. 1), as the predictive capacity of the variables and the model in general (Martínez-Navalón, Gelashvili, and Saura, 2020).

In the first of the analyses described above, all the variables in the study are reflective. This characteristic indicates that the analysis process of the measurement scale should have the following studies: individual reliability, composite reliability, convergent validity, and discriminant validity. The data obtained from these analyses will make it possible to validate each of the questions asked in the questionnaire and, therefore, validate the scale. These analyses can be seen in Tables 2 and 3.

In the individual reliability analysis, each question's loadings (λ) must be studied. To be validated, the value of the loadings must be higher than 0.707 (Carmines and Zeller, 1979); (Del-Castillo-Feito, Cachón-Rodríguez, and Paz-Gil, Politi-cal Disaffection, Sociodemographic, and Psychographic Variables as State Legitimacy Determinants in the European Union, 2020). In this analysis, all the items proposed to pass the test in the case of the composite reliability study where Cronbach's Alpha should be analyzed following the criteria of Nunnally and Bernstein (1994). The cut-off level of the Alpha is 0.707. Once this process has been analyzed, it could be concluded that there is high reliability in the study. However, as it has a variable above 0.85, it is advisable to carry out the study (Dijkstra and Henseler, 2015). In this analysis, the ratio (rho_A) is analyzed, and the cut-off value of the variable is set at 0.7 (Gelashvili, Vera, Martínez-Navalón, and Saura, 2021). All the items proposed in the study have passed the three analyses carried out so far.

Fourthly, convergent validity analysis is carried out, that is, the analysis known as average variance extracted (AVE). This analysis, carried out according to the criteria of (Fornell and Larcker, 1981), sets a cut-off point for AVE at 0.5. This cut-off indicates that the variables must have at least 50% of the explanation of the underlying variables (Hair, Risher, Sarstedt, and Ringle, 2019).

Table 2. Measurement items

Constructs	Items	Correlation loading	CA	rho_A	CR	AVE
Evironmental sustainability	(ENS-1) Las empresas turísticas que sigo en redes sociales tienen políticas de reciclaje	0.782***	0.897	0.901	0.924	0.709
	(ENS-2) Las cuentas de redes sociales de la empresa turística que sigo promueven la ética ambiental positiva entre todos	0.861***				
	(ENS-3) Las empresas turísticas que sigo en redes sociales valoran y protegen al medio ambiente	0.869***				
	(ENS-4) Las redes sociales de las empresas turísticas que sigo publican mensajes de concentración contra la contaminación	0.844***				

(continued)

Table 2. (*continued*)

Constructs	Items	Correlation loading	CA	rho_A	CR	AVE
	(ENS-5) Las redes sociales de las empresas turísticas que sigo defienden la diversidad de la naturaleza, promoviendo que sea valorada y protegida	0.852***				
Satisfaction	(SAT-1) Me siento satisfecho con los conocimientos que me aportan las redes sociales de las empresas turísticas a las que sigo	0.854***	0.825	0.826	0.896	0.741
	(SAT-2) En términos generales estoy satisfecho con las redes sociales de las empresas turísticas a las que sigo	0.862***				
	(SAT-3) Las redes sociales de empresas turísticas a las que sigo cubren mis expectativas	0.867***				
Loyalty	(LOY-1) Tengo intención de continuar siguiendo a las mismas empresas turísticas en redes sociales	0.854***	0.792	0.801	0.878	0.706
	(LOY-2) Si pudiera, dedicaría más tiempo a seguir a las empresas turísticas en redes sociales	0.793***				
	(LOY-3) Recomendaría a otras personas a seguir en redes sociales a las empresas turísticas que sigo	0.868***				

To complete the validation of the measurement scale, it is necessary to carry out a final process, that of discriminant validity. This process analyzes the variable's variance from the items that make it up. The contribution of the items must be more significant than that which these items may share with other variables in the model (Hair, Risher, Sarstedt, and Ringle, 2019). The Fornell and Larcker (1981) criterion has traditionally been used to carry out this study. Many researchers in their work have used these criteria. However, it has recently been found that it is not a very demanding study, so Hair et al. (2019) recommend using another more recent and more demanding criterion that allows for greater robustness in this analysis (Del-Castillo-Feito, Blanco-González, and

González-Vázquez, The relationship between image and reputation in the Spanish public university., 2019). This second criterion is the Heterotraitmonotrait ratio (HTMT). This analysis sets the cut-off index at the maximum value of 0.9. These indicate that the variables in the model analyzed would be empirically different (Dijkstra and Henseler, 2015). Once the analyses have been carried out, it can be seen in Table 3 that all items meet both criteria.

Table 3. Measurement discriminant validity

Constructs	Fornell-Lakert			Heterotrait-Monotrait ratio (HTMT)		
	Loyalty	Satisfaction	Environmental sustainability	Loyalty	Satisfaction	Environmental sustainability
Loyalty	**0.840**					
Satisfaction	0.713	**0.861**		0.878		
Environmental sustainability	0.590	0.592	**0.842**	0.694	0.686	

Finally, it can be affirmed that the measurement scale proposed in the model and made up of the questions on the variables environmental sustainability, satisfaction, and loyalty is a valid and reliable scale of measurement. The questions asked in the study are valid for measuring the proposed variables and the relationships between them.

5.2 Structural Model Analysis

To finalize the analysis of the results, a study of the model must be carried out, studying the influences proposed in the model and its prediction. In order to carry out this study, a bootstrapping of 50,000 samples will be performed. This analysis allows standard errors and t-statistics to be obtained (Cachon Rodriguez, Blanco-González, Prado-Román, and Diez-Martin, 2021).

Before starting with the analysis, it is necessary to analyze whether there is multi-linearity in the structural model. This analysis applies the VIF value criterion that shows whether such collinearity exists in the model. If values of less than five are obtained, it can be affirmed that there is no multicollinearity in the model (Gelashvili, Vera, Martínez-Navalón, and Saura, 2021). Once this criterion has been applied, the relationships of the study have values equal to 1, so there is no multicollinearity, and we can proceed to measure the relationship between the variables and the predictive power of the model.

In the analysis of the model, we can see how both hypotheses are accepted, as we can see in Table 4. In the same way, we can see how the original sample of the relationship is high, as well as the t-statistics being 37.619 for H.1 and 57.871 for H.2, which indicates the strong influence of the relationship. Similarly, the third criterion for validating the relationships is confidence intervals. These also show the validation of the relationships satisfactorily.

Regarding the explained variance (R2) of the model, it can be seen that the prediction results are promising. Both explained variances have a medium predictive power (Chin,

1998). Similarly, the effect size (f2), the degree to which an exogenous variable contributes to explaining an endogenous variable, has a significant effect, and the predictive relevance of the model (Q2) is obtained by blindfolding analysis. This shows that the model has a medium predictive validity, being very close to a high predictive relevance (Hair, Risher, Sarstedt, and Ringle, 2019) (Fig. 2).

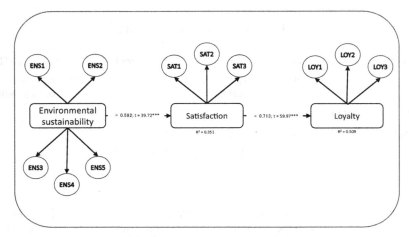

Fig. 2. Proposed research model

Table 4. Comparation of hypotheses

	Path coeff (β)	Statistics t (β/STDEV)	f²	Confidence interval	
				5.0%	95.0%
H1. Enviromental Sustainability → Satisfaction	0.592***	39.72	0.540	0.567	0.615
H2. Satisfaction → Loyalty	0.713***	59.96	1.036	0.693	0.732

R^2: Loyalty = 0.509; Satisfaction = 0.351
Q^2: Loyalty = 0.355; Satisfación = 0.258

Notes: For n = 50000 subsamples. Students in single queue ***p < 0,001;

6   Conclusions

The study confirms the direct and positive relationship between environmentally sustainable content on social networks and the level of customer satisfaction of the companies analyzed so that the decisions of tourism companies related to environmentally friendly actions and their communication through social networks can generate a positive image that could be capitalized with higher revenues because of high levels of satisfaction. Ecuador is a country that presents itself to the world as a natural destination, which is why foreign tourists take sustainability very much into account as a factor in choosing a destination or a tourism company.

Although there is theoretical and empirical evidence on the relationship between satisfaction and trust, this study presents a particular approach by analyzing the satisfaction of social network users and its direct and positive relationship with the trust they may have in the tourism companies studied in Ecuador. The design of communication strategies through social networks should consider that these are a way to develop trust in customers, strengthening their positioning and the quality of their relationship with their customers.

This study has limitations regarding the sample design, which was not probabilistic, and therefore does not allow inferences to be made about the population. Despite this, the number of companies studied is relevant, as the object of study, which was the city of Quito, is considered one of the most representative heritage cities in Latin America.

References

Alalwan, A.A., Rana, N., Dwivedi, Y., Algharabat, R.: Social media in marketing: A review and analysis of the existing literature. Telematics Inform. (2017). https://doi.org/10.1016/j.tele.2017.05.008

Alismail, S., Zhang, H.: Exploring and understanding participants' perceptions of facial emoji Likert scales in online surveys: a qualitative study. ACM Trans. Soc. Comput. **3**, 1–12 (2020)

Brown, B., Hanson, M., Liverman, D., Merideth, R.: Global sustainability: Toward definition. Environ. Manag. **11**, 713–719 (1987). https://doi.org/10.1007/BF01867238

Rodríguez, C.G., Blanco-González, A., Prado-Román, C., Diez-Martin, F.: Sustainability actions, employee loyalty, and the awareness: the mediating effect of organization legitimacy. Manag. Decis. Econ. **25**(3) (2021). https://doi.org/10.1016/J.IEDEEN.2019.04.005

Campón, A., Baptista, H., Hernández, J.: El marketing relacional en el sector turístico, el caso del turismo rural: un enfoque teórico. In: XXIII Congreso Anual AEDEM, España, pp. 1–15 (2009)

Carmines, E., Zeller, R.: Reliability and Validity Assessment. Sage Publication, Thousand Oaks (1979)

Chou, M.C.: Does tourism development promote economic growth in transition countries? A panel data analysis. Econ. Model. **33**, 226–232 (2013). https://doi.org/10.1016/j.econmod.2013.04.024

Chica, M., Hernández, J., Perc, M.: Sustainability in tourism determined by an asymmetric game with mobility. J. Clean. Prod. (2022). https://doi.org/10.1016/j.jclepro.2022.131662

Chin, W.W.: The partial least squares approach to structural equation modeling. In: Marcoulides, G.A., Lawrence, E., Modern Methods for Business Research, vol. 295, pp. 295–336 (1998)

Del-Castillo-Feito, C., Blanco-González, A., González-Vázquez, E.: The relationship between image and reputation in the Spanish public university. Eur. Res. Manag. Bus. Econ. **25**(2), 87–92 (2019). https://doi.org/10.1016/j.iedeen.2019.01.001

Del-Castillo-Feito, C., Cachón-Rodríguez, G., Paz-Gil, I.: political disaffection, sociodemographic, and psychographic variables as state legitimacy determinants in the European union. Am. Behav. Sci. **66**, 86–105 (2020). https://doi.org/10.1177/0002764220981116

Dijkstra, T.K., Henseler, J.: Consistent partial least squares path modeling. MIS Q. **39**(2), 297–316 (2015). https://www.jstor.org/stable/26628355

Du, S., Yalcinkaya, G., Bstieler, L.: Sustainability, social media driven open innovation, and new product development performance. J. Prod. Innov. Manag. (2016). https://doi.org/10.1111/jpim. 12334

Fornell, C., Larcker, D.F.: Structure equation models: LISREL and PLS applied to customer exist-voice theory. J. Mark. Res. **18**(2), 39–50 (1981)

Fuxman, L., Mohr, I., Mahmoud, A., Grigoriou, N.: The new 3Ps of sustainability marketing: the case of fashion. Sustain. Prod.0 Consum. (2022). https://doi.org/10.1016/j.spc.2022.03.004

Gelashvili, V., Martínez-Navalón, J.G., Herrera-Enríquez, G.: How stress and anxiety when using mobile restaurant reservation apps influence users' satisfaction and trust. J. Indian Bus. Res. **13**, 395–412 (2021). https://doi.org/10.1108/JIBR-08-2020-0276

Gelashvili, V., Martínez-Navalón, J.G., Saura, J.R.: Using partial least squares structural equation modeling to measure the moderating effect of gender: an empirical study. Mathematics **9**, 3150 (2021). https://doi.org/10.3390/MATH9243150

Hair, J.F., Risher, J.J., Sarstedt, M., Ringle, C.M.: When to use and how to report the results of PLS-SEM. Eur. Bus. Rev. **31**, 2–24 (2019). https://doi.org/10.1108/EBR-11-2018-0203

Henseler, J., Ringle, C.M., Sarstedt, M.: A new criterion for assessing discriminant validity in variance-based structural equation modelling. J. Acad. Mark. Sci. **43**(1), 115–135 (2014). https://doi.org/10.1007/s11747-014-0403-8

Kassim, N., Abdullah, N.A.: The effect of perceived service quality dimensions on customer satisfaction, trust, and loyalty in e-commerce settings: across cultural analysis. Asia Pac. J. Mark. Logist. (2010). https://doi.org/10.1108/13555851011062269

Kotler, P., Kartajaya, H., Setiawan, I.: Marketing 3.0: from Products to Customers to the Human Spirit. Wiley, New Jersey (2010)

Lee, Y.-C.: Corporate sustainable development and marketing communications on social media: fortune 500 enterprises. Bus. Strateg. Environ. (2016). https://doi.org/10.1002/bse.1936

Liengaard, B.D., et al.: Prediction: coveted, yet forsaken? introducing a cross-validated predictive ability test in partial least squares path modelling. Decis. Sci. **52**, 362–392 (2021)

Martínez-Navalón, J.G., Gelashvili, V., Saura, J.R.: The impact of environmental social media publications on user satisfaction with and trust in tourism businesses. Int. J. Environ. Res. Public Health **17**, 5417 (2020). https://doi.org/10.3390/ijerph17155417

Ministerio de Turismo. Geo Portal. Innovación Turística (2022). https://servicios.turismo.gob.ec/ index.php/turismo-cifras/

Nunnally, J.C., Bernstein, I.H.: Psychometric theory (3 Ed.). (MCGraw- Hil, Ed.) (1994)

Ribbink, D., van Riel, A., Liljander, V., Streokens, S.: Comfort your online customer: quality, trust and loyalty on the internet. Manag. Ser. Q. Int. J. (2004).https://doi.org/10.1108/096045 20410569784

Signitzer, B., Prexl, A.: Corporate sustainability marketing communications: aspects of theory and professionalization. J. Public Relat. **20**, 1–19 (2008). https://doi.org/10.1080/106272607 01726996

Walch, P., Dodds, R.: Measuring the Choice of Environmental Sustainability Strategies in Creating a Competitive Advantage. Bus. Strategy Environ. **26**, 672–687 (2017). https://doi.org/10.1002/ bse.1949

Yul Lee, J., Soo Yang, Y., Ghauri, P., Park, B.: The impact of social media and digital platforms experience on SME international orientation: the moderating role of COVID-19 pandemic. J. Int. Manag. (2022). https://doi.org/10.1016/j.intman.2022.100950

Zeng, B., Gerritsen, R.: What do we know about social media in tourism? a review. Tourism Manag. Perspect. **10**, 27–36 (2014). https://doi.org/10.1016/j.tmp.2014.01.001

Zhang, L., Zhang, J.: Perception of small tourism enterprises in Lao PDR regarding social sustainability under the influence of social network. Tour. Manage. (2018). https://doi.org/10.1016/j.tourman.2018.05.012

Zhang, X., Zhong, L., Yu, H.: Sustainability assessment of tourism in protected areas: a relational perspective. Global Ecol. Conser. (2022). https://doi.org/10.1016/j.gecco.2022.e02074

Web 3.0 Resources in the Development of Autonomous Work of Higher Education Students in Times of Covid-19 Pandemic

Sonia Armas-Arias[1]([✉]) [ID], Kléber Augusto Jaramillo-Galarza[2] [ID],
Verónica Freire-Palacios[2] [ID], and Juan Pablo Andrade[1] [ID]

[1] Facultad de Ciencias Humanas y de la Educación, Universidad Técnica de Ambato, Ambato, Ecuador
{sp.armas,jp.andrade}@uta.edu.ec
[2] Universidad Nacional de Chimborazo, Riobamba, Ecuador
{kjaramillo,vfreire}@unach.edu.ec

Abstract. This research on web 3.0 tools and autonomous work analyzes new and interactive possibilities for the generation of educational content in web environments. The research aims to determine the use of web 3.0 tools and the autonomous work of higher education students in times of pandemic. The research methodology was of an experimental type through a quantitative approach, with a documentary bibliographic modality for the understanding of the variables and field where direct contact was maintained with the study population. For the collection of information, the survey technique was used based on a questionnaire on a Likert scale. The study population was 68 students of the Tourism major, a population to which the experimentation was applied based on the ADDIE methodology for the development of digital tools and the application of the TAM model survey. The statistic used to test the hypothesis is Kolmogorov-Smirnov with a value less than 0.05. The results of this research were that the students favorably accepted the technology, that is, the web 3.0 tools in autonomous work since they contribute to generating self-learning skills, motivation, and commitment to the construction of knowledge in a playful way.

Keywords: TAC · Web 3.0 tools · Author resources · Virtual education · Autonomous work

1 Introduction

[1] author of the study "Pedagogical use of web 3.0 to dynamize teaching practice" seeks to point out the didactic alternatives of web 3.0 in the curriculum of the Faculty of Communication (Medellín, Colombia) through a mixed research approach. He reflects that there must be a balance between the technological possibility, the role of the student, the role of the teacher and the pedagogical model to initiate a bidirectional sketch of a virtual learning environment adapted to a variety of situations inside and outside the educational field. Within the results, two main limits are exhibited for the pedagogical management of web 3.0 in the development of classes:

© The Author(s), under exclusive license to Springer Nature Switzerland AG 2023
M. Botto-Tobar et al. (Eds.): ICAT 2022, CCIS 1757, pp. 82–92, 2023.
https://doi.org/10.1007/978-3-031-24978-5_8

1. Lack of tangible resources (computers, mobiles, etc.)
2. Digital illiteracy of teachers

For this reason, the researcher concludes and identifies the need for teaching literacy in pedagogical digital media that allows it to guide, share and transfer viable and reliable information to students as a key source of construction of significant knowledge in a critical, recursive, autonomous, and collaborative way.

[2] considers in his study that "M-Learning in the autonomous learning process" is a multimedia learning method that allows the individual to learn anywhere, at any time through mobile devices (tablets, mobile phones)., handheld devices, etc.) if you have wireless connectivity. The author concludes with four significant advantages when carrying out educational practices of M-Learning such as:

● Stimulates the use of ICT (Information and Communication Technologies).
● Provides flexibility in content and interaction between student and teacher.
● Promotes the interest, motivation, and concentration of students in-class sessions.
● Strengthens group and individual experiences in virtual environments.

Therefore, mobile devices facilitate individual learning, since each learner is a unique being with their own abilities, skills, needs, and interests in terms of their learning process, thus offering students great flexibility to follow their own pace and learning style which could enhance their motivation to learn.

[3] reflect that facing a new digital generation, the educational system must be focused on investigating new ways of conceiving a more personalized, flexible education and the use of mobile devices as an added value. Much of our daily life requires the use of the Internet in different fields, especially in the educational field [4]. These mobile resources provide an ideal framework and/or environment for the teacher and the student to interact through devices, giving way to increasing autonomy, competitiveness, and critical - constructive vision besides having immediate and continuous progress of the students during the teaching and learning process.

With the appearance of the (TEP) Technologies for Empowerment and Participation, [5] defines them as the set of digital tools that facilitate communication, social cohesion, commitment, and participation, sharing ideas in a virtual environment. Thus, collaboration is encouraged within the framework of reflection, interaction, and the joint construction of knowledge to contextualize and locate them according to the learning needs of each student in the educational community [6].

In a pedagogical sense, if we learn to use ICT, TAC, and TEP to motivate students, develop their creativity, and take advantage of synergies between teachers and students, we will create extended learning in which students work proactively, and independently, guided by their curiosity for lifelong learning. They learn to use the extraordinary potential of technology as a source of information, teaching methodology and constant educational stimulus [7].

2   State of the Art

Web tools are the set of programs or applications that are hosted directly on a page and/or website to facilitate access to information regardless of the site of origin [8]. Over time, the web continues to evolve, offering improved network connectivity, new network access points, and endless changes to meet needs, particularly access to information and communication.

For the evolution of the web over time, there are three different stages known as the "web" and then the numbers 1.0, 2.0, 3.0 (Fig. 1).

Web 1.0 Content delivey	Web 2.0 Sharing content	Web 3.0 Semantic contect
• Meet • Preserv • Communicate • Introduce	• Manipulate • Model • Check • Edit	• Extract • Interpretate • Analyze • Sructure

Fig. 1. Evolution of web

However, this evolution of the WEB depends on its content and the possibility of accessing, maintaining, and optimizing the information that users have, giving rise to three generations of the web. Thus, Web 1.0 provides information, Web 2.0 overloads the data network, and Web 3.0 offers information control [3].

2.1   Web Tools Used in Education

In this digital universe, there are innumerable tools that are framed within the WEB, including a variety of applications that can be used from any device, or location and are focused on educational purposes, while most stand out for being free [9] (Fig. 2).

Fig. 2. Education web tools

2.2   Web 3.0 Tools

The web 3.0 concept first emerged in 2006 in an article by Zeldman. Web 3.0, also known as the "Semantic Web" which, in general, refers to a variety of tools (google, mobile devices, augmented reality, etc.) with procedures and languages that can interpret certain styles of users, allowing them to access a variety of images, content, videos, documents, files and multimedia content through hyperlinks and/or hyperlinks [9]. So, it is linked to the term personalization, since it aims to offer a range of content and information adapted to our preferences based on a framework of flexibility and versatility that allows us to overcome barriers of structure and format [10].

In this sense, the generalities of web 3.0 tools were exposed to understand their origin and conceptualization. The immersion of this type of tools in the educational field has shown that it can contribute to a new concept of teaching where the motivation and creativity of teachers, students and parents in the educational process are encouraged [11].

2.3   Web 3.0 Tools in Education

The Semantic Web in education would then focus on the design and development of meta programs such as logical, attachable information systems, with a complete and individually executable computational structure aimed at both students and teachers. Given this scenario, there is an unavoidable need to involve all members of the educational community (students, teachers, parents, directors, among others) in the production of innovative pedagogical proposals to address the great benefits offered by technological advances, considering that there must be constant training and monitoring of changes that are taking place in this context [12].

[13] mentions that there are advantages to the application of web 3.0 tools in the educational field such as:

1. Environment simulators (laboratories, classrooms, class sessions).
2. Hypertext, which allows the user to create content within the address that he imagines interesting.
3. Multimedia capabilities, which allow exchanging content internally in different ways.
4. Tools that facilitate communication through emails, chat, and forums.
5. Ability to form working groups. 6. Student motivation and interest in learning.

2.4   Characteristics of Web 3.0 in Education

Web 3.0 tools are facilitators of the process of transformation and innovation of educational praxis, so they have important characteristics. [14] mentions the following (Fig. 3):

Universal use
Personal learning network
Mobile learning
Digital competence
3D website

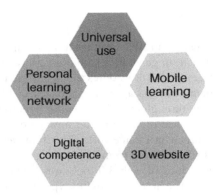

Fig. 3. Web 3.0 characteristics in education

2.5 Autonomous Work

Autonomous work is the faculty of self-interest that the student must systematically manage, plan, control, and evaluate their cognitive and socio-affective processes based on the use of their own strategies, that is, go beyond what is seen in the class session. to develop their skills, and abilities in a conscious, autonomous way to achieve specific goals. In this process, aspects such as self-regulation (control and awareness of one's own learning), the role played by the teacher (counselor), and the development of the student's autonomous thinking and learning are present [15].

In this case, the pedagogical effort is aimed at training students focused on solving specific aspects of their own learning activities, and not only solving a specific task, in other words, guiding the student and learning to plan, monitor, and self-assess their own pace of learning consciously [16] defines the three precise aspects (Fig. 4):

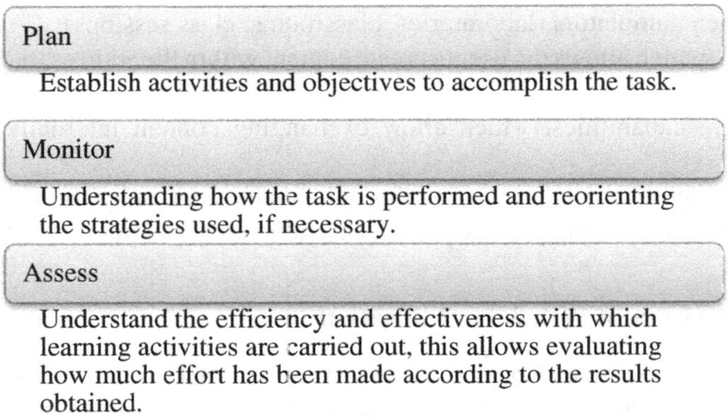

Plan
Establish activities and objectives to accomplish the task.
Monitor
Understanding how the task is performed and reorienting the strategies used, if necessary.
Assess
Understand the efficiency and effectiveness with which learning activities are carried out, this allows evaluating how much effort has been made according to the results obtained.

Fig. 4. Autonomous work

In contrast, the teaching process aimed at autonomous work and therefore autonomous learning has the purpose of expanding behaviors that promote a high degree of understanding and control of learning in and by students adapted to individual characteristics, needs and interests for taking timely decisions and problem-solving.

The world cannot fail to recognize the current technological reality, even more from the emergence of virtual education also understood as an interactive and dynamic learning method based on collaborative work. Teachers and students will continue accomplishing objectives set forth in the national curriculum, which is comprehensive and holistic training, even if there is a certain distance that prevents physical contact between educational actors [17].

From this perspective, web 3.0 tools have modified the educational process, as they are known as the web of time and space that allows organizing the search for content and information through connections between the web and the real world [18]. Then, the teacher must innovate their pedagogical plans rich in virtual environments that simulate laboratories, classrooms, etc. In addition to providing interactive games, virtual reality, one-way graphics, webcams, and more components where the student is motivated to learn and interact with the teacher and classmates to share knowledge, encouraging the management and development of creativity and imagination [19].

3 Methodology

The research is experimental because it applied author resources based on web 3.0 tools. First, a diagnosis was made that consisted of two parts. The first consisted of a test on the use of web 3.0 tools in self-employment for university students; Finally, the TAM Model was applied, with the intention of knowing and measuring the degree of satisfaction that students present in the use of this technological tool intended for learning. In the same way, it is considered exploratory because this study allowed to have an approximation on the use of Web 3.0 resources in self-employment, which allowed obtaining preliminary information as an approach to have an overview of the research.

The hypothesis that was proposed for this research is: web 3.0 resources improve the development of autonomous learning.

It has a mixed approach in seeking both quantitative and qualitative data. By applying the web 3.0 resources test and the TAM Model with their respective instruments, the aim was to measure the level of development of students' autonomous work and thus obtain quantitative data; to then obtain the qualitative part on the perceptions and acceptance of the use of technology in the population under study.

Based on an analysis prior to the development of web 3.0 tools aimed at autonomous work in students, the various types of appropriate and adaptable tools to the contents of the subject were examined, which promote motivation, responsibility, critical thinking, and learning. Significant on the various topics, for that, the selected tools focus on the acquisition of abilities, skills, and an autonomous learning process in playful and interactive virtual environments. So, it is important to emphasize the difficulty that lies in this whole process. It is the navigation and manipulation of many platforms, tools, or virtual environments, which generates in students a certain degree of demotivation or moments of distraction due to the great demand for information, and therefore the lack of interest in examining and acquiring academic content focused on technological knowledge.

Currently, most students rely on the use and management of Microsoft Teams as a unique communication platform for the development of their classes, as well as the presentation of information or academic activities. They are addressed with tools that do not show greater interaction in their presentation such as Word, PowerPoint, educational platforms or in the same books or notebooks. This generates monotonous classes and boredom in students. Therefore, it is necessary for educators to integrate digital tools that streamline the teaching and learning process, in which the teacher-student binomial must be willing to face the challenge of producing significant knowledge in a playful, digital, and interactive way.

4   Results

Among the results obtained, three web 3.0 tools were taken into consideration, focused on autonomous learning in students of the Tourism career, which were used in virtual classes against the Covid-19 pandemic, which are detailed below (Table 1):

Table 1. Web 3.0 for autonomous work

	Why to use them?	Benefits
Educaplay	• Preparation of multimedia academic activities • Various educational scenarios: word search, crossword puzzles, riddles, etc • You can add audio files, images • Easy and attractive tool to handle	• Promotes creativity, imagination in the flow of ideas • Promotes motivation to fulfill the tasks suggested by the teacher • Self-management of actions and procedures • Activates imagination and critical thinking
Canva	• Interactive teaching and learning • Online design tool • Content creation: videos, presentations, infographics, etc • Presentation of concise, playful, and attractive information	• Helps them express themselves more confidently and learn from feedback (recordings) • Visibility of creative processes • Way to stimulate creativity, collaboration and optimize work • Adaptable to all types of users
Kahoot	• Tool to gamify the teaching and learning process • Activities personalized to the needs and interests of the student • Allows you to create quiz games with multiple answers • Objective: learn by playing	• Link between fun and learning • Broadens the level of participation • Dynamic and enjoyable learning different from conventional learning • Renewing, dynamic vision

Table 2. Useful tools in virtual classes

Options	Frequency	Percentage
Strongly disagree	5	7,4
Disagree	7	10,3
Agree	24	35,3
Strongly agree	32	47,1
Total	**68**	**100,0**

Question 5. In general, I find that these tools are useful in my work in virtual classes.

Of a total of 68 surveyed students that correspond to 100%, 47.1% strongly agree that technological tools are useful in their work in virtual classes, 35.3% agree, 10.3% disagree and 7.4% strongly disagree. The results indicate that, for the most part, the students strongly agree that technological tools are useful in their work in virtual classes since they provide learners with autonomy, flexibility adapted to their learning rhythms and content based on the quick navigation in diverse digital spaces (Table 2).

Question 2. In general, I find that web 3.0 and gamification tools improve autonomous work in virtual classes.

Table 3. Use of 3.0 Web tools and gamification

Options	Frequency	Percentage
Strongly disagree	3	4,4
Disagree	10	14,7
Neither agree nor disagree	10	14,7
Agree	29	42,6
Strongly agree	16	23,5
Total	**68**	**100,0**

Of a total of 68 students surveyed that corresponds to 100%, 42.6% agree that web 3.0 and gamification tools improve autonomous work in virtual classes, 23.5% totally agree, 14.7% are undecided and disagree and 4.4% totally disagree. The results indicate that, for the most part, the students agree that web 3.0 tools are easy to use due to the existence of multiple interactive, innovative, and playful tools with easy access that generate curiosity in students about their manipulation and activity development (Table 3).

Question 12. The use of web 3.0 and gamification tools allows for friendlier communication with my environment, both synchronously and asynchronously (classmates and teacher).

Table 4. Web 3.0 and gamification for communication

Options	Frequency	Percentage
Strongly disagree	6	8,8
Disagree	8	11,8
Neither agree nor disagree	10	14,7
Agree	24	35,3
Strongly agree	20	29,4
Total	**68**	**100,0**

Of the 68 students surveyed that corresponds to 100%, 35.3% agree that the use of 3.0 and gamification tools supports more friendly communication, 29.4% totally agree, 14.7% are undecided, 11.8% disagree and 8.8% totally disagree. The results indicate that, for the most part, the students agree that the use of 3.0 and gamification tools supports friendlier communication through games, playful activities, and real-time interaction between teachers and students provided by technology (Table 4).

Question 15. I would like to use this type of tool more frequently outside the virtual classroom.

Table 5. Tools used outside virtual classes

Options	Frequency	Percentage
Strongly disagree	6	8,8
Disagree	7	10,3
Neither agree nor disagree	9	13,2
Agree	22	32,4
Strongly agree	24	35,3
Total	**68**	**100,0**

35.3% totally agree they would like to use tools outside the virtual class more frequently, 32.4% agree, 13.2% are undecided, 10.3% disagree and 8.8% totally disagree. The results indicate that, for the most part, the students fully agree that they would like to use tools outside the virtual class more frequently because they could self-manage their procedures and academic activities, that is, self-educate based on the implementation of playful digital tools, needs and pace of learning (Table 5).

For the Wilcoxon test statistic, the two representative questions were considered: question number 5: In general, I find that these tools are useful in my work in virtual classes and question number 11: Technological tools help me to work efficiently in an autonomous way. It can be determined that, according to the application of the

TAM model (Technology Acceptance Models), technological tools help students to work autonomously. Then, having a P value (.000) less than the value of 0.05, the null hypothesis is rejected, and the alternative hypothesis is accepted, therefore, the web 3.0 tools applied to the autonomous work of children are acceptable, because they allow them to work autonomously and are useful for their virtual classes (Table 6).

Table 6. Wilcoxon test

	Technological tools help me work autonomously more often. In general, I find that these tools are useful in my work in virtual classes
Z	$3,531^b$
Asymptotic Sig. (bilateral)	,000
a. Wilcoxon test of signed ranks	
b. It is based on positive ranges	

5 Conclusions

Web 3.0 resources for the development of autonomous work provide various dynamic scenarios that, due to their singularities, catch the attention of students and this contributes to the teaching-learning process. In this way, students are not passive receivers of information, but also have the possibility of searching and sharing, as well as creating content in a creative way that can be used at any time during the class or specifically to work on reading comprehension, but in a fun way.

This is how new web 3.0 resources are constantly generated with various characteristics regarding their use, communication, and collaboration according to their purpose.

The digital author resources presented a great acceptance by the students since they are encouraged to improve their communication, creativity when carrying out autonomous work, both synchronous and asynchronous, in a fun way.

It is not intended to carry out a summative evaluation only for a quantitative grade, but in this case a formative assessment, in which students can play and learn at the same time. This is how these types of resources are essential for the teacher because they are attractive, modifiable and can be used inside and outside the class so that the student exercises their reading comprehension.

References

1. Achury, A.: Trabajo autónmo del estudiante. Junio (2018). https://cuestioneseducativas.uex ternado.edu.co/el-trabajo-autonomo-del-estudiante/
2. Zamora, R.: M-learning en el proceso autnónomo de aprendizaje. ReHuso: Revista de Ciencias Humanísticas y Sociales, 2–8 (2019)

3. Alcívar, C.: Uso de las TIC en el porceso enseñanza y aprendizaje. Espacios, 2–6 (2019)
4. Velarde, A.L., Paredes, R.I., Quinde, C.P., Torre, A.: Task based learning to enhance the oral production: study case chimborazo. In: Auer, M.E., Tsiatsos, T. (eds.) ICL 2018. AISC, vol. 916, pp. 194–201. Springer, Cham (2018). https://doi.org/10.1007/978-3-030-11932-4_20
5. Mayorga, M.d.l.Á.: Conocimiento, aplicación e integración de las TIC, TAC y TEP. Rev. Tecnológica Educativa Docentes, 2–5 (2020)
6. Pérez., Á., Hernando, A.: El trabajo autónomo del alumno universitario. Dialnet, 6–12 (2018)
7. Romero, C.: Formación mediante modelos TIC, TAC, TEP. (2018). https://repositorio.uta.edu.ec/bitstream/123456789/28894/1/1719235077%20CRISTIAN%20RAMIRO%20ROMERO%20TIGMASA.pdf
8. Chávez, U.: Herramientas tecnológicas en el proceso de enseñanza y aprendizaje. Scielo, 3–7 (2020)
9. Cabero, J.: Historia de las web (2018). https://d1wqtxts1xzle7.cloudfront.net/59947315/74_Historia_de_la_Web20190706-123188-141xd95-with-cover-page-v2.pdf?Expires=1635433071&Signature=DdOyMd8iQ3yBa8cN2nwq7Fy7jxbzt47jzNPfdhbds4IQG3Ms7rEhetB8-RO18ShIKz~YaYz~OkZLkxhBIYg~YanxNn3MqzDrBMu8eqywTZstuRt
10. Peinado, J.: Experiencias del profesorado acerca del aprendizaje autónomo. RIDE: Rev. Iberoam.para la Investig.y el Desarro. Educ. **10**, 3–7 (2020)
11. Cárcel, F.: Desarrollo de habilidades mediante el aprendizaje autónomo. Empresa, Investigación y pensamiento crítico, 2–7 (2019)
12. Suárez, M.: Herramientas web 3.0 para el desarrollo del competencias investigativas. Revista: Pensamiento y Acción, 5–9 (2020)
13. Guix, E.: Aplicaciones web 3.0 en el ciclo formativo. DIM: Didáctica, Innovación y Multimedia, 4–9 (2019)
14. Rosa, L.: Recursos web 3.0 - Mirada desde los docentes informáticos. (2018). http://www.eduqa.net/eduqa2017/images/ponencias/eje1/1_30_de_la_Rosa_Leida_VP_.pdf
15. Katz, M.: La técnica de la encuesta: características. (2019). http://metodologiadelainvestigacion.sociales.uba.ar/wp-content/uploads/sites/117/2019/03/Cuaderno-N-7-La-t%C3%A9cnica-de-encuesta.pdf
16. Solórzano, Y.: Aprendizaje autónomo y competencias. Dominio de las Ciencias, 3.8 (2018)
17. Alvarado, A.: El proceso de enseñanz – aprendizaje. MENDIVE: Revista de Educación, 2–6 (2019)
18. Coronado, F.: Cuadro comparativo de la web (2019). https://issuu.com/felipecoronado19.02/docs/peludo_1.0.pptx
19. Latorre, L., Castro, K.: Las TIC, las TAC y las TEP: innovación educativa (2018). https://repository.usergioarboleda.edu.co/bitstream/handle/11232/1219/TIC%20TAC%20TEP.pdf?sequence=1&isAllowed=y

Technology for Learning and Knowledge Strategies in Virtual Education: A Case Study of Higher Education

Diego Vinicio López-Aguilar(✉) ⓘ, Wilmer Efraín Burbano-Anacona ⓘ,
Diego Isaías Granja-Peñaherrera ⓘ, and Juan Francisco Parreño-Freire ⓘ

Universidad Tecnológica Indoamérica Ambato, Ambato, Ecuador
{diegolopez,wilmerburbano,isaiasgranja,juanparrenio}@uti.edu.ec

Abstract. This research is oriented to the application of Information and Communication Technologies based on Learning and Knowledge Technologies, for the development of virtual environments that improve concentration, creativity, and student interest in virtual or face-to-face classes. The objective pursued by the research is to relate ICT and TAC in the development of personal learning environments in students of higher education. The methodology used is experimental, exploratory through a quantitative approach. The technique used was the survey, using two instruments; a structured questionnaire focused on web 3.0 tools used as a pre-test, made up of 24 questions, later the previously validated instrument was applied as a post-test based on the Technology Acceptance Model (TAM) made up of 15 questions in which measures the acceptance of digital resources. The instruments were validated using the Cronbach's Alpha statistic, having high-reliability values. The population used for this research was 49 students: obtaining as a result the acceptance of the Moodle educational platform. Recognizing that ICT and TAC are fundamental in the educational field since they demonstrate an innovative educational strategy that fosters interaction with free web 3.0 tools available on the Internet, where students prefer to work with TAC tools on gamification platforms due to their ease of use demonstrating greater interest in collaborative work, optimizing time and resources.

Keywords: ICT · TAC · Virtual education · Pedagogy · Strategies

1 Introduction

The evolution of society and the innovation of technology that daily creates and designs new resources and digital tools for all areas of personal and professional use, has made it necessary for educational institutions to continuously train teaching staff for the management, control, and design of educational material from an innovative approach consistent with current technology [1].

The research develops an experimental work, which serves as the basis for the articulation of system and plan of virtual training, which facilitates the professional development of teachers in resource issues with Information and Communication Technologies (ICT), for the efficient development of the teaching-learning process in students.

© The Author(s), under exclusive license to Springer Nature Switzerland AG 2023
M. Botto-Tobar et al. (Eds.): ICAT 2022, CCIS 1757, pp. 93–105, 2023.
https://doi.org/10.1007/978-3-031-24978-5_9

The need for the academic training of a human being is an important parameter in the evolutionary process that lasts a lifetime; personal development and acquiring new knowledge is of vital importance to complete the goal set since childhood. In teaching, it is not enough to share the knowledge acquired in their professional training, but it is also important to continuously update and discover new tools and original pedagogical resources, which have a direct impact on the academic satisfaction of students and are connected to new approaches [2], methodologies and technological resources.

The pandemic and the health emergency declared by the World Health Organization (WHO), has revealed several deficiencies in educational systems worldwide, and in a particular way in our country Ecuador, according to surveys developed by UNESCO, UNICEF [3] quoted by [4], and the World Bank. Only half of the total number of countries surveyed offered training processes focused on the management of info-pedagogical resources.

UNESCO, in its study, reveals results that indicate that 81% and 78% of primary and secondary teachers, respectively, worldwide, barely meet the minimum requirements to carry out their work as educators. In the case of the Latin American population, the problem is even more alarming since the results reflect that 83% and 84% of primary and secondary teachers, respectively, do not have or handle the basic tools to face the challenge imposed by the new virtual education modality [5] quote by [6].

Lifelong learning is an important aspect that guarantees quality comprehensive academic training, which endorses significant knowledge, where TIC TAC TEP takes a fundamental place. The impact is that the student feels motivated through the educational process in a personal learning environment suitable for the development of skills. The problem is evident with the use only of ICT in the educational field, therefore, it is intended to improve the didactic strategies used in the teaching of English, in which teachers must change their conventional pedagogical practices in interaction with the student, applying technologies to build knowledge [7].

In this context, the originality of this project is aimed at relating ICT and TAC to obtain content in a more dynamic and flexible way, involving different learning styles and responding to the current needs of the Educational Institution, enhancing training and continuing education according to with the study variables. In Ecuador, the Ministry of Education undertook an online training project for the entire teaching staff at the national level in 2016, after the declaration of the health emergency in 2020, an emerging training process was activated with several training courses that aimed to support teachers to face the challenge of virtual education [8]. The objective pursued by the research is to relate ICT and TAC in the development of personal learning environments in students of higher education. The methodology used is experimental, exploratory through a quantitative approach.

2 State of the Art

The development of new technologies allows the elimination or reduction of time and barriers between individuals, shortening the geographical distance around the world, even outside it for almost instantaneous communication. What a few years ago was developed as a complement, today has become an undeniable necessity, because if we look around us it is easy to notice that we are surrounded by technology and interconnected through it. This process of technological and telecommunications development has allowed the creation of new working fields and the development and improvement of the standard of living of society [6].

ICTs are technologies that, with information technology, microelectronics, and telecommunications, create innovative forms and methods of information exchange, using tools and devices of a communicational and technological nature. This information processing method has managed to combine information technologies (IT) and communication technologies (CT); CTs are made up of media such as television, radio, and even mobile telecommunication, while IT is focused on information processing through digital methods and content management [9].

By combining these technologies, a network of communication channels is developed without time limits or distance barriers, making it possible for people to see and hear situations or events that occur anywhere in the world almost instantly. A practical example of the use of these communication networks is the new modality of teleworking and Tele-education that the society had to face due to the declaration of a health emergency and subsequent confinement worldwide due to COVID 19 during the years 2020 and 2021 [10].

TACs are constituted in two great areas of attention: the computer and communicational nomenclature. On the other hand, the process of transmitting knowledge to facilitate understanding in the various areas of development of a society or organization it is exploring positive actions that generate knowledge, thus allowing true digital inclusion, where teachers share with their students an entire accumulation of necessary information in real-time [11]. All this by assigning categories from which the initial interest that each teacher has about ICT and the use of tools such as individual blogs, collective blogs, and blogs in the classroom are fostered.

Also considering that, in this research, a technological literacy was given to strengthen the skills and abilities in the management of technological knowledge that allows greater integration of teachers for cooperative work, both in their lines of research and in their extension activities [12].

Within the educational environment, there are also applications of TACs in the development of inclusive practices implemented with students who present an attention deficit hyperactivity disorder, in which they refer to the use that students can make of this medium for the improvement of your learning. The potential that TACs have in an educational environment, especially for students with specific educational needs, is very remarkable since they make it possible to scaffold many of the difficulties student learning [13].

Considering the interest, the majority of children have for Learning and Knowledge Technologies (TAC), the educational strategy based on learning centers where working with technology is included will increase the incentive towards learning. It is important to take advantage of all the resources at their disposal in order to ensure that the student understands the contents around the center of interest in a relevant and attractive way [14].

The primary objective of education is intended in offering the student the possibility of creating their own knowledge based on their experiences. For the educational system, it is essential to have methodologies that facilitate the process and learning can be obtained with all the information acquired from various sources such as radio programs, television and physical documentation generated by educational entities or by the teacher himself (Bravo Mancero & Varguillas Carmona, 2020; United Nations - ECLAC, 2020).

The use of ICT in the educational process is essential to maintain the constant relationship between teacher and student since they can transform, improve, and complement education. One of the hypermedia that has facilitated remote work is virtual education, which consists of maintaining lines of communication through technologies that facilitate the exchange of digital resources. The activities that take place in a virtual environment must necessarily encourage students to autonomously build their knowledge.

All these changes have made educators be committed to the skills in digital resources management in order to improve the experience of virtual education. Thus, breaking the paradigm of the use of technology in the educational process by making using platforms such as Moodle or Blackboard that facilitates the application and development of pedagogical strategies, which in some cases are new since they are not fully familiar with them [15].

Within the technological advances at the educational level, virtual learning environments have a greater acceptance in the teaching process due to the benefits they provide. Technological exploration has become a challenge for current pedagogical models increasing the application of innovative strategies that favor the development of skills that allow students to foster a critical and reflective capacity of essential knowledge in different media.

These environments have the purpose of becoming a space that enables a diversification of the different teaching modalities in all the different educational levels. One characteristic that virtual learning environments have is the functionalities that facilitate communication between the participants, which ends up promoting new roles for the teacher, seeking to play the role of guide and moderator: while for students, through a more active role in the construction of knowledge. All this is possible thanks to the fact that these areas offer work and collaboration spaces for the different research teams [16].

Education has changed since the moment new technologies were incorporated in the 90s, through the generation of new programs and the incorporation of technological mediations, as a complement to face-to-face programs, making it possible to reconfigure teaching-learning methodologies and propose new strategies.

Lines of education have been developed hand in hand with lines of educational research, which seek to strengthen the teaching-learning process through technology. In previous research studies, the need to expand the field of study where virtual environments are applied is evident, as well as considering experiences developed in other countries as a reference [17].

Students use this software with other media resources in order to achieve educational goals; due to their benefits as they are open, flexible, and can be incorporated into any situation of the teaching-learning process. They can be supported in constructivist, behavioral, or cognitive environments, which favor collaborative and cooperative learning. It is understood then those virtual environments are spaces for the teaching and learning process under face-to-face, virtual, and mixed modalities, in which communication processes are carried out through ICT both synchronously and asynchronously, to allow the exchange of information through processes of cooperation, monitoring, and continuous evaluation of teachers, including students [18].

Virtual teaching is supported by various digital resources, among which are the use of educational platforms, thanks to the advancement of technology and the Internet, several institutions have distance education courses, as an alternative to traditional education, giving way to the management of ICT tools through educational platforms.

In this case, the Moodle platform represents a very useful technological tool, by enabling the use of resources adaptable to different teaching-learning environments, together with methodologies that allow learning to be managed, and communication and collaboration between teachers and students to be facilitated.

When using this platform in the learning of English, positive results were obtained because the use of these virtual platforms contributes favorably to the attitude that students take towards behavioral learning, also it reinforces students' intrinsic motivation [19].

One important issue that must be considered when using the Moodle platform is in terms of functionality since experts emphasize the importance of designing its environment, which must be intuitive, easy to handle, and correct with the objective of facilitating access and interaction to users. Emphasizing the importance of both synchronous and asynchronous communication channels. Its main benefit is that it is an open-source tool, so it can be adjusted to the needs of users, as well as providing ease of use managing to connect study with work and thus favor relationships of reciprocal enrichment [20].

3 Methodology

The research was carried out with the students of Higher Education of Zone 3, has private support, which is in the urban area, with a morning shift.

This research is experimental because it developed a virtual learning environment in the Moodle educational platform and was used as an experiment for teaching English. The PACIE methodology was applied, using free tools of the web 3.0. The experimental method proposes the following procedure: the statement of the problem, the hypothesis, observation, experimentation, verification, and generalization.

The use of the pedagogy wheel for this research was essential since tools focused on Bloom's taxonomy were used with a change in the wheel that allows the use of gamification resources in virtual education as an important tool to select the appropriate applications for being used in accordance with the learning skills to be achieved.

For the verification of the hypothesis, the results are obtained considering the selection of the three most representative questions within the investigation, in this case, they are by the independent variable (VI) P23 and P24 and by the dependent variable (DV) P12 that are detailed below:

- Q23: Do you consider that the development of web 3.0 resources is important to improve virtual teaching and collaborative work?
- Q24: Do you think that the correct application and use of web 3.0 tools promote the interest, participation and motivation of students in collaborative work?

- Q12: How often do teachers use 3.0 tools to teach?

The most representative questions were considered when considering the development of web 3.0 resources by the teacher to improve virtual education and collaborative work. In the same way, the correct application and use of web 3.0 tools promote interest, participation, and motivation of students in collaborative work, which refer to the independent variable, ICT and TAC; and according to the dependent variable, the development of personal learning environments is used to know the frequency teachers apply 3.0 tools.

Table 1. Hypothesis summary.

Null hypothesis	Test	Sig.	Decision
The categories of Do you consider that the development of web 3.0 resources by the teacher is important to improve teaching occur with equal probabilities	One-Sample Chi-Square Test	,000	Reject the null hypothesis
The categories of Do you believe that the correct application and use of web 3.0 tools promote interest occur with equal probabilities	One-Sample Chi-Square Test	,000	Reject the null hypothesis
The categories of How often do teachers use 3.0 tools to teach occur with equal probabilities	One-Sample Chi-Square Test	,000	Reject the null hypothesis

Table 1. shows the summary of the hypothesis test, according to the chi-square test statistic of a sample, the rejection of the null hypothesis is taken as a decision and the alternative hypothesis is accepted, with a level of significance of 0.5 and asymptotic significance.

To check the summary of the hypothesis, the three most representative questions detailed above were taken into consideration, and the Kolmogorov Smirnov statistic K-S of a sample was used, therefore, the following Hypotheses are established:

- H0: Learning technologies and knowledge as learning strategies do not contribute to virtual education.
- H1: Learning technologies and knowledge as learning strategies contribute to virtual education

Table 2. Kolmogorov-smirnov test.

Kolmogorov-Smirnov Test for one sample			Do you consider that the development of web 3.0 resources by the teacher is important to improve teaching	Do you believe that the correct application and use of web 3.0 tools promote interest?	How often do teachers use 3.0 tools to teach
N			49	49	49
Normal Range[a,b]	Media		3,98	3,02	3,94
	Standard deviation		,829	1,266	,659
Extreme differences	Absolute		,306	,291	,374
	Positive		,245	,199	,320
	Negative		-,306	-,291	-,374
Z de Kolmogorov-Smirnov			2,140	2,034	2,616
Sig. asintót. (bilateral)			,000	,001	,000

a. Contrast distribution is normal.
b. It is been calculated from data.

Table 2 verifies the hypothesis considering the P-value of the relative questions for the experimentation that is, having a P value less than 0.05 in the three cases, the null hypothesis is rejected, and the alternative hypothesis is accepted.

Therefore, the scores that were obtained within the experimentation have a normal distribution and at the same time, they allowed to measure the degree of concordance that the distribution of the data and its experimentation had, finally it was possible to contrast that the development of the applied personal learning environments to the population gave positive results.

4   Results

To demonstrate the results obtained within the investigation, the most representative questions were considered and from which the most relevant data for the investigation and its results were obtained (Table 3.) (Fig. 1).

Question 1: What type of web 3.0 tools do you use to make conceptual and mental maps in virtual classes?

Table 3. Web 3.0 tools to create conceptual and mental maps.

		Frequency	Percentage
Valid	Creatly	12	24,5
	Lucidchart	32	65,3
	Mindmodo	2	4,1
	Bubbl.us	2	4,1
	Mind meinster	1	2,0
	Total	49	100,0

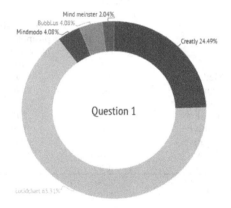

Fig. 1. Tools to create conceptual and mental maps.

Of a total of 49 students, 32 students, which corresponds to 65.30% mention that the web 3.0 tool used to make conceptual and mental maps is Lucidchart. The 24.50%, which are 12 young people, indicate that the tool used is Creatly. The 4.10%, who are 2 young people, indicate that the tool used is Bubbl.us, the other 4.10%, who are 2 young people, indicate that the tool used is Mindmodo and the remaining 2.0%, which is equivalent to 1 student, affirm that the tool used is Mind meinster. In these results, it is observed that the students in most works corresponding to the development of conceptual and mental maps use the Lucidchart tool (Table 4.) (Fig. 2).

Question 2. What kind of web 3.0 tools does your teacher use for the evaluation of synchronous and asynchronous classes?

Table 4. Web 3.0 tools used for assessment.

		Frequency	Porcentage
Valid	Educaplay	1	2,0
	Kahoot	48	98,0
	Total	49	100,0

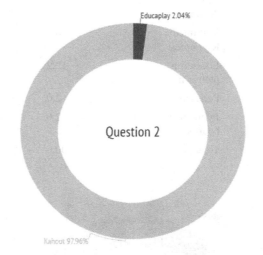

Fig. 2. Tools used for assessment.

Of a total of 49 students who represent 100%, 48 students that correspond to 98.00% affirm that the tool used by the teacher for the evaluation is Kahoot and the remaining 2.00% that corresponds to 1 student mentions that the platform used is Educaplay. Results allow us to know that teachers use the Kahoot platform more frequently for the evaluation of knowledge in their students (Table 5.) (Fig. 3).

Question 18. From the following list, which tools does your teacher use for learning purposes in synchronous classes?

Table 5. Tools used by teachers for the learning process

		Frequency	Percentage
Valid	Blogs	7	14,3
	Wikis	4	8,2
	Social network	3	6,1
	Digital documents	25	51,0
	Multimedia Resources	2	4,1
	Education platform	6	12,2
	Podcasts	1	2,0
	Interactive boards	1	2,0
	Total	49	100,0

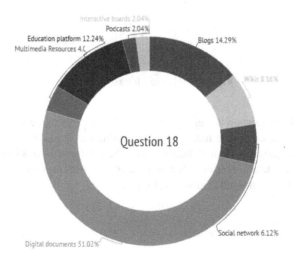

Fig. 3. Tools used by teachers for the learning process

Of a total of 49 students who represent 100%, 25 students that correspond to 51.00% affirm that the tool used by the teacher for learning purposes is Digital Documents. The 14.30% that are 7 students mentioned that they use tools such as Blogs. The 12.20% of which are 6 students mention that they use educational platforms, 8.20% of which are 4 students mention that they use Wikis. The 6.10% of which are 3 students mention that they use social networks, 2 .00%, which is 1 student, mentions that they use Podcasts and the remaining 2%, which corresponds to 1 student, affirms that they use Digital Whiteboard. Results allow us to know that teachers use digital documents more frequently for learning purposes due to the advantage of having valuable bibliographies in scientific databases (Table 6.) (Fig. 4).

Question 19. How important is the use of web 3.0 tools in your learning in virtual classes?

Table 6. Importance of Web 3.0 tools in the learning process

		Frequency	Percentage
Valid	Low importance	1	2,0
	Slightly important	8	16,3
	Important	19	38,8
	Very Important	21	42,9
	Total	49	100,0

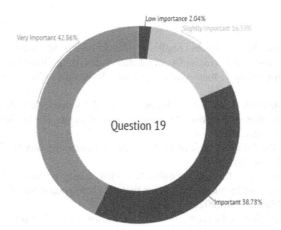

Fig. 4. Importance of Web 3.0 tools

Of a total of 49 students, 21 students, which corresponds to 42.90%, state that the use of web 3.0 tools in learning processes is very important. The 38.80%, which are 19 young people, mention that it is important, 16.30% that is equivalent to 8 students affirm that it is moderately important and 2.00% that is equivalent to 1 person indicates that it is of little importance. It can be affirmed that most of the students consider that the use of web 3.0 tools in their learning is very important because of the advantages they obtain by using the different technological tools available.

5 Discussion

The current situation forces teachers to innovate the methodological and didactic strategies used in the teaching-learning process of English, allowing them to take advantage of the resources, creativity, and skills of the student in virtual classes. Technology constitutes fundamental support demonstrating a favorable response in the development of ICT and TAC in learning in a participatory and dynamic way. Personal learning environments based on TACs are fundamental since they present an innovative educational strategy that fosters adequate interaction with several free web 3.0 tools available on the Internet, facilitating understanding and the student's experience of learning at their own pace and style.

All the information analyzed through statistical tables and graphs after the application of the technology acceptance model generated important results correlating the perceptions of the population with respect to the experimentation carried out through a training instrument. The results obtained represent beneficial information that contributed significantly to the verification of the hypothesis, which focuses on the relationship between teacher training and meaningful learning. The analysis carried out with the data allowed the design and creation of an online platform for teacher training in five digital tools that were relevant in the experimentation in the population.

References

1. Peralbo-Uzquiano, M., Fernández-Abella, R., Durán-Bouza, M., Brenlla-Blanco, J., Cotos-Yáñez, J.: Evaluation of the effects of a virtual intervention programme on cognitive flexibility, inhibitory control and basic math skills in childhood education. Comput. Educ. **159**, 104006 (2020)
2. Radianti, J., Majchrzak, T., Fromm, J., Wohlgenannt, I.: A systematic review of immersive virtual reality applications for higher education: Design elements, lessons learned, and research agenda. Comput. Educ. **147**, 103778 (2020)
3. Heyneman, S.: The future of UNESCO: Strategies for attracting new resources. Int. J. Educ. Dev. **31**(3), 313–314 (2011)
4. Mróz, A., Ocetkiewicz, I., Tomaszewska, B.: What should be included in education programmes – the socio-education analysis for sustainable management of natural resources. J. Cleaner Prod. **250**, 119556 (2020)
5. Burnett, N.: UNESCO education: political or technical? Reflections on recent personal experience. Int. J. Educ. Dev. **31**(3), 315–318 (2011)
6. Chang, S.C., Hsu, T.C., Jong, M.S.Y.: Integration of the peer assessment approach with a virtual reality design system for learning earth science. Comput. Educ. **146**, 103758 (2020)
7. Pal, K.B., et al.: Education system of Nepal: impacts and future perspectives of COVID-19 pandemic. Heliyon **7**(9), e08014 (2021)
8. MINEDUC, Mecapacito (2022). https://mecapacito.educacion.gob.ec/
9. Kozlova, D., Pikhart, M.: The use of ICT in higher education from the perspective of the university students. Procedia Comput. Sci. **192**, 2309–2317 (2021)

10. Ramírez-Rueda, M., Cózar-Gutiérrez, R., Roblizo Colmenero, M., González-Calero, J.: Towards a coordinated vision of ICT in education: a comparative analysis of preschool and primary education teachers' and parents' perceptions. Teach. Teach. Educ. **100**, 103300 (2021)
11. Tuma, F., Nituica, C., Mansuri, O., Kamel, M.K., McKenna, J., Blebea, J.: The academic experience in distance (virtual) rounding and education of emergency surgery during COVID-19 pandemic. Surg. Open Sci. **5**, 6–9 (2021)
12. Abumalloh, R., et al.: The impact of coronavirus pandemic (COVID-19) on education: the role of virtual and remote laboratories in education. Technol. Soc. **67**, 101728 (2021)
13. Zainuddin, Z., Shujahat, M., Haruna, H., Chu, S.K.W.: The role of gamified e-quizzes on student learning and engagement: an interactive gamification solution for a formative assessment system. Comput. Educ. **145**, 103729 (2020)
14. Potkonjak, V., et al.: Virtual laboratories for education in science, technology, and engineering: a review. Comput. Educ. **95**, 309–327 (2016)
15. Shen, S., Xu, K., Sotiriadis, M., Wang, Y.: Exploring the factors influencing the adoption and usage of augmented reality and virtual reality applications in tourism education within the context of COVID-19 pandemic. J. Hospitality Leisure Sport Tourism Educ. **30**, 100373 (2022)
16. Pal, D., Vanijja, V.: Perceived usability evaluation of microsoft teams as an online learning platform during COVID-19 using system usability scale and technology acceptance model in India. Child. Youth Serv. Rev. **119**, 105535 (2020)
17. Klement, M.: Models of integration of virtualization in education: virtualization technology and possibilities of its use in educationKlement. Comput. Educ. **105**, 31–43 (2017)
18. de la Peña, D., Lizcano, D., Martínez-Álvarez, I.: Learning through play: gamification model in university-level distance learning. Entertainment Comput. **39**, 100430 (2021)
19. Donnermann, M., et al.: Social robots and gamification for technology supported learning: an empirical study on engagement and motivation. Comput. Human Behav. **121**, 106792 (2021)
20. Jodoi, K., Takenaka, N., Uchida, S., Nakagawa, S., Inoue, N.: Developing an active-learning app to improve critical thinking: item selection and gamification effects. Heliyon **7**, e08256 (2021)

Abrasion Thermo-transference Fabric Vinyl Resistance and Its Application in Haptics Perception Stimuli

Omar V. Godoy-Collaguazo[ID], Ana Umaquinga-Criollo[✉][ID], Marco Naranjo-Toro, Ronny M. Flores, and Katherin Chulde

Universidad Técnica del Norte, Gral. José María Córdova, Av. 17 de Julio 5-21, Ibarra, Ecuador
{ovgodoy,acumaquinga,rmflorest,kgchuldec}@utn.edu.ec

Abstract. In this research a comparative analysis is performed to determine thermo-transference vinyl finish abrasion resistance in select texture under the ISO 12947–2: 2016 Abrasion resistance test with upper limit 100000 cycles. The comparative analysis studies 2 types of fabric performance: Knitting fabric: (i) White Jersey (ii) Red fleece (iii) White Pique and Flat knit: (iv) Pink knit, (v) White print knit, (vi) 4 types Gabardine fabric: (a) 90-micron Fine vinyl (b)110 -micron Average vinyl, (c) 325-micron Glitter vinyl (d) 600-microne Embossed vinyl considering time, temperature, pressure and transfer method applying the Midi Martindale equipment. Additionally, the study of embossed textile products stimulates the sense of touch in individuals with a light degree of visual impairment or completely visually impaired. This information is based on an analog test –Snellen methodology to measure visual acuity adapted to smooth surfaces like embossment or shine, micron finesse and three detail complexity levels in characters: basic figures, alphanumeric and complex designed with Adobe Illustrator Cs6. Since used vinyl is thermoplastic together with substrate allows for user sensory perception magnification through finger tips nerve endings emitting electrical impulses to the brain turning into information giving rise to haptics perception.

Keywords: Haptics perception · Thermo-transference vinyl fabric · Fabric abrasion · Inclusive fashion · Resistance

1 Introduction

Haptics perception is the combination of sense of touch and kinesthetic learning through embossment, smoothness or material rigidity. [1, 2]. The aim of this research work is to determine whether a thermo-transference vinyl fabric finish may resist the demands of abrasion generated by haptics perception on the visually impaired.

Among the haptics techniques, printing of different types of thickness or thermo-transferable vinyl in fabric. The fabric finish allows for the fabric to be stimuli-sensitive to touch forming binder films in the surface changing its texture [3] the application method improves resistance and the detection of a series of elements through a transfer plate [4].

M. Botto-Tobar et al. (Eds.): ICAT 2022, CCIS 1757, pp. 106–120, 2023.
https://doi.org/10.1007/978-3-031-24978-5_10

In this study a substrate vinyl resistance comparative analysis is performed, subject to abrasive cycle procedures that determine superficial durability through a number of tests [5] [6]. Then, figures will be designed according to the visually impaired needs [7].

1.1   Thermo-transferable Vinyl Fabric

Technological advances have given way to the acquisition of new products therefore, plastic application is on the rise having a versatile and innovative use. As far as the fabric field, textile fabric is a thermo-plastic polymer keeping a heat-fixed thermo-adhesive film with variations according on micron structure so it may be applied to diverse finishes to obtain embossment effect in the printing process [8]. One of its best assets is its thermostable assets, agile production and recyclable nature, thickness, light transmission, film transparency, color analysis and mechanical properties among others [9]. However, traditional fusion process restricts composite parts size and thickness [10].

Vinyl strong performance results in the production of fabrics from this synthetic material having increased usability features specifically in the printing processes, producing a wide range of fabrics [11]. In the finish area, vinyl fabric is used to transfer a substrate to a design through heat application of a thermo-plastic product until it reaches fusion temperature, generally between 10 – 30 s thus achieving a physical bonding between vinyl and fabric substrate so that it solidifies at the cooling process [12, 11].

Fabric vinyl is applicable to cotton, polyester garments, acrylic fabrics, and mixtures. In terms of application processes, fabric composition and vinyl type should be taken into account since there is a wide variety of vinyl [13]. Influencing characteristics in the printing process are: fabric type, quality, resistance, durability, touch, elasticity and color. However, the use of handkerchiefs, elastic garments, caps is not advisable since in the vinyl printing there is no total adhesion causing garment damage [14].

Since the fabric industry is the most polluting industry, therefore waste management is desirable, nevertheless vinyl is considered a recyclable material when handled well so as to avoid the unnecessary waste of this material so other purposes should be considered. [15] The more abrasion resistance, tone durability the better adaptability to fabric, so the finish results in better quality. However, the biggest drawback of this technique is washing resistance [16].

1.2   Surface Abrasion Resistance

Textile fabrics are frequently subject to abrasion [17]. Natural, synthetic, and regenerated fabric have a certain level of resistance to abrasion resulting in decreased peeling and fabric wear depending on fabric quality and type. Nowadays, there are several abrasion resistance methods "whichever the abrasion testing method is, fabric wear will occur in the end" [18, 17, 19], furthermore, depending on mass per unit area, thickness is not a crucial element [20], what should be considered important is fabric substrate technical characteristics since they determine quality and resistance at the moment of wearing. The main characteristic necessary to know is resistance to other material friction.

Abrasion resistance is a study method in which different factors are involved such as fiction coefficient, heat spreading among others analyzed through several tests with the purpose of obtaining comparative values [21]. Abrasion takes place in two ways, fabric rubbing together or fabric substrate with other elements. It is worth mentioning that fabrics with little resistance to abrasion tend to wear and in certain instances, tearing. During the abrasion resistance process, fracture elongation and traction resistance characteristics are evaluated [22].

Abrasion resistance test performed to polymerics may or may be printed, use different mechanisms. One of the advantages of these kinds of abrasion resistance tests is that evaluated fabrics may be analyzed in different ways [23], among them, the computational analysis of image processing algorithms in the evaluation of the abrasion of textile fabrics [24]. Mechanisms and performed test are evaluated based on wear resistance and described by several international norms. The mechanism used for abrasion resistance test es called Martindale according to the International Organization for Standardization ISO 12947–2 [25] standard consisting of performing a particular rubbing or fiction by alternate movements. It is important to note that by performing the abrasion process, diverse samples can be evaluated simultaneously.

A drawback evident in these simple systems is the adhesiveness fragility between the coating and textile substrate. The technique used in the chemical interfacial bonding, substrate surface and the micro-nano structure was built by a $SiO2$ coating re-coated and embedded in the fabric Surface [26].

Abrasion wear occurs due to friction and the sliding of objects on fabric substrate Surface. This form of wear observed in tests applied on fabric print, which occurs as force exertion is applied due to the fabric-surface relative movement and the Martindale testing instrument [20]. Moreover, Martindale tests not only identifies fabric resistance since fabric subject to friction using the Martindale mechanical tool commonly contributes to variations in fabric substrate look giving it an old unattractive look, showing tear and change in fabric sheen and color. Similarly, certain substrate fabric resistance properties may be altered causing fracture or fabric breaking. For good fabric resistance, yarn twisting, lineal density and chemical or mechanical treatment is crucial [27].

1.3 Haptics Perception

Haptics perception comes from the Greek word *"haptohapthestai"* which in essence means touch, human sensations and perceptions when touching an object or surface [28] hand in hand with dimension or object characteristics like temperature, weight, roughness, smoothness and durability among others [29] identified by the sense of touch unrelated to visual perception [30]. Skin receptors in fingertips and other parts of the body achieve successful haptics perception with the help of *Paccini* and *Meissner* corpuscles as well as *Ruffini* nerve endings surface variations may be identified reacting as nerve impulses traveling to the brain so that it is transformed into information. Variations that exist on a surface can be identified, which, in turn react with [31, 28, 32].

This is how traditionally speaking, three information processes over objects and enhanced patterns make learning possible by the sense of touch [28]. These processes such as touch perception—referring to information exclusively gathered by cutaneous sense. Kinesthetic perception is information provided by muscles and tendons whereas the main perception previously mentioned is haptics [33]. As touch and kinesthetic components complement, they provide receptors valuable information regarding what is at immediate distance through sensory stimuli captured through the sense of touch so that stimuli reach the brain [33].

A clear example is when actions performed by touch perception occur together with nerve endings and muscles found in the palm of hands, given way to a Motor Action with individual or social purposes considering place, space and reach [34]. In other words, the touch sensory system provides the necessary information in regards to size, texture, temperature, weight and durability; on the other hand existing qualities like roughness, dryness, whiteness and softness involving the 2 types of senses above, may be applied entering the haptics perception world causing that memories and emotions take place [35].

2 Materials and Methods

Next, a Workflow Research shows phase one, where a survey, study and a 12947–2: 2016 standard analysis take place. After that, Abrasion Resistance haptics perception is shown in phase 2 as well as team formation, appropriate configurations and the experimental run take place, while in phase 3 an analysis from results obtained is performed. (See Fig. 1).

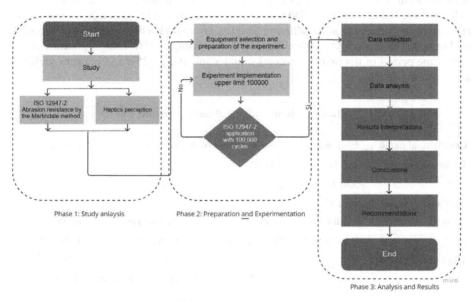

Fig. 1. Workflow reseach

Equipment used is a transfer plate, whose configurations may be up 53 mm thickness and adjustable precision to the fabric material having security elements from the beginning to the end of the process, such as automatic warning after the transferring of design to the fabric. Pressure depends on compressor power adjusting accurately through the use of the pressure gauge. (See Fig. 2).

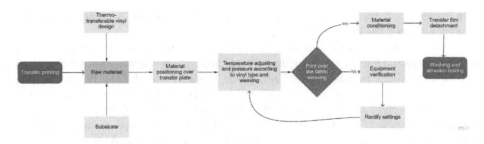

Fig. 2. Printing process through transferring

In the process, 4 vinyl types are used, easy weed easy weed sub-blog, Brik 600 and 1 glitter. Each one having their respecting thickness for testing, which revealed distinct embossments. Temperature applied to each knit and woven fabric substrate is determined by each fabric weaving. Vinyl composition is polyurethane, given in 90,110, 600 and 325 microns, achieving smooth, high embossment, sheer effect print.

It is essential that curing temperature for the first sample is set to 150 °C average pressure resulting in smooth embossment. However, the second sample at 130 °C temperature during the same time set, yielded the same result although thickness increased to 110 microns. Using vinyl Brik 600 temperature is raised to 155 °C in a 20 s-time period at medium-high pressure so as adhering a 600-micron vinyl, a high-texture embossment is obtained. The last sample used glitter-vinyl, increasing to 160 °C high-pressure at the same time period of the first and second samples involving 325-vinyl microns yielding a sheer-effect finish.

Table 1. Temperature and curing pressure

Commercial name	Easy weed	Easy weed sub blog	Brik 600	Glitter
Temperature (°C, °F)	150 °C	130 °C	155 °C	160 °C
	350°F	265°F	311 °C	320 °F
Application time (s)	10 a 15	10 a 15	20	10 a 15
Pressure	Media	Media	Media/ High	High
Composition	Polyurethane	Polyurethane	Polyurethane	Polyurethane
Thickness (microns)	90	110	600	325
Finish	Smooth	Smooth	High embossment	Sheer effect

2.1 Methods

Method applied is based on the ISO 12947–2 standard upper limit 100000 cycles, when the upper limit is reached the test end, which determines abrasion resistance to substrate by Martindale equipment rubbing through a standard circular abrasive medium whose results are determined by wear intervals obtained, kPa unit pressure according to weaving type as in work-clothing or upholstery. 12kPa is used for house linens or bedding at 9 kPa pressure [36]. The norm is reached after a particular number of cycling testing after time applied with the aim of getting to the sample tear point so that abrasion sensed by the visually impaired user results are analyzed considering set limitations.

2.2 Sampling Preparation

Substrate must be conditioned for at least a 18-h period to manipulate and extend samples without the use of tension, showing the weaving front. For print weaving two small samples are taken from different design that should be extracted from 100 mm away from the edge of the fabric, in turn it needs to have the most relevant characteristics from the pattern and select points in the sample where the most elements or patterns are located. Provided there are diverse weaving in the same model, the of highlighting its properties and characteristics is vital to identify weak points such as floating yarns [36].

2.3 Dimensions

Sampling requires 38 mm minimum diameter; however, it should not pass that measure. As for abrasive dimensions (disk and combed woold) a 140 mm minimum diameter is required to cover the abrasive table and adequately adhere.

2.4 Martindale Equipment

Martindale (Fig. 3) is a kind of equipment that determines abrasion resistance and peeling. Because of the machine's versatility is possible to practice this type of testing on a wide range of fabric types, in addition to testing on fabrics having a coating or finish. Moreover, it has testing instruments and aiding elements such as template, magnifying device, mounting device for highly flexible fabric. Furthermore, test devices and ancillary components such as templates, magnifying device, and a high flexibility textile mounting device are included. Peeling is an additional testing for the device determining resistance to formation of changes damaging weaving surface [25].

Template is mask-shaped characterized by a hard and transparent material characterized. It also has a hole between 2.5 ± 0.1 mm, which allows the observation of the sample test. The magnifying device provides enhanced print visualization from 8* to 10* maximum to single out broken thread or curl formation so that forming wear can be analyzed in the sample. The mounting device function for elastic weaving is to provide stability avoiding the destabilizing of the circular adhesion area when preparing the fabric which deforms due to elasticity capacity exerted on it [25].

2.5 Process

During the experimental phase the following is considered:

1. Team work assigning of experimentation and research—Professor participation (3) students (2) beneficiaries of the project.

Fig. 3. Martindale   **Fig. 4.** Fabric sampling

2. Weaving fabric selection: (i) Jersey knit fabric (commonly used in T-shirts), (ii) Fleece perched knit (sweaters and sport-clothing) (iii) Pique knit (polo shirts) (iv) Plain fabric (shirts) (v) Plain fabric (clothing), (vi) Plain fabric (canvas). (See Fig. 3).
3. Area cut for each of the samples-- 15 cm wide x 15 cm high according to used norm.
4. Textura and size selection which should contain vinyl in different size (2) diverse thickness and textures for the study. Structure organization is performed by Adobe illustrator Cs6, aiming to determine the pattern to be created (Fig. 5, Fig. 6).

Fig. 5. Pattern Design 1

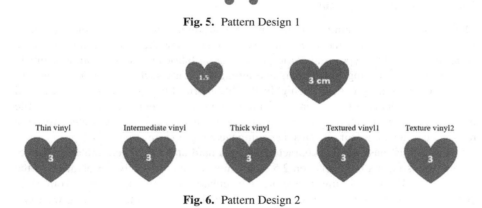

Fig. 6. Pattern Design 2

5. Cut is made inside out. Vinyl fabric is placed on the plotter inside out cutting the interior and not the exterior.
6. A 45° blade is used and suitable for cutting since fabric vinyl is sheer.
7. Being cautious about speed, pressure and blade Depth is essential.
8. Proceed to design cut discarding extra fabric to keep the respective vinyl signage.
9. After that, vinyl design is positioned touch the weaving and the conveyor blade is face up.

10. Extra peeling is cut diagonally.
11. Then, the plate is adjusted considering temperature, pressure and regulating time according to weaving type.
12. Cooling finishes the process.

2.6 Cycles

Complying with ISO 12947–2 standards, the number of cycles is relative to 100.000, i.e., the process stops when the fabric to which abrasion testing is performed overtake breakage. As seen in Table 2, White Jersey knit and red fleece cannot reach over 100.000 cycles, nor fine vinyl or glitter, knitted and woven fabrics. Conversely, there is a difference between Jersey knit and Fleece where vinyl thickness applied varies among fine, average, glitter and embossed, resulting in vinyl embossed applied knit for both, Jersey and Fleece withstand 100.00 abrasion cycles before showing breakage or wear.

For other types of knit like White Pique, Flat Pink, Print Flat White and Gabardine the opposite occurs not retracting from the type of vinyl applied to fine, glitter and embossed since they are capable of tolerating abrasion cycles without tearing or breaking.

Table 2. Abrasion testing- Number of cycles withstood by fabric

Type	Name	Fine vinyl 90 microns	Average vinyl 110 microns 130 °C	Glitter vinyl 325 microns -55 °C	Embossed vinyl 600 microns
		Cycle	Cycle	Cycle	Cycle
Knitting	White Jersey	77000	77000	33000	100000
	Red fleece	55000	25000	33000	100000
	White Pique	100000	100000	100000	100000
Flat weaving	Flat Pink	100000	100000	100000	100000
	Print Flat White	100000	100000	100000	100000
	Gabardine	100000	100000	100000	100000

2.7 Socialization

The Project in the initial phase has 13 students identified with partial or complete visual impairment currently enrolled in *Universidad Técnica del Norte*. Knit samples together with thermo-transferring vinyl utilizes kinesthetic learning and sense of touch (haptics perception) where different-color knit print and embossments allows for the identification of texture and content based on analog testing from Snellen methodology to measure visual acuity, but adapting such acuity to smooth textured-figures like embossment or sheer; micron-finesse and three character detail complexity levels: basic figures, alphanumeric characters and complex figures (Fig. 7 a-b-c-d.)

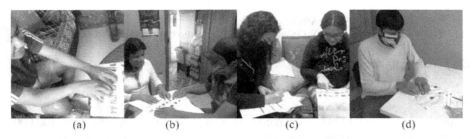

(a)   (b)   (c)   (d)

Fig. 7. Haptics perception project socialization

3   Results

90- micron fine vinyl—see Fig. 8 shows that flat woven has greater abrasive resistance compared to knitting however, knitting fabric (Jersey) showed more resistance to fleece so thermo-transferring vinyl is recommended in flat woven and knitting since it has more resistance to friction. During the development of this study the beneficiaries— suffering from visual impairments had difficulty in recognizing different elements due to the obtention of a smooth print.

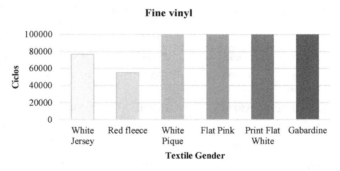

Fig. 8. Fine vinyl

110 -micron average vinyl, see Fig. 9, knit fabrics with diverse ligaments were welcome in flat fabrics since during abrasion testing quality results were satisfactory as it was in Pique weaving showing a similar resistance to knitting, which knitting did not show. As for vinyl micron increase in the print, the result was similar to the mentioned above as the only difference is the degree of curing temperature—130 °C (Table 1).

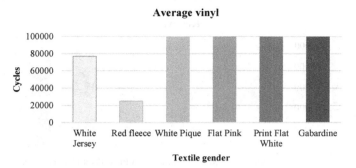

Fig. 9. Average vinyl

At the same time, 325- micron vinyl glitter, see Fig. 10 compared to different fabric types, has optimum results in regards to flat fabric. Nevertheless, Pique knit had a resistant abrasion to print since both Jersey and Fleece did not display an optimum grade during performed testing. Likewise, time and temperature were the same as in Table 1, where increasing the level of microns curing required a 155 °C temperature and a longer period of time compared to the rest of the samples producing a sheer - high embossment.

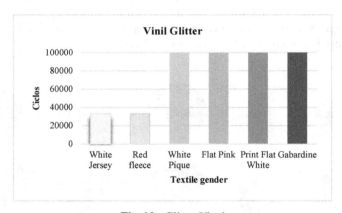

Fig. 10. Glitter Vinyl

Samples showed higher embossment, since 600 microns thermo-transferable vinyl was applied to a wide range of knits yielding optimum results in all substrates. Brik 600 performed best at abrasion resistance showing an equal number of cycles allowing for durable print when being hand-rubbed (Fig. 11).

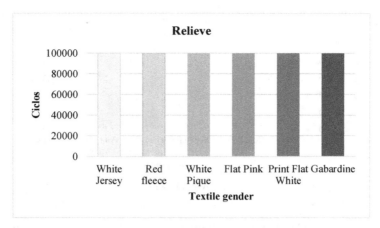

Fig. 11. Embossment

Final results, see Fig. 12, Martindale equipment provided better visualization of generated ware during testing causing damage to vinyl adhered to knit surface especially in glitter because of its sheer print losing its luster but not in embossed effect. Regarding 90 – 110- micron fine vinyl, Jersey and Fleece did not perform well since the finish surface ended up with an old and unaesthetic look although usage efficiency is expected, giving priority to high-embossed Brik vinyl for showing an acceptable abrasion resistance quality in every knit used in the experimental process.

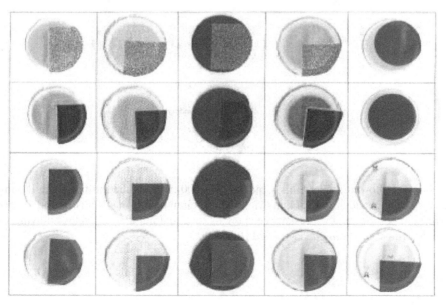

Fig. 12. Vinyl Sampling

4 Conclusions

This study allows an approach to the abrasion resistance analysis therefore, fabric substrate is examined. Through abrasion analyses performed to each of the samples selected, the maximum breakage point or tear is identified allowing for the study of friction between the visually impaired and knitting constant contact in addition to being able to verify color and texture perceived at that moment.

Fabric vinyl is an easily manageable material which obtains embossment effect finishes in print. Advantages of such polymer provide better tenacity, faster production and is recyclable. However, one of the disadvantages is washing resistance techniques. The application of this material, specifically to print, an extremely wide range of colors in textile products emerges. Characteristics pertaining to fabric substrate in vinyl application should be made of resisting, durable, elastic material in addition to quality so that print can be made to T-shirts, Polo shirts, publicity garment type among others—knitted fabrics and flat knitting fabrics should be used.

In the case of fine vinyl, White Jersey and red Fleece knitted fabrics have less abrasion resistance from 55000 to 77000 cycles compared to White Pique knit which soared 100000 cycles as well as flat knit with fine vinyl which withstood up to 100000 cycles in abrasion testing.

As far as average vinyl the lowest value was identified i.e. red Fleece displayed the least abrasion resistance with average vinyl resisting up to 25000 cycles. Alternatively, it was verified that White Jersey with average vinyl has intermediate abrasion resistance i.e. abrasion testing reached 77000 cycles and knit fabric reached 100000 cycles.

Referring to White knit and red Fleece with Glitter vinyl, they presented a cycle resistance to 33000 cycles probing that they have little abrasion resistance unable to endure a 100000 -fabric cycle.

White Piqué knit with any vinyl variant have high abrasion resistance as well as all flat knit subject in the testing reaching 100000 Martindale cycles, therefore are optimum to be used in haptics perception since they will not show wear as felt by finger tips.

It is evidenced that haptics perception is a way of interpreting and recognizing information through nerve ending impulse in the palm of hands; mainly finger surface which allows for the perception of immediate information around. Such perception, aligned with kinesthetic perception would not be as crucial for those suffering from partial or total visual impairment.

By means of this experimental research, it may be concluded that the vinyl that has the most significant abrasion resistance is embossment vinyl because of its physical characteristics withstanding 1000000 cycles in resistance testing, i.e., when the visually impaired perform haptic perception with embossed vinyl fabrics, it will not readily degrade since it has high resistance to constant friction / rubbing in this case in the fingertips of the visually impaired.

Acknowledgements. Special thanks to *Universidad Técnica del Norte* library, to the Department of University Wellness for the information received regarding the number of visually impaired students. Also, to the group of students from several majors who helped in the data-gathering process and support of the experimental process and, especially to professor- technicians in charge of the physical and chemical processes in the Textile College Degree.

References

1. Wu, X., et al.: Artificial multisensory integration nervous system with haptic and iconic perception behaviors. Nano Energy **85**, 106000 (2021). https://doi.org/10.1016/j.nanoen.2021.106000
2. Preißler, L., Jovanovic, B., Munzert, J., Schmidt, F., Fleming, R.W., Schwarzer, G.: Effects of visual and visual-haptic perception of material rigidity on reaching and grasping in the course of development. Acta Psychol. (Amst). **221** (2021). https://doi.org/10.1016/j.actpsy.2021.103457
3. Yang, Y., Li, M., Fu, S.: Screen-printed photochromic textiles with high fastness prepared by self-adhesive polymer latex particles, vol. 158 (2021)
4. Liu, M., Zhang, C., Liu, F.: Understanding wax screen-printing: A novel patterning process for microfluidic cloth-based analytical devices. Anal. Chim. Acta. **891**, 234–246 (2015). https://doi.org/10.1016/J.ACA.2015.06.034
5. Cao, M., Liu, Z., Xie, C.: Effectiveness of calcium carbonate whiskers in mortar for improving the abrasion resistance. Constr. Build. Mater. **295**, 123583 (2021). https://doi.org/10.1016/j.conbuildmat.2021.123583
6. Zhao, H., et al.: Robust sandwich micro-structure coating layer for wear-resistant conductive polyester fabrics. Appl. Surf. Sci. **494**, 969–976 (2019). https://doi.org/10.1016/j.apsusc.2019.07.103
7. Baumgartner, E., Wiebel, C.B., Gegenfurtner, K.R.: A comparison of haptic material perception in blind and sighted individuals. Vision Res. **115**, 238–245 (2015). https://doi.org/10.1016/j.visres.2015.02.006
8. Gonzalez, J.S., Maiolo, A.S., Hoppe, C.E., Alvarez, V.A.: Composite Gels Based on Poly (Vinyl alcohol) for Biomedical Uses. Procedia Mater. Sci. **1**, 483–490 (2012). https://doi.org/10.1016/j.mspro.2012.06.065
9. Braga, L.R., Pérez, L.M., Soazo, M. del V., Machado, F.: Evaluation of the antimicrobial, antioxidant and physicochemical properties of Poly(Vinyl chloride) films containing quercetin and silver nanoparticles. Lwt. **101**, 491–498 (2019). https://doi.org/10.1016/j.lwt.2018.11.082
10. van Rijswijk, K., Bersee, H.E.N.: Reactive processing of textile fiber-reinforced thermoplastic composites – An overview. Compos. Part A Appl. Sci. Manuf. **38**, 666–681 (2007). https://doi.org/10.1016/J.COMPOSITESA.2006.05.007
11. Wadatkar, N.S., Waghuley, S.A.: Characterizing the electro-optical properties of polyaniline/poly(vinyl acetate) composite films as-synthesized through chemical route. Res. Surf. Interf. **4**, 100016 (2021)
12. Mudzi, P., Wu, R., Firouzi, D., Ching, C.Y., Farncombe, T.H., Ravi Selvaganapathy, P.: Use of patterned thermoplastic hot film to create flexible ballistic composite laminates from UHMWPE fabric. Mater. Des. **214**, 110403 (2022). https://doi.org/10.1016/j.matdes.2022.110403
13. Du, Y., Xu, J., Paul, B., Eklund, P.: Flexible thermoelectric materials and devices (2018). https://doi.org/10.1016/j.apmt.2018.07.004
14. Kane, F.: Nonwovens in smart clothes and wearable technologies. Smart Clothes Wearable Technol. 156–182 (2009). https://doi.org/10.1533/9781845695668.2.156
15. Hilary, L.N., Sultana, S., Islam, Z., Sarker, M.K.U., Abedin, M.J., Haque, M.M.: Recycling of waste poly(vinyl chloride) fill materials to produce new polymer composites with propylene glycol plasticizer and waste sawdust of Albizia lebbeck wood. Curr. Res. Green Sustain. Chem. 4, (2021). https://doi.org/10.1016/j.crgsc.2021.100221

16. Li, W., Ye, X., Wang, Z., Zhang, J., Chao, J.: The preparation and performance characteristics of polyvinyl chloride-co-vinyl acetate modified membranes. In: Energy Procedia. pp. 1158–1162. Elsevier Ltd. (2011). https://doi.org/10.1016/j.egypro.2011.03.203
17. Wortmann, M., Frese, N., Hes, L., Gölzhäuser, A., Moritzer, E., Ehrmann, A.: Improved abrasion resistance of textile fabrics due to polymer coatings. J. Ind. Text. **49**, 572–583 (2019). https://doi.org/10.1177/1528083718792655
18. Thumsorn, S., Srisawat, N.: Influence of ethylene vinyl acetate contents on properties and crease recovery of slit yarn from polypropylene/high density polyethylene blend. Energy Procedia. **56**, 334–341 (2014). https://doi.org/10.1016/j.egypro.2014.07.165
19. Jokisch, S., Scheibel, T.: Spider silk foam coating of fabric. Pure Appl. Chem. **89**, 1769–1776 (2017). https://doi.org/10.1515/PAC-2017-0601
20. Ramujee, K., Potharaju, M.: Abrasion Resistance of Geopolymer Composites. Procedia Mater. Sci. **6**, 1961–1966 (2014). https://doi.org/10.1016/j.mspro.2014.07.230
21. Strength, T., Yuksel, I.: Blast-furnace slag Advanced testing of silk fibers , yarns , and fabrics (2018)
22. Fiber, T., Sinclair, R.: Understanding Textile Fibres and Their Properties Adding Functionality to Garments textiles and clothing (2020)
23. Zhang, W., Wei, L., Ma, J.: The antibacterial property and abrasion resistence of polyacrylate/graphene composites in finished leather. In: Proceedings of 34th IULTCS Congr. Sci. Technology Sustain. Leather, pp. 108–115 (2017)
24. Jasińska, I.: The algorithms of image processing and analysis in the textile fabrics abrasion assessment. Appl. Sci. **9** (2019). https://doi.org/10.3390/APP9183791
25. ISO: ISO 12947–2:2016(en), Textiles — Determination of the abrasion resistance of fabrics by the Martindale method — Part 2: Determination of specimen breakdown, https://www.iso.org/obp/ui/#iso:std:iso:12947:-2:ed-2:v1:en, (Accessed06 Apr 2022)
26. Liu, Y., Yuan, Y., Liu, J., Hua, J.: High wear-resisting, superhydrophobic coating with well aging resistance and ultrahigh corrosion resistant on high vinyl polybutadiene rubber substrate by thiol-ene click chemistry. Polym. Test. **101**, 107312 (2021). https://doi.org/10.1016/j.polymertesting.2021.107312
27. Coldea, A.M., Vlad, D.: Research Regarding the Physical-Mechanical Properties of Knits for Garments - Abrasion Resistance. Procedia Eng. **181**, 330–337 (2017). https://doi.org/10.1016/j.proeng.2017.02.397
28. Valencia, D.E.: Resolución de localización espacial háptica mediante estimulación eléctrica en la yema de los dedos Resolution of spatial localization haptic. **29**, 18–26 (2021)
29. Rodríguez-Guerrero, C., Fraile, J.C., Pérez-Turiel, J., Rivera Farina, P.: Robot Biocooperativo con Modulación Háptica para Tareas de Neurorehabilitación de los Miembros Superiores. Rev. Iberoam. Automática e Informática Ind. RIAI. **8**, 63–70 (2011). https://doi.org/10.1016/s1697-7912(11)70027-9
30. Bartocci, M.: Moderately and late preterms have problem recognizing faces after birth. J. Pediatr. Versão em Port. **93**, 4–5 (2017). https://doi.org/10.1016/j.jpedp.2016.10.003
31. Basset, N.: Estudios y rehabilitación de los trastornos de la sensibilidad de la mano. EMC - Kinesiterapia - Med. Física. **42**, 1–13 (2021). https://doi.org/10.1016/S1293-2965(21)45680-X
32. Ibáñez-Hernández, M.Á., Mora-González, F., Acosta-González, R., Alvarado-Castillo, B., Casillas-Chavarín, N.L.: Implante de lente intraocular trifocal difractivo: análisis y resultado de la agudeza visual. Rev. Mex. Oftalmol. **91**, 235–240 (2017). https://doi.org/10.1016/J.MEXOFT.2016.06.010
33. Ballesteros Jiménez, S.: Percepción haptica de objetos y patrones realzados: una revisión (1993)

34. Leclere, N.X., Sarlegna, F.R., Coello, Y., Bourdin, C.: Gradual exposure to Coriolis force induces sensorimotor adaptation with no change in peripersonal space. Sci. Rep. **12**, 1–13 (2022). https://doi.org/10.1038/s41598-022-04961-1

35. Dezcallar Sáez, T.: Relación entre procesos mentales y sentido háptico: Emociones y recuerdos mediante el análisis empírico de texturas. TDX (Tesis Dr. en Xarxa). 322 (2012)

36. ISO 12947–2:2016(E) ii COPYRIGHT PROTECTED DOCUMENT (2016)

Gamification, Nearpod Platform in Academic Performance in Virtual Classes for Higher Education Students

Sonia Armas-Arias[1]([✉]) [iD], Patricio Miranda-Ramos[1] [iD],
Kléber Augusto Jaramillo-Galarza[2] [iD], and Carlos A. Hernández-Dávila[1] [iD]

[1] Facultad de Ciencias Humanas y de la Educación, Universidad Técnica de Ambato, Ambato,
Ecuador
{sp.armas,dp.miranda,ca.hernandez}@uta.edu.ec
[2] Universidad Nacional de Chimborazo, Riobamba, Ecuador
kjaramillo@unach.edu.ec

Abstract. Currently, the use of technological tools constitutes a determining factor in virtual education, considering that now of acquiring significant learning in the student, it is necessary that they be motivated, interested, and carry out collaborative work. Therefore, the teacher oversees making use of innovative strategies such as gamification together with technology as a support instrument in the teaching-learning of the various contents.

The objective of this research is to determine the contribution provided by the Nearpod platform in virtual classes for Higher education students. Experimental research was applied with a parts approach through the application of two instruments that were validated by Cronbach's Alpha; they had a structure of questions with multiple choice on a Likert scale of five points, in addition to the application of the Technological Acceptance Model (TAM) to verify the level of acceptance of new technology or resource. The study population is 30 students of the Tourism Major of the Technical University of Ambato. For the validation of the hypothesis, the Friedman Chi-square statistic was applied to the most representative questions to determine which hypothesis to accept and finally check with the Kolmogorov Smirnov (KS) statistic, reaching the conclusion that the Nearpod platform as a gamification resource contributes to the teaching of university students in virtual classes, promoting inclusion, active participation, and collaborative work. It also allows the teacher to be the guide or mediator of the learning process and the student feels motivated and above all generates knowledge.

Keywords: Gamification · Author resources · Nearpod · Education · Academic performance

1 Introduction

Everyday innovation ensures that the teaching-learning process is updated and can keep pace with a world that is constantly changing. Traditional methodologies have already

M. Botto-Tobar et al. (Eds.): ICAT 2022, CCIS 1757, pp. 121–132, 2023.
https://doi.org/10.1007/978-3-031-24978-5_11

lost their golden days and are now considered obsolete or do not allow the comprehensive development of students. With this, gamification "applies game techniques to other processes to facilitate their realization and/or understanding" [1]. In other words, gamification presents innovative strategies and techniques that could drastically improve student performance in our country, which for years has presented drawbacks and low results in educational evaluations.

Learning games go through a series of processes and investigations, to qualify them as significant in the teaching-learning process. It is considered that gamification seeks the inclusion of the game as part of a new, innovative, and interesting learning that encourages creativity, authenticity, and autonomy in children. Limits, rules, procedures, and various activities that allow the independence of the students, when relating to their peers and solving a series of problems by themselves, are established.

Gamification in recent years has spread rapidly in terms of how teaching is represented as an educational process. In addition, it has been accepted in educational centers as a new and improved methodology, which does not allow the repetition of knowledge but the construction of it and mainly it is student-centered [2]. It can be implemented in a positive way in student life so that it influences emotionally and cognitively, who for one or more reasons cannot learn with traditional and ambiguous methodologies.

In recreational activities in the classroom, balanced environments can be presented, which encourage student participation. The educational process is related to games, in a very intrinsic way. Teachers and students must try to find the perfect balance between games and learning. So that with this, a relationship of mutual benefit can be established [3]. Gamification can be understood as a method that improves the motivation and ability of students, combining learning with play.

Games' procedures are implemented to achieve positive results, internalization of knowledge, and development of skills. They are based on obtaining rewards that serve as incentives for the student. The teacher who gamifies his academic activities has in his hands the possibility of transforming the education he/she teaches, daily activities are combined with playful procedures that generate greater interest. Of course, by gamifying the activities there is a risk that the student will be distracted and not comply with what was agreed, so the teacher must correctly plan each activity, expressing what and how it will be carried out [4].

Modern times impose the constant training of teachers. When technology is properly implemented as a didactic resource, positive results must be generated in terms of autonomous work with solid learning in students. Without forgetting that its bad practice could generate physical or behavioral problems. This considers the barriers that would prevent technology from being a central part of education, those institutions that do not have the necessary technological material, a lack of relevant infrastructure, and the non-existent internet connection.

In their research, [5] emphasize that "the advantages of thinking technologically imply greater speed and effectiveness in decision-making", postmodernism already implies a resounding change in how the person thinks and reasons. In this, the action of multimedia is manifested, as a factor that affects the opening of several cognitive windows in the student. Education has as its principle the linear educational process, centered on the teacher, now it leads to a non-linear form, that is, it has been dispersed giving way to the chaotic creativity of the student to learn.

Evaluations must be key allies to be able to quantify how much and how the student learns and if the knowledge has been internalized or not. At the same time, it talks about how educational quality affects the development of the members of society since the parameter of their training or instruction is established. Rodríguez (1981) cited by [6] mentions that academic performance requires the convergence of three factors: social, educational – institutional, and economic. In the social factor, "the educational institution has the obligation to guarantee the leveling of social inequalities", in that regard, it is understood that the institution must not judge the student by their social stratum, on the contrary, it must allow the homogeneity of opportunities for each of its students.

Academic results should not be affected by social inequalities. The educational and institutional factor, "tries to elucidate how adequate are the forms in which the educational future is developed to achieve the proposed objectives" that the methods, programs, organization, and teaching classification intervene directly in the student's academic performance. Although it is conceived that these actions are not allowing the student to achieve the objectives established in a hurry, they must be changed or improved, limiting that educational quality promotes good teaching and institutional action, which fulfills its role as a trainer.

Finally, the economic factor is analyzed, which radically affects academic performance. It is important to find out how willing the institution is to invest in improving its educational process, teacher education, and training, implementation of material resources, and technology, among others. In addition to considering the parent's investment in their child's education, seen as a long-term investment or an unnecessary expense. This will clearly affect academic performance, in terms of how the student may feel when they see that their parents or the institution do not invest in their academic training.

2 State of the Art

Due to the COVID 19 pandemic, face-to-face education was affected and took a drastic turn into virtual education. Considering that the implementation of TAC and ICT in the educational process is not a new topic, it is still an under-explored issue in our context. Traditional teaching, which does not implement so many technological resources, is still considered relevant since the lack of infrastructure and materials is often evident in the urban or rural sector. Now, education since March 2020 changed, creating the opportunity to work in a virtual environment, which although it generated various inconveniences in its beginning, has also offered the possibility of a transformation of teachers and their technological training.

We must not forget that the native digitals know how to use technology better than the digital immigrant, who had to face this big change and must learn immediately to be able to carry out their classes in the best way. If memory does not fail, it must be remembered that each transformation entails collateral damage, sacrifices, and moments of uncertainty and discomfort. That is, learn from scratch, without fearing the challenges that are present, teachers through training have gradually learned or improved their technical skills and abilities, through programs, web pages, resources, and digital tools.

Gamification is a great opportunity to take advantage of the education field and make it the central role in education, understanding that knowledge is adapted to the process of the game, with the aim of motivating the student, improving their concentration, participation, academic performance, and their motivation [7] understands gamification as a didactic strategy that incorporates the game in the teaching process, not so much as the game itself, but rather its mechanics, narratives, and rewards, expressed in a way that monotonous activities are innovated. Harus and Fox (2015) cited by [1] mention that gamification can establish direct links between the student and the content to be learned, based on a different perspective, with the aim of effectively understanding knowledge and improving skills and abilities. in the student.

Gamification provides students with the necessary resources for them to participate in the creation of their learning community, gives them freedom, and allows them to learn from mistakes in pleasant learning environments [8]. This does not mean that the scores are dropped, on the contrary, the students develop a spirit of healthy competition, and teamwork and are also motivated by knowing that by completing the activities they will obtain small rewards and a score that measures their effort and dedication.

Since the beginning, the internet has presented constant changes and improvements. In the history of communication, decades ago the only way that existed for digital communication was the telegraph. It was invented in 1840 and used electrical signals that communicated a point of origin and destination, through Morse code. Years passed and people considered generating something that could connect in real-time to several places at the same time, in this way little by little what is now known as the internet was created. In 1980, computers were already being developed experimentally giving way to a phenomenon known as email, which was very useful for communication.

Web 2.0 arrived and allowed us to access information in a globalized way, however, it did not allow us to interact with it. Therefore, in Web 3.0, not only access to information was easy, but also its manipulation in real-time, thus interacting with various people regardless of geographic profile. The semantic web, in a nutshell, is understood as the instruction of languages and procedures, which generate or allow the user to be offered a personalized interface. Web 3.0 already allows intelligent search, based on user preferences, linked to the needs and characteristics of the individual. Social networks are increasing, allowing real-time communication among people all over the world, Facebook, WhatsApp, Instagram, YouTube, Telegram, and Tik Tok, capture the attention of millions of people in the world.

In simple words, academic performance falls on quantitative qualifications that a student obtains; however [9] agrees that these numerical data should not only be analyzed to classify a student as good, fair, or poor since there are several factors that can affect low results. At present, academic performance takes a concept more in line with student productivity, the fulfillment of educational objectives, and the quality of the result obtained from the development of activities in class and at home (Fig. 1).

Among the factors that affect academic performance are exogenous and endogenous factors, which express how both external and internal factors have a direct relationship with the academic performance of students. In other words, the family, social, economic situation will infer the results obtained by the student in his learning process. Hence the importance of not only considering summative evaluations since they can generate

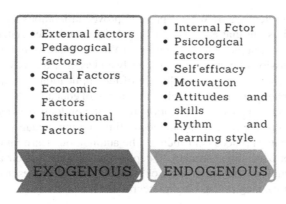

Fig. 1. Exogenous and endogenous factors

erroneous results when evaluating knowledge. Likewise, the psychological factor, attitudes, and skills of the student can redeem that their academic performance is not the best in terms of punctuation since this goes hand in hand with the rhythms and styles of learning [10].

Another factor that influences academic performance according to Bravo et al. (2017) is the importance of family expectations, that is, the family plays a fundamental role in the learning process. The socioeconomic and cultural level, and reading habits, will have a great impact on the students. If the child does not perceive that reading is important, it will be difficult for him to generate a reading habit. Contrary to homes in which reading is encouraged in participation in recreational activities, organizing family nights of games such as chess, sudoku, and word search, among others.

Certainly, when implementing web 3.0 tools for virtual education, the teacher becomes a guide, overseeing investigating, planning, and executing various activities that consolidate student learning. Likewise, it contributes to generating self-learning skills, motivation, commitment, opting for a playful character, becoming an active subject committed to their comprehensive training to stimulate the construction of basic knowledge in a playful and recreational way in the various subjects of Basic General Education [7].

With a descriptive approach [4] in his article "Autonomous work strategies for students", determines that implementing self-regulated autonomous and active learning participation strategies in adaptable work environments allows the development of skills and competencies of the student, strengthening interdisciplinarity in the construction of their self-study. Based on a descriptive methodology using the survey technique, the results indicate that the most used strategies are exam preparation, and intellectual content work, while the expansion strategy (exploration and construction of activities and materials) is the least used. Executed by students. Therefore, it concludes that the teaching performance in the face of this new perspective is not limited to the transmission of content, but to expanding the ability of students to decipher the information, organize it, create content, and improve their educational experience from key training actions and motivational that benefits your academic profile.

[11] in their article "Use of WhatsApp to improve autonomous learning in university students", points out that education in a globalized and interrelated world to ICT (Information and Communication Technologies) allows the creation of flexible training spaces, the transmission of content synchronously and asynchronously between teacher - students. Furthermore, it states that the use of the application is frequent because it enables the learner and educator to establish new forms of educational tutorials, access to literature, effective and rapid communication, resolution of doubts, active and participatory methodology outside the classroom, and optimizing individual work. It concludes that the use of WhatsApp does contribute to the autonomous learning of students as a compliment and/or educational strategy to deploy the capacity for self-regulation, self-learning, metacognition, and use of tools or technological resources according to their needs to face their training process in an integral and holistic way.

3 Methodology

The research is experimental-exploratory. Experimental because the use of the Nearpod platform was applied to the academic performance of university students in the Tourism career of the Technical University of Ambato, for this the pre-test was carried out with the structured questionnaire of the research project; then the TAM model was applied, which made it possible to measure the degree of satisfaction with the use of the resources created in Nearpod, the same ones that were used in virtual classes due to the COVID-19 Pandemic. It is exploratory because it allowed the Nearpod study to be carried out as a gamification resource by investigating and identifying the particularities of the study variables, knowing their causes and effects using effective techniques for collecting information.

The survey was used as a research technique based on questions linked to the research.

The questionnaire as a research instrument was structured by 24 questions classified as:

- 5 sociodemographic questions
- 17 questions on a Likert scale
- 2 dichotomous questions

The instrument was of great help in collecting accurate and real data and information since it allowed possible conclusions to be drawn from the results obtained with their corresponding analysis and interpretation.

We worked with a parts approach: quantitative through the processing of statistical information, frequencies, and percentages through the application of two instruments: a questionnaire structured as a diagnostic test and the TAM model, to subsequently obtain the qualitative part on the perceptions of measure the degree of acceptance and/or satisfaction of the use of web 3.0 tools focused on the autonomous work of students in the subject of Social Studies.

3.1 ADDIE Methodology

The ADDIE methodology is an alternative to educational planning of a generic and flexible nature that allows managing not only the design and development of thematic units or subjects from the virtual world but also the evaluation of the implementation to continuously improve its efficiency and effectiveness. The basic objective of its application is to create interactive educational experiences and environments that promote the acquisition of skills and the production of educational skills. ADDIE consists of 5 phases:

Analysis. This first phase of analysis of the ADDIE methodology was carried out in Tourism Career at the Technical University of Ambato through the application of a structured survey of 24 questions carried out in Google Forms, with the purpose of knowing the current situation on the use of web 3.0 tools focused on the autonomous work of students, for this the population that was taken into consideration for the application of the survey is 68 students.

Design. In the design phase, a sketch of the author's resources for the collaborative and autonomous work of the students was made, as stated in the objective which points out the development of web 3.0 tools. Within each tool, there are creative and innovative activities based on improving academic performance.

Development. For the development of the presentation, the Nearpod gamification tool was used by clicking on the following connection link: https://nearpod.com or you can also type the word Nearpod in the Google search engine and select the first option, where the following window appears as shown in Fig. 2.

Fig. 2. Nearpod platform

Once the presentation has been prepared, the name must be entered and click on save and exit Fig. 2 or, at the same time, the presentation can be viewed as students, which allows them to see how it will be observed when working live.

Fig. 3. Upload presentation

The presentation is ready to be shared with the students (Fig. 3).

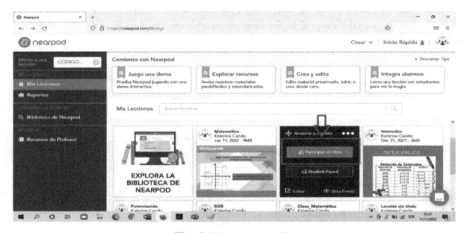

Fig. 4. Live presentation

Implementation. At this stage, Nearpod was applied as a gamification tool for the students, making use of the previously designed presentation. To access the Nearpod platform, the student only needs to have internet access and the code or connection link, which is obtained. By placing the cursor over the presentation, choosing the option to participate live, click on copy code or link and send to the Microsoft Teams chat, without the need to project the screen, the student can view the presentation Fig. 4.

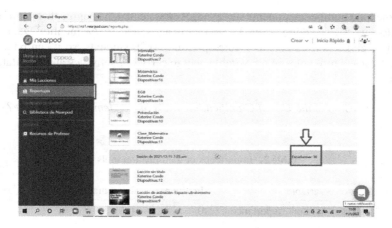

Fig. 5. Evaluation

Evaluation. To determine the results of the experimentation process, the Technological Acceptance Model known as TAM was applied, which is based on a structured questionnaire that contains 14 questions on the Likert scale, which are supported by the utility factor UP and ease of use FUP which allows measuring the degree of user acceptance before the implementation of new technology; through the use of the Google Form, the information was collected that allowed determining the degree of perception, acceptance, or rejection that the student has after the use of Nearpod as a gamification tool in virtual classes (Fig. 5).

4   Results

The results obtained from the application of the TAM model to 30 students of the Tourism career at Technical University of Ambato are presented to analyze and interpret if the resources developed in the Nearpod platform during virtual classes were beneficial, interesting, entertaining, and contributed significantly to academic performance.

1. *Using Web 3.0 Tools Allows Me to Get My Work Done Faster*

Table 1. Use of web 3.0 tools

Variable	Frequency	Percentage
Strongly disagree	0	0,0
Disagree	0	0,0
Neither agree or disagree	5	16,7
Agree	15	50,0
Strongly agree	10	33,3
Total	**30**	**100**

Of the total number of students surveyed, 50% state that they agree that gamification tools allow work to be done faster, 33.3% totally agree and 16.7% mention that they are undecided, giving a total of 100% corresponding to 30 students, so it can be ensured that the Nearpod tool helps in a favorable way to carry out activities and facilitate their solution.

2. *How Important is the Use of Gamification Tools in Academic Performance?*

Table 2. Importance of gamification tools

Variable	Frequency	Percentage
Without importance	0	0,0
Of little importance	0	0,0
moderately important	0	0,0
Important	3	10
Very important	27	90
Total	**30**	**100**

90% of the population state that the use of gamification tools in academic performance is very important and 10% mention that it is important; giving a total of 100% that corresponds to 30 students, so it can be ensured that for the teaching-learning process these tools improve the transmission of content and improve student participation.

3. *Consider that the Use of Gamification Tools in Collaborative Learning is:*

Table 3. Use of web 3.0 tools

Variable	Frequency	Percentage
It is a determine factor in student learning	22	73,33
It is a fashion, due to the technological age in which we live	0	0,0
It is an alternative support tool for teaching the various contents	8	26,67
It is a totally expendable tool	0	0,0
It is an alternative that does not necessarily influence student learning	0	0,0
Facilitates group work, collaboration, and inclusion with your students	0	0,0
Reduces time and resources	0	0,0
Helps search information faster	0	0,0
Total	**30**	**100**

Of the total number of students surveyed, 73.33% state that gamification tools are an alternative support tool for teaching the various contents, 26.67% affirm that it is a determining factor in student learning; giving a total of 100% corresponding to 30 students, so it can be ensured that the use of gamified tools facilitates the teaching of content, providing alternative support to the teaching methodology.

The calculation of statistic that is used to verify the hypothesis established in the research is Kolmogorov Smirnov, which measures the tendency that exists between experimentation and satisfaction with the use of technology, the same that allows for improving student performance (Tables 1, 2 and 3).

Table 4. Hypothesis verification

Kolmogorov-Smirnov test for one sample					
		The use of technological tools in virtual classes is better	In general, I find these tools to be useful	The use of web 30 and gamification tools allows	I feel satisfied at the time of carrying out activities
N		30	30	30	30
Normal range	Media	3,97	4,17	4,03	4,03
	Standard deviation	,890	,747	,999	,964
Differences more extreme	Absolute	,315	,278	,320	,286
	Positive	,218	,255	,180	,180
	Negative	-,315	-,278	-,320	-,286
Z de Kolmogorov-Smirnov		1,725	1,525	1,753	1,568
Sig. Asintót. (bilateral)		,005	,019	,004	,015

a. Contrast distribution is normal
b. Calculated from data

The Kolmogorov Smirnov statistic applied to the 4 most representative questions determines the p value, giving the following results as shown in Table 4, therefore, the p value of each question is less than 0.05, therefore the result is verified rejecting the null hypothesis and accepting the alternative hypothesis, verifying that the Nearpod platform improves the performance of students in virtual classes of university students.

5 Conclusions

Gamification-based tools have modified the educational process, making it more creative, practical and, above all, participatory, becoming the teacher's best ally, as they are known as the web of time and space that allows organizing the search for content and information through connections between the web and the real world.

From its immersion in education, it has been shown that it contributes to the autonomous work of the student based on criteria of self-discipline, self-regulation and self-management of their own actions and procedures, in such a way that they develop critical, reflective, technological, and become an innovative being capable of working independently with the help and application of ICT.

The implementation of web 3.0 tools to enhance academic performance in the educational field is relevant because when developing activities, workshops, and extracurricular work based on tools and/or digital environments, a new teaching and learning concept is created where motivation is encouraged. And creativity of the learner, in addition to giving way to work proactively, independently, guided by their curiosity for learning from a framework of flexibility and versatility that allows overcoming barriers of structure and pre-established form.

References

1. Sullivan, P., Sergi-McBrayer, J., Miller, S., Fallon, K.: An Examination of the use of computer-based formative assessments. Comput. Educ. **173**, 104274 (2021)
2. Dong, Y., Shizheng-Du, H., Wang, A.: The effects of flipped classroom characterized by situational and collaborative learning in a community nursing course: A quasi-experimental design. Nurse Educ. Today **105**, 105037 (2021)
3. Guntha, R., Hariharan, B., Rangan, P.: Analysis of multimedia communication issues in the immersive smart classroom system – a control center approach. Proc. Comput. Sci. 2600–2609 (2020)
4. Kozlova, D., Pikhart, M.: The use of ICT in higher education from the perspective of the university students. Proc. Comput. Sci. 2309–2317 (2021)
5. Legaki, N., Karpouzis, K., Assimakopoulos, V., Hamari, J.: Gamification to avoid cognitive biases: An experiment of gamifying a forecasting course. Technol. Forecast. Soc. Change **167**, 120725 (2021)
6. Palazón-Herrera J., Soria-Vílchez, A.: Students' perception and academic performance in a flipped classroom model within Early Childhood educ. Degree. Heliyon **7**(4), e06702 (2021)
7. Shao-Chen, C., Ting-Chia, H., Siu-Yung, M.: Integration of the peer assessment approach with a virtual reality design system for learning earth science. Comput. Educ. 103758 (2020)
8. Páez-Quinde, C., Infante-Paredes, R., Chimbo-Cáceres, M., Barragán-Mejía, E.: Educaplay: una herramienta de gamificación para el rendimiento académico en la educación virtual durante la pandemia covid-19. Catedra **5**(1), 32–46 (2022)
9. Morán-Barrios, J., Ruiz de Gauna, P., Ruiz-Lázaro, P., Calvo, R.: Complementary learning methodologies for the acquisition of competencies in postgraduate medical education and Entrustable Professional Activities (EPAs). Educación Médica **21**(5), 328–337 (2020)
10. Manzano-León, Rodríguez Ferrer, J., Aguilar-Parra, J., Fernández-Campoy, J., Trigueros, R., Martínez-Martínez, A.: Play and learn: Influence of gamification and game-based learning in the reading processes of secondary school students. Revista de Psicodidáctica (English ed.) **27**(1), 38–46 (2022)
11. Weepiu Samekash, M.L: Uso de whatsapp para mejorar el aprendizaje autónomo en los jóvenes universitarios. EDUCARE ET COMUNICARE: Revista De investigación De La Facultad De Humanidades **8**(1), 78–87 (2020)
12. de la Peña, D., Lizcano, D., Martínez-Álvarez, I.: Learning through play: Gamification model in university-level distance learning. Entertain. Comput. 100430 (2021)

Gamification in the Development of Meaningful Mathematics Learning in Students with Unfinished Schooling

Luis Pujos-Zumbana$^{(\boxtimes)}$ (iD) and Cristina Paez-Quinde (iD)

Pontificia Universidad Católica del Ecuador, Ambato, Ecuador
{lapujos,mpaez}@pucesa.edu.ec

Abstract. This article presents the experience of a meaningful learning proposal through the Classcraft platform with interactive activities for 20 students with unfinished upper basic schooling from Hispano America School about first-grade inequalities. It has as its main objective the implementation of gamification resources for the strengthening of meaningful learning of mathematics, this study is quasi-experimental research with a descriptive scope and quantitative approach. The instruments applied were the questionnaire (pretest and posttest) and the survey that was applied through the TAM model to know the degree of technological acceptance of the students, for which 4 objective questions were analyzed to know the effectiveness, usefulness, ease, and satisfaction of using technological tools to achieve meaningful learning in mathematics. The results of this research are favorable in the learning of mathematics, even more so in students with unfinished schooling since they can improve their academic performance by using gamification tools, which are available all the time so that their performance improves.

Keywords: TAC · Gamification · Web 3.0 tools · Virtual Education · Unfinished Schooling · Meaningful Learning

1 Introduction

Technological progress has been involved in all fields and education is no exception, in the educational context there is the Learning and Knowledge Technologies (LKT), which have become extremely important with the forced insertion of technology virtual education. Online education has led the teacher and student to seek ways and strategies for better learning, and with the insertion of TAC, gamification is used to help students maintain interest in mathematics and achieve meaningful learning.

Gamification is constituted as the implementation of games in a context that is not a game to stimulate the acquisition of knowledge, it is a topic that is studied a lot today since the students' lack of interest is evident, this resource is very useful for application in class, which can be virtual or face-to-face [1].

© The Author(s), under exclusive license to Springer Nature Switzerland AG 2023
M. Botto-Tobar et al. (Eds.): ICAT 2022, CCIS 1757, pp. 133–144, 2023.
https://doi.org/10.1007/978-3-031-24978-5_12

Achieving meaningful learning through gamification in any area is a challenge for the community in the educational context, it is for this situation to concisely understand the process to achieve it, to speak of meaningful learning is to involve the students as the main author who must have the full predisposition followed by the content taught by the teacher. Ausubel's theory [2] states that this training precedes the constructive integration of thoughts, feelings, and actions, which directs human enrichment, forges a feeling of satisfaction and increases the disposition for the acquisition of new knowledge.

Mathematics has always been a challenge to keep students' attention. For this reason, implementing game strategies in the educational field is necessary to obtain enriching results. One of the tools that has contributed to the implementation of gamification in the educational field is Classcraft. This is constituted as an online educational tool that allows to gamify the classroom and gives role-playing overtones to the learning experience, it is the central part of the educational proposal exposed in this article [3].

The implementation of Genially within this educational tool is an addition to strengthen knowledge and stimulate learning, this tool allows us to generate interactive digital content without programming and without design knowledge, it has a wide section of templates that helps us to create quality content.

Another resource that is added to gamification is Nearpod, which is constituted as a multiplatform student participation website that entertains students with interactive activities, connecting them through collaborative discussions and offering an instant view of their learning [4].

1.1 Unfinished Schooling

The current situation regarding student desertion is still evident in Ecuador where 5.4 million people have unfinished schooling. Of this total, 2.9 million have not completed higher basic education and 965,000 high school [5]. The lack of resources and other factors have led those students to integrate into institutions in order to complete their studies and have access to a better quality of working life. Hence the need to integrate LKTs into virtual and face-to-face education to help the academic process continue.

During pandemics, the integration of technology has favored the education of students with unfinished schooling, this has led teachers to use this advance to further enrich the content that is taught to students, with this comes the proposal of integrating interactive activities immersed in a gamification [6].

1.2 How Will Gamification Be Applied?

The gamification was developed in the classcraft platform, which helps to organize consecutive content as missions, it integrates the students in the game with a personalized avatar that will accompany them throughout the teaching-learning process, and resources are integrated within it interactive created in Genially and Nearpod that helped in the motivation of the students [7].

The game was about first-grade inequalities which respond to the learning objective of the Ministry of Education. Once the subject was presented, the teachers provide the profile sheet to each student for their registration on the platform. Therefore the teacher will guide the entire process and each of the missions and activities to be developed within them in order to acquire knowledge and reach a final evaluation that allows knowing the level of assimilation of the contents.

2 State of the Art

LKTs have been included in recent years in academic training, resulting in favor of students, since they prefer to search for information using their mobile devices, leaving aside visits to libraries. According to [8], it is necessary to talk about TACs as dynamic pedagogical use to guarantee the teaching-learning process and the construction of new knowledge. This will allow teachers to maintain the attention of their students, who will work on the development of understanding in a comfortable way.

According to [9] for the correct use of ICT-LKT in face-to-face or virtual classes, it is necessary to consider the domain of teachers, students and family members who are part of the educational field. The teacher as a learning guide shows lack of training on tools and theoretical knowledge that help develop inclusive pedagogical practices in the classroom [10]. Therefore, training is the primary link to acquiring technological competence and understanding the educational process of their environment, this can be evidenced in the acquisition of mobile phones by many people, the same that cannot be verified if they use these devices as educational support.

In the study carried out by [11] the implementation of the gamified resource in the classcraft platform in the area of language and literature is evidenced. It uses this tool that acts as a background for students to immerse themselves in the reality of gamified learning, the main objective is to facilitate the acquisition of basic English grammar when using Classcraft platform and motivate students with gamification strategies, resulting in significant learning that also enhances group work.

In the work by [12], entitled gamification and game-based learning, a compilation of platforms and tools are presented that help improves game-based learning of geology by making academic content attractive and motivating for students. It reflects the strong intervention of emotions as a fundamental part to attract the attention of students.

[13] carried out a study entitled Gamification tools: effect on meaningful learning, engagement and student stress. Its purpose is to examine the perception of university students, in the results is found that the students perceive that the use of gamification tools has allowed them to achieve significant learning since the average values obtained in the different indicators have exceeded by more than 80% of students, obtaining grades greater than 8. This dictates that the resource implemented by teachers is innovative for immersion in classes.

2.1 Gamification

According to [14] in their work Gamification to encourage the activation of students in their learning point out that it is an active strategy to motivate students. It makes the study of several works of literature that show the experiences put to the test, obtaining, as a result, the action of learning through gamified activities taking into account sociodemographic indicators that do not affect the objective achieved.

2.2 Web 3.0 Tools

The integration of web 3.0 tools continues to take ownership and gain strength, which is why it has become a necessity and not an option [15] in research on 3.0 creative writing websites for high school students of the third year of Basic General Education. They use the website JIMDO platform based on 3.0 technology for the students of the "Maria Troncatti" School and thus improve writing through virtual interactivity. In the result evidence is reflected of the proper use in the participation of ICT within the teaching-learning process, as well as the access to technological resources of both students and the teacher could be evidenced.

For the construction of web resources, the use of ICT is essential, the same as in the field of mathematics has been more useful in recent times since this area presents a greater degree of difficulty due to the concepts and procedures, the same ones that require practice, and technology contributes in this aspect thanks to interactive activities [15]. Research on ICT in the Development of Mathematical Competencies in Virtual University Education shows the achievement of mathematical skills acquired in training, using software such as Winplot, Derive, Matlab, Maple, GeoGebra that help to calculate symbols and complex numbers, through which you can learn thanks to its strength to show mathematical procedures in detail [16].

The creation of gamified activities does not guarantee the development of meaningful learning (SA) of mathematics, although it is known that this area has been cataloged as one of those that present the greatest confusion of understanding on the part of the apprentices at the different levels of education. According to [17] in their work on the paradigmatic complexity in meaningful learning of mathematics, they value the scientific evidence found regarding the AS of mathematics and its structure from the paradigm of confusion Therefore, it is concluded that it is necessary to use educational strategies to reduce the difficulty of understanding [18].

2.3 Unfinished Schooling

Just as the intervention of gamification in meaningful learning is known, it should be seen how influential the proposal is, taking into account the flexibility, availability and learning styles of students with unfinished schooling [2]. In this way [7] carried out research entitled "The employment of duolingo app for the oral production of the English language for adult learners with unfinished schooling of 10th level EGB." Its objective is to determine the applicability of Duolingo App in the development of audio-verbal skills in adult students with unfinished schooling through pre and post-tests which helped to demonstrate that Duolingo, a gamification app, allowed improving oral production of the English language. According to this work, the positive aspect of including gamified activities in work on unfinished schooling is evident.

2.4   Virtual Education

The virtual education established at the time of COVID 19 brought with it positive and negative aspects, among which the forced adaptation to the technological age of all people must be highlighted, and students with unfinished schooling have strengthened their learning through this virtuality. According to [3], in his work on "Virtualized education in critical thinking for people with unfinished schooling at Everest School in the Riobamba canton". He highlights the good development of virtual training not only in a specific area since, thanks to this technology, but students also have the facility to access their educational files from anywhere in the world at any time of the day, in addition, to learning autonomy in decision-making helps to strengthen the critical aspect of learning [9].

3   Methodology

For the innovative proposal, the Classcraft platform was selected, which helped with the participation of 20 students with unfinished schooling belonging to the upper basic education level of the Hispano America School, the topic worked on was first-grade inequalities, the class objective was to solve and graph inequalities of the first degree. The same one that led to gamification requiring the use of interactive activities carried out in Genially and Nearpod, also relying on the Symbolab website to verify mathematical processes and results (Fig. 1).

3.1   Gamification Proposal

Fig. 1. Classcraft teacher profile

Once the theme, objectives and class activities have been considered, the gamified proposal called "The power of inequalities" is developed, which is divided into three stages of activities with a total time of 70 min described below (Table 1):

Table 1. Lesson plan

Stage	Description	Activities
Beginning 15 min	The activity begins with a warm-up activity, then the introduction and registration of the participants on the Classcraft are done on the platform	From Havana a ship arrives full of: They must repeat and mention an object from a group and so the next one will mention the one they listen to plus the one they add
Procedure 40 min	We entered to work on the different missions, each with a score of 200, which in the end will show 1000 points, which is equivalent to a rating of 10 points: Mission 1: "THE BEGINNING OF POWER" Mission 2: "STRENGTHENING THE MIND" Mission 3: "AN UNKNOWN ENCOUNTER" Mission 4: "SOURCE OF POWER" Mission 5: "GETTING THE POWER"	Genially: content about inequalities Nearpod: Inequalities Symbology Pairing Genially: content about first-degree inequalities Nearpod: canvas activity to solve an exercise Symbolab: to verify the mathematical procedure
Evaluation 15 min	The gamified evaluation is developed on the Nearpod platform	Nearpod: final test to know the simulation level of knowledge

For the development of this activity, mobile technology was used through the Google Chrome browser, which facilitates internet access provided by the educational institution. For a more optimal result, students are required to use a computer where they can monitor their progress.

3.2 Type of Research

This research has a descriptive scope, it is based on a quasi-experimental type, since the purpose is to implement the proposal regarding the search for theoretical information of each of the variables of a group and is based on a quantitative model which helps to collect and analyze of statistical data to obtain the results.

The techniques for collecting information were the survey and the instrument, a questionnaire structured by 10 multiple-choice questions with the contents established in the Ministry of Education for the respective level of the area of mathematics and additional, an instrument validated on the model was used. TAM based on 15 questions on the Likert scale. The study sample was 20 students from the quasi-experimental group.

4   Results

Once the survey was applied to the 20 students with unfinished schooling at the upper basic level, the following results were obtained:

There was a total of 20 students in the socialization, among which 12 are women who represent 60%, and 40% who incorporate the remaining 8 men. The ages of the students vary between 21 and 40 years, the same one that has an average age of 32.15 years.

4.1   Analysis of the Evaluation Questionnaire

The applied questionnaire consists of 10 questions, of which 4 of the most relevant have been selected to analyze the average response of the classroom.

Question 1: Theoretical Knowledge (Table 2)

Table 2. What is inequality?

Answer	Answer: It is inequality between unknowns and numbers related by arithmetic operations	
Instrument	Pretest	Postest
Wrong answer	12	0
Right answer	8	20
Average	4	10

According to the correct answers obtained in the pretest and in the post-test of the experimental population, the following results were obtained. In the diagnostic test for the 20 students, 12 of them representing 60% of the sample answered incorrectly obtaining a grade equal to 0, the other 40% are 8 remaining students had a note of 10 points for the correct answers, giving an average in the pretest of 4 points. After having applied the experimentation of the Classcraft tool, the following qualifications of the question were obtained, of the total of 20 collegiates, 100% of the population improved their learning by obtaining a perfect qualification in the question regarding the theoretical introduction, this after having interacted with the activities reflected in the gamification.

In conclusion, all of the students in this question improved their knowledge using the gamified tool on the Classcraft web platform, obtaining a general average of 10 points in the theoretical knowledge question.

Question 2: Theoretical Knowldege (Table 3)

Table 3. Question 2 Analysis -questionnaire

Question	Question 2: Complete the concept of first-degree inequality? The _____ of the first degree are those whose _____, in this case unique, has an exponent	
Instrument	Pretest	Postest
Wrong answer	9	0
Right answer	11	20
Average	5,5	10

During the pretest of this question the following results were obtained, of the total of 20 students, 9 representing 45% of the population answered incorrectly, whose rating is 0 and the remaining 55%, which are the 11 students, answered satisfactorily to the question with a grade of 10, thus giving a general average of the pretest 5.5 points. Once the gamification was socialized, in the results of the post-test it was possible to observe that 100% of the students who are 20 responded satisfactorily, which implies that the theoretical knowledge has been provided and acquired efficiently by the students.

The outcome of this question shows that the classcraft gamification resource and the interactive activities help the absorption of knowledge.

Question 3: Practical Knowledge (Table 4)

Table 4. Cost of using agroforestry agricultural medicines in

Instrument	Pretest	Postest
Wrong answer	12	0
Right answer	8	20
Average	4	10

Once the diagnostic test (pretest) was carried out, the following results were obtained: Of the 20 students, 12 of them who represent 60% of the population have answered incorrectly and obtained a grade equal to 0, while 40% that are 8 students got 10 points by responding correctly, giving, the total average of 4 points. After the presentation of the classcraft web platform with interactive resources, progress was observed in the post-test carried out, in which a total of 20 students, which is 100% of the sample, obtained a perfect average of 10 points to recognize the order to follow to solve exercises on first-degree inequality.

This allows recognition of the importance of applying a gamification resource in the area of mathematics since they came to recognize the detailed process for the construction and solution of exercises.

Question 4: Practical Knowledge (Table 5)

Table 5. Practical knowledge

Question	Question 4: Develop the first-degree inequality exercise $(7x + 5 < 2x - 10)$ and select your result	
Answer	Answer: $X < -3$: $(-\infty, -3)$	
Instrument	Pretest	Postest
Wrong answer	11	1
Right answer	9	19
Average	4.5	9.5

After having carried out the pretest, within this question the following results were obtained: 11 students representing 55% of the sample answered incorrectly and obtained a score of 0 points, on the contrary, 9 students who are 45% of the population responded satisfactorily to the question, reaching a total of 10 points, this gives an average of 4.5 points. Therefore, the gamified proposal is presented in classcraft with the intervention of interactive activities in which 95% of the population, which are 19 students, carry out the exercise correctly and 5%, which represents a student, do not manage to answer it.

In conclusion, the gamified resource contributes significantly to educational progress since a large percentage of the population satisfactorily develops first-degree inequalities exercises.

4.2   Analysis of the TAM Model

Question 1: Meaningful Learning (Table 6)

Table 6. Table 1. Question 1 analysis - survey

[The use of web 3.0 tools (platforms with interaction) allows me to carry out my work more quickly]		
1	Extremely satisfied	19
2	Satisfied	1
3	Neither satisfied nor dissatisfied	0
4	Dissatisfied	0
5	Extremely dissatisfied	0

According to the question: The use of web 3.0 tools (platforms with interaction) allows carrying work out faster. 19 students representing 95% of the population consider it highly satisfactory, ruling out the complexity that exists in the use of content in web 3.0 tools in class. A student who represents 5% states that these tools are satisfactory to get the job done quickly.

Question 3: Gamification (Table 7)

Table 7. Table 2. Question 3 analysis- survey

[Learning to use gamification and technological tools is easy for me.]		
1	Extremely satisfied	19
2	Satisfied	1
3	Neither satisfied nor dissatisfied	0
4	Dissatisfied	0
5	Extremely dissatisfied	0

In the following question: Learning to use the gamification and technological tools is easy for me, where 95% of the population, which is the total of 19 students, express highly satisfactorily results the ease of learning with gamified activities. On the other hand, the 5% that corresponds to 1 student shows the degree of satisfaction with the gamified interactive activities in classcraft.

Question 4: Gamification (Table 8).

Table 8. Question 4 analysis- survey

13 [I have felt satisfied when carrying out activities with web 3.0 tools (platform with interaction) or gamification]		
1	Extremely satisfied	17
2	Satisfied	3
3	Neither satisfied nor dissatisfied	0
4	Dissatisfied	0
5	Extremely dissatisfied	0

Finally, this question: I have felt satisfied when carrying out activities with web 3.0 tools (platform with interaction) or gamification, where 17 students, which is 85% of the population, show relevant results in highly satisfactory work with activities interactive gamified, therefore, the remaining 15% that represent 3 students satisfactorily show the degree of interest in manipulating it, motivating learning.

4.3 Hypothesis Verification

Logic Model

Gamification contributes to the development of meaningful learning of mathematics for students with unfinished upper basic education from Hispano America School.

Null Hypothesis

Gamification does NOT contribute to the development of meaningful learning of mathematics for students with unfinished upper basic education from Hispano America School.

5 Conclusion

The Classcraft web resource used for the development of the gamified class turns out to be efficient due to the scenarios it reflects that obtains a plus thanks to the integration of interactive activities designed in Genially and Nearpod, where it is shown that its realization and progress in the different missions are highly effective in dynamizing the class. This could be evidenced thanks to the diagnostic test (pretest) and evaluative test (Post-test) whose averages are 4.5 and 9.8 respectively, this after analyzing 4 objective questions that help strengthen the learning of theoretical and practical knowledge about first-degree inequalities. The different interactive activities inserted in Classcraft motivate students thanks to its competitive game interface in which students immerse themselves to acquire their knowledge during class.

The TAM model has helped to recognize the results obtained according to the research data, the efficacy, usefulness, ease, and satisfaction that the gamification proposal has had to strengthen the meaningful learning of mathematics. This is evidenced by a large number of responses inclined towards the high level of satisfaction obtained after applying the survey instrument. This was obtained after analyzing 4 of the 15 objective questions that helped to recognize the level of learning through the effectiveness in terms of content presented in the resource, ease of maneuvering activities, usefulness to present in the classroom and the satisfaction of the students when manipulating it.

The proposal was implemented correctly since there was a stable internet connection through a point established by the teacher, to which the students do not have free access, all the members were able to use their smartphones to develop each gamified activity. In addition, relevant results were obtained through observation, since the students reflected satisfaction when using the gamified resource, which was presented as a game at the beginning of the classes. Furthermore, some of the students became familiar with the environment thanks to their player history in the fire-fire app, which looks similar in the game environment.

In this way, it is concluded that the students of the Hispanic America School see it as an innovative process when making use of gamified and interactive resources, by increasing their participation in a dynamic way, thus promoting meaningful learning.

References

1. R. Anjarwati, S. Setiawan y K. Laksono, «Experiential meaning as meaning making choice in article writing: A case study of female and male writers,» Heliyon, p. e06909, 2021
2. C. Assuad, N. Tvenge y K. Martinsen, «System dynamics modelling and learning factories for manufacturing systems education,» Procedia CIRP, pp. 15–18, 2020
3. K. Bahadur Pal, B. Bahadur-Basnet, R. Raj-Pant, K. Bishwakarma, K. Kafle, N. Dhami, M. Lal-Sharma, L. Thapa, B. Bhattarai y Y. Bhatta, «Education system of Nepal: impacts and future perspectives of COVID-19 pandemic,» Heliyon, vol. 7, n° 9, p. e08014, 2021
4. Q. Cao, H. Hao, S. R y V. Thanjai, «Occupational stress management of college English teachers under flipped classroom teaching model,» Aggression and Violent Behavior, p. 101712, 2021
5. E. Telegrafo, «EL TELEGRAFO,» 31 03 2022. [En línea]. Available: https://www.eltelegrafo. com.ec/noticias/sociedad/6/5-4-millones-escolaridad-inconclusa
6. Y. Dong, H. Shizheng-Du y A. Wang, «The effects of flipped classroom characterized by situational and collaborative learning in a community nursing course: A quasi-experimental design,» Nurse Education Today, vol. 105, p. 105037, 2021
7. D. Emm, «Gamification – can it be applied to security awareness training?,» Network Security, vol. 2021, n° 4, pp. 16–18, 2021
8. V. Farinango-Lema y E. Pardo Paredes, «Propuesta de perfil del educador para centros de acogimiento institucional. Caso de estudio.,» Veritas & Research, vol. 3, n° 2, pp. 111–112, 2021
9. R. Guntha, B. Hariharan y P. Rangan, «Analysis of Multimedia Communication Issues in the Immersive Smart Classroom System – A Control Center Approach,» Procedia Computer Science, pp. 2600–2609, 2020
10. D. Kozlova y M. Pikhart, «The Use of ICT in Higher Education from the Perspective of the University Students,» Procedia Computer Science, pp. 2309–2317, 2021
11. MINEDUC, «Mecapacito,» 2022. [En línea]. Available: https://mecapacito.educacion.gob.ec/
12. D. Pal y V. Vanijja, «Perceived usability evaluation of Microsoft Teams as an online learning platform during COVID-19 using system usability scale and technology acceptance model in India,» Children and Youth Services Review, p. 105535, 2020
13. M. Peralbo-Uzquianoa, R. Fernández-Abella, M. Durán-Bouza, J. Brenlla-Blanco y J. Cotos-Yáñez, «Evaluation of the effects of a virtual intervention programme on cognitive flexibility, inhibitory control and basic math skills in childhood education,» Computers & Education, vol. 159, p. 104006, 2020
14. Saleh-Metwally, L. Nacke, M. Chang, Y. Wang y A. Fahmy-Yousef, «Revealing the hotspots of educational gamification: An umbrella review,» International Journal of Educational Research, p. 101832, 2021
15. P. Sullivan, J. Sergi-McBrayer, S. Miller y K. Fallon, «An Examination of the use of computer-based formative assessments,» Computers & Education, vol. 173, p. 104274, 2021
16. Z. Zainuddin, M. Shujahat, H. Haruna y S. WahChu, «The role of gamified e-quizzes on student learning and engagement: An interactive gamification solution for a formative assessment system,» Computers & Education, p. 103729, 2020
17. D. de la Peña, D. Lizcano y I. Martínez-Álvarez, «Learning through play: Gamification model in university-level distance learning,» Entertainment Computing, p. 100430, 2021
18. S. Álvarez-Dardet, B. Lara y J. Pérez-Padilla, «Older adults and ICT adoption: Analysis of the use and attitudes toward computers in elderly Spanish people,» Computers in Human Behavior, p. 106377, 2020
19. UNESCO, «Uso de las TIC en la educación,» 2020. [En línea]. Available: https://es.unesco. org/themes/tic-educacion/accion

Gambling as a Methodological Strategy of Probabilities in University Students

Cristian Roberto Moncayo Espín[1] and Emilia Daniela Aimacaña Sánchez[2(✉)]

[1] Departamento de Ciencias Exactas, Universidad de las Fuerzas Armadas ESPE,
Latacunga, Ecuador
crmoncayo@espe.edu.ec
[2] Unidad Educativa Rumiñahui, Ambato, Ecuador
eaimacana@hotmail.com

Abstract. The article aims to analyze how students, when putting statistical knowledge into practice, can formulate problems applied to games of chance that involve probabilities, as a teaching strategy to promote constructivist learning. The strategy of creating practical spaces with applied problems tries to collect student experiences and the results show students' understanding of basic concepts of statistics.

Keywords: Gambling · Probability · Automotive statistics · Problem setting

1 Introduction

The statistics dictated to university students have several problems. One of them is that the basic concept of probability lacks practical sense for them, although it is true that in an introductory course it is not intended to turn them into experts, if it is to get them to apply statistics in real-world situations. (Garfield et al. 2000).

The definition we obtain of probability by students who have already taken the subject is not satisfactory, considering it a sufficient reason to propose a strategy that contextualizes statistical concepts, Díaz and Hernández (2002) point out that statistics and their teaching does not work with day-to-day situations and that it leaves aside logical reasoning to focus on merely theoretical concepts.

The new approaches to the teaching of mathematics and mainly statistics emphasize proposals based on concepts such as chance that is associated with probability. Penalva (2010) mentions that problem-solving and the resolution process allow the student to abstract knowledge by himself by promoting the learning of statistics through clear concepts of probability.

Students are not clear about the concepts of probability or their practical application, which makes it more difficult to enter the learning process (Batanero 2013a). There

M. Botto-Tobar et al. (Eds.): ICAT 2022, CCIS 1757, pp. 145–151, 2023.
https://doi.org/10.1007/978-3-031-24978-5_13

is research that emphasizes the lack of formality with which students carry the concepts of statistics and the little rigor with which they perform calculations related to the probability of an event (Díaz and Hernández 2002; Batanero 2013a; Jones 2007).

Conceptual Framework

The analysis of mathematical thinking and mainly the one that involves the probabilities and randomness of events has been developed by several researchers since the 50s by Piaget and Inhelder (1951) where they identify the stages of knowledge according to the age of the students, although it is true that it does not correspond to an investigation purely of the teaching of probabilities if it has allowed to expand the investigations.

Education in probabilities can be taken to a practical field with the use of meaningful and constructivist learning techniques that promotes in students the development of skills Díaz (2002), in this case the proposal of "Automotive roulette", aims to give the concept of probability a physical space where it can be applied; during recent research the implementation of basic theories of gambling and randomness to the teaching of probabilities have generated important proposals in the field of teaching statistics Jones (2007).

According to Batanero (2013b) in the article Understanding probability in children, it states that the basis for acquiring probability knowledge in the classroom is through games of chance that promote mathematical thinking and therefore the intuitive acquisition of knowledge applied to real situations, that is, contextualized knowledge.

Malaspina (2013) promotes the creation of problems as a strategy to acquire knowledge, two types are mentioned; the one that allows a new problem to be formulated from a known one and the one that is formulated from a given situation.

According to UNESCO (2017) it indicates that within the Sustainable Development Goals (SDGs) is a quality education and education for sustainable development (ESD), and mentions that education given to students of any level can and should contribute to a vision of development and provides a general guide for all educators to contribute to this end.

It is for this reason that Alsina and Vásquez (2020) mention that it is important that all citizens have resources and strategies within the statistical and probabilistic field. Creating tools that allow decisions to be made in situations where there is uncertainty and data that are relevant in daily life.

2 Materials and Methods

The article that is presented investigates aspects of the approach and resolution of problems posed by the Department of Exact Sciences to a group of university students of the Automotive Engineering career of the "Universidad de las Fuerzas Armadas ESPE" headquarters Latacunga, focused on the analysis of probabilities using a problem already known that is the game of roulette, but modifying it to promote the use of automotive tools such as dice and nuts.

The teacher in charge of the subject of statistics, as a final project proposed to the students the creation of a practical problem where the concept of probability, o that after its application they can exchange experiences related to the intuitive perception of probability and the real one.

Fig. 1. 2nd fair of exact sciences.

In classes the teacher explained the operation and probability applied to various games of chance and situations of daily life.

2.1 Automotive Roulette

After carrying out the evaluation of the projects, the selected work was the one entitled "Automotive Roulette" that participated in the Second Fair of Exact Sciences organized by the institution.

The game of Automotive Roulette is about appraising dice, you have thirteen nuts and thirteen nuts remover with their respective measurements, roulette with divisions from 1 to 16; to start the player spins the roulette and must obtain as a result an even number to participate, if that is the case, he chooses a nut of thirteen available and tries to match it with the corresponding nut remover in terms of measure with which the participant wins the game.

Figure 1 shows the finished project with the roulette options with the thirteen nuts and thirteen nuts remover to be able to cup them and win the game (Fig. 2).

2.2 Statistics and Probabilities

The problem posed in class answered the following question: What is the probability of obtaining an even number in the game of roulette, the students manage to modify the problem posed and now the game is divided into two moments, that of participating (A) and that of winning the game (B).

2.3 Calculation

The game of Automotive Roulette now raises the question: What is the possibility to participate and win the game, the probability calculation is shown below:

$$P(A \cup B) = P(A) + P(B) - P(A \cap B) \tag{1}$$

Fig. 2. Automotive Roulette. It has 13 Nuts remover socket located at the top of the box, 13 nuts in the inner of the box, 16 divisions with numbers.

$$P(A) = Probability\ to\ participate$$

$$PA = \frac{even\ numbers}{total\ of\ numbers} \tag{2}$$

$$P(A) = \frac{8}{16} = \frac{1}{2}$$

$$P(B) = Probability\ to\ win$$

$$P(B) = \frac{1}{13}$$

$$P(A \cap B) = Probability\ of\ intersection$$

$$P(A \cap B) = P\left(\frac{A}{B}\right) * P(B) \tag{3}$$

$$P(A \cap B) = \left(\frac{\frac{1}{2}}{\frac{1}{13}}\right) * \left(\frac{1}{13}\right)$$

$$P(A \cap B) = \frac{1}{2}$$

$$P(A \cup B) = \left(\frac{1}{2}\right) + \left(\frac{1}{13}\right) - \left(\frac{1}{2}\right)$$

$$P(A \cup B) = \frac{1}{13}$$

When pretending to solve the question of participating and winning in the game of Automotive Roulette, it is necessary to apply the general rule of addition (1) for probabilities; where the classical probability P(A) of success or failure is used, that is, the possibility that when turning the roulette wheel the number obtained is even, P(B) corresponds to the possibility that when pricing the dice in the nuts a success is obtained and P(AUB) corresponds to the probability of intersection of independent events (3) (Table 1).

Table 1. Table of probabilities

Probability	Probability value
1. Probability of entering to the game	$P(A) = \frac{1}{2}$
2. Probability of winning	$P(B) = \frac{1}{13}$
3. Intersection of events	$P(A \cap B) = \frac{1}{2}$
4. Probability of entering and win	$P(A \cup B) = \frac{1}{13}$

2.4 Results and Discussion

The research presented in this article shows the project selected to participate in the Second Fair of Exact Sciences organized at the Universidad de las Fuerzas Armadas ESPE headquarters Latacunga, where they applied concepts of probability in the game of automotive roulette identifying basic concepts of statistics.

The most important observation is that the concept of probability is contextualized with a real and active problem, where both students of the subject and the general public who visited the fair can participate, generating a teaching strategy that goes beyond the classrooms.

By allowing students to choose and build their project, it fosters creativity, problem-solving and the emergence of new questions, related not only to probability but also to statistics and their application.

The methodological strategy of generating practical projects to exhibit at fairs in order to demonstrate knowledge acquired throughout the semester is an advantage to involve both students of the subject and the public.

According to the researchers cited throughout the article, the study of statistics must be transformed from being formal to practical, with contextual elements that place the student in both the mathematical field and the application, being an introductory course to statistics is not intended to train experts, but levels of knowledge applied to the future.

By asking questions to problems raised or modified, they provide the student with mathematical abilities that contribute to their learning and not only in the subject of statistics.

According to Arias et al. (2021), they mention that teaching was affected by covid-19 restrictions. Time in which teachers had to develop new ways of teaching so that learning the concepts of statistics and probability made sense far beyond theoretical knowledge, but rather practical.

Vásquez (2020), also mentions that an important aspect for teachers to consider is to carry out tasks and activities that allow students of all ages, not only university students, to identify solutions to statistical problems using tangible tools or based on software.

Allowing in this way that all the knowledge acquired is put into practice, and have a greater impact on it, which is not only teaching but also a playful and relaxation activity during COVID-19.

3   Conclusion

The creation of problems associated with mathematical concepts promotes a development in the thinking of students and their way of seeing what surrounds in this particular case the theory of probabilities, however and despite the efforts there is still more interaction with real problems that promote in student's real experiences of what really happens in the mathematical world.

The objective of looking at mathematics as the problem solver and not the problem, through practical exercises such as gambling and its application in statistics goes from being an exercise to a learning experience, which according to research promotes the constructivist learning that we need to develop critical students.

The game aims to demonstrate the importance of teaching probability and that this serves to make known that probabilistic reasoning is necessary to face chance in everyday life and improve the intuitions of students.

Acknowledgements. Thanks to the teachers, students, classmates and friends who made the development of this research possible.

References

Arias, J., Barquero, C., Meroño, L., Morales, M.: Enseñanza comprensiva de contenidos socio motrices con estudiantes universitarios atendiendo a las restricciones por la COVID-19. Nuevos retos educativos en la enseñanza superior frente al desafío COVID-19 1, 5–10 (2021). http://hdl.handle.net/10045/119290

Alsina, Á., Vásquez Ortiz, C.A., Muñiz-Rodríguez, L., Rodríguez Muñiz, L.J.: ¿Cómo promover la alfabetización estadística y probabilística en contexto? Estrategias y recursos a partir de la COVID-19 para Educación Primaria. © Epsilon Revista de la Sociedad Andaluza de Educación Matemática **104**, 99–128 (2020)

Batanero, C.: Sentido estadístico: Componentes y desarrollo. Actas de las Jornadas Virtuales en Didáctica de la Estadística, Probabilidad y Combinatoria 1, 55–61 (2013a)

Batanero, C.: La comprensión de la probabilidad en los niños:¿ qué podemos aprender de la investigación. In: Atas do III Encontro de probabilidades e estatistica na escola, pp. 9–21 (2013b)

Díaz, F., Hernández, G.: Estrategias docentes para un aprendizaje significativo: Una interpretación constructivista. McGraw Hill, México (2002)

Garfield, et al.: Position paper prepared for the Undergraduate Statistics Education Initiative. First Courses in Statistical Science Working Group. Recuperado (20 de agosto de 2020) (2000). https://ww2.amstat.org/meetings/jsm/2000/usei/usei_1st.PDF

Jones, G. A., Langrall, C.W., Money, E.S.: Research in probability: responding to classroom realities. In: Lester, F.K. (ed.), The Second Handbook of Research on Mathematics Teaching and Learning, pp. 909–955. Information Age Publishing, Charlotte (2007)

Malaspina, U.: La creación de problemas de matemáticas en la formación de profesores. In: SEMUR, Sociedad de Educación Matemática Uruguaya (ed.), VII Congreso Iberoamericano de Educación Matemática, pp. 129–140 (2013)

Penalva, M.C., Posadas, J.A., Roig, A.I.: Resolución y planteamiento de problemas: Contextos para el aprendizaje de la probabilidad. Educación Matemática 22(3), 23–54 (2010). [fecha de Consulta 22 de Agosto de 2020]. ISSN: 0187–8298. https://www.redalyc.org/articulo.oa?id=405/40516678003

Piaget, J., Inhelder, B.: La genèse de l'idèe de hasard chez l'enfant. Presses Universitaires de France, Paris (1951)

UNESCO. Educación para los objetivos de desarrollo sostenible: objetivos de aprendizaje. Francia: Organización de las Naciones Unidas para la Educación, la Ciencia y la Cultura (2017)

Vásquez Ortiz, C.: Estrategias y recursos para la enseñanza de la probabilidad y la estadística en el aula escolar en el contexto de la emergencia sanitaria de la COVID-19. I Ciclo de seminarios "Aprender y enseñar matemáticas desde casa". Pontificia Universidad Católica de Chile (2020). http://funes.uniandes.edu.co/22632/1/Vasquez2020Estrategias.pdf

Thermo-transferable Vinyl as High Embossment Textile Finish for the Visually Impaired Pattern Recognition by Haptics Perception - Case Study

Omar Godoy-Collaguazo$^{(\boxtimes)}$ ⓘ, Ana Umaquinga-Criollo ⓘ, and Marco Naranjo-Toro

Universidad Técnica del Norte, Av. 17 de Julio 5-21, Ibarra, Ecuador
{ovgodoy,acumaquinga,mfnaranjo}@utn.edu.ec

Abstract. This research performs a quantitative, descriptive and documental study analyzing the following factors (i) preference (ii) perception (iii) textile surface character-identification; through a vinyl thermo-transference finish complying with an inclusive fashion approach for the visually impaired. In order to achieve this process, a study case was performed at Universidad Técnica del Norte with a group of visually impaired students. Data is gathered through a survey and templates designed with letters, numbers, symbols, diverse shapes, *braille writing*, 4 types of textures and embossment thickness from 90, 110, 325 to 600 μ. Application time fluctuates between 10–20 s at 155 °C.

Keywords: Thermo-transferable · Inclusive fashion · Touch

1 Introduction

History has defined fashion as an individual's essence, a symbol of status, creed and sense of belonging according to time and space [1, 2]. Clothing provides self-sufficiency but at the same time, instills a series of inclusive and exclusive stereotypes [3]. Frequently, clothing designed according to the wearer of clothing's need not only should look good, but also should conform to the body [4]. In this context, the designer has to potentialize human diversity and residual capacities of the general public, that is to say those who overcome "sensorial channels" shortcomings [5, 6].

Clothing has an intimate relationship with each individual, beyond being a necessity, not to mention the visually impaired who represent an economically active population increasingly getting inclusively involved in normal activities of society hence challenge to design new products and services [7, 8]. At the beginning of the XVIII century, clothing was tailor made by hand [9]; Today individuals with functional diversity have access to required social benefits, including clothing.

Perhaps the concept of thinness and beauty is internalized differently among the visually impaired since having a kind of disability, deficient memory and reasoning may result in a hurdle in understanding space and environment. Such individuals may prefer to remain in one place instead of going out and explore [10–12] therefore, a designed

M. Botto-Tobar et al. (Eds.): ICAT 2022, CCIS 1757, pp. 152–166, 2023.
https://doi.org/10.1007/978-3-031-24978-5_14

centered in the upper and lower part of the body and garment selection to form an outfit is desired [13].

As inclusive fashion consolidates as a field of interest, new efforts like inclusive fashion shows to increase and develop methods and tools that fulfill the need of this interest group prove that participants help the development of proposed fashion collections, methods and techniques applied to fashion design fulfilling requirements that many fashion designers disregard [14, 15]. Although fashion companies focus on fulfilling diverse segments of consumers, the need for studies and development regarding the visually impaired is vital [16]. While there are "variables" and complex challenges in this interest group, the approach of several research work is aimed to the visually impaired environment and the development of gadgets and new technology according to their needs [17, 18].

Although efforts are made to keep the designed closely linked to choice and preference [19] it should be noted that firstly, products offered to the impaired meet their expectations, secondly that inclusive garments have information not affecting the attractiveness of the garment or quality material [20].

Body senses have been extensively studied by psychologists, now it is being studied by modern science [21]; eyesight is essential for human beings, but not indispensable; the visual sensorial perception allows for the gathering, integration and data memorizing in extremely limited time, while surface and texture causes stimuli, irregularity turns into vibrations as touched by fingers traveling through two types of mechanoreceptors: *Meissner and Paccini* corpuscles signaling tactile-vibro signals perceiving minimal changes in the surface of a particular element [22–24].

Braille reading system is a consequence of *Louis Braille's* own blindness-the inventor of this the first embossment approach translating alphabet visual environments into tactile form [25]. Meeting the "criteria" for subjective and visual aspects of fashion such as color and fabric combinations presents a challenge [15, 26].

Finally, with the development of this research, it is intended to establish the relationship between the type of relief and the ease of identification of patterns by people with visual disabilities. This pursues a primary objective that is that improvements can be granted in the degree of autonomy in the blind individual with the development of products that stimulate perception by touch [16, 27, 28].

2 Materials and Methods

The methodology applied is focused on the case study consisting of a 13-visually disabled student interview at *Universidad Técnica del Norte* (UTN), with the purpose of establishing whether the vinyl thermo-transference high embossment finish may influence of information-recognition through haptics perception as well as the identification of possible strengths so that the development of inclusive fashion textiles based on the visually impaired is highly likely in the immediate future. The study center is in Ibarra city, Ecuador geographical coordinates (0.37816764316765145, -78.12318267916226) with 35 undergraduate careers covering the northern area having a large influx of students. (See Table 1).

Table 1. Student population UTN

Academic period	Female	Masculine	Total
September-February 2022	5757	5193	10950

2.1 Instrument Construction

Work Plan Outline—after getting feedback from the socialization project students, questionnaire is generated with questions aimed to determine haptics perception levels. Team work is comprised by 3 research professors, 2 technical professors and 3 students so field work has 4 pollsters. Work material has: (i) printed forms (ii) 2 vinyl finishing-fabric sampling kits (Figs. 1 and 2).

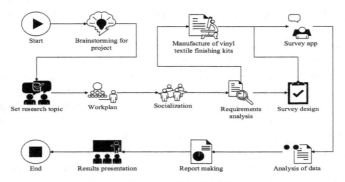

Fig. 1. Research work-plan diagram

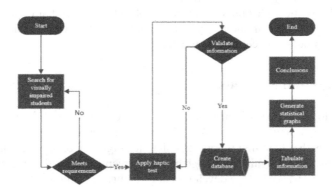

Fig. 2. Research flowchart

A survey data-gathering instrument was created and denominated: "Manufacturing of textile products based on inclusive fashion for the haptics perception analysis".

The document has 5 well-defined sections: a) Respondent profile b) visual impairment information c) fabric preference d) texture and size perception) symbol recognition and information by haptics perception. The instrument has Likert-scale type of questions ranging from 1–5 (1 minimum level and 5 the best), close-ended YES/NO questions to include open-ended varied questions.

Kit's Design Based on Thermo-Transference for Haptics Perception. Kit A, (shown in Fig. 3), is intended to determine the sensibility degree that a visually impaired individual develops over time to the use of textiles, the respondent should strive to recognize textile conditions such as softness or roughness, as for fabric density thinness or thickness.

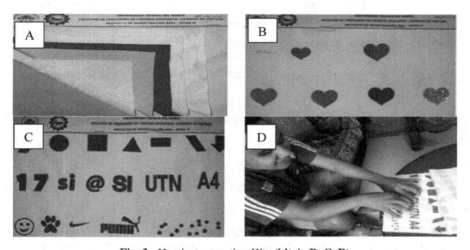

Fig. 3. Haptics perception Kits (**kit A, B, C, D**)

Textile substrate used for the preference are detailed in Table 2 are made of materials, and knitting in the most common daily wear garment presentations.

Kit B has vinyl finishes. In the upper part there is a "heart" symbol in two sizes 1, 5 cm and 3 cm., while in the lower part of the film there are vinyl thermo-transference finishes in 4 presentations: 90-micron smooth, 110-micron smooth, 600-micron highly embossed smooth finish and 325-micron, shinny-effect finish. This spreadsheet is intended to study the degree of sensitivity by size, embossment and texture.

Perception by Size. Determines whether a shape is adhered to the knitting surface and also enlightens the effects that size have on sensitivity degree and how it may influence the information presented.

Embossment and Texture Perception- with the help of touch the visually impaired can determine the type of vinyl adhered to a surface thus enhanced shape recognition.

Information Identification—Kit C has 3 geometric shapes rows, alphanumeric characters and symbols. A different type of finishing vinyl is assigned to each film intended to determine if the information complexity has an influence on processing and identifying characters by sense of touch.

Table 2. Textile Substrate characteristics

Textile substrate	Category	Composition	Woven fabric-density (g/m2)	Common use
Knit fabric	Jersey	Pes/Co 65/35	117	T-shirts, underwear,
	Perched fleece	Pes 100%	250	Sports clothing
	Piqué	Pes/Co 65/35	268	Polo shirts
Flat cloth	Fine taffeta	Co 100%	107	Shirts, blouses (formal wear)
	Average taffeta	Co 100%	155	Table linen, bed sheet (house linens)
	Industrial trench coat	Pes/Co 65/35	219	Work clothes

2.2 Participants

Before the study a general university population is performed to establish whether there are students registered as "visually impaired" as shown in Table 3 meeting the ideal analysis profile.

2.3 Selection and Preparation Material for Vinyl Based Thermo-Transference

Preparation and Vinyl Design Cut—Vinyl graphic design is performed with the Adobe Illustrator Cs6 vectorial program.

Design Cut Over Vinyl—A cut-plotter is used for Grapfteccorp CE6000–60 vinyl, the vinyl films and the cutting blade are set up in a 45 to 65 inclination degree. A stiletto separates the area to be thermo-transferred to waste.

Cut Vinyl Application Over Textile Products—A transfer plate applies heat which activates vinyl's adhesive over the fabric web under conditions presented in Table 4.

2.4 Research Questions

Under the determined structure in [29], questions are raised to establish the following degrees: (i) preference (ii) texture and size perception (iii) thermo-transference textile based products information identification by embossment.

Table 3. Frequency chart—respondents information

Respondents' characteristics		n	%	% Accumulated
Gender	Women	6	46, 2	46, 2
	Men	7	53, 8	100
Age	18–28	9	69, 2	69, 2
	1	1	7, 7	76, 9
	40–50	2	15, 4	92, 3
	51–61	1	7,7	100
Program	Applied science engineering	1	7,7	7,7
	Education, science and technology	9	69, 2	76, 9
	Administrative and financial sciences	2	23, 1	100
Type	In-person	7	53,8	53,8
	Blended learning	1	7, 7	61, 5
	Online	5	38, 5	100
Impairment degree	Low	7	53,8	53,8
	Moderate	4	30, 8	84, 6
	Severe	2	15, 4	100

Table 4. Technical vinyl datasheet: Application [27].

Commercial name	Easy weed	Easy wed Sub-blog	Brick 600	Glitter
Temperature (°C; °F)	150 °C 305 °F	130 °C 265 °F	155 °C 311 °F	160 °C 320 °F
Application time (s)	10–15	10–15	20	10–15
Pressure	Average	Average	Average/high	Highs
Composition	Polyurethane	Polyurethane	Polyurethane	Polyurethane
Thickness (microns)	90	110	600	325
Finish	Smooth	Smooth	High embossment	Shiny effect

Preference Analysis Questions. Do the visually impaired address their textile preference based on information sensed by touch?

In the survey, questions a - g grades this item.

Size Perception Analysis Questions. Are haptics perception determinant factors closely related to shape size?

In the survey, questions "h", "i" y "j" grades this item.

Texture Perception Analysis Questions Texture embossment in a thermo-transference vinyl textile product influence on selecting of them?

In the survey, questions "k", "l" y "m" grades this item.

Vinyl Thermo-Transference by Embossment Textile-Based Products Identification of Information Analysis Questions. Does the complexity of the information in thermo-transference vinyl hinder the visually impaired a degree of autonomy when selecting textile products?

3 Results and Discussion

The thermo-transference vinyl haptics perception survey is subject to a statistical analysis using IBM SPSS Statistics software; reliability results from the instrument using Cronbach alpha preference sections in respect to textiles, size perception and texture, finally information identification by haptics perception are classified within robust and reliability ranges [30] (Table 5).

Table 5. Reliability analysis

Survey section	Cronbach alpha
Preference	0,851
Perception	0,826
Information identification	0,933

3.1 Preference

The first elements refere to the visually impaired students among low, moderate and severe who regularly attend class 53,8% men and 46,2% women. The age category in this group is mainly comprised by young adults between 18 and 28 years old, representing 69,2% of total respondents whereas the remaining respondents ranged between 29–39, 40–50 years old and 51–61 hold 7,7%, 15,4% and 7,7% respectively.

Qa data gathered, determined that respondents associate texture with colors vital to identify the garment to be worn; they consider this factor as essential—46,15% while only 7,69% of respondents said that texture is not important. Therefore, a visually impaired individual prefers a textile fabric or functional product as seen in **Qb** since 53,85% of respondents favor detail, while usability and fashion are not meaningful having each factor a percentage value of 23,08% (Fig. 4).

Fabric softness, roughness, thinness and thickness are important points to be considered since, according to data gathered in **Qc**, the visually impaired associate these elements for daily garment selection, that is, they identify textile substrate and their characteristics determined by weigh per unit area (g/m^2), surface finish and /or woven type.

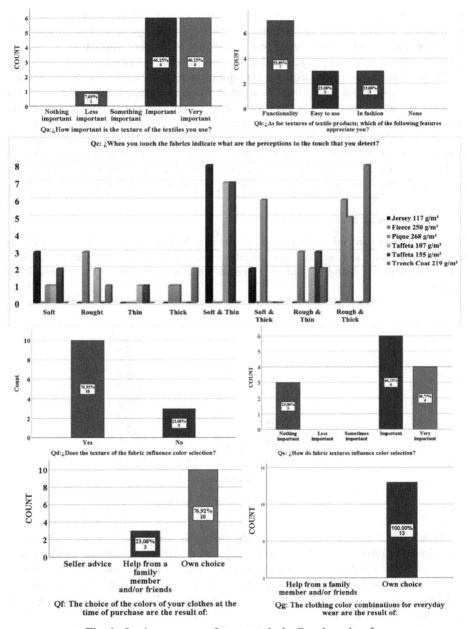

Fig. 4. Section-survey preference analysis; Q: a, b, c, d, e, f, g

Qd statistical results show that fabric texture serves as a guide to determine color to be worn, 76,2% of respondents agree to this reality while the rest, that is 23,08% do not take into account texture for color association. According to information collected, there are dark tones not associated to delicate textures and to the contrary, White color for instance is associated to fine textures, concept enforced by the analysis in question **Qe where respondents considered important and extremely important** texture for color association, obtaining percentual figures 46,15% and 30,77% respectively.

Finally, preference results associated to questions Qf and Qg indicate that a visually impaired individual has a considerable autonomy degree since, when asked about color combination at the time of purchasing clothing 76,92% get their clothing voluntarily and by their own taste, while 23,08% buys clothing suggested by family members.

As per daily use according to color combination, 100% of the visually impaired choose garments voluntarily owing to their memory associating distinct elements in each garment such as texture, accessories, embossed identifiable elements allowing for a comprehensive concept what they wish to express through the clothing worn.

3.2 Perception by Size

Related questions intend to determine whether each individual's grade of sensibility has an impact on the selection, interpretation and information identification through embossed elements, using thermo-transference vinyl directly linked to size and texture (Fig. 5).

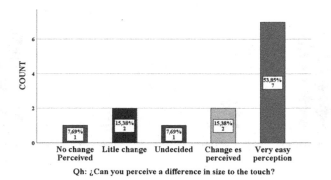

Qh: ¿Can you perceive a difference in size to the touch?

Fig. 5. Perception survey analysis Q: h

To this effect, as observed in **Qh** regarding symbols sensed by touch, the respondents may identify information related to shape size using thermo-transference vinyl. Results show that 53,85% are able to easily identify information sensed, likewise 15,38% perceive certain changes while 15,38% perceive small changes helping identify elements and 7,69% of respondents do not perceive any changes. Finally, 1% of visually impaired students are undecided (Fig. 6).

Analysis results in question **Qi** rule that thinness, embossment level and texture facilitate information identification. "Easy weed" vinyl sampling (90 microns) and "easy weed" sub-blog vinyl (110 microns) do not generate enough embossment level on textile substrate making information identification difficult therefore, 7,69% cannot achieve information identification whereas 15,38% poorly defines information and 23,08% is uncertain when identifying information.

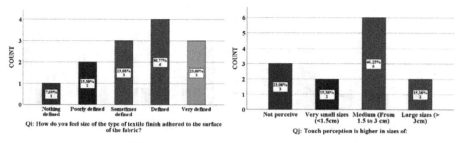

Fig. 6. Perception survey analysis Q: i, j

On the other hand, Brick vinyl (600 microns) facilitates symbol recognition with 30,77% positive responded. Similarly, Glitter vinyl (325 microns) is perceived as explicitly defined identifying and interpreting information easily. **Qj** results prove that 46,15% of respondents sense changes in the textile product measuring between 1,5 and 3 cm while diminutive or huge shapes perception hinders information identification obtaining 15,38% results for each type of referred size comparable to 23,08% who did not differentiate size in vinyl finish.

3.3 Texture Perception

An important factor to consider consists of finding out whether the texture type that thermo-transference vinyl has facilitates the interpretation of characters or even information.

In this context, results indicate that the type of texture is essential for touch stimuli. Forty-six of percent of respondents (46,15%) easily identify information while 30,77% perceive changes, in 1% of each option no changes are perceived and respondents feel a slight change or are undecisive (Fig. 7).

When analyzing **Qk, Ql** y **Qm** it was determined that the smoother the finish is through thermo-transference, the easier the character interpretation. In terms of percentages, 69,23% has difficulty in identifying 90 and 110-micron vinyl information. Equally, vinyl with pronounced thickness like **Brick 600** and 300-micron **glitter** facilitate typography on fabrics owing to embossment and texture found in the previously mentioned vinyl. Finally, as respondents were asked about different vinyl information identification 46,15% think this type of finish has a powerful impact on this finish, while 23,08% says the type of texture is notable definitely influencing the decision process when identifying information. 15,38% believe that vinyl texture sometimes may have an influence on character interpretation and the position of no-influence or somehow influence is perceived by 7,69%.

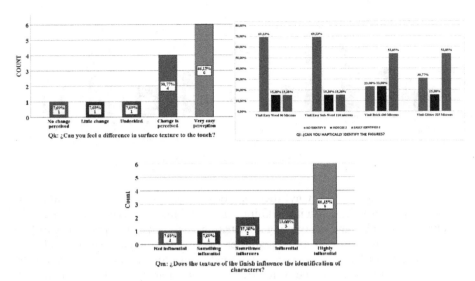

Fig. 7. Texture perception graph

3.4 Information Identification

The third part of the haptics perception evaluation instrument is aimed to determine whether the type of finish in thermo-transference vinyl affects information identification used on a daily basis by a student. For this purpose, thermo-transference-based characters correlate three scenarios: basic shapes, alphanumeric characters and symbology—unusual for the visually impaired, in other words complex information. Firstly, the level of information identification relies on 2 well-defined elements such as thermo-transference vinyl type and the kind of information in themselves.

As seen in Fig. 8-A The better the thermo-transference vinyl has embossment or texture characteristics as the ones found in *Brick 600 or glitter*, the better the degree of correctness regarding the symbology presented to each respondent. Likewise, when associated to commonly memorized basic symbology learned at an early age used on a daily basis, the degree of correctness improves making the information homogeneous.

In the case of Fig. 8-B, alphanumeric characters are not readily identifiable since there are unusual elements students are unfamiliarized with, however once memorized may facilitate information identification.

In Fig. 8-C results determined that the degree of correctness is reduced compared to previously analyzed characters. This allows determining that a visually impaired individual is not familiarized with characters a person not having this disability is, i.e., emoticons, clothes brands, and varied information owing to the little or no use of such elements by the visually impaired. However, cognitive memory quickly stores character shapes, thus making possible identification information.

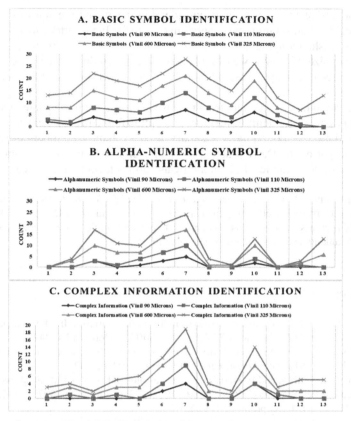

Fig. 8. Análisis de Identificación de caracteres

4   Conclusions

Visually impaired inclusive fashion para personas based on thermo-transference vinyl is considered a textile finish modern option. Moreover, this study is the first of its kind even using textile as a sustainable alternative for haptics stimuli.

As far as daily clothing worn by a visually impaired individual, the decision is by self-choice and / or by family and friends' assistance. In a certain way, the influence of fashion does not affect their personality, nonetheless it is related to customs and society. Although garment selection depends on the occasion, these individuals respect conventional dress code ruled by society. For instance, dark colors and formal wear are common in parties so they try to fit in by respecting outfit rules.

Toch evaluations performed by the visually impaired on several textile substrates make it clear that for them that functionality and usability are critical; having a notable development in the sense of touch able to recognize textures, thickness, softness and elasticity effortlessly; situation that a person with no disability would not be able to recognize, neither the use of cognitive memory for patter recognition.

Respondents of this survey have considerably developed the sense of touch thus they are capable of detect minimal changes in texture facilitate pattern-identification and shapes over finished vinyl textile substrates. Moreover, they are able to neatly identify diverse shapes size. However, we should acknowledge that this is relative, since without previous storage of a shape in an individual's mind, he will not be able to describe the element displayed.

The color-combination system from the visually impaired is associated with pattern, texture, shapes or decor cognitive memory perception found in a garment complemented by the association of colloquial vocabulary used by family members creating color references to garments. Daily practice of color memory and texture, grant a visually impaired person a certain level of autonomy as outfit selection takes place.

Acknowledgements. Most sincere thanks to *Universidad Técnica del Norte*, particularly to the Department of University Well-being, the University Library and to the University IT Integrated System (SIIU) professors, specialists, students, field pollsters, project volunteers and specially to the group of students whom this study is dedicated to.

References

1. Choi, K.-H., Lewis, V.D.: An inclusive system for fashion criticism. Int. J. Fash. Des. Technol. Educ. **11**(1), 12–21 (2018). https://dci.org/10.1080/17543266.2017.1284272
2. Williams, D.: Fashion design as a means to recognize and build communities-in-place. She Ji **4**(1), 75–90 (2018). https://doi.org/10.1016/j.sheji.2018.02.009
3. L. Schiehll, I. Simões, and F. M. da Silva, "Kinesiological Analysis of the Dressing Process in Musculoskeletal Patients," *Procedia Manuf.*, vol. 3, no. Ahfe, pp. 5979–5986, 2015, doi: https://doi.org/10.1016/j.promfg.2015.07.695
4. Bragança, S., Fontes, L., Arezes, P., Edelman, E.R., Carvalho, M.: The Impact of Work Clothing Design on Workers' Comfort. Procedia Manuf. **3**(Ahfe), 5889–5896 (2015). https://doi.org/10.1016/j.promfg.2015.07.898
5. Camplone, S., Di Bucchianico, G.: Shopping experience for all: social inclusion through the multisensorial design of daily activities. Procedia Manuf. **3**(Ahfe), 5373–5380 (2015). https://doi.org/10.1016/j.promfg.2015.07.651
6. McIntyre, M.P.: Shame, blame, and passion: affects of (un)sustainable wardrobes. Fash. Theory - J. Dress Body Cult. **25**(6), 735–755 (2021). https://doi.org/10.1080/1362704X.2019.1676506
7. Andrade, P.S., Martins, L.B.: Tactile reality: the perception of space in the cultural heritage for people with visual impairments. Procedia Manuf. **3**(Ahfe), 6013–6019 (2015). https://doi.org/10.1016/j.promfg.2015.07.714
8. Evans, D.M.: What is consumption, where has it been going, and does it still matter? Sociol. Rev. **67**(3), 499–517 (2019). https://doi.org/10.1177/0038026118764028
9. Gupta, D., Zakaria, N.: Anthopometry, Aparel sixing and design (2014)
10. Márquez-Ramírez, G.: University students with visual functional diversity: their challenges. Rev. Iberoam. Educ. Super. **6**(17), 135–158 (2015). https://doi.org/10.1016/j.rides.2015.02.002
11. Peres, R.J., Do Espírito-Santo, G., Do Espírito, F.R., Ferreira, N.T., De Assis, M.R.: Insatis-fação com a imagem corporal entre pessoas com deficiência visual. Rev. Bras. Ciencias do Esporte **37**(4), 362–366 (2015). https://doi.org/10.1016/j.rbce.2015.08.013

12. Salleh, N.M., Ali, M.M.: Students with visual impairments and additional disabilities. Procedia Soc. Behav. Sci. **7**(2), 714–719 (2010). https://doi.org/10.1016/j.sbspro.2010.10.097

13. Zhang, M., Andrew, S., Gill, S.: Exploring fashion choice criteria for older chinese female consumers: a wardrobe study approach. In: Di Bucchianico, G., Kercher, P.F. (eds.) AHFE 2017. AISC, vol. 587, pp. 109–121. Springer, Cham (2018). https://doi.org/10.1007/978-3-319-60597-5_10

14. Brogin, B., Okimoto, M.L.L.R.: Functional fashion and co-creation for people with disabilities. In: Bagnara, S., Tartaglia, R., Albolino, S., Alexander, T., Fujita, Y. (eds.) IEA 2018. AISC, vol. 824, pp. 850–867. Springer, Cham (2019). https://doi.org/10.1007/978-3-319-96071-5_88

15. Burton, M.A.: Fashion for the blind: a study of perspectives. In: ASSETS 2011: Proceedings of the 13th International ACM SIGACCESS Conference on Computers and Accessibility, pp. 315–316 (2011). https://doi.org/10.1145/2049536.2049625

16. Clark, D., Frankel, L.: The challenges of interdisciplinary participation and anti-oppressive principles. In: Di Bucchianico, G., Shin, C.S., Shim, S., Fukuda, S., Montagna, G., Carvalho, C. (eds.) AHFE 2020. AISC, vol. 1202, pp. 370–377. Springer, Cham (2020). https://doi.org/10.1007/978-3-030-51194-4_49

17. Kursun, S.: Wearable Obstacle Avoidance System Integrated With Conductive. Université Lille 1 (2011). http://doc.univ-lille1.fr

18. Di Bucchianico, G., Kercher, P. (eds.): Advances in Design for Inclusion Proceedings of the AHFE 2016 International Conference on Design for Inclusion, Walt Disney World®, Florida, USA.pdf, 27–31 July 2016 (2016)

19. Goodman-Deane, J., Ward, J., Hosking, I., Clarkson, P.J.: A comparison of methods currently used in inclusive design. Appl. Ergon. **45**(4), 886–894 (2014). https://doi.org/10.1016/j.apergo.2013.11.005

20. Liu, S.F., Lee, H.C., Lien, N.H.: Do fast fashion consumers prefer foreign brands? the moderating roles of sensory perception and consumer personality on purchase intentions. Asia Pac. Manag. Rev. **26**(2), 103–111 (2021). https://doi.org/10.1016/j.apmrv.2020.09.001

21. Ramos, O.S.: Cuerpo y sentidos: el análisis sociológico de la percepción. Debate Fem. **51**, 63–80 (2016). https://doi.org/10.1016/j.df.2016.04.002

22. Preißler, L., Jovanovic, B., Munzert, J., Schmidt, F., Fleming, R.W., Schwarzer, G.: Effects of visual and visual-haptic perception of material rigidity on reaching and grasping in the course of development. Acta Psychol. (Amst). **221** (2021). https://doi.org/10.1016/j.actpsy.2021.103457

23. Wu, X., et al.: Artificial multisensory integration nervous system with haptic and iconic perception behaviors. Nano Energy **85**(February), 106000 (2021). https://doi.org/10.1016/j.nanoen.2021.106000

24. Overvliet, K.E., Sayim, B.: Perceptual grouping determines haptic contextual modulation. Vision Res. **126**, 52–58 (2016). https://doi.org/10.1016/j.visres.2015.04.016

25. Lundgard, A., Lee, C., Satyanarayan, A.: Sociotechnical considerations for accessible visualization design. In: 2019 IEEE Visualization Conference, VIS 2019, pp. 16–20 (2019). https://doi.org/10.1109/VISUAL.2019.8933762

26. Cooper, T., Claxton, S.: Garment failure causes and solutions: Slowing the cycles for circular fashion. J. Clean. Prod. **351** (2022). https://doi.org/10.1016/j.jclepro.2022.131394

27. Serimax, S.R.L.: Poli1flex Printable 4010 Blockout. Poli-Tape Group (2014). http://www.serimax.com.py/poli-tape.html. Accessed 17 Feb 2022

28. Gómez, A.: El estampado transfer y su aplicación (2021). http://repositorio.une.edu.pe/handle/UNE/3436

29. Havelka, A.: Measuring selected properties of materials of military clothing for their possible innovation. **28**(4), 102–110 (2021)
30. Taber, K.S.: The use of cronbach's alpha when developing and reporting research instruments in science education. Res. Sci. Educ. **48**(6), 1273–1296 (2016). https://doi.org/10.1007/s11 165-016-9602-2

Performance Evaluation of Psychology Teachers of a Private University in Lima – Peru: An Experience in Emergency Remote Teaching

Giannina Cuadra, Karina Chirinos, Hugo Del Rosario, Judyth Morales, and Ivan Iraola-Real[✉] [iD]

Universidad de Ciencias y Humanidades, Lima 15314, Perú
{gcuadra,kchirinos,hdelrosario,jmorales,iiraola}@uch.edu.pe

Abstract. The performance evaluation of university teachers is an opportunity to align the training activity to the demands of the higher education system. The paper analyzes the results of the performance evaluation in a university in the city of Lima, considering dimensions such as course mastery, teaching-learning process, student-student relationship, ethics and humanistic; this evaluation is within the regulatory framework that seeks to improve the quality of education and innovation in the Peruvian university sector. The sample is made up of teachers of the academic program of the Psychology career, made up of 23 teachers, 52% women and 48% men. It is concluded that the teachers obtain a homogeneous performance in all the dimensions evaluated, the highest being the ethical dimension and the lowest the student-student relationship dimension.

Keywords: Teaching evaluation performance · Psychology · Educational evaluation

1 Introduction

Providing a comprehensive training that contemplates all dimensions of the human being has become a goal for higher education institutions, therefore, teachers should focus their task in training students in the contents of the professional career and in cross-cutting issues related to ethical, humanistic, socioemotional aspects. Psychology as an applied science contributes to the personal and social development of human beings in all areas of interaction, as explained by different theoretical approaches such as humanistic, sociocultural or systemic; therefore, psychology is one of the professional careers in which a profile that contemplates the various dimensions of comprehensive training is required, since the psychologist is in constant relationship with people who require his attention and service, and because one of its purposes is to ensure mental health [1].

In the field of higher education, we speak of the community of students and teachers who interact and learn from each other, living together harmoniously [2]. How to train integral psychologists? The answer seems to be obvious, with competent teachers, who meet the qualities of the graduate profile and who know how to transmit these qualities to their students [3].

M. Botto-Tobar et al. (Eds.): ICAT 2022, CCIS 1757, pp. 167–176, 2023.
https://doi.org/10.1007/978-3-031-24978-5_15

1.1 Educational Quality Standards in the Peruvian Context

At the beginning of the 1960s in Peru, there was a fixed and classical conception of educational quality, where learning and teaching quality were based mainly on the exclusivity of teachers and students, on material resources and on the traditions of the institutions. However, over the years, the concept of quality in the university sector became the subject of multiple discussions and became increasingly relevant [4]. Because of one of the various debates, it was concluded, "To speak of quality is to allude to the purpose pursued, which in the case of education is the formation of the individual" (SINEACE, p. 6). Accordingly, the objective of Peruvian education is the formation of well-rounded individuals who can build a democratic society based on cultural diversity [5].

Along the same lines, through Supreme Decree No. 016–2015, the Quality Assurance Policy for University Higher Education was approved, whose objective is to guarantee access to a quality university service and whose principles are: responsible autonomy and stewardship; the student as the center; inclusion and equity; quality and academic excellence and development of the country. Likewise, this policy is based on four pillars of reform to build a quality assurance system: reliable and timely information, promotion to improve performance, accreditation for continuous improvement and licensing as a guarantee of basic quality conditions [6].

In order to comply with the quality objectives, the National Superintendence of University Higher Education (SUNEDU) exists, an entity that promotes compliance with standards that guarantee the quality of the educational service provided by universities. Likewise, through Law 28044, General Education Law, in 2003, the SINEACE (National System of Evaluation, Accreditation and Certification of Educational Quality) was created [7], whose model requires strengthening the organizational culture, systematizing administrative and academic processes for better control and continuous improvement process, incorporating stakeholders in the development of the career and implementing a quality management system. For this purpose, SINEACE has an evaluation matrix composed of 4 dimensions, 12 factors and 34 standards, to which the different study programs must respond [5] (see Fig. 1).

One of the dimensions stipulated in the SINEACE evaluation matrix is comprehensive training, which is composed of five factors: teaching-learning process, teacher management, student monitoring, research, technological development and innovation, and university responsibility. Thus, with respect to the factor "teacher management", its standard "selection, evaluation, training and improvement" considers the need for the respective curriculum to have the relevant mechanisms to evaluate the performance of teachers and to be able to identify requirements for improvement, training or even a subsequent separation [8].

In compliance with the above, as of March 2020, 29 universities had at least one accredited program of study [9]. Currently, according to the list of accredited programs, nine programs corresponding to Psychology are accredited [10].

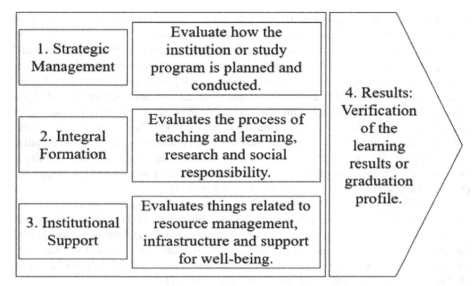

Fig. 1. SINEACE standards.

1.2 Evaluation of Teaching Performance in the Psychology Program

The Peruvian higher education system has undergone a series of modifications in the last ten years. As part of the transformation process, adequate infrastructure, students with a solid level of school education and qualified teachers were established as conditions [11]. This last aspect is subject to evaluation in the curricular area, whose importance lies in achieving the quality required in the higher education sector, in addition to representing an opportunity for the improvement of teaching and learning processes [12].

Teacher performance evaluation is a process that requires planning, execution, evaluation and feedback. In addition, according to Peruvian regulations, it should consider the following dimensions: scientific dimension, thematic dimension, methodological dimension and ethical dimension [13]. It has also been suggested that students are the ones who should evaluate teachers, as they are "on-site observers", since they are in direct contact with them and can account for their ability to express themselves, their mastery of the course and their role in general [14]. However, other members of the educational community must also be part of the evaluation process, as proposed in the University Law 30220 [15].

In the educational institution where the study is being carried out, the evaluation of teaching performance is considered the process in which the fulfillment of the teacher's profile is identified. Which is established according to the institutional educational project, its mission and vision, its principles and values, and more specifically to the needs and demands of the professional career. It includes the evaluation of the teacher's professional competencies and transversal competencies that are related to the educational community, to their own development and to topics of great interest to the university, such as research, the integral approach, conceptual bases, tutoring, social responsibility, innovation for the achievement of competencies in the professional training of students

[16]. The dimensions evaluated are the following: Course mastery, teaching-learning process, student-teacher relationship, ethical and humanistic.

In the process of evaluating teaching performance, student participation offers useful information, as was found in a study in which 164 university students from Lambayeque participated, 110 of whom belonged to the psychology program. Of these, 90% believe that a higher education center should be classified as a "quality university" if it has "quality teachers". Thus, most of them consider that the main criterion for measuring the educational quality of a university is to have qualified teachers. To this end, students value in their teachers, as a priority, the thematic dimension concerning mastery and updating in the subjects they are in charge of (37%), followed by the methodological (ability to generate new learning in students), scientific (mastery of research methodology) and ethical (practice and teaching of values) dimensions [17].

In addition, a study of a group of 70 students in the mathematics course of the psychology faculty of a private university in Lima found that good teaching performance will be a predictor of student academic performance characterized not only by cognitive but also by non-cognitive achievements. That is, a motivating, trained teacher, with didactic teaching strategies and efficient evaluation processes will have a positive impact on student learning, active participation and motivation [18].

1.3 Objectives

Therefore, the objective of this research is to evaluate the performance of a sample of teachers in a professional psychology program at a private university in Lima-Peru. Specifically, it is intended to:

– Identify and describe the dimensions within the evaluation of teaching performance presented by professors at a private university in Lima.

2 Methodology

In the present study, a descriptive quantitative analysis methodology [19] was used, assuming an evaluative research orientation [20].

2.1 Participants

Participated 112 students who evaluated 23 teachers in charge of training future psychologists. Of the total, 12 were women (52%) and 11 men (48%); all of them work in a private university in Lima, Peru.

2.2 Instrument

Teaching Performance Survey. This survey evaluates teaching performance in five dimensions: course mastery, teaching and learning process, teacher-student relationship, ethical dimension, and humanistic dimension. It consists of 16 items with 5 response dimensions on a Likert scale (very low, low, regular, high and very high). The present survey was constructed by the teaching team and subjected to a process of analysis by expert judgment [21].

2.3 Process

The present investigation was carried out based on bibliographical research. Then, the Peruvian regulations related to the Peruvian University Law [12], and what was established by SINEACE [20], were analyzed. Based on this information, a documentary analysis was carried out on the teacher performance evaluation surveys of the first three study cycles of the new professional career in Psychology. The analysis was performed with the Statistical Package for the Social Sciences (SPSS) software [22]. Then, the exploratory analyzes were presented in which the levels of teaching performance were determined according to the established dimensions (see Fig. 2). According to the ethical research criteria, the personal data [23] of the teachers evaluated and the students surveyed were handled confidentially. Which is also in accordance with the Personal Data Protection Law of Peru [24]. Then, the final report was written discussing the results.

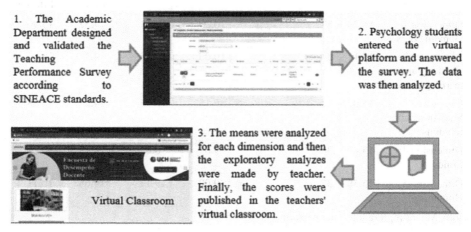

Fig. 2. Methodological process.

3 Results

Because the study is evaluative [20], an analysis was carried out with descriptive statistics [25] in order to obtain a general average of teaching performance. However, due to the need for a more personalized approach, exploratory analyzes were performed using box plots [26].

3.1 Average Score by Dimension

Therefore, Table 1 shows the averages, which range from 15.07 to 15.49. It can also be seen that the highest averages correspond to the ethical and humanistic dimension. However, the lowest score corresponds to the student-teacher relationship dimension. Table 1 indicates that in the group of Psychology professors, the results of both the final average and the average score in the different dimensions, analyzed independently, reach the same average score, with no dimension standing out or being very low.

Table 1. Average per dimension.

Dimensions	Mean	Standard error of the mean	Minimum	Maximum	Int. confidence 95% mean	
					Lim low	Lim sup
Dimension 1: Domain course	15.24	.37	10.00	18.61	14.52	15.96
Dimension 2: Teaching and learning process	15.14	.34	10.00	18.45	14.47	15.81
Dimension 3: Student-teacher relationship	15.07	.41	6.15	18.75	14.25	15.88
Dimension 4: Ethics	15.49	.36	9.67	18.89	14.79	16.2
Dimension 5: Humanistic	15.38	.37	9.00	19.17	14.65	16.11

Note. Means represent teacher performance

Then, Fig. 3 shows the analysis with box plots for both the final average and for each of the dimensions an atypical case was identified, showing performance well below that of the rest of the professors teaching in Psychology (cycle-shift-course-teaching). The central cases of teachers and the highest values (75% of teachers evaluated), exceed the score of 12.5. Only one teacher evaluated appears as an atypical case with a failing score of less than 7.5 (see Fig. 3).

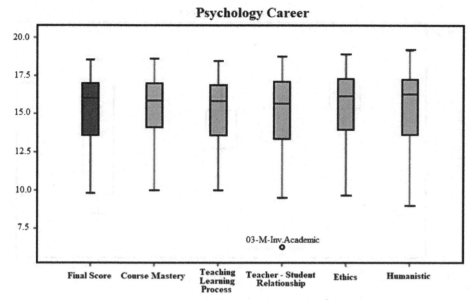

Fig. 3. Box plot showing the final average score by dimension and identification of atypical cases.

3.2 Comparison of Averages by Cycle

Since it is a professional career that began its activities in the university evaluated in March 2020, it has three academic cycles. Therefore, Table 2 shows the averages per cycle, which range from 14.04 to 16.54, with an overall average of 15.38.

Table 2. Mean analysis.

Cycle	Nro	Mean	SD	Minimum	Maximum
01	21	16.54	0.31	13.26	18.19
02	12	14.69	0.45	12.73	17.27
03	12	14.04	1.07	9.00	19.17
Total	45	15.38	.37	9.00	19.17

Note. Means represent teacher performance

Finally, Fig. 4 shows the box plot of the final average of the professors grouped by the cycle of the course they teach. In the boxes, at the bottom are identified some professors whose scores are well below the Psychology professors (cycle-shift-course-professor) within the courses of the same cycle. The most worrying case is the third cycle in which it is observed that the central cases of the box, and the minimum values descend to disapproving levels (see Fig. 4).

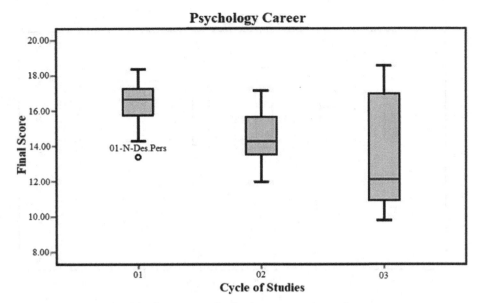

Fig. 4. Comparative final mean score by cycle.

4 Discussion

When we speak of teacher performance evaluation, we refer to a process that requires planning, execution, evaluation and feedback, and according to Peruvian regulations, the following dimensions are evaluated: scientific, thematic, methodological and ethical dimensions [13]. Likewise, it has been suggested that students are the ones who should evaluate teachers, as they are "on-site observers" [14]. Thus, the instrument used for performance evaluation meets the aforementioned requirements; the dimensions are reflected in the survey applied to students. Likewise, according to the competency-based education systems as a proposal for university education [3] in the evaluation of teaching performance, it was identified that in the dimensions established in the university studied, teachers have a higher score in the ethical, humanistic and course mastery dimensions. Thus, we consider that a motivating, trained teacher, with didactic teaching strategies and efficient evaluation processes will have a positive impact on learning, active participation and motivation of the student body [18]. However, we observe that the student-teacher relationship dimension obtains a low score, so it will be necessary to strengthen this closeness and trust with the students that will have an impact on the improvement of the teaching-learning process.

On the other hand, students in the first cycle placed higher-grade scores in relation to students in the second and third cycles. These evaluation dimensions are also considered by SINEACE [13] to establish educational quality. According to these criteria, when analyzing the general results of the teaching performance survey, it was identified that teachers are in an average that places them at an Adequate level (UCH Survey Statistics Report - 2021 I), results that are in accordance with the antecedents raised on the evaluation of teaching performance in university students in other institutions.

5 Conclusions and Future Works

After the analysis (at a general level), we can conclude that, at a general level, as a result of the application of the teacher performance survey, teachers obtain a score that places them at an adequate level, obtaining the highest scores in the ethical and humanistic dimensions and low scores in the student-teacher relationship dimension. Likewise, students in the first cycle rate their teachers with higher scores than students in the second and third cycles. Finally, we believe that our study will contribute to future research that explores these results in greater depth.

Then, (at a particular level), with the exploratory analyzes it was possible to identify particular cases of teachers who presented performance far from the average. In the analysis by dimensions, a case was identified of a teacher who showed a disapproving grade in the dimension of the teacher-student relationship, demonstrating a possible difficulty in dealing with students. In addition, in the exploratory analyzes worrying data was observed with the teachers evaluated in the third cycle, who descended to disapproving evaluations. Finally, to solve the difficulties, it is intended to provide support to teachers with low qualifications. For example, talks about social skills to students or teaching strategies to improve the teaching of their subjects.

References

1. Arias, W.: Reseña histórica de la Psicología Peruana desde la época Republicana hasta la Actualidad. Revista de Psicología **1**, 73–94 (2011)
2. Garcés, N., Orellana, C., Pesantes, M., Salazar, G.: Eco formación del docente universitario y su modelo ecológico de la universidad de Guayaquil. Innova Res. J. **3**(12), 167–176 (2018)
3. British Council. The Reform of the Peruvian University System: Internationalisation, progress, challenges and opportunities (2016). https://www.britishcouncil.pe/sites/default/files/the_reform_of_the_peruvian_university_system_interactive_version_23_02_2017.pdf. Accessed 10 Feb 2018
4. Díaz, R.: Factores condicionantes de la calidad en la educación universitaria peruana. Lex Revista de la Facultad de Derecho y Ciencias Políticas **13**(15), 307–331 (2015)
5. Sistema Nacional de Evaluación, Acreditación y Certificación de la Calidad Educativa (SINEACE), Modelo de Acreditación para Programas de Estudios de Educación Superior Universitaria, Lima. Perú (2016)
6. Montenegro, J.: La calidad en la docencia universitaria. Una aproximación desde la percepción de los estudiantes. Educación **29**(56) (2020). http://www.scielo.org.pe/scielo.php?script=sci_arttext&pid=S1019-94032020000100116. Accessed 10 Feb 2018
7. Alarcón, H., Flores, K., Alarcón, G.: Perú: Políticas que aseguran la calidad en la Educación superior. InterMeio: Revista do Programa de Pós-Graduação em Educação, Campo Grande, MS **24**(47), 17–30 (2018)
8. Gobierno del Perú.: Cerca de 30 universidades cuentan con carreras acreditadas (2020) https://www.gob.pe/institucion/sineace/noticias/208563-cerca-de-30-universidades-cuentan-con-carreras-acreditadas, Accessed 26 Sept 2018

9. Sistema Nacional de Evaluación, Acreditación y Certificación de la Calidad Educativa (SINEACE), Padrón de Programas Acreditados (2021). https://app.sineace.gob.pe/RegistroN acional/appAcreditacion_new.aspx, Accessed 22 Aug 2021
10. Di Domenico, C., Hermosilla, A.: The accreditation of psychology degree in Argentina. Nuevas prospectivas (2019). https://www.redalyc.org/journal/4835/483568603001/html/. Accessed 08 Jan 2020
11. Puya, A., Castillo, C.: La evaluación del desempeño docente: una práctica de mejora continua en la Universidad Estatal Península de Santa Elena. Revista de Ciencias Pedagógicas e Innovación 5(1), 90–98 (2017). https://incyt.upse.edu.ec/pedagogia/revistas/index.php/rcpi/article/view/159/148. Accessed 23 Nov 2018
12. Congreso de la República del Perú.: Ley Universitaria – Ley No 30220 (2014). http://www.minedu.gob.pe/reforma-universitaria/pdf/ley_universitaria.pdf. Accessed 07 June 2022
13. Universidad de Ciencias y Humanidades, Plan curricular de la Carrera Profesional de Psicología (2021). https://www.uch.edu.pe/carrera/psicologia/planestudios. Accessed 25 May 2021
14. Díaz, R.: Factores condicionantes de la calidad en la educación universitaria peruana. Lex Revista de la Facultad de Derecho y Ciencias Políticas 13(15), 307–331 (2015). Homepage, http://revistas.uap.edu.pe/ojs/index.php/LEX/article/view/726/840, Accessed 07 Oct 2020
15. Alarcón, H., Flores, K., Alarcón, G.: PERÚ: Políticas que aseguran la calidad en la Educación superior. InterMeio: Revista do Programa de Pós-Graduação em Educação, Campo Grande, MS 24(47), 17–33 (2018). https://periodicos.ufms.br/index.php/intm/article/view/5902/4355. Accessed 16 Apr 2020
16. Sistema Nacional de Evaluación, Acreditación y Certificación de la Calidad Educativa (SINEACE), Educación Superior en el Perú: Retos para el Aseguramiento de la Calidad (2013). https://www.sineace.gob.pe/wp-content/uploads/2013/08/Retos-para-el-asegur amiento-de-la-calidad.pdf. Accessed 30 Apr 2022
17. Gobierno de la República del Perú.: Cerca de 30 universidades cuentan con carreras acreditadas. Lima. Perú (2020). https://www.gob.pe/institucion/sineace/noticias/208563-cerca-de-30-universidades-cuentan-con-carreras-acreditadas. Accessed 15 Jan 2021
18. Sistema Nacional de Evaluación, Acreditación y Certificación de la Calidad Educativa (SINEACE), Plan anual de supervición 2021 del SINEACE, Lima, Lima: Ministerio de Educación (2021). https://cdn.www.gob.pe/uploads/document/file/1693108/Modificaci%C3%B3n%20de%20la%20Directiva%20N%C2%B0002-2018-SINEACEP-ST.pdf.pdf. Accessed 21 Aug 2021
19. Appelbaum, M., Cooper, M., Kline, R., Mayo-Wilson, K., Nezu, A., Rao, S.: Journal article reporting standards for quantitative research in psychology: the APA publications and communications board task force report. Am. Psychol. Assoc. 73(1), 3–25 (2018)
20. Stufflebeam, L., Shinkfield, S.: Evaluation Theory, Models, and Applications. Jossey-Bass, San Francisco (2007)
21. Escobar-Pérez, J., Cuervo-Martínez, A.: Validez de contenido y juicio de expertos: una aproximación a su utilización. Avances en medición 6(1), 27–36 (2008)
22. International Business Machines. Software SPSS (2022). https://www.ibm.com/pe-es/analyt ics/spss-statistics-software. Accessed 15 Jan 2022
23. Goodwin, J.: Research in psychology: methods and design. Córdova, Brujas (2010)
24. Congreso de la República. Ley de protección de datos personales. Ley N°. 29733. Lima. Perú (2013). https://diariooficial.elperuano.pe/pdf/0036/ley-proteccion-datos-person ales.pdf. Accessed 14 Mar 2022
25. Field, A.: Discovering Statistics Using SPSS, 3era edn. Sage Publications, Lóndres (2009)
26. Helsel, D.: Statistics for Consored Environmental Data Using MINITAB and R, 2nd edn. Wiley, Denver (2011)

Using Gamification to Develop Vocabulary and Grammar Among A1 Level of English Students: A Quasi-Experimental Design

Mónica R. Tamayo[1]([✉]) [ID], Diego Cajas[2] [ID], and David D. Sotomayor[3] [ID]

[1] Universidad de las Fuerzas Armadas ESPE, Sangolquí, Ecuador
mrtamayo@espe.edu.ec
[2] Universidad Nacional de Educación UNAE, Azogues, Ecuador
diego.cajas@unae.edu.ec
[3] Instituto Superior Tecnológico CENESTUR, Quito, Ecuador
david.sotomayor@cenestur.edu.ec

Abstract. Gamification is an emerging strategy for teaching English as a foreign language and has helped teachers empower and motivate students. It also promotes students' participation while engaging and supporting their autonomous learning. The purpose of this quasi-experimental is to investigate the effects of gamification on the developing vocabulary and grammar of A1-level English students. The researchers administered a pre-test to 28 Ecuadorian learners that were part of an experimental group (EG) and a control group (CG). The EG was exposed to gamified-based instruction, whereas the CG to traditional instruction. After the intervention, the students took a post-test to determine how much the use of gamification has improved their knowledge. Based on the p values obtained in this study, the alternative hypothesis was accepted, which led to the conclusion that gamification positively affects vocabulary and grammar development. The results of this research can be used to facilitate the students with innovative ways to learn English.

Keywords: Gamification · English as a foreign language · Vocabulary and grammar learning

1 Introduction

With the advancement of technology, maintaining students' attention and interest in learning has become challenging for teachers who must innovate and shift from traditional to advanced teaching methods [1], such as gamification. This methodology has gained prominence in educational contexts due to its potential to engage students in significant learning experiences. The gamification features have allowed teachers and academics to create diverse learning environments drawing increasing interest in this area [2, 3]. Recent studies have shown that this teaching approach positively impacts students' motivation, collaboration, and persistence, fostering students' creativity and experimentation [4, 5].

© The Author(s), under exclusive license to Springer Nature Switzerland AG 2023
M. Botto-Tobar et al. (Eds.): ICAT 2022, CCIS 1757, pp. 177–190, 2023.
https://doi.org/10.1007/978-3-031-24978-5_16

Gamification should not be equated to just having fun. Some research shows that it can also be used in various industries and disciplines, including marketing [6], production and logistics [7], and information systems. Gamification has attracted teachers' interest due to the positive effect that well-designed games can have on students' productivity and creativity and positive attitudes toward the subject matter [8]. [9, 10] highlighted the impact that gamification has on learners' intrinsic motivation and effectiveness in their learning. They found out that the game's challenging nature became an important factor that motivated students to actively participate in a game. Furthermore, playing and learning, in this context, highly contribute to students' performance by providing a practice space for goal-oriented challenges as well as rewards that characterize the experience of being a part of a game [11, 12].

Gamification refers to the application of game-design elements and characteristics to non-game settings to create engaging, interesting, and stimulating learning experiences [13–15]. [15] further defines it as "the process of making activities more game-like" by employing game concepts, mechanics, and dynamics in educational settings to boost students' critical thinking, concentration, and other beneficial outcomes seen in all games [16].

In tandem with the game-like settings, the mechanics in gamification contain a set of predefined procedures and rules that lead players – in this case, students - throughout the game to achieve a goal. Game mechanics also provide students with comfortable scenarios to interact and follow the rules while playing the game using different levels, badges, leaderboards, quests, challenges, virtual goods, points, and customization, among others [17]. These elements are essential to improving academic achievement since they aid in stimulating students' interests [18].

Another component of gamification is game dynamics. This refers to the outcome of the game, which must be achieved at the end of the activity. [19] details how game dynamics can elicit and motivate learners' emotions to participate in a game. These include "status, achievement, reward, self-expression, competition, altruism, challenge, enjoyment, and satisfaction". He adds that games are powerful tools to interact with learning goals. This means that gamification cannot be disconnected from the curriculum and students' learning outcomes to be relevant. When teachers use gamification as their main teaching and learning tool, its components allow them to create an aesthetic experience for their students [20] and ultimately have successful teaching.

1.1 Gamification in Teaching and Learning English

Many academics have acknowledged the value of gamification in foreign language teaching. It offers an excellent response to two typical problems that teachers and learners generally encounter in their classrooms: demotivation and detachment [21]. [22] asserted that game learning environments and their elements enhance learners' interest to learn English, decrease their feelings of anxiety and fear of interacting in another language, and promote high interactivity and continuous peer-based feedback including social elements of teamwork and communication [23]. Ultimately, [24] debunks the idea that gamification is only related to game elements; he adds that it promotes empowerment and engagement aspects that can motivate the language learner.

[25] looked at the benefits of gamification and discovered that it could maximize learners' motivation, engagement, and social influence when they interact. According to [26], students' motivation increases as the result of competition, challenges, sociability, and imagination, allowing them to achieve academic success [27–29]. Furthermore, students feel encouraged and committed to their learning when they exchange virtual items or presents with their peers during their learning activity [30].

Gamification allows students to have active participation in classes regardless of their content. For instance, [31] mentions that most students learn vocabulary passively without interacting with others and they just wait for the teachers to provide the translation of the words. [31] showed in his study that games like "Hangman," engage students in the language learning process. In another related study, [32] highlights that students learned more English words and correct structures when they are engaged in games. It is claimed that gamification produces an inexplicable learning experience where students are eager to learn new words. Furthermore, the results obtained by [33] in his study, revealed that gamification-based techniques promote learners´ English vocabulary abilities at different levels. In a similar vein, [34] found out that gamified learning is also more effective in terms of grammar achievement than the traditional method since students have access to online language games without limitations and they can check their own progress.

[35] adds that gamification facilitates assessment, which significantly increases students' academic performance compared to the non-gamified traditional classrooms. In the same line, [29] claimed that using gamification as a learning method in foreign language learning significantly improves student academic achievement. Similarly, [36] also suggested that gamification can certainly affect the retention of students´ knowledge.

According to [37], gamification is frequently used by foreign language teachers to motivate the practice of the language, and it has several benefits, including modification in the mood within the classroom; stimulation of students' feelings of happiness and engagement; freedom to try, fail, and explore, and goal-oriented activity. [38] for example, applied Kinect technology to investigate game-based learning tools on self-efficiency for learning English as a foreign language. The experimental group showed an improvement in the self-efficiency attitude compared to the control group. This finding is in line with the results found by [39] where the Kahoot platform demonstrated its effectiveness in teaching English for specific purposes to technical university students. They were not only actively engaged but also obtained a high level of achievement. Apart from motivation and engagement, gamified environments for learning English could provide students with the confidence to practice the language without fearing failure. As a result, gamified strategies should be designed to create relaxing and participatory experiences, and motivational situations, either by creating new content or transforming existing content. In addition, students should feel confident during learning and evaluation, and creativity and sociability should also be encouraged [40].

In addition, gamification can be considered a useful tool and an extra incentive in the teaching process [41]. When gamification is applied in a language classroom, learning tasks should consider aspects such as students' age, level, personality, game dynamics, and elements. These elements must be based on the study objectives and content of the curriculum, and finally, clear rules so that students can carry out the activities without difficulty [42]. Thus, a well-designed gamified environment should allow for a progressive comprehension of the content and consider how the learning goals implemented provide the possibility of evaluating to what extent the games are effective to achieve these goals and help students improve their language performance [43]. [44] claims that even though designing gamified applications may become time-consuming, the evidence showed a correlation between the learners' perception and design usefulness.

Despite being a new concept in educational domains, gamification seems to impact teaching and learning [28]. The objective of the present study was to examine the effectiveness of using gamification in a higher education context in terms of its ability to: 1) facilitate the development of vocabulary and grammar among A1-level English students. 2) improve English language learning.

2   Materials and Methods

2.1   Research Design and Participants

The research question that this study aimed to answer was: to what extent does gamification improve vocabulary and grammar learning in A1 level of English students? And the hypothesis for this study is: the use of gamification facilitates the development of vocabulary and grammar among A1 level of English students.

This study was carried out at an Ecuadorian private higher education institution offering on-campus and online technological programs. The methodology employed was a quasi-experimental design since the participants of the experimental and control groups were intentionally assigned by the researchers. Each group comprised fourteen students enrolled in the A1 level of the English proficiency program. The treatment of this experiment lasted for five weeks. Students in the experimental group were exposed to gamification-based ELT activities in their classes. Students in the control group had their classes with the traditional ELT methods employed by the EFL teachers in their institution.

The researchers asked permission and consent from the institution and the students to participate in this study. The researchers informed the students that their participation was voluntary and assured them that their confidentiality and anonymity were guaranteed.

2.2   Instructional Environment

The institution where the research took place offers online programs in various areas and courses for the learning of English as a foreign language. The learning contents of all the online programs are uploaded to the NEO LMS, which students have access to with a username and a password. In addition, the contents for the foreign language English program level A1 according to the Common European Framework of Reference for Languages are uploaded to Pearson's My English Lab platform. Apart from the study lessons and content uploaded into the platform, the students are assigned activities for each unit based on the academic calendar. Pearson's online English learning programs are defined as "Stand alone", which means that the student can develop skills in the use and understanding of English autonomously. Evaluations are also done on this platform asynchronously. In addition, two weekly synchronous tutoring sessions that last one hour and 30 min each are also provided by the tutors through Google Meet.

2.3 Data Collection Procedure

Following the experimental research methodology, the researchers administered a pre and post-test to the students in both groups. The tests focused on vocabulary and grammar of an A1 level of English. To ensure the validity and reliability of the tests, the researchers opted to use the tests constructed by the publisher that provides the textbooks to the institution. According to the publisher, the tests they provide to the institutions that use their material globally have gone through a rigorous process of validity and reliability. The pre and the post-tests contained forty items: twelve revolved around vocabulary and twenty- eight around grammar. In addition, the same test applied in the pre-test was used as a post-test.

At the end of each week, participants from the two groups were asked to take a quiz. Its objective was to measure their progress throughout the experiment. Each of these quizzes focused on vocabulary and grammar in line with the dependent variables.

2.4 Description of the Experiment (Treatment)

Gamified Environment

The participants of the experimental groups had to connect to the NEO LMS platform with their user data. The links for all the sessions (with the support of Google Meet) were published in "Calendar", along with the missions and challenges planned for each week of training. In addition, the NEO platform allowed participants to customize their workspace; for example, the settings of their accounts (background colors, language, avatars, etc.). Through this platform, the participants kept in touch with their class teacher, received their rewards, learned their level, and were placed on the leader board.

The gamification elements available in the NEO LMS platform were: a Game Guide that explains the generalities of the game, including the narrative, the rules, the level table, etc., a Canvas Module A, B, C that describes in detail all the aspects related to the training circuits such as, context, relationship with the curriculum, timing, narrative, players, levels and experience points, components, and a map of badges that presents all the possible badges as well as the conditions for obtaining them. Additionally, the participants had to work with the Pearson's My English Lab platform to develop the training circuits and to be able to track their progress, thus being one of the most important resources in the game.

The model suggested by [45] was used to plan the treatment. This model suggests 1. Understanding the target audience and the context 2. Defining learning objectives. 3. Structuring the experience. 4. Identifying resources. 5. Applying gamification elements. Based on these steps, the students who were part of the gamified environment worked in the same online learning environment, studied the same content, and aimed toward the same learning objectives. The difference was in how the experience was structured or designed to apply the gamified elements.

Structure or Design of the Experience

Narrative: The experience was designed as a contest game and was named by the designer as "Code A1: The challenge!". The students, called "participants," took three modules; each one was divided into five training circuits to demonstrate their progress in learning English. Each module lasts four weeks. All participants started their training from scratch. The designer of the experience or the class teacher assumed the role of "host coach" who accompanied and provided "action feedback" to the participants throughout the process, facilitating input to achieve their goals.

The host coach communicated to the participants the start of a mission or a challenge on the NEO and My English Lab platforms, including instructions, objectives, compliance conditions, deadlines, rewards, etc. The participants had access to a welcoming tutorial through Google Meet to become familiar with the system. During this tutorial, credentials to the training platform were delivered, the game's rules were explained, the main gamification elements were delivered (the game guide, Canvas module, and a map of badges), and the first assignment was released.

Game Rules: The participants had to meet the challenges and missions proposed by their host coach in each circuit. For example, to graphically indicate the direction to follow, when assigning a mission, an icon or a reference was generated on the NEO platform. As the game progresses, the participants could earn experience points and increase their level, depending on the degree of fulfillment of the challenges and missions. After completing each step, the participants received badges and recognition as evidence of their achievements, generating a change in the leader board and their status as a participant. The following are the students' rewards based on the points of experience:

Points of experience	Level	Participant badge
100	D	Bronze runner
200	C	Silver gauntlet
300	B	Golden crown
400 or more	**A**	**Platinum mortarboard**

All participants had the opportunity to reach level "A" until the end of the game and get the Platinum mortarboard badge. The brave ones who succeeded showed off their knowledge of the English language, but they were also able to directly access the next level of the game by obtaining 450 experience points, one of the greatest benefits (Fig. 1).

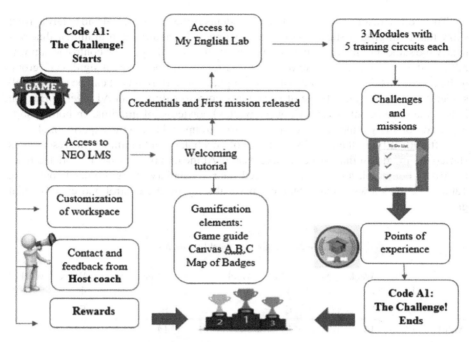

Fig. 1. Flowchart of the Gamified environment

3   Results and Discussion

Descriptive statistics were employed to describe the average of the results of the trials and the pre and post-tests. Also, a Paired Sample T-test was also used to measure the differences between the control and experimental groups. This is to accept or reject the alternative hypothesis. The data was processed using the JASP software.

Students took a pre-test that measured vocabulary and grammar to start this study, as presented in Table 1.

Table 1. Pre–test results of vocabulary and grammar knowledge

	Vocabulary		Grammar	
	Control	Experimental	Control	Experimental
Valid	14	14	14	14
Mean*	8.9	8.8	6.6	6.2

*Max value = 10

The pre-test results administered to 28 students in the experimental and control group show that both groups started with a knowledge of vocabulary and grammar that was nearly the same. For instance, the mean obtained in vocabulary by the control group was 8.9 and the experimental group 8.8. The two results did not show a significant group difference. Considering that the test was computed over 10 points, it can be said that all students had a good knowledge of vocabulary corresponding to an A1 level of English before the experiment started. Conversely, the knowledge of grammar in both groups was low, obtaining a mean of 6.6 in the control group and 6.2 in the experimental.

After identifying the initial knowledge of vocabulary and grammar, the researchers started the treatment that lasted for five weeks. At the end of each week, students from the two groups took a quiz that measured their vocabulary and grammar knowledge. Table 2 below shows results obtained in vocabulary by the control and experimental group.

Table 2. Vocabulary weekly quiz results

	Week 1	Week 2	Week 3	Week 4	Week 5	Week 1	Week 2	Week 3	Week 4	Week 5
	C	E	C	E	C	C	E	C	E	C
Valid	14	14	14	14	14	14	14	14	14	14
Mean*	5.6	6.8	9.6	9.6	9.3	9.4	9.8	9.8	8.8	9.2

*Max Value = 10
C = Control, E = Experimental

Table 2 shows that, the results obtained in the weekly vocabulary quizzes by the students belonging to the control and experimental groups (14 in each) do not show, in general, a significant group difference. However, in the first week of the intervention, students of both groups did not obtain good results in the quiz. These results are the lowest of the five quizzes and lower than the pre-test. Furthermore, there was a difference of 1.2 points between the control and experimental groups (5.6 in the control and 6.8 in the experimental groups) this week.

During weeks 2, 3, and 4, students from the two groups scored high in the vocabulary quiz, and their results were the same in weeks 2 and 4. There was a minimal group difference in week 3 where the control group's mean was 9.3 and 9.4 in the experimental group. In week 5, results were different in the two groups. Students in the control group show a slight difference of 0.4 points compared to the experimental group (8.8 the experimental group and 9.2 the control group).

Excepting week 1, students from the experimental and control group showed a high level of vocabulary knowledge corresponding to an A1 level of English. In most quizzes, the results were the same in the two groups except for weeks 1 and 5, where the control group had relatively lower results.

Apart from vocabulary quizzes, all students took a grammar quiz at the end of each week. These results are presented in Table 3.

Table 3. Grammar weekly quiz results

	Week 1	Week 2	Week 3	Week 4	Week 5	Week 1	Week 2	Week 3	Week 4	Week 5
	C	E	C	E	C	C	E	C	E	C
Valid	14	14	14	14	14	14	14	14	14	14
Mean*	8.8	8.6	6.3	6.6	6.4	6.6	6.9	7.7	7.3	7.5

Max Value = 10
C = Control, E = Experimental

Table 3 shows that there is no significant difference between the means corresponding to the control and experimental groups. This means that both groups developed this skill almost equally in terms of grammar knowledge. An apparent noticeable difference between the control and the experimental group is the one that occurred on week 4. This week, the control group's mean was 6.9 and 7.7 in the experimental group.

It is important to note that the data do not show progress in the knowledge of grammar in any of the two groups during the implementation of the experiment. For instance, the highest results obtained by the students from the two groups occurred in week 1. After this week, the results decreased. See Table 3.

After finishing the treatment, students from the control and the experimental group took a post-test that measured their knowledge of vocabulary and grammar in an A1 level of English. These results are shown below in Tables 4 and 5.

Table 4. Pre and post–test results of vocabulary knowledge

	Pre-test	Post-test	Pre-test	Post-test
	Control	Control	Experimental	Experimental
Mean*	8.9	9.3	8.8	9.5

Max Value = 10

Table 5. Pre and post–test results of grammar knowledge

	Pre-test	Post-test	Pre-test	Post-test
	Control	Control	Experimental	Experimental
Mean*	6.6	7.3	6.2	7.5

Max Value = 10

Tables 4 and 5 show the means of the pre and post-tests administered to students in the control and experimental groups. Table 4 shows the students' knowledge of vocabulary. Based on the data, it can be said that there is not a significant difference between the control and experimental groups. In the pre-test, the mean obtained by the two groups was high (see Table 4). After the experiment, both groups show slight progress in vocabulary knowledge. However, this progress does not differ much from each group. Students in the control group showed an increase of 0.4 points and students in the experimental group 0.7 (see Table 4).

In line with the results obtained in vocabulary learning, Table 5 shows no significant difference between the control and the experimental group regarding grammar knowledge (see Table 5).

Data in Table 5 shows that the control group had a small difference of 0.4 points at the beginning of the experiment. After the experiment, both groups improved their knowledge of grammar. However, the results show a negligible difference of 0.2 points between the control and experimental groups (see Table 5).

Hypothesis Testing

To accept or reject the null hypothesis (H_0) a paired sample T-test was employed. This test was chosen since in this experiment; the researchers aimed to "compare" the mean of two matched groups of people or cases … examined at two different points in time" [46]. The results of this test are presented in Table 6.

The null hypothesis (H0) for this study is that gamification does not facilitate the development of vocabulary and grammar among A1 level of English students.

The alternative hypothesis (Ha) is that gamification facilitates the development of vocabulary and grammar among A1 level of English students.

Table 6. Paired samples T-test

Measure 1	Measure 2	t	df	p
Vocabulary pre-test	Vocabulary post-test	−2.268	27	032
Grammar pre-test	Grammar pre-test	−3.309	27	003

This study had one independent variable (gamification) and two dependent variables (a. vocabulary knowledge and b. grammar knowledge). Table 6 shows the paired sample t-test for each of the dependent variables.

Regarding vocabulary, the means of the pre-test ($M = 8.81, SD = 1.34$) and the post-test ($M = 9.41, SD = 0.64$) show a difference. Therefore, it can be assumed that students performed better after the treatment. The results of the t-test show a *p-value* of *0.032*.

In relation to grammar, the means of the pre-test ($M = 6.43, SD = 2.09$) and the post-test ($M = 7.38, SD = 1.64$), also, show a difference. So, it can be assumed that students performed better after the treatment. The results of the t-test show a value of *0.032*.

Based on the p values obtained in this study (see Table 6), the null hypothesis is rejected, and the alternative hypothesis is accepted. Thus, it can be said that gamification has a positive effect on vocabulary and grammar development.

4 Conclusion

Gamification has great potential as an educational strategy to learn a foreign language. This study aimed to determine to what extent gamification improves vocabulary and grammar learning in A1 level English students. The experiment reveals that even though there is not a marked significant difference between the means of the pretest and posttest scores of the experimental and control groups for vocabulary and grammar development, the alternative hypothesis is accepted. Therefore, it can be implied that gamification facilitates the development of vocabulary and grammar among A1 level English students.

When compared to the traditional method, gamification can have a positive influence on student achievement. Thus, teachers can be recommended to use the gamification method to enhance student learning.

Upon consideration of the benefits of gamification, teachers should consider evaluating how they can attract learners' attention, reduce the fear of failure, and create scenarios to communicate in real life. In addition, most vocabulary and grammar activities in the English language courses are conducted using textbooks, and there is an urgent need for innovative and flexible teaching materials to supplement textbooks. In these regards, the application of gamified environments can help deal with issues regarding time constraints and resources so that students can be provided with more opportunities for autonomous learning, language practice, and producing language outputs.

Gamification can be a supportive tool for online learning; however, institutions need to make sure that there is accessibility to the internet and technological devices for students to connect and carry out the planned activities. Meaningful assessments must also be developed to ensure that students are achieving their learning goals. Additionally, the application of these innovative strategies is necessary for higher education contexts to meet the interests and needs of tertiary-level students.

Future research should analyze the effects of gamification on additional English language skills such as, writing, speaking, reading, and listening. Similar studies may also be conducted to make comparisons with gamification approaches that are not technology-oriented.

References

1. Renandya, W.A., Widodo, H.P. (eds.): English Language Teaching Today Linking Theory and Practice English Language Education. ELE, vol. 5. Springer, Cham (2016). https://doi.org/10.1007/978-3-319-38834-2
2. Kyewski, E., Krämer, N.C.: To gamify or not to gamify? An experimental field study of the influence of badges on motivation, activity, and performance in an online learning course. Comput. Educ. **118**, 25–37 (2018). https://doi.org/10.1016/j.compedu.2017.11.006
3. Tsay, C.H.H., Kofinas, A., Luo, J.: Enhancing student learning experience with technology-mediated gamification: an empirical study. Comput. Educ. **121**, 1–17 (2018). https://doi.org/10.1016/j.compedu.2018.01.009
4. Groening, C., Binnewies, C.: Achievement unlocked! – the impact of digital achievements as a gamification element on motivation and performance. Comput. Hum. Behav. **97**, 151–166 (2019). https://doi.org/10.1016/j.chb.2019.02.026
5. Lopez, C.E., Tucker, C.S.: The effects of player type on performance: a gamification case study. Comput. Hum. Behav. **91**, 333–345 (2019). https://doi.org/10.1016/j.chb.2018.10.005

6. Thorpe, A.S., Roper, S.: The ethics of gamification in a marketing context. J. Bus. Ethics **155**(2), 597–609 (2017). https://doi.org/10.1007/s10551-017-3501-y

7. Warmelink, H., Koivisto, J., Mayer, I., Vesa, M., Hamari, J.: Gamification of production and logistics operations: status quo and future directions. J. Bus. Res. **106**, 331–340 (2018). https://doi.org/10.1016/j.jbusres.2018.09.011

8. Caporarello, L., Magni, M., Pennarola, F.: One game does not fit all. gamification and learning: overview and future directions. In: Lazazzara, A., Nacamulli, R.C.D., Rossignoli, C., Za, S. (eds.) Organizing for Digital Innovation. LNISO, vol. 27, pp. 179–188. Springer, Cham (2019). https://doi.org/10.1007/978-3-319-90500-6_14

9. Landers, R.N., Armstrong, M.B.: Enhancing instructional outcomes with gamification: an empirical test of the Technology Enhanced Training Effectiveness Model. Comput. Hum. Behav. **71**, 499–507 (2017). https://doi.org/10.1016/j.chb.2015.07.031

10. Jurgelaitis, M., Ceponiene, L., Ceponis, J., Drungilas, V: Implementing gamification in a university-level UML modeling course: a case study. Comput. Appl. Eng. Educ. **27**, 332–343 (2019) https://doi.org/10.1002/cae.22077

11. Bai, S.; Hew, K.F.; Huang, B.: Does gamification improve student learning outcome? Evidence from a meta-analysis and synthesis of qualitative data in educational contexts. Educ. Res. Rev. **30** (2020) https://doi.org/10.1016/j.edurev.2020.100322

12. Park, S., Kim, S.: Is sustainable online learning possible with gamification? -the effect of gamified online learning on student learning. Sustainability. **13**(8), 4267 (2021). https://doi.org/10.3390/su13084267

13. Baptista, G., Oliveira, T.: Gamification and serious games: a literature meta-analysis and integrative model. Comput, Hum. Behav. **92**, 306–315 (2018). https://doi.org/10.1016/j.chb.2018.11.030

14. Rapp, A., Hopfgartner, F., Hamari, J., Linehan, C., Cena, F.: Strengthening gamification studies: current trends and future opportunities of gamification research. Int. J. Hum. Comput. Stud. **127**, 1–6 (2019). https://doi.org/10.1016/j.ijhcs.2018.11.007

15. Werbach, K., Hunter, D.: The Gamification Toolkit: Dynamics, Mechanics, and Components for the Win. Wharton School Press, Philadelphia (2015)

16. Rachels, J.R., Rockinson-Szapkiw, A.J.: The effects of a mobile gamification app on elementary students' Spanish achievement and self-efficacy. Comput. Assist. Lang. Learn. **31**(1–2), 72–89 (2018). https://doi.org/10.1080/09588221.2017.1382536

17. Barata, G., Gama, S., Jorge, J., Gonçalves, D.: Studying student differentiation in gamified education: a long-term study. Comput. Hum. Behav **71**, 550–585 (2017). https://doi.org/10.1016/j.chb.2016.08.049

18. Buckley, P., Doyle, E.: Individualising gamification: an investigation of the impact of learning styles and personality traits on the efficacy of gamification using a prediction market. Comput. Educ. **106**, 43–55 (2017). https://doi.org/10.1016/j.compedu.2016.11.009

19. Ding, L.: Applying gamifications to asynchronous online discussions: a mixed methods study. Comput. Hum. Behav. **91**, 1–11 (2019). https://doi.org/10.1016/j.chb.2018.09.022

20. Hernández-Fernández, A., Olmedo-Torre, N., Peña, M.: Is classroom gamification opposed to performance? Sustainability **12**(23), 9958 (2020). https://doi.org/10.3390/su12239958

21. Millis, K., Forsyth, C., Wallace, P., Graesser, A.C., Timmins, G.: The impact of game-like features on learning from an intelligent tutoring system. Technol. Knowl. Learn. **22**(1), 1–22 (2016). https://doi.org/10.1007/s10758-016-9289-5

22. Wu, T.-T., Huang, Y.-M.: A mobile game-based English vocabulary practice system based on portfolio analysis. J. Educ. Technol. Soc. **20**(2), 265–277 (2017). http://www.jstor.org/stable/90002180

23. Bouchrika, I., Harrati, N., Wanick, V., Wills, G.: Exploring the impact of gamification on student engagement and involvement with e-learning systems. Interact. Learn. Environ. **29**, 1–14 (2019). https://doi.org/10.1080/10494820.2019.1623267

24. Flores, J.: Using gamification to enhance second language learning. Digit. Educ. Rev. **27**, 32–54 (2015). https://revistes.ub.edu/index.php/der/article/view/11912
25. Zainuddin, Z., Chu, S.K.W., Shujahat, M., Perera, C.J.: The impact of gamification on learning and instruction: a systematic review of empirical evidence. Educ. Res. Rev. **30**, 100326 (2020). https://doi.org/10.1016/j.edurev.2020.100326
26. Aldemir, T., Celik, B., Kaplan, G.: A qualitative investigation of student perceptions of game elements in a gamified course. Comput. Hum. Behav. **78**, 235–254 (2018). https://doi.org/10.1016/j.chb.2017.10.001
27. Davis, K., Sridharan, H., Koepke, L., Singh, S., Boiko, R.: Learning and engagement in a gamified course: investigating the effects of student characteristics. J. Comput. Assist. Learn. **34**(5), 492–503 (2018). https://doi.org/10.1111/jcal.12254
28. Göksün, D.O., Gürsoy, G.: Comparing success and engagement in gamified learning experiences via Kahoot and Quizizz. Comput. Educ. **135**, 15–29 (2019). https://doi.org/10.1016/j.compedu.2019.02.015
29. Groening, C., Binnewies, C.: 'Achievement unlocked!' – the impact of digital achievements as a gamification element on motivation and performance. Comput. Hum. Behav. **97**, 151–166 (2019). https://doi.org/10.1016/j.chb.2019.02.026
30. Kyewski, E., Kramer, N.C.: To gamify or not to gamify? An experimental field study of the influence of badges on motivation, activity, and performance in an online learning course. Comput. Educ. **118**, 25–37 (2018). https://doi.org/10.1016/j.compedu.2017.11.006
31. Kayseroglu, M.A., Samur, Y.: Vocabulary learning through a gamified question and answer application. J. Learn. Teach. Digit. Age. **3**(2), 27–41 (2018). ISSN:2458-8350. https://dergipark.org.tr/tr/download/article-file/1175639
32. Tamtama, G.I.W., Suryanto, P., Suyoto, S.: Design of English vocabulary mobile apps using gamification: an Indonesian case study for kindergarten. Int. J. Eng. Pedagogy (IJEP) **10**(1), 150–162 (2020). https://doi.org/10.3991/ijep.v10i1.11551
33. Boyinbode, O.:Development of a gamification based English vocabulary mobile learning system. *International Journal of Computer Science and Mobile Computing*, 7(8), 183–191. (2018). https://ijcsmc.com/docs/papers/August2018/V7I8201835.pdf
34. Hashim, H., Rafiqah, M., Rafiq, K., Md. Yunus, M.: Improving ESL 'learners' grammar with gamified-learning. SSRN Electr. J. **5**, 41–50. (2019). https://doi.org/10.2139/ssrn.3431736
35. Huang, B., Hew, K.F., Lo, C.K.: Investigating the effects of gamification enhanced flipped learning on undergraduate students' behavioral and cognitive engagement. Interact. Learn. Environ. **27**(8), 1106–1126 (2019). https://doi.org/10.1080/10494820.2018.1495653
36. Putz, L.-M., Hofbauer, F., Treiblmaier, H.: Can gamification help to improve education? Findings from a longitudinal study. Comput. Hum. Behav. **110**, 106392 (2020). https://doi.org/10.1016/j.chb.2020.106392
37. Veljković Michos, M.: Gamification in foreign language teaching: do you Kahoot?.In: International Scientific Conference on Information Technology and Data Related Research, pp. 511–516 (2017). https://doi.org/10.15308/Sinteza-2017-511-516
38. Yukselturk, E., Altıok, S., Başer, Z.: Using game-based learning with Kinect technology in foreign language education course. J. Educ. Technol. Soc. **21**(3), 159–173. (2018). https://drive.google.com/file/d/1a-JRVjXx7VNpGg-Kp80ic8DPdYourHze/view
39. Głowacki, J., Kriukova, Y., Avshenyuk, N.: Gamification in higher education: experience of Poland and Ukraine. Adv. Educ. **10**, 105–110. https://doi.org/10.20535/2410-8286.151143
40. Tazouti, Y., Boulaknadel, S., Fakhri, Y.: ImALeG: a serious game for Amazigh language learning. Int. J. Emerg. Technol. Learn. (IJET) **14**(18), 28–38 (2019). https://doi.org/10.3991/ijet.v14i18.10854
41. Al-Dosakee, K. ., Ozdamli, F.: Gamification in teaching and learning languages: a systematic literature review. Rev. Roman. Pentru Educ. Multidim. **13**(2), 559–577 (2021) https://doi.org/10.18662/rrem/13.2/436

42. Denisova, A., Cairns, P., Guckelsberger, C., Zendle, D.: Measuring perceived challenge in digital games: development & validation of the challenge originating from recent gameplay interaction scale (CORGIS). Int. J. Hum. Comput. Stud. **137**, 102383 (2020). https://doi.org/10.1016/j.ijhcs.2019.102383

43. Ahmed, H.D., Asiksoy, G.: The effects of gamified flipped learning method on student's innovation skills, self-efficacy towards virtual physics lab course and perceptions. Sustainability **13**(18), 10163 (2021). https://doi.org/10.3390/su131810163

44. Klimova, B., Polakova, P.: Students' perceptions of an EFL vocabulary learning mobile application. Educ. Sci. **10**(2), 37 (2020). https://doi.org/10.3390/educsci10020037

45. Hsin-Yuan Huang, W., Soman, D.: A practitioner's guide to gamification of education. Research Report Series Behavioural Economics in Action – Rotman School of Management. University Of Toronto. (2013). https://mybrainware.com/wp-content/uploads/2017/11/Gamification-in-Education-Huang.pdf

46. Ross, A., Willson, V.L.: Paired samples T-Test. In: Basic and Advanced Statistical Tests Writing Results Sections and Creating Tables and Figures, pp. 17–19. SensePublishers, Rotterdam (2017). https://doi.org/10.1007/978-94-6351-086-8_4

Statistical Analysis of University Academic Performance in the Area of Exact Sciences, Before and During the Covid-19 Pandemic

Rodrigo Bastidas-Chalán[1]([✉]) [ID], Gisella Mantilla-Morales[1] [ID], Fernando Vinueza-Escobar[1] [ID], and Christian Coronel-Guerrero[2] [ID]

[1] Departamento de Ciencias Exactas, Universidad de Las Fuerzas Armadas ESPE. Sede Santo Domingo, Vía Santo Domingo-Quevedo Km 24, Santo Domingo de los Tsáchilas, Ecuador
`{rvbastidas,gbmantilla,nfvinueza}@espe.edu.ec`
[2] Departamento de Ciencias de La Computación, Universidad de Las Fuerzas Armadas ESPE. Sede Santo Domingo, Vía Santo Domingo-Quevedo Km 24, Santo Domingo de los Tsáchilas, Ecuador
`cacoronel@espe.edu.ec`

Abstract. The pandemic caused by Covid-19 at the end of 2019 affected the development of academic activities in educational institutions at all levels. This article focuses its interest on analyzing the academic performance, failure and dropout of the students of the Universidad de las Fuerzas Armadas ESPE, Santo Domingo, before and during the pandemic. The analyzed data was collected from the academic results matrices of the Departamento de Ciencias Exactas of the ordinary academic periods: 201950, 201951, 202050, 202051, 202150 and 202151. The information was analyzed with a descriptive approach, using bar charts, which indicate the evolution of the areas of knowledge in the indicated periods. For the variation of academic performance, the ANOVA method was used, obtaining a $p - value = 0.126$, which indicated that there is no significant variation between the means of the analyzed data. In addition, it was determined that between academic periods the assumptions of normality and homoscedasty with values $p - value > 0.05$ are met. In the linear correlation analysis, the Pearson coefficient was calculated, whose value indicated a strong negative correlation between the academic performance and the percentage of failure (values of 0.887, 0.796), while between the academic performance and the percentage of abandonment there was a moderate negative correlation (values of 0.428, 0.636). Finally, models based on linear regression are proposed in the areas of knowledge analyzed, to predict the academic performance of the new academic period 202250.

Keywords: Academic performance · University education · Linear regression · ANOVA

1 Introduction

It has been approximately one hundred years since humanity was engulfed in a global pandemic [1]. On March 11, 2020, a new generation was affected by the virus called

SARS-CoV-2, which was declared a pandemic by the World Health Organization (WHO).

As a preventive measure, institutions, organizations and governments started contingency plans to prevent the spread of the virus. The Government of Ecuador was no exception, declaring a state of emergency on March 16, 2020, the date on which the closure and suspension of all face-to-face activities that were not a priority for public welfare were decreed.

In the educational field at all levels, the suspension of face-to-face activities was ordered in order to prevent the spread of the virus and reduce its impact. According to data from the United Nations Educational, Scientific and Cultural Organization (UNESCO), by mid-May 2020 more than 1.2 billion students at all levels of education, worldwide, had stopped having face-to-face classes at school. Of these, more than 160 million were students from Latin America and the Caribbean [2].

Educational institutions had to take measures to allow them to continue with their activities, which gave rise to the deployment of distance learning modalities, using a variety of formats and platforms. This modality demanded a new challenge, since in a short time it was necessary to adapt face-to-face study programs to the virtual modality.

Virtual education reduces certain problems that face-to-face education presents, such as geographical problems, since it is not necessary to travel anywhere; time problems, since it favors combining studies and work activities; and demand problems, since it is possible to access training programs that are not available in nearby educational institutions. However, it also has its drawbacks: little interactivity between teachers and students; feedback can be very slow; it is more difficult to rectify errors in materials, evaluations, etc.; there are more dropouts than in face-to-face teaching [3].

One of the variables used to measure the quality of education is academic performance. Educational institutions analyze the results of this variable to develop action and improvement plans, trying to evaluate academic performance and improve it, implies considering the following socioeconomic factors, scope of study programs, teaching methodologies, difficulty of using a personalized teaching, mastery of previous concepts and modality of face-to-face or virtual studies can affect it [4].

The objective of this research is to analyze the academic performance of the students who attend first levels in the exact sciences subjects at the Universidad de las Fuerzas Armadas ESPE, Santo Domingo, an institution of higher education in Ecuador, for which the information of the academic results of the periods of ordinary classes 201950, 201951, 202050, 202051, 202150 and 202151 of the Department of Exact Sciences was used. The hypotheses raised are:

H1: There is no significant difference between the average academic performance of the periods analyzed.
H2: There is a Strong Linear Correlation Between the Averages of Each Area of Knowledge and the Percentages of Abandonment and Failure.

The main contribution of this research is to provide higher education institutions (HEI) and the educational community with a descriptive and inferential analysis of the results of the academic performance of students of the first levels of the Universidad de las Fuerzas Armadas ESPE, Santo Domingo, before and during the confinement caused by the pandemic, through the use of python software.

2 Related Works

The pandemic has affected almost all Instituciones de Educación Superior (IES) in Ecuador, for which an accelerated change towards the virtual modality was generated, modifying the teaching-learning process along with other processes in the educational environment, posing enormous challenges in the technological environment for both teachers and students. [5].

Maintaining continuity in educational activities during the pandemic has required the incorporation of virtual learning environments supported by Information and Communication Technologies (ICTs). This new learning context has required the development of digital skills and it is estimated that it has produced effects particularly on the academic performance of students. According to the case study in a higher education institution in Mexico and its affiliated institutions, 90 percent considered that they need to improve their digital skills, as well as that the resulting academic performance is subjective. [6].

Other research identified the correlation between critical thinking skills and academic performance in first-semester college students, using the W-GCTA Critical Thinking Assessment short test to record that students with average academic performance have critical thinking skills. Pearson's correlation coefficient found that these skills and academic performance are related. In addition, the ANOVA test was used to verify the difference between the means of the variances [7].

Particularly, the subjects belonging to the Knowledge Areas of Exact Sciences have a high component of participation in the curricular meshes for the careers of Engineering, Technology, Sciences and particularly during the first years of training, their in-depth study is required as part of the basic formation of the professional profile. The results of greater failure are evident in exact science subjects with respect to the subjects of the career. Among the main causes, as described in a research carried out [8], it can be the product of the difficulty of adaptation of the student who enters the university system, low level of previous knowledge, problems of study habits, which has led to propose initiatives to mitigate the disapproval as in the case of the National Technological Institute of Mexico in Celaya, with the Advisory Program for Repeating or Special Students (PASARE), by the Department of Basic Sciences.

In an investigation, the academic results of 2 cohorts of university students were analyzed in May 2019–2020 and May 2020–2021, the first in face-to-face mode, the other during the pandemic in virtual mode. It was evidenced that the results of the grade point average were higher for the cohort in virtual modality, however the main disadvantage reported by the students was the non-execution of practical activities of their career [9]. It is necessary to limit that it cannot be directly inferred that a better average implies a greater internalization of knowledge; In this sense, it is necessary to carry out other investigations that include more variables of the teaching-learning process that change in the virtual context, one of them is the incidence of the evaluation by the type of available instruments, as well as the accessibility by the students to unauthorized or controlled extra resources, in contrast to face-to-face evaluations.

According to another study carried out based on the perception of students from a university institution in Colombia, the virtual learning modality was one of the factors that affected the results of academic performance during the pandemic, with a slight association between virtuality and impact on learning. Academic performance, while the family coexistence factor presented a moderate association with the affectation of academic performance [10].

In a similar investigation, applied to students of the leveling course of a university institution in Ecuador, which analyzed face-to-face and virtual study modalities as a factor, significant differences were found. The results showed a superior academic performance for those who took the basic science subjects of the first leveling course, executed particularly for the first time in the virtual modality, with respect to the previous courses executed in face-to-face mode, however, the authors point out that the superior values do not necessarily imply a better level or depth of knowledge[11]. In this research, unlike the one cited above, the results of academic performance for students of the first levels in six consecutive academic periods were analyzed, of which the last four periods were executed completely in virtual modality, obtaining that there is no significant difference for the means in academic performance between the face-to-face and virtual modalities.

3   Materials and Methods

For the analysis of the research, the information on the academic performance, failure and dropout of the students who take exact science subjects was considered, information that is compiled by the Department of Exact Sciences of the Santo Domingo campus (DCEX-SS). The subjects are grouped into the knowledge areas of: Functional Analysis, Mathematical Analysis, Physics, Statistics and Chemistry.

The academic periods considered are: 201950, 201951 executed in face-to-face mode and the periods 202050, 202051, 202150, 202151 executed in virtual mode.

The institution's academic regulations stipulate that students pass a subject with an average equal to or greater than 14 out of 20 points, otherwise they fail. For this study, dropout is considered as a student who does not present homework, frequent tests and exams, without officially canceling their enrollment record.

For the descriptive and inferential analysis, the phyton software was used in the online version of Colab, since this resource facilitates the collaborative work of the group and reduces the use of computer resources in data processing.

This study aims to develop a quantitative research approach; the methodology focused on a descriptive-predictive type analysis, which allowed the grouping, representation and interpretation of the results. In addition to determining the association between some variables of interest in the educational field such as: performance, failure and dropout and analyzing their possible dependence.The following hypotheses are proposed:

H1: There is no significant difference between the average academic performance of the periods analyzed.

H2: There is a strong linear correlation between the averages of each area of knowledge and the dropout and failure rates.

To verify H1, the average performance per academic period was considered as a variable, in order to verify that the averages of the five areas of knowledge are maintained or show variation, applying an ANOVA test. The assumptions of normality and homoscedasticity must be met before applying the ANOVA test, the Shapiro Test was applied for normality and the Bartlett Test to analyze homoscedasticity.

To verify H2, the average performance per academic period, the failure rate and the dropout rate were considered as variables in order to verify the linear correlation with the Pearson Coefficient. To generate the prediction model, linear regression was used in order to obtain the performance averages in each area of knowledge in subsequent academic periods.

3.1 Data Collection

Table 1 shows the performance averages by area of knowledge (Functional Analysis, Mathematical Analysis, Physics, Statistics, Chemistry) based on the last six academic periods analyzed, while in Table 2 shows the failure percentages by area of knowledge. In the Table 3 shows the dropout percentages for each area of knowledge:

Table 1. Academic performance according to academic periods

Area-Period	201950	201951	202050	202051	202150	202151
Functional analysis	15.32	14.40	15.00	14.87	14.65	14.59
Analysis	15.31	13.36	14.08	13.34	13.57	13.33
Statistics	15.44	14.12	15.24	15.54	15.27	15.50
Physics	15.16	12.07	13.86	N/A	14.27	14.91
Chemistry	15.16	13.96	14.38	13.38	14.11	13.74

Table 2. Percentage of loss based on academic periods

Area-Period	201950	201951	202050	202051	202150	202151
Functional analysis	8,00%	27,59%	16,85%	15,17%	15,70%	18,83%
Analysis	27,10%	33,33%	24,51%	30,43%	29,90%	33,45%
Statistics	23,23%	25,36%	9,33%	11,46%	9,38%	12,82%
Physics	26,57%	47,66%	17,82%	N/A	18,56%	14,71%
Chemistry	25,86%	31,94%	24,85%	30,65%	26,10%	29,50%

Table 3. Abandonment rate based on academic periods

Area-Period	201950	201951	202050	202051	202150	202151
Functional analysis	1,33%	4,60%	5,62%	3,32%	3,41%	3,14%
Analysis	8,13%	7,14%	5,07%	12,46%	5,14%	16,89%
Statistics	4,04%	6,52%	1,33%	3,13%	3,13%	0,85%
Physics	2,80%	8,41%	9,90%	N/A	3,09%	5,88%
Chemistry	5,01%	8,06%	12,27%	11,74%	3,52%	10,32%

Table 4. Normality and homoscedasticity test

Period	Shapiro test	Bartlett test
	p-value	p-value
201950	0.74	
201951	0.71	
202050	0.63	0.05
202051	0.81	
202150	0.0003	

4   Results and Discussions

4.1   Descriptive Statistics of Academic Performance

In Fig. 1 through bar diagrams, the evolution of performance is presented academic, obtaining that the averages for each area of knowledge do not show a significant variation between the periods: 201950, 201951, 202050, 202051, 202150 and 202151. Particularly, in the period 202051, in the area of Physics average was not generated because its subjects were not taught by readjustment of academic meshes.

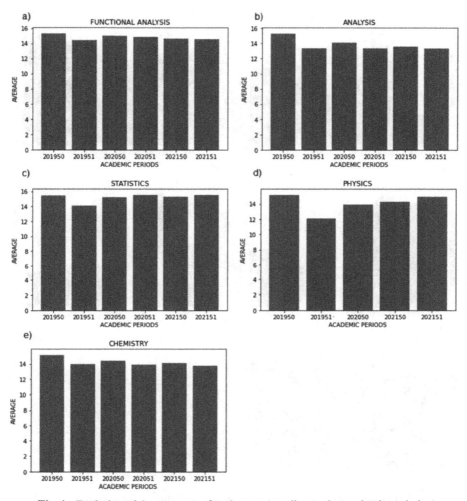

Fig. 1. Evolution of the averages of each area according to the academic periods.

In Fig. 2 using bar diagrams, the evolution of the reprobation percentage is described, obtaining that in the areas of knowledge of Physics and Statistically, this value decreased significantly during the pandemic, for periods: 202050, 202051, 202150 and 202151. While in the area of Chemistry and Analysis there was no consistent variation between pre and post periods pandemic. Particularly, in the period 202051, in the area of Physics, no was the percentage of reprobation due to the fact that their subjects were not taught for readjustment of academic meshes.

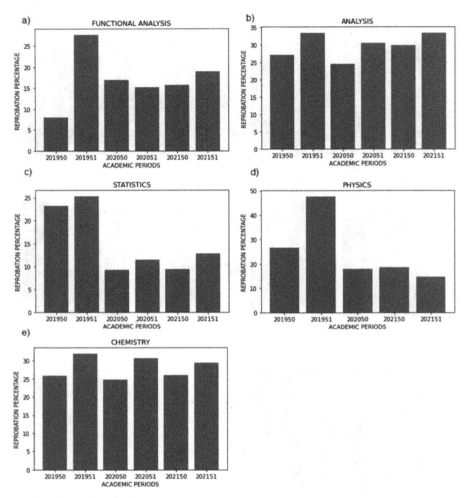

Fig. 2. Evolution of the reprobation of each area according to the academic periods.

In Fig. 3 shows the evolution of the dropout rate by means of bar diagrams, obtaining that in the area of knowledge of Statistics this value decreased significantly during the academic periods developed in the pandemic: 202050, 202051, 202150 and 202151. In the other areas of knowledge there was no defined trend of increase or decrease of the percentage of abandonment in the pre and post pandemic periods.

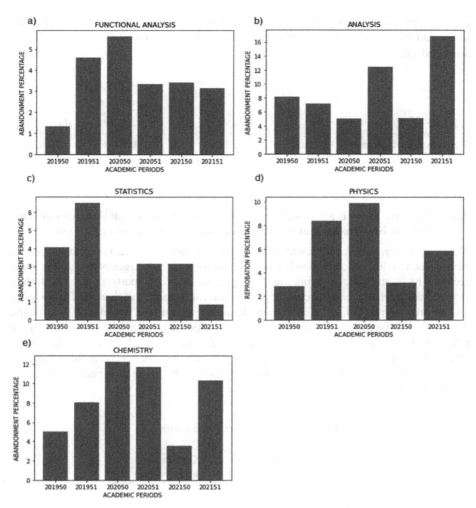

Fig. 3. Evolution of the abandonment of each area according to the academic periods.

4.2 Verification of the Hypotheses and Discussion

4.2.1 H1 test: There is No Significant Difference in the Average Academic Performance of the Academic Periods

Prior to obtaining the results, the Shapiro test (Normality) and Bartlett test (homoscedasticity) was used, as indicated in Table 4. For a value of $\alpha = 0.05$ there is sufficient evidence to affirm that all academic periods meet the assumptions of normality and homoscedasticity with a value $p - value > 0.05$, except for the period 202150:

The ANOVA test applied to the academic performance averages by period are shown in Table 5, obtaining sufficient evidence to affirm that there is no significant difference in the performance averages. In this way, studies can be complemented in which the experimental and control groups, Shapiro's test and mean difference with a Bartlett test were used in this research, surpassing other investigations in which the assumption of homocedasticity is not verified [12].

Table 5. ANOVA test

Variable	ANOVA (F)	ANOVA (p-value)
Performance of all areas of knowledge	2.13	0.12

4.2.2 H2 Test: There is a Strong Linear Correlation Between the Averages of Each Area of Knowledge and the Percentages of Abandonment and Failure

The Pearson correlation coefficients are presented in Table 6. It was found that there is a strong negative linear correlation between the performance averages of each knowledge area and its failure rate, implying that the higher the academic performance, the failure rate decreases. However, between the performance averages of each area of knowledge and its dropout percentage, there is a moderate negative linear correlation, that is, the dropout percentages are not only related to the performance averages, but could also be related to Other factors are outside the scope of this research. In this way, the results obtained in other investigations were passed, in which the Shapiro (normality) and Levene (homocedasticity) tests were performed. However, the correlation part involves only two variables [13].

Table 6. Pearson's correlation coefficient

Area	Correlation Reprobation	Correlation abandonment
Functional Analysis	−0.887	−0.447
Analysis	−0.669	−0.332
Physics	−0.796	−0.636
Statistics	−0.609	−0.769
Chemistry	−0.654	−0.428

Additionally, by means of linear regression, a prediction model was obtained to obtain performance averages in each area of knowledge, as indicates in the Table 7. The predictions that were found correspond to the new period 202250, including a model for the Physics area.

Table 7. Linear regression model

Period	Linear regression model	Prediction
Functional Analysis	$y = 0 - .08657143x + 15.108$	14.502
Analysis	$y = -0.286x + 14.8327$	12.831
Physics	$y = 0.17x + 13.544$	14.564
Statistics	$y = 0.11571429x + 14.78$	15.59
Chemistry	$y = -0.20428571x + 14.92$	13.49

5 Conclusions and Future Work

This study determined through the ANOVA test that there is no variation significant in the performance averages by academic period, before and during the pandemic. The information at the level of the areas was taken as a base. of knowledge: Functional Analysis, Mathematical Analysis, Physics, Statistics and Chemistry.

Pearson's correlation indices indicated a strong negative correlation difference between the average academic performance and the failure rate, while between the average academic performance and the percentage of abandonment there was a moderate negative correlation.

The models obtained through linear regression will allow predicting academic performance in future ordinary academic periods, indicating possible trends of increase or decrease in the averages of the areas of knowledge of the Department of Exact Sciences of the University of the Armed Forces, Santo Domingo. In the future, actions may be taken in the areas of knowledge with the greatest tendency to reduce academic performance.

To complement this research with future work, it would be pertinent to analyze other relevant factors (social, economic, etc.), which can be related as a cause of abandonment and desertion of studies.

Other research could delve into the effect of not doing laboratory activities during the pandemic on subjects that have a practical component and its impact on academic performance. In addition, if a deepening of knowledge was achieved in these subjects.

Finally, the use of descriptive and inferential statistics made it possible to visualize the temporal evolution of the data obtained in the areas of knowledge of the Department of Exact Sciences, achieving the objectives set in this study.

Acknowledgment. The authors thank the Department of Exact Sciences of the Universidad de las Fuerzas Armadas Sede Santo Domingo (DCEX-SS), for providing access to the matrices that contain information from the academic periods analyzed in this work. A special thanks to the teachers who are part of it.

References

1. CastañedaGuillot, C., Ramos, G.: Principales pandemias en la historia de la humanidad. Revista Cubana de Pediatría. **92**, 1–11 (2020)

2. CEPAL: Organización de las Naciones Unidas, and UNESCO. La educación en tiempos de la pandemia de covid-19. Technical report (2020)
3. Rodríguez Gallego, A., Martínez Caro, E.: Estilos de aprendizaje y elearning. hacia un mayor rendimiento académico. Revista de Educación a Distancia (RED). **7**, 1–9 (2003)
4. Navarro, R.E.: El rendimiento académico: concepto, investigación y desarrollo. REICE. Revista Iberoamericana sobre Calidad, Eficacia y Cam- bio en Educación. **1**(2), 1–16 (2003)
5. SantanaSardi, G., GutiérrezSantana, J., ZambranoPalacios, V., CastroCoello, R.: La educación superior ecuatoriana en tiempo de la pan- demia del covid-19. Dominio de las Ciencias **6**(3), 757–775 (2020)
6. Zimbrón, A., Gutiérrez, E., et al.: Rendimiento académico en ambientes vir- tuales del aprendizaje durante la pandemia covid-19 en educación superior (2021)
7. ShirleyLorenaAlquichire, R., Arrieta, J.C.: Relación entre habilidades de pensamiento crítico y rendimiento académico. Voces y Silencios. Revista Latinoamericana de Educación **9**(1), 28–52 (2018). https://doi.org/10.18175/vys9.1.2018.03
8. Oliver, E., Serrano, M., Ramírez, M.: Estrategias virtuales de pandemia para abatir los índices de reprobación en asignaturas de ciencias básicas. Revista Mapa **5**(24), 1–21 (2021)
9. Benitez Martinez, S., Cabrera Soriano, L.: Impacto de la pandemia Covid- 19 en el rendimiento estudiantil a través del teleaprendizaje en estudiantes de la Carrera de Enfermería. Ph.D. thesis, Universidad de Guayaquil, Fac- ultad de Ciencias Medicas, Carrera de Enfermería (2020)
10. Valdivieso, M.A., Victor, M., Angela, S.: Percepción de estudiantes universitarios colom- bianos sobre el efecto del confinamiento por el coronavirus, y su rendimiento académico. Espacios **41**(42), 269–281 (2020). https://doi.org/10.48082/espacios-a20v41n42p23
11. Sánchez-Almeida, T., Naranjo, D., Reina, J.: Análisis del desempeño académico de estu- diantes de una institución de educación superior en ecuador, antes y durante la pandemia. Technical report, Universidad de Zaragoza, Servicio de Publicaciones (2021)
12. Bastidas-Chalán, R., Mantilla-Morales, G., et al.: Inferential statistical anal- ysis in e-learning university education in latin america in times of covid-19. Commun. Comput. Inf. Sci. **1535**, 97–107 (2022)
13. Mingorance, A.C., Trujillo, J.M., Cáceres, P., Torres, C.: Mejora del rendimiento académico a través de la metodología de aula in- vertida centrada en el aprendizaje activo del estudiante universitario defi- ciencias de la educación. J. Sport Health Res. **9**(1), 129–136 (2017)

Performance in the Practice of Mountain Biking Using the Samsung Health App: An Experience in Physical Education with University Students

Edwin Iraola-Real[1] (ID), Alonso Iraola-Arroyo[2] (ID), Keita Nakamine[3], Daniel Iraola[3], Nicole Iraola-Arroyo[2], and Ivan Iraola-Real[3](✉) (ID)

[1] Universidad Nacional de Educación Enrique Guzmán y Valle, Lima 15472, Perú
[2] Universidad Tecnológica del Perú, Lima 15046, Perú
[3] Universidad de Ciencias y Humanidades, Lima 15314, Perú
ivanir701@hotmail.com

Abstract. Mountain biking is a sport that is physically demanding and at the same time beneficial for health; therefore, it can be implemented in university education by monitoring achievements. For this reason, the present study aims to analyze the university performance of the physical education course through the practice of mountain biking through the Samsung Health app. 12 university students between 16 and 25 years of age participated ($M_{age} = 21.78$, $SD = 1.40$) from Lima-Peru. The record of the sport performance was 7 sessions of training with a pace as a peloton. The results showed that there was an increase in average and maximum speed, altitude, and mileage. Then, the analysis of the coefficients of variation showed moderate homogeneity of the means of maximum and average speed, as well as altitude per day. But it was heterogeneous with respect to the distance covered, showing an increase in the performance of the students.

Keywords: Physical education · Sport · Athletes · Mountain biking · Physical activity · Samsung Health App · Mobile health

1 Introduction

Mountain biking is one of the most popular outdoor sports [1]. Although its origin as off-road cycling is associated with the decade of the 70s of the twentieth century, it was incorporated as a competitive sport in the 1996 Olympic Games in Atlanta [2]. This was the year when its popularity and the number of people who practice it increased [3]. Due to its popularity, it can be said that currently as a sport it is classified into cross-country cycling, endure (all mountain) cycling, downhill cycling, cyclocross, and freeride. And likewise, each classification requires a bicycle with specialized equipment [1]. However, it is important to consider that as a physical activity it is characterized by its high intensity and high aerobic and anaerobic demands [3]. These demands are due to the simultaneous coordination of the muscles of the whole body, particularly the arms and legs to achieve traction and stability of the bicycle [4]. These demands are

M. Botto-Tobar et al. (Eds.): ICAT 2022, CCIS 1757, pp. 203–213, 2023.
https://doi.org/10.1007/978-3-031-24978-5_18

sometimes increased if cyclists use bicycles with shock absorbers, which tend to absorb the muscular force of the legs when pedaling; being more demanding for the cyclist [5].

These high physical demands that cycling involves [3], generate health benefits. And in this regard, there are studies that claim that cycling is beneficial for muscular and cardiorespiratory fitness; reducing the risk of overweight, premature death, cardiovascular problems, blood pressure problems, hyperlipidemia, breast, and colon cancer, and even type 2 diabetes [1]. For example, a British study conducted in 2017 with a sample of 250,000 participants confirmed that cycling reduces the likelihood of suffering from cardiovascular disease, cancer, and mortality [6].

Therefore, according to the analysis of mountain biking as a highly demanding sport [4] due to the high demand of energy consumption and muscular work [3], it is necessary for cyclists to monitor their performance during their training. In this way, it is necessary to keep track of the rhythm of their activity and physical effort, as well as to follow up their vital signs. Thus, as athletes, they can set new goals in their training by monitoring their health status. Therefore, it is important to keep a more and more professional control with technological applications such as the Samsung Health app [7].

1.1 About the Samsung Health App

Usually, sports practices such as athletics or cycling lacked a thorough monitoring of the performance achieved by each athlete. However, nowadays, technological applications (apps) have been developed that allow athletes to perform an increasingly professional monitoring of their performance and vital signs. Being useful for physical education teachers who want to monitor the performance of university students. Among these innovative applications is Samsung Health, which was developed for athletes and cyclists and is gradually increasing the number of users due to the information it records and reports to the user (see Fig. 1). In this way, Samsung Health app provides information about the speed reached (minimum and maximum), the highest and lowest elevation points above sea level, the average heart rate, etc. Thus, this application allows the athlete to turn his IPhone and Android into a technological resource for sports monitoring; also obtaining statistics on his performance [7].

Samsung Health is an application for smartphones that has proven to be valid for monitoring physical performance; especially when used with smartwatches to capture vital signs at the body level in the arm and hands. Due to its popularity it has achieved millions of downloads through Google Play, and is currently considered pre-installed on Samsung cell phones [8]. Samsung Health app has been shown to have great accuracy in reporting walking even though the location of the smartphone affects the accuracy [9], or the type of activity, such as uphill or downhill walking [10].

However, it is considered an application that adequately reports performance levels for independent athletes. Although there are several studies using the Samsung Health app in the last 5 years, these studies report the performance of walking athletes [8–10]. For these reasons, it is important to conduct studies using the Samsung Health app [7] for monitoring the performance of university students who practice mountain biking during training in their physical education courses.

Fig. 1. Registration of the Samsung Health app in a training route in the university physical education course.

1.2   Importance of Monitoring Mountain Biking Performance in Peru

Peru is one of the countries with a varied geography and culture that makes it one of the perfect places to practice mountain biking. It is a country that has a wide network of trails and dirt roads optimal to provide satisfaction to beginners and professional cyclists. These mountain biking routes can be found mainly in the highlands, with the Sacred Valley of the Incas in Cusco as a destination [11]. Part of its geography shows eight natural regions ranging from the Coast or Chala from sea level to 500 m above sea level (mosl) to the Janca or Cordillera region from 4800 (mosl) to 6768 (mosl) [12]. But, due to the particularities of the geography, in a distance of less than 25 km a mountain biker can go from the Coast or Chala region to the valleys of the Yunga region from 500 (mosl) to 2300 (mosl). This represents a great physical effort and also the need to have an adequate level of physical performance due to the change in altitude.

This geographical variety that characterizes Peru [11], can cause temperatures ranging from 11 degrees Celsius with a sky covered with fog, but with a humidity level of up to 85% in the coastal region or Chala [13]. And when moving to the Yunga region, temperatures ranging from 27 degrees Celsius with a sky partially covered with clouds, but with a humidity level of up to 41% [14]. It should be considered that the routes for mountain biking in Peru can be dirt and stone roads, or bridle paths. But additionally, these routes range from flat roads (0% elevation gain) to very challenging roads (more than 16% elevation gain) [15], which may represent less or more physical effort for athletes. For these reasons, it is essential to monitor the performance of athletes (as well as their physical condition), and even more so if it is to be implemented in university education as a physical education course.

1.3 Implementing Mountain Biking in University Physical Education

Peruvian university education is oriented towards the comprehensive training of professionals. This proposal is based on Competency-Based Education that was implemented in Peruvian universities since the university reform since 2014 [16]. This university reform was achieved with the implementation of the current University Law 30220, which requires universities to develop professional skills from general courses and specialty courses [17]. In these subjects, the implementation of university leveling courses, research courses, specialty courses, artistic training and physical education are contemplated. In order to comply with this university reform, in Peru the National System of Evaluation, Accreditation and Certification of Educational Quality (SINEACE) monitors the universities' compliance with the University Law [18]. The SINEACE complies with the provisions of the General Law of Education 28044 in which in article 9 it is proposed that training a person is intended to develop their ethical, intellectual, artistic, cultural, affective, religious and physical capacities to adequately exercise their citizenship and to be linked to the world of work [19]. Therefore, according to the implementation of these regulations and policies, it is justified that physical education courses have been implemented, even as a pilot test with new sports that universities do not usually work on, such as cycling.

The previously exposed arguments on the particularities of Peruvian university education, on policies [17], and the implementation of sports activities in the university curriculum. Also, about the geographical variety of Peru [12], as well as the variants of the climate [13, 14], make mountain biking very demanding in many cases [4]. For obvious reasons, this requires high energy consumption for cyclists [3]. Therefore, it is necessary to monitor performance with a technological application such as the Samsung Health app [7]. Thus, the objective of this study is to analyze the university performance of the physical education course through the practice of mountain biking through the Samsung Health app [8].

In order to achieve the proposed study objective, the research methodology is explained below.

2 Methodology

The study assumes a quantitative approach methodology [20] because they analyze the records in terms of speed, distance, height, etc. reported by the Samsung Health app. At the same time, because it refers to a study with a small sample and in a short time it corresponds to a case study [21].

2.1 Sample

The sample consisted of 5 mountain bikers belonging to the Qhapaq Peru from a public university in Lima - Peru. Due to the context of the Co-vid-19 pandemic, there was a small group of students from the first cycles in order to correctly develop the pilot of the physical education course. All participants were male and ranged between 16 and 25 years old (Mage = 21.78, SD = 1.40) from the districts of Lurigancho Chosica and

Chaclacayo in Lima-Peru. Students trained in a peloton-style formation from the district of Chaclacayo in the province of Lima to the district of Santa Eulalia in the province of Huarochirí.

2.2 Measures

Performance monitoring was done jointly. To do this, a checklist was created to record the data provided by the Samsung Health app of the student team. The purpose of this checklist was to facilitate the monitoring of the cyclists' training pace and sports performance. In this way, a database was generated in which the progress of the mountain bikers could be tracked. The data recorded were the following: altitude level above sea level, average speed and maximum speed, mileage and ride time. In addition, the temperature was recorded (see Fig. 2). It is important to clarify that the record was obtained for the whole team and not individually in training circuits (see Fig. 3).

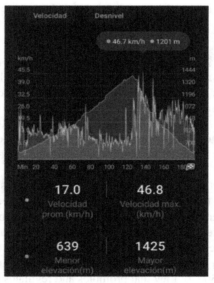

Fig. 2. Display of the Samsung Health app log on a training route. Report of the seventh day of training in which you specified the average and maximum speed, altitude level, etc.

2.3 Methodological Procedures

For the present study, coordination was carried out with the university authorities for the curricular implementation through a physical education course that includes two units of 7 sessions with mountain biking practices for students of the first cycles of study. The ethical research criteria were respected, specifically that of voluntary participation and confidentiality [22]. Thus, according to these ethical criteria, we proceeded in accordance

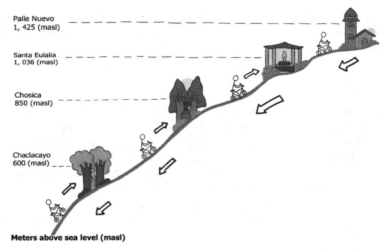

Fig. 3. Training Circuits, names of the towns and altitude level above sea level. Source: Nicole Iraola-Arroyo.

with Peruvian Law No. 29733 on Personal Data Protection, which refers to keeping the identities of the participants confidential [23]. Regarding the voluntary and confidential participation of cyclists aged 16 and 17 years, considered adolescents (not adults), we acted in accordance with Peruvian Law No. 27337 known as the Civil Code of the Child and Adolescent of Peru. This regulation states that those over 16 years of age have the psychological maturity to decide without the influence of other people [24]; for example, to decide to participate freely in the training sessions and to participate in the present study.

After defining the ethical criteria, the training program was defined. This program consisted of 7 sessions training routines. The participants agreed to train on Saturday mornings. Thus, a schedule was established starting at 8:00 am to make preparations (clothing, warm-up, safety accessories, tools, food, etc.). And at 9:00 a.m. the training route began. At this time the registration of the Samsung Health app [7] was started. It is important to clarify that throughout the driving process the requirements established in the Peruvian Law No. 30936, Law that promotes and regulates the use of bicycles as a means of sustainable transport were met, mainly Article 11 of protection to pedestrians, the driver himself and third parties [25] because the training route included urban areas with traffic signs. The protocols to avoid the spread of Covid-19 were followed, so the training sessions were conducted wearing masks and keeping the respective distance from other people [26].

The data recorded by the Samsung Health app were entered into a database with the Statistical Package for the Social Sciences software (SPSS, version 26) [27]. In this way, descriptive statistical analyses were performed and to identify the significance of the possible increase or decrease of the training pace and sports performance, the means were analyzed with the coefficients of variation (CV) assuming the criteria of Rustom (2012) that range from high homogeneity to high heterogeneity [28].

3 Results

Following the description of the methodology, ethical aspects and procedures, the results are presented below.

3.1 Report of the Samsung Health App

Table 1 shows the record of the Samsung Health app. The progress of the mountain bikers in terms of average speed, maximum speed, altitude, kilometers traveled and temperature can be observed.

Table 1. Report of the Samsung Health app.

Training	Average speed	Maximum speed	Lower altitude	Higher altitude	Km	Temperature
First training	12,90	32,30	623,00	829,00	22,44	18,00
Second training	13,80	34,40	652,00	985,00	32,12	21,00
Third training	16,70	30,50	645,00	982,00	33,30	27,00
Fourth training	15,60	42,20	486,00	1300,00	52,22	19,00
Fifth training	15,70	46,50	632,00	1268,00	48,68	17,00
Sixth training	18,20	43,10	597,00	1335,00	53,32	21,00
Seventh training	17,00	46,80	639,00	1425,00	55,26	19,00

3.2 Descriptive Statistics and Variation Coefficients

Table 2 shows the means, standard deviations and coefficients of variation. To determine the increase in sports performance, the criteria of Rustom (2012) were taken into account, who establishes that if the coefficient of variation (CV) is less than 5% it is considered highly homogeneous, if the CV ranges between 5% to 20% it indicates moderate homogeneity, if the CV is between 20% to 50% it is heterogeneous, and if the CV is greater than 50% it is considered highly heterogeneous [28].

Therefore it can be seen that the average speed has a CV of 11.74%, the maximum speed has a CV of 17.38, the performance explained in the altitude as a minimum point has a CV of 9.46%, and the maximum altitude shows a CV of 19.39%; these sports performance criteria prove to be moderately homogeneous. However, the mileage covered during the 7 sessions of training shows a CV of 30.50%, which is heterogeneous, evidencing an increase of the distance, covered in each day of training.

Table 2. Descriptive statistics and variation coefficients.

Sport performance		Minimum	Maximum	Mean	SD	VC
1	Average speed	12,90	18,20	15,70	1,844	0.1174 (11.74%)
2	Maximum speed	30,50	46,80	39,40	6,847	0.1738 (17.38%)
3	Lower altitude	486,00	652,00	610,57	57,772	0.0946 (9.46%)
4	Higher altitude	829,00	1425,00	1160,57	225,086	0.1939 (19.39%)
5	Km	22,44	55,26	42,48	12,957	0.3050 (30.50%)
6	Temperature	17,00	27,00	20,29	3,302	0.1627 (16.27%)

3.3 Dispersion Diagram

Once the heterogeneity with respect to mileage run was identified, an analysis was performed with a scatter diagram in which the variable mileage was entered (Y axis), then training day (X axis) and average speed (Z axis) (see Fig. 4). Thus, the scatter plot and the coefficient of variation confirm the clear trend of a gradual increase in sports performance expressed in distance covered, which could be evidence of better physical endurance or better management of muscular energy during the training days.

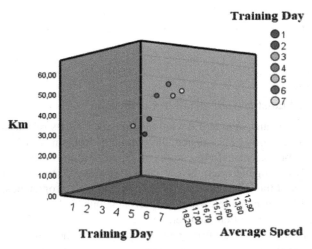

Fig. 4. Dispersion diagram showing the evolution of the mileage traveled according to the 7 training sessions in the physical education course.

4 Discussion

The case study developed that oriented according to the objective to analyze the university performance of the physical education course through the practice of mountain biking through the Samsung Health app. This educational performance was evaluated thanks to the reports of average and maximum speed, distance traveled (KM) and altitude levels reached indicated by the Samsung Health app [7]. Although it is known that the app has presented accuracy difficulties in walking athletes, there are studies that conclude that it has achieved efficient results to record the performance of athletes [9, 10]. And in the evaluation of the sports performance of the universities cyclists, the app provided efficient records. The records obtained were confirmed with maps, traffic signs and information from geographical documents.

In the results, it was possible to show that in terms of the records obtained, it was evidenced that the team reached a gradual increase in speed, distance and height reached in the seven training sessions of the physical education course. This performance may have been due to the level of difficulty of the route, characteristic of the geography of the route that goes from the coast to the Peruvian highlands [12]. This generated a gradual increase in sporting performance due to the demands of mountain biking itself [4] and the energy demand for the university students [3]. However, it is important to highlight that it was expected to obtain a level of heterogeneity in sports performance in order to identify a more differentiated increase in each day of training. However, the result showed moderate homogeneity in the average and maximum speed and in the height attained (mosl). It could be observed that the use of masks to prevent Covid-19 [26] was important to prevent cyclists from catching Covid-19. Although cycling requires high energy consumption [3], cyclists indicated that the use of masks exhausted them, reducing their oxygenation and even generating dizziness. Therefore, the results in speed and altitude did not differ much on each training day.

Finally, in terms of mileage, a differentiated (heterogeneous) increase was identified. This result allows to understand that, despite the homogeneous performance in speed and altitude achieved, the distance covered in training was greater day by day of training due to various factors such as the gradient or the weather. Also, the same speed allows to manage one's own energy consumption each time the training route became more familiar.

5 Conclusions and Future Works

The training and sports performance of the group of university students who practiced mountain biking was efficiently monitored with the Samsung Health app. The app showed adequate levels of accuracy in terms of speed, altitude and distance traveled, and these app records were confirmed with geographic data. Then, in terms of sports performance, it showed an increase in each day of training. In some way, difficulties characteristic of the Peruvian geography and the use of masks as a protocol for the prevention of Covid-19 infections were evidenced. However, sports performance increased particularly in the distance traveled, proving to be an appropriate option to develop sports courses with cycling monitored by apps. For future studies, from the university proposal, it is suggested to carry out a follow-up in more training routines, with a greater number of participants, with different training circuits. So also using other devices such as watches to monitor heart rate. Additionally, it is expected to expand the study with qualitative research techniques to record better appreciations of mountain bikers about the use of apps and the training itself.

References

1. Dillard, S.C.: Mountain Biking as a Means to Encourage Public Health and Wellbeing. Wright State University, Dayton, Ohio. (2017). Homepage, https://corescholar.libraries.wright.edu/cgi/viewcontent.cgi?article=1201&context=mph. Accessed 20 June 2021
2. Berto, F.J.: Origins of Mountain Biking: The Birth of Dirt. Van der Plas Publications, San Francisco (1999)
3. Burr, J., Drury, T., Ivey, A., Warburton, D.: Physiological demands of downhill mountain biking. J. Sports Sci. **1**, 1–9 (2012)
4. Impellizzeri, F.M., Marcora, S.M.: The physiology of mountain biking. Sports Med. (Auckland, N.Z.), **37**(1), 59–71 (2007)
5. Berry, M.J., Woodard, C.M., Dunn, C.J., Edwards, D.G., Pittman, C.L.: The effects of a mountain bike suspension system on metabolic energy expenditure. Cycling Sci. Spring, 8–14 (1993)
6. Celis-Morales, C.A., et al.: Association between active commuting and incident cardiovascular disease, cancer, and mortality: Prospective cohort study. BMJ (Clinical Research Ed.), **357**, j1456 (2017). https://doi.org/10.1136/bmj.j1456
7. Samsung.: Feel good with Samsung Health (2021). Homepage. https://www.samsung.com/global/galaxy/apps/samsung-health/. Accessed 20 June 2021
8. Beltrán-Carrillo, V., Jiménez-Loaisa, A., Alarcón-López, M., Elvira, J.: Validity of the "Samsung Health" application to measure steps: a study with two different Samsung smartphones. J. Sports Sci. **37**(7), 788–794 (2019). https://doi.org/10.1080/02640414.2018.1527199
9. Johnson, M., Turek, J., Dornfeld, C., Drews, J., Hansen, N.: Validity of the Samsung Phone S health application for assessing steps and energy expenditure during walking and running: does phone placement matter? Digit. Health **2**, 1–8 (2016)
10. Šinkovec, M., Rugelj, D.: Accuracy of the "S Health" pedometer application during walking and stair climbing. Baltic J. Health Phys. Act. **12**(4), 93–104 (2020). Homepage. https://manus.zf.uni-lj.si/biomeh/lab/Clanki/2020_BJHPA_S_Health_Rugelj.pdf. Acessed 10 July 2021
11. Peru for Less: Cycling in Peru: A complete bike guide to Peru. (2021). Homepage. https://www.peruforless.com/blog/cycling-in-peru/. Acessed 10 July 2021
12. Escobal, J., Torero, M.: Adverse Geography and differences in welfare in Peru. World Institute for Development Economics Research, p. 73 (1992). Homepage. https://www.researchgate.net/publication/23780541_Adverse_Geography_and_Differences_in_Welfare_in_Peru. Acessed 10 July 2021
13. Ministerio del Ambiente del Perú: Pronóstico del tiempo para Lima Oeste (Lima). (2021). Homepage. https://www.senamhi.gob.pe/main.php?p=pronostico-detalle&dp=lima&localidad=0001/. Accessed 10 July 2021
14. The Weather Channel.: Pronóstico para 10 días – Distrito de Santa Eulalia (2021). Homepage. https://weather.com/es-BO/tiempo/10dias/l/Distrito+de+Santa+Eulalia+Lima+Per%C3%BA?canonicalCityId=3c87fb0126ab840cafad17179d049abb826d1f02e1a91a5c8a7f7ba3ac545cb5/. Acessed 11 July 2021

15. The Climbing Cyclist.: Gradients and cycling: an introduction. (2013). Homepage, http://the climbingcyclist.com/gradients-and-cycling-an-introduction/. Acessed 11 July 2021
16. British Council. The Reform of the Peruvian University System: Internationalization, progress, challenges and opportunities (2016). Homepage. https://www.britishco uncil.pe/sites/default/files/the_reform_of_the_peruvian_university_system_interactive_ver sion_23_02_2017_fg.pdf. Acessed 9 July 2021
17. Congreso de la República del Perú. Nueva Ley Universitaria. Ley N° 30220. Lima. Perú (2014)
18. Sistema Nacional de Evaluación, Acreditación y Certificación de la Calidad Educativa. Modelo de Acreditación para Programas de Estudios de Educación Superior Universitaria. Lima. Perú, SINEACE (2016)
19. Congreso de la República del Perú. Ley General de Educación. Ley N°. 28044. Lima. Perú (2003)
20. Leavy, P.: Research Design: Quantitative, Qualitative, Mixed Methods, Arts-Based, and Community-Based Participatory Research Approaches. The Guilford Press, London (2017)
21. Creswell, J.: Research Design: Qualitative, Quantitative, and Mixed Methods Approaches, 4th edn. Sage, Los Ángeles (2014)
22. Goodwin, J.: Research in Psychology: Methods and Design. Córdova, Brujas (2010)
23. Congreso de la República del Perú. Ley de Protección de datos personales. Ley N°. 29733. Lima. Perú (2013)
24. Congreso de la República del Perú. Código del Niño y del Adolescente. Ley N°. 27337. Lima. Perú (2000)
25. Congreso de la República del Perú. Ley que promueve y regula el uso de la bicicleta como medio de transporte sostenible. Ley N°. 30936. Lima. Perú (2019)
26. Ministerio de Salud del Perú.: No bajes la guardia ante la Covid-19: Evita enfermarte. Uso de las mascarillas para ayudar a desacelerar la propagación de la Covid-19 (2020). Homepage. http://www.minsa.gob.pe/covid-19/?op=31. Accessed 25 May 2021
27. IBM Knowledge Center. (2020). Ibm.com. Homepage. http://www.ibm.com/support/knowle dgecenter/SSLVMB_26.0.0/spss/product_landing.dita. Accessed 1 Aug 2020
28. Rustom, A.: Estadística descriptiva, probabilidad e inferencia: Una visión conceptual y aplicada. Universidad de Chile, Santiago (2012)

Analysis and Incidents in the Professional Practices of IT University Students in the Context of the COVID-19 Pandemic

Christian Coronel-Guerrero[1]([✉]) [ID], Rodrigo Bastidas-Chalán[2] [ID],
Gisella Mantilla-Morales[2] [ID], Fernando Vinueza-Escobar[2] [ID],
Margoth Guaraca-Moyota[1] [ID], and Luis Castillo-Salinas[1] [ID]

[1] Departamento de Ciencias de la Computación, Universidad de las Fuerzas Armadas ESPE Sede Santo Domingo, Vía Santo Domingo-Quevedo km 24, Santo Domingo de los Tsáchilas, Ecuador
{cacoronel,meguaraca,lacastillo12}@espe.edu.ec
[2] Departamento de Ciencias Exactas, Universidad de las Fuerzas Armadas ESPE Sede Santo Domingo, Vía Santo Domingo-Quevedo km 24, Santo Domingo de los Tsáchilas, Ecuador
{rvbastidas,gbmantilla,nfvinueza}@espe.edu.ec

Abstract. The objective of this research is to analyze the level of satisfaction and effectiveness of pre-professional practices in university students, before and during the pandemic. The analyzed data was collected through surveys applied to 67 students. The data was analyzed with a descriptive approach, using tables to summarize the results, while in the analysis of the difference in means in the effectiveness and satisfaction scales, the ANOVA method was used, obtaining a $p-value = 0.1134$, the same as indicated that there is no variation in the means of the scales. For the correlation analysis, the Pearson coefficient was calculated, whose value indicated a strong correlation between the satisfaction scale of the place where the practice was carried out and the level of satisfaction (0.637). Finally, a web page model is proposed that is capable of better guiding the choice of the place where the students will carry out the pre-professional practices.

Keywords: Pre professional practices · ANOVA · Pearson's coefficient

1 Introduction

COVID-19 appeared as a strain originating from SARS-CoV-2 in Wuhan-China at the end of 2019 when several cases of severe pneumonia were reported [1]. Due to the rapid expansion and excessive contagion of this virus in some countries, it was declared a global pandemic by the World Health Organization (WHO) in March 2020. Since then, several biosecurity measures have been established to prevent the spread of the virus COVID-19, such as lockdown and social distancing for an indefinite time [2]. This prevented people from leaving their homes,

M. Botto-Tobar et al. (Eds.): ICAT 2022, CCIS 1757, pp. 214–225, 2023.
https://doi.org/10.1007/978-3-031-24978-5_19

causing them to opt for new alternatives to carry out their work and educational activities.

As a consequence, the COVID-19 pandemic left many workers unemployed and in many cases they were forced to work from home, using technological tools such as a computer and the internet [3]. Much of the jobs that was transferred to the home was administrative labour, educational, technological, communication, marketing, finance and law [4]. On the other hand, labor pressures grew out of control, the intensification of teleworking increased, forcing employees to employees to be 'online' and 'available' all the time [5].

The COVID-19 pandemic also affected students, educational institutions were forced to suspend the face-to-face modality, forcing them to opt for online teaching and virtual education [6]. According to the United Nations Educational, Scientific and Cultural Organization (UNESCO), 87% of the student population in the world was affected by the closure of educational institutions due to COVID-19 [7]. Despite the fact that higher education institutions expedited the replacement of face-to-face classes with online training, the significant learning of students had a transformation that was not successfully planned [8]. However, online learning gradually became one of the best alternatives for education. Information technologies provided more than a stopgap solution during the COVID-19 pandemic crisis [9].

This research aims to determine the relationship between the effectiveness and satisfaction of the internships of university students in the engineering career in information technologies (ITIN). The hypotheses are:

H1: There is variation in the mean of the effectiveness and satisfaction scales.

H2: There is a correlation between the effectiveness and satisfaction scales.

The main contribution of this research is to provide the community university with a descriptive and inferential analysis, with python software, the results of surveys on effectiveness and satisfaction in ITIN student internships.

2   Related Works

On the other hand, pre-professional practices are the set of tasks focused on the formation of professional knowledge, skills and abilities that a student must obtain during their learning stage [10]. These practices are part of the fundamental requirements that must be met during the academic period, so that students can graduate from Higher Education. The Universities offer the academic credit to the students so that they can carry out their activities in the organizations, during a certain number of hours that is equivalent to the number of class hours [11].

At the Universidad de las Fuerzas Armadas ESPE, the guidelines were approved to carry out pre-professional internships under sanitary conditions imposed by the COVID-19 pandemic in March 2021. Among these guidelines are the face-to-face, semi-face-to-face and non-face-to-face modalities to carry out professional practices. For the face-to-face modality, it is established that both the receiving Institutions and the University must guarantee the protection of people by carrying out the biosafety protocols, as for the blended and non-face-to-face modalities, the practices can be carried out with the use of telematic tools [12].

The Information Technology Engineering career at ESPE has the responsibility to train professionals according to their graduation profile, therefore it is committed to organizing and evaluating the periods of pre-professional practices, for that reason, this study focuses in determining the effectiveness of the pre-professional practices that their students have carried out during the pandemic period.

University students face numerous challenges during their professional training. They have to prepare for the work environment by applying the knowledge acquired during their academic stage. Pre-professional internships are the closest link that students have with the world of work, in which they use their skills and learning in order to achieve practical training and work-related experience [13]. The pre-professional internship is the starting point in the professional career of each student, a space in which experience is gained on the role to be played and the skills to solve situations typical of their profession [14].

However, pre-professional internships are not always developed properly, because students do not carry out activities in the areas that correspond to their professional profile. In some cases, the receiving companies or institutions do not give the interns the opportunity to do important tasks that are more difficult, either because of the little experience they may have and the fear that an incident may occur within the institution, for Therefore, they assign students irrelevant activities that have no importance and are not related to their career [15].

In a case study from Pakistan, the Impact of internship programs on the professional and personal development of students is measured, weaknesses exposed by the respondents were found. The lack of organization between companies and academic tutors; Companies only assign insignificant tasks to students in an uncomfortable environment to teach what they really need to learn; and companies do not offer adequate feedback to their interns or academic supervisors [16].

According to Parola, in his research he also states that there are several obstacles in the formation of pre-professional practices. He mentions the link between the organization and the effectiveness of pre-professional practices. Ensures that there are many variables at stake to improve the planning and implementation of internships, both companies and institutions can be considered as obstacles or as a learning opportunity for students [17].

An investigation carried out at the National University of Education (UNAE) by Pesántez, analyzes the pre-professional practices carried out in the virtual modality during the COVID-19 pandemic. In this research it is determined that the activities of pre-professional practices carried out in a virtual way reduce the direct contact between tutors and students. On the other hand, connectivity impedes the effectiveness of internships by limiting students from obtaining the work experience they need for their professional training [18].

3   Materials and Methods

3.1   Survey Design

For the data of this study, a survey was conducted on 65 university students of the Information Technology engineering career at the Universidad de las Fuerzas Armadas ESPE.

3.2   Data Collection

The survey was structured in 4 sections, which focus on: software, Networks and Telecommunications, Help Desk and Backoffice, Satisfaction of professional practices. These sections show on the area where the students carried out their work practice activities, in this case 4 questions about the area of Software, 5 questions about Networks and Telecommunications were evaluated; and 5 from Help Desk and Backoffice. The last section of the survey was made up of 6 satisfaction questions based on the Likert scale, as can be seen from Tables 1, 2, 3 and 4.

Table 1. Questions about the Software area

1. In which programming language did you work when you did your internship in the area of software development? (TB1)
2. In which phase of the software development cycle did you have the opportunity to work in your internship? (TB2)
3. In what type of software development did you carry out your internship activities? (TB3)
4. In the company where you did your software internship, what assets or tools did you have access to? (TB4)

For the hypotheses that were raised, they were analyzed with the python software:

H1: There is variation in the mean of the effectiveness and satisfaction scales.

H2: There is a correlation between the effectiveness and satisfaction scales.

To verify H1, it was necessary to weight the Likert scale responses between 1 to 5, and apply the ANOVA test.

To verify H2, it was necessary to calculate the Pearson correlation coefficient between the 4 scales TE1, TE2, TE3 and TE4.

Table 2. Questions about the area of Networks and Telecommunications

1. In what type of network did you carry out activities or solve problems when you did your internship? (TC1)
2. Which of these common failures in the area of networks have you solved in your professional practices? (TC2)
3. What tools did you use to detect or solve problems in the network of the company where you did your internship? (TC3)
4. One of the most common problems in the area of networks is punching network cables. Indicate with what standard you punched out a network cable? (TC4)
5. In which categories did you try to solve network problems in your professional practices? (TC5)

Table 3. Questions about the Help Desk and Backoffice area

1. What type of service or support did you provide in the Help Desk area when you did your internship? (TD1)
2. What kind of activities did you carry out in your Help Desk professional practices? (TD2)
3. What tools did you use to detect, support or solve IT problems when you did your internship? (TD3)
4. Indicate how many computers you performed preventive or corrective maintenance on in your professional practices? (TD4)
5. At what level of technical support did you carry out your professional internship activities? (TD5)

Table 4. Questions about Satisfaction of professional practices

1. Did you learn useful things during your pre-professional internship? (TE1)
2. After completing your internship, do you feel competent to work as a technician in a company in the sector? (TE2)
3. Was the environment where you did your internship the right one? (TE3)
4. What is your level of satisfaction regarding the pre-professional internships that you carried out? (TE4)
5. Would you recommend other students of the degree to do their internships in the company where you did them? (TE5)
6. What could improve expectations about carrying out professional internships at the headquarters? (TE6)

4   Results and Discussions

The data obtained from the surveys is shown in this section in two parts. The first consists in exposing the results to the questions while the The following corresponds to the statistical analysis applied.

4.1   General Results

The general results are shown in Tables 5, 6, 7 y 8:

Table 5. About the software area

Question	Options	Quantity
TB1	Python	2
	Java	7
	PHP	11
	C	7
	Java	9
	Angular	6
	React JS	6
	Visual	3
TB2	Gathering information	13
	Design	12
	Development, testing and documentation	9
	Maintenance	10
	Help desk	7
TB3	Accounting applications	0
	Databases	9
	API development	1
	Application Maintenance	4
	Data migration	4
	Reports from a database	2
	Web applications	8
	Data backup	2
	Creation of webpages	11
	Macro with Excel	2
	Any application	1
	Mobile applications	2
TB4	Web server	11
	Database	8
	Database test tables	6
	Hosting	8
	Computer	7

Specifically in the Table 5 the following results were obtained: For TB1 it was found that the most used language is PHP, while for TB2 the phase in which the most work was done was Information gathering. For TB3 there is a greater number of students who developed web pages, and for TB4 the majority of students had access to the web server.

For the Table 6, the following relevant results were obtained: in TC1 it was obtained that the majority of students carried out Local Area Networks activities, in TC2 the majority of problems were presented with Conflict with IP addresses, while for TC3 the tools that were most used to detect or solve network problems was Any Desk. For TC4 students They performed mostly cable punching according to the EIA/TIA-568B standard and in TC5 it was found that most network problems are associated with Router Configuration.

Table 6. About the area of Networks and Telecommunications

Question	Options	Quantity
TC1	Personal Area Networks (PAN)	1
	Local Area Networks (LAN)	5
	Wide Area Networks (WAN)	2
TC2	Conflict with IP addresses	4
	Switch level failures	3
	Insufficient broadband	2
	Active Directory permissions	2
	Installation of network cards	3
	Slow navigation	2
	Deny or enable access to web pages	2
	Configuration of network equipment	3
	Antivirus or firewall issues	3
	Configure access point	1
	Punch down network cables or structured cabling problems	2
TC3	Wireshark	2
	Telnet/SSH	2
	Virtual Machine	1
	Any Desk	5
	Ping	2
	Ipconfig	5
	Traceroute	1
TC4	EIA/TIA-568A	0
	EIA/TIA-568B	5
	OSI	0
	TCP/IP	3
TC5	Configure IP phone	3
	Computer does not ping	2
	Fiber optic problems	1
	Switch Configuration	3
	Router Configuration	5
	Structured cabling	4

For the Table 7 the following results were obtained: for TD1 most of the services were performed in Preventive Maintenance or corrective, for TD2 the activities were focused on Format a hard drive, for TD3 the most used tool was Blowtorch, screwdrivers, cleaning kit. For TD4, the number of computers that were repaired the most was 0–10 and for TD5 the support level that was mostly performed was Level 1 (Basic Incidents).

Table 7. About the Help Desk and Backoffice area

Question	Options	Quantity
TD1	Preventive Maintenance or corrective	32
	Attention to users by window or phone	4
	Solution to software or hardware problems	16
	Attention to users in the position of work	9
	Track tickets in Help Desk	1
	Technological inventory	13
TD2	Support for network problems	13
	Installation of driver cards	5
	Check why the computer is slow	16
	Setting up a network printer	12
	Debugging or installing software	12
	Virus problems	8
	Format a hard drive	19
	Punch down network cables	8
	Answer mail or phone to users	4
	Reset keys	4
	Provide information on an IT product	13
TD3	Windows or Linux installers	21
	Virtual Box	3
	Anti virus installers	12
	Remote desktop programs	11
	Network cable crimper	6
	Ghost to clone hard drives	4
	Blowtorch, screwdrivers, cleaning kit	22
	Change of spare parts	9
TD4	0-10	12
	10-20	11
	20-50	6
	more than 50	6
TD5	Level 1: Basic Incidents	24
	Level 2: LAN networks, programming, computer repairs, databases	9
	Level 3: systems complexes, WAN networks and servers	2

4.1.1 H1: There Is Variation in the Mean of the Effectiveness and Satisfaction Scales.
In the Table 8, questions TE1, TE2, TE3 and TE4 represent the effectiveness and satisfaction scales.

To determine the variation of the mean in the scales of effectiveness and satisfaction faction, it is first necessary to weight the Likert scale, establishing five in the most positive value until reaching one for the most negative value of the scale. The averages obtained in the four scales are shown in Table 9:

Table 8. About the satisfaction of professional practices

Question	Options	Quantity
TE1	Strongly agree	24
	Agree	29
	Neither agree nor disagree	11
	In disagreement	2
	Strongly disagree	1
TE2	Strongly agree	14
	Agree	32
	Neither agree nor disagree	14
	In disagreement	6
	Strongly disagree	1
TE3	Strongly agree	20
	Agree	36
	Neither agree nor disagree	8
	In disagreement	2
	Strongly disagree	1
TE4	Very satisfied	12
	Satisfied	42
	Indifferent	10
	Dissatisfied	3
	Very unsatisfied	0
TE5	Yes	52
	No	15

Table 9. Averages of effectiveness and satisfaction surveys

Scale	Mean
TE1: useful learning	4.089
TE2: feeling of competition	3.776
TE3: suitable place of practice	4.074
TE4: level of satisfaction with practices	3.940

Next, the ANOVA test was applied to determine the mean variation between the four scales, as indicated in the Table 10. The result obtained, stated that with a $p-value = 0.1134$ and $\alpha = 0.05$ there is sufficient evidence to affirm that there is no significant difference in the means of the effectiveness and satisfaction scales. In this way, results obtained in other investigations are complemented, In this way, the results obtained in other investigations are complemented, in which only averages are analyzed with tests of the difference between means [19].

Table 10. ANOVA test

Variable	ANOVA Test (F)	ANOVA Test (p-value)
Performance of all areas of knowledge	2.004	0.1134

4.1.2   H2: There Is a Correlation Between the Effectiveness and Satisfaction Scales. Pearson's correlation coefficients are shown in Table 11. The result obtained determined that there is a strong linear correlation between the satisfaction scale of the place where the practice was carried out and the level of satisfaction (0.755). There was also a strong linear correlation between the satisfaction scale of the place where the practice was carried out and the feeling of feeling competent (0.637). The other correlations are moderate among themselves. This complements research work, in which only the difference in means is analyzed without developing the correlations [20].

Table 11. Pearson's correlation indices between the effectiveness and satisfaction scales

Scale	TE1	TE2	TE3	TE4
TE1: useful learning	1	0.520	0.554	0.632
TE2: feeling of competition	0.520	1	0.594	0.637
TE3: suitable place of practice	0.554	0.594	1	0.755
TE4: level of satisfaction with practices	0.632	0.637	0.755	1

5   Conclusions and Future Work

This study made it possible to determine that in carrying out pre-professional practices, there is a strong correlation between the place where the practices are carried out and the level of satisfaction, which allows the creation of metrics that help to better locate the students. The rest of the scales presented a moderate linear correlation.

The averages of the four scales analyzed did not present a significant difference because the data obtained were analyzed with responses from pre-professional practices before and during the pandemic. However, it could be complemented with studies with hypothesis tests that compare the means, separately, before and after the pandemic.

This research allows laying the foundations to develop a page (https://ppp-espe.elementfx.com/#home), that is orientation of pre-professional practices. Research instruments such as surveys could then be applied to validate their improvement.

Finally, the use of statistics and effectiveness and satisfaction scales made it possible to better analyze the data collected, achieving the objectives set out in this research.

Data Availability Statement. Python code and data used in this study is available in: https://drive.google.com/drive/folders/1BL2uudkvZTGCWMUzBFv56CFsLSVB m-Ac?usp=sharing

References

1. Vargas, C.M., Acosta, R.G., Bernilla, A.T.: El nuevo coronavirus y la pandemia del covid-19. Rev. Médica Herediana **31**(2), 125–131 (2020)
2. Ciotti, M., et al.: The Covid-19 pandemic. Crit. Rev. Clin. Lab. Sci. **57**(6), 365–388 (2020)
3. Hodder, A.: New technology, work and employment in the era of Covid-19: reflecting on legacies of research. N. Technol. Work. Employ. **35**(3), 262–275 (2020)
4. Bloom, N.: How Working from Home Works Out. Institute for Economic Policy Research (SIEPR). Policy Brief June, 2020
5. Kniffin, K.M., et al.: Covid-19 and the workplace: implications, issues, and insights for future research and action. Am. Psychol. **76**(1), 63 (2021)
6. Sir John Daniel: Education and the Covid-19 pandemic. Prospects **49**(1), 91–96 (2020)
7. Tadesse, S., Muluye, W.: The impact of Covid-19 pandemic on education system in developing countries: a review. Open J. Soc. Sci. **8**(10), 159–170 (2020)
8. Singh, S.: Impact of Covid-19 pandemic on education system. Tathapi **19**(26), 58–63 (2020)
9. Schleicher, A.: The impact of Covid-19 on education: insights from education at a glance 2020. Retrieved from OECD. org website (2020). https://www.oecd. org/education/the-impact-of-COVID-19-on-education-insights-education-at-a-glance-2020.pdf
10. Consejo de Educación Superior. Reglamento de régimen académico rpcso-08-no. 111–2019 (2019). Recuperado de https://procuraduria.utpl.edu.ec/sitios/ documentos/NormativasPublicas/
11. Galbraith, D., Mondal, S.: The potential power of internships and the impact on career preparation. Res. High. Educ. J. **38**, 9 (2020)
12. Universidad de las Fuerzas Armadas ESPE. Lineamientos para el desarrollo de proyectos de vinculación con la sociedad y prácticas preprofesionales a partir del aõo 2021, bajo condiciones sanitarias impuestas por la pandemia de covid-19 (2021). Recuperado de https://ugvc.espe.edu.ec/wp-content/uploads/2021/09/ Lineamientos-proyectos_vinculacion_y_practicas_2021-Agosto.pdf
13. O'Higgins, N., Pinedo, L., et al.: Interns and outcomes just how effective are internships as a bridge to stable employment? Technical report, International Labour Organization (2018)

14. Ruiz, J.R.T., Bermeo, L.J.L., García, C.C.C.: La práctica preprofesional integradora: concepción para la formación profesional en las carreras de educación. Opuntia Brava **11**(1), 270–278 (2019)

15. Steve Guarnizo Crespo: Importancia de las prácticas preprofesionales para los estudiantes de educación superior en la universidad de guayaquil. INNOVA Res. J. **3**(8), 14–26 (2018)

16. Anjum, S.: Impact of internship programs on professional and personal development of business students: a case study from pakistan. Fut. Bus. J. **6**(1), 1–13 (2020)

17. Noemí Parola, R.: Problematizando las prácticas preprofesionales en trabajo social. desafíos y perspectivas. Prospectiva, pp. 73–88 (2020)

18. Palacios, M.D.P., Alvarado, P.A.C.: Pre-professional practice at UNAE: analysis and reflections on the virtual modality in times of pandemic. Actualidades Investigativas en Educación **22**(1), 36–64 (2022)

19. Bastidas-Chalán, R., Mantilla-Morales, G., et al.: Inferential statistical analysis in e-learning university education in Latin America in times of Covid-19. Commun. Comput. Inf. Sci. **1535**, 97–107 (2022)

20. Trujillo, H.M., Valero, F.J.: Estrés y situaciones de transición al mercado laboral. el caso de las prácticas profesionales en empresa. Psicología Conductual, **15**(2), 267–279 (2007)

Written Corrective Feedback: A Case Study of the Effectiveness of Direct, Indirect Coded, and Indirect Uncoded Feedback

Alexandra Zapata[1]([✉]) [iD] and Evelyn Almeida[1,2] [iD]

[1] Universidad de Las Fuerzas Armadas Espe, Sangolqui, Ecuador
cazapata@espe.edu.ec
[2] Universidad Central del Ecuador, Quito, Ecuador

Abstract. This study aims to determine the effects and benefits of direct feedback with coded and uncoded indirect feedback as a strategy to improve the writing skill of an adult EFL learner. It is a descriptive case study that involves an adult Spanish speaker during an eight-week process that focused on providing direct feedback and indirect feedback with its coded and uncoded subtypes. Based on initial instruments of writing tasks, which allowed the identification of errors, followed by a process of feedback with the development of writing tasks which facilitated comparisons, as well as an objective analysis related to errors' improvement. Showing that the three types of feedback facilitated the correction of different types of errors. So, the learner's motivation and the applied strategies granted the participant to acquire language features leading to effective corrections.

Keywords: Written corrective feedback · Direct feedback · Indirect feedback

1 Introduction

One of the key components of language teaching and learning is feedback. The study of the feedback's different forms and benefits become of significant interest to teachers, researchers, educational institutions, and administrators over recent years. However, there is little literature related to feedback on the development of writing skill in the context of EFL learning in Ecuador. In this sense, this study seeks to understand how effective the incorporation of direct, indirect coded, and indirect uncoded feedback is to improve the writing skill of an adult EFL learner.

Writing is the most complex language skill to develop compared to speaking, reading, and listening in the context of EFL acquisition because learners have to focus not only on language features but also on a process that involves the use of additional skills such as the capacity to plan and arrange ideas to obtain a product with fluency Srinivas [1]. As Krashen [2] states writing facilitates learners to solve problems since it encourages cognitive development. In fact, this skill is one of the significant components of applied linguistics which has enhanced important research focused on its development. Considering that a great number of studies determine that corrective feedback guarantees the improvement of writing skill in L2 learners by developing an oriented process that requires sequential revision [3].

Corrective feedback has shown usefulness because it enhances learners of L2 to work on a process of errors revision based on the given feedback [4]. Likewise, Allman [5] states that feedback leads to improving the quality of learning. Thus, feedback for students is valuable since it makes them notice their development, weaknesses, and what needs to be improved. Teachers also obtain information about students' strengths and weaknesses which facilitates them to establish the language features that require a process of orientation.

Different early studies base their feedback in an unfocused manner, it is every error receives feedback instead of categorizing errors. The main disadvantage of this process is that learners are not provided with elaborate feedback that facilitates them to identify the area in which they need the teacher's assistance. Without mentioning the lack of interest that they might express in the amounts of corrections [6].

Related to the development of writing skill, written feedback is a strategy that focuses on improving the accuracy of language features, content, and organization of ideas with high quality [4]. Additionally, written feedback can be adapted to the learner's learning pace since it is less cognitively demanding because the time to process this type of feedback is more flexible compared to the type required for speaking skill. Indeed, [7] claims that feedback leads learners to keep checking and restructuring language items that promote the construction of knowledge and the development of language production.

Regarding the types of feedback, [8] identified two main WCF types: direct and indirect. Direct feedback (DC) refers to explicit corrections while indirect feedback is implicit and does not provide correct forms [6]. Additionally, indirect feedback has two categories: indirect coded feedback (CF) which underlines and identifies the type of error with a symbol, while indirect uncoded feedback (UF) identifies the error with no other input [19].

Moreover, the strategy of feedback implementation is determinative because the combination of direct and indirect feedback maintains selective feedback by giving suggestions for corrections or just stating corrections directly [9]. Abbas and Tawfeeq [10] focused on establishing the positive effects of direct and indirect feedback on English writing accuracy, showing a closer relationship between error correction and the development of writing skill accuracy.

On the one hand, Bitchener and Knoch's [8] study found that both, direct and indirect feedback show positive effects in the short term, but more significant long-term effects are provided by direct error correction. Also, Vyatkina's [11]study compared direct feedback with coded feedback establishing that the first was more beneficial and determining that implicit feedback might mislead learners to wrong inferences and deductions.

On the other hand, Pham's [12] study determines that grammatical errors were reduced significantly after a process of indirect feedback showing a higher reduction of errors compared with direct feedback. However, the poor practice of reading shown by participants was a factor that influenced the success of feedback negatively, so it led this author to establish that feedback by itself has restrictions in the process of linguistics acquisition.

Elham [13] states that indirect feedback outstripped direct feedback. Likewise, Westmacott [14] study determined that indirect feedback was more beneficial as it encourages deeper cognitive processing and learning. The author also stated that indirect feedback reinforced grammatical knowledge and fostered students' autonomous learning.

Finally, different studies establish the positiveness of direct feedback and indirect feedback but it is important to highlight that there are other factors that affect the effectiveness of feedback such as motivation [15], perseverance, learning context, and individual differences [14].

2 Methodology

2.1 Study Design

A descriptive case study was carried out to analyze the effectiveness of combining different types of feedback (direct feedback, indirect coded and indirect uncoded) to improve writing skill in an EFL learner. This case study provides detailed data and analysis of the process of writing improvement through different types of feedback.

The participant of this study was an adult Spanish speaker whose age is around forty, with an English language background that belongs to the following aspects: level of A2[1] according to the European Common Framework of References for Languages [16]. The individual former English training that the learner received in the past was limited, additionally, it is valuable to highlight the anxiety about writing and speaking.

The current training process consisted of one-to-one classes since the participant's interest focused on achieving a B1 level immediately. The process took eight weeks, with forty hours in which direct feedback was used for four weeks, then indirect coded and indirect uncoded feedback were used in the following four weeks as can be seen in Table. 1.

The initial stage started with written narratives that used past simple, present simple, and present perfect (last relevant vacation trip). This stage permitted to determine the weaknesses in the writing skill and also to identify specific errors.

The direct feedback stage was developed through writing tasks about narrative stories that used different tenses such as past simple, present simple, and present perfect with a variety of themes (last vacation, memories, anecdote, semi-formal emails). Tasks in which errors were underlined and not only correct options were provided but also a detailed explanation about language use was given, constituting a refined direct explicit feedback.

Regarding the other four weeks, indirect feedback CF and UF were used. A writing task was developed weekly centered on a variety of themes (semi-formal emails, biographies, news reports, memories). The stage of CF took two weeks, this stage consisted of underlining errors and coding them with a specific symbol, e.g. Sp. For spelling. Then,

---

[1] The learner can understand sentences and frequently used expressions related to areas of most intermediate areas, such as shopping, family, employment, etc.; communicate in simple and routine tasks requiring a simple and direct exchange of information on familiar and routine matters; and describe in simple terms aspects of their background, immediate environment, and matters in areas of immediate need.

Table 1. Applied feedback process

Initial stage	Writing drafts	
First week	Direct feedback DC	5 h
Second week	Direct feedback DC	5 h
Third week	Direct feedback DC	5 h
Fourth week	Direct feedback DC	5 h
Fifth week	Indirect feedback: Coded CF	5 h
Sixth week	Indirect feedback Coded CF	5 h
Seventh week	Indirect feedback Uncoded UF	5 h
Eight week	Indirect feedback Uncoded UF	5h

during the last two weeks, UF was applied and devoted to a process in which the errors were underlined without any explicit correction or comment.

The categorization of the errors in this study was based on James's [17] classification of syntactic errors (phrase structure, clause errors, sentence errors, and prepositions); morphological errors (omission, misplacement, over inclusions, and misselection); discourse errors (sequential coherence and sentence coherence), and substantial errors (spelling, punctuation, and capitalization). While the semantic errors were categorized according to [18] into direct translation from L1 and collocation.

2.2 Data Analysis

The stage of analysis basically is related to focusing on the accuracy rate that every type of feedback provided. Direct feedback (DC), indirect coded feedback (CF), and indirect uncoded feedback (UF) gave different percentages that represent the number of corrections throughout this study. The following Table. 2. Presents the identified errors which are underlined:

Related to the semantic type, the most frequent identified errors are collocations (e.g. *see tv)* and direct translation from Spanish, keeping the L1 pattern in most cases e.g. *people use traditional clothes,* instead of *people wear traditional clothes.*

The syntactic errors included the subcategories of phrase structure, clause and sentence, and preposition errors e.g. *I could to know many cities. News about of business.*

Morphological errors included misselection and misordering by the wrong use of sentence pattern and wrong choice of language features e.g. *People can be better, you think.* Instead of *I think people can be better.* Omission errors with the wrong use of verbal derivations *(studing),* noun inflections *(place* instead of *places),* and the lack of subject pronoun *(is good to know).* The repeated errors of misselection responded to the

Table 2. Type of errors

Type of Errors	Sub-categories	Examples
Semantic errors	*Collocations*:	I <u>see</u> tv. I am <u>in</u> home
		the <u>name building is</u> Hilton
	Direct translation from L1	People <u>use</u> traditional clothes
		he was dismissed <u>of</u> his company
Syntactic errors	*Phrase structure*	You <u>can to see</u> the most important things
	Clause errors	I will live near a my work and <u>It</u> is <u>more big</u>
	Sentence errors	I could <u>to knew</u> many <u>cityies</u>
	Prepositions	I prefer to eat <u>in</u> home
		the concert is <u>near of</u> Hilton Colon hotel
		they have news <u>about of</u> business
Morphological errors	*Misselection and misordering*	People can better <u>you</u> think
		You can to see
	Omission:	-studing, " y" is omitted
		-I have many virtual class "es" omitted
		-is ok "it" omitted
		-is good to know "it" omitted
		-There are many touristic place(s) "s" omitted
	Misselection	-I <u>will want study</u>
		-let me <u>to</u> know news <u>of</u> you
		- Ecuador <u>have</u> many traditional festivals
		- I like <u>dance</u>
		- The restaurant <u>have</u> a great view
	Misplacement	People can better <u>you</u> think
	Over inclusion	-different<u>s</u> animals "s" extra
		-traditional<u>s</u> food "s" extra,
Discourse errors	*Sequential and sentence coherence*	-<u>People can learn use your money and better your life</u>
		-<u>I write for to tell you that now I am move to a new flat</u>
		-<u>The most important in enjoy all the people of the class</u>
Substantial errors	*Capitalization*:	<u>f</u>riday- <u>s</u>aturday / <u>j</u>uly / <u>i</u> like this movie / Best <u>R</u>egards
	Spelling	diferent,montain,beatiful,perfomed,funy, pandemy,schol,daughter,cityes

(*continued*)

Table 2. (*continued*)

Type of Errors	Sub-categories	Examples
	Punctuation	-Best regards(x) no comma -Hi John(x) no comma for salutation in emails - Some sentences without full stop

wrong choice of verbal derivations and prepositions, and the category of over-inclusion showed the wrong use of adjective derivations, e.g. *differents* instead of *different*.

Sequential and sentence coherence errors in the category of discourse were identified with the wrong use of verbal forms, possessive adjectives, and the lack and wrong use of verbal forms and nouns e.g. *I write for to tell you that now I am move to a new flat.*

Among substantial errors, capitalization, spelling and punctuation were identified e.g. *friday, saturday*, and the wrong use of *"i"* instead of *I*. Spelling for example *pandemi, school, beautiful,* and punctuation with the *omission of commas* and *full stops* especially in semi-formal contexts.

3   Discussion

Chen's [19] establishes that direct feedback is more effective for errors related to word choice, sentence structure, and discourse errors compared with other types of errors, and this study reveals similar findings. Therefore, incorporating direct feedback to improve writing skill might be valuable. Hedgcock and Lefkowitz [20], also determined that specific feedback is more beneficial than unspecified feedback on content because addressing errors in specific and explicit ways offers notorious improvement.

With this premise, Table. 3. Shows the number of morphological, semantic, and syntactic errors found in the first drafts compared with the number of improvements reached in the final writing task, which permits establishing the corrections in each category of errors after the process of DC. The percentage that belongs to the accuracy rate of correction is calculated according to the formula of [19] (Accuracy rate = Total No. of correct improvements of each error / Total No. of each type of errors × 100%).

These results show that direct feedback DC allowed the learner to correct 70 percent as average compared to the initial errors. In detail, the errors that were best addressed are related to prepositions (90%), direct translation from L1 (80%), phrase structure (80%), and misselection (83%). This significant improvement can be attributed to the explicit feedback provided through underlined errors, giving the correct options, and providing additional reinforcement with specific explanations. This strategy facilitated the learner not only to correct the errors but also to improve his knowledge related to morphology, semantics, and syntax to be able to apply it to different contexts in which using writing skill might be required.

Even though the accuracy rate reached in the other categories is lower than the previously mentioned, with percentages that go from 50 to 75, these percentages reveal a significant number of corrections in terms of improvement. It is that all types of errors

Table 3. Errors corrected with direct feedback DC

Types of errors	Subcategories	Errors in the first drafts	No. of correct improvements in the final writings	Accuracy rate of correction
Semantic Errors	collocations	8	6	75%
	direct translation from L1	5	4	80%
Syntactic Errors	Phrase structure	5	4	80%
	clause errors	7	5	71%
	sentence errors	8	3	75%
	prepositions	20	16	90%
Morphological Errors	Omission	26	13	50%
	misplacement	15	7	53%
	overinclusions	14	10	71%
	misselection	12	10	83%
Discourse errors	sequential coherence	6	3	50%
	sentence coherence	10	6	60%
Substantial errors	spelling errors	13	8	61%
	punctuation errors	10	7	70%
	capitalization	16	12	75%
Average				70%

were corrected by at least 50 percent. However, it is important to notice the substantial errors in the subcategories of spelling, punctuation, and capitalization, the accuracy rate of errors obtained percentages between 61 and 75. These percentages suggest that there is no total correction as expected, considering that these types of errors might not need remarkable teacher's comments and specific explanations.

According to the accuracy rate of correction shown in Table. 4., coded feedback CF facilitated the learner to correct errors by 58 percent on average. Indeed, working with errors of omission, over- inclusions, spelling, and capitalization in a more efficient way than DC, these errors were corrected 100 percent. CF consisted of underlining and identifying the type of error with a symbol (e.g., *Sp.* For spelling, *C.* for capitalization, *Oi.* For over inclusions, and *Om.* For omission). Therefore, it might be claimed that CF improves writing skills because the learner focuses more on those errors in which he had to work by himself, analyzing and establishing correct options. Lalande's [21] study supports these findings pointing out the advantage of CF compared to DC because it challenges the learner to establish corrections and works as an effective strategy.

Additionally, [22] established relevant differences between indirect coded feedback and direct feedback. Thus, the first type of feedback CF provided more efficient corrections than the second one DC.

Table 4. Indirect coded feedback CF

	Types of errors	Errors in the first drafts	No. of correct improvements in the revised drafts	Accuracy rate of correction
Semantic Errors	collocations	4	2	50%
	direct translation from L1	4	2	50%
Syntactic Errors	Phrase structure	4	1	25%
	clause errors	3	1	33%
	sentence errors	5	1	20%
	prepositions	4	3	75%
Morphological Errors	Omission	5	5	100%
	misplacement	3	2	66%
	Over-inclusions	4	4	100%
	misselection	5	1	20%
Discourse errors	sequential Coherence	2	0	0
	sentence coherence	5	0	0
Substantial errors	spelling	5	5	100%
	punctuation	3	2	66%
	capitalization	3	3	100%
Average				58%

In Table. 5. The results led to determine that Uncoded Feedback UF helped the learner in 45,16 percent on average to correct errors, highlighting that this type of feedback works better with spelling and capitalization corrections, obtaining an accuracy rate of 100 percent. However, in this type of feedback, the teacher limited the input to underline the errors. It seems to be as effective as CF, in which errors are underlined and identified with symbols for the corresponding category. For instance, the learner's engagement with the process of UF promotes independence, discrimination, and analysis, in order to determine the correct options.

Table. 5. Also shows a relevant finding related to the failure of improvement regarding discourse errors with the subcategories of overinclusion, and sequential coherence errors with UF. It might be because the learner needed not only to identify wrong utterances,

Table 5. Indirect uncoded feedback UF

Types of errors	Subcategories	Errors in the first drafts	No. of correct improvements in the revised drafts	Accuracy rate of correction
Semantic Errors	collocations	4	2	50%
	direct translation from L1	4	1	25%
Syntactic Errors	Phrase structure	4	2	50%
	clause errors	3	1	33%
	sentence errors	5	1	20%
	prepositions	4	1	25%
Morphological Errors	Omission	5	1	20%
	misplacement	3	1	33%
	Over-inclusions	4	0	0
Discourse errors	sequential Coherence	2	0	0
	sentence coherence	5	1	20%
Substantial errors	spelling	5	5	100%
	punctuation	3	2	66%
	capitalization	3	3	100%
Average				45.16

but also needed support to correct errors as well as additional explanations to accomplish communicational, and linguistic features correct use.

4 Conclusions

The results obtained by combining the three types of feedback, direct DC, indirect coded CF, and indirect uncoded UF contributed to writing accuracy showing outstanding benefits. Thus, DC facilitated a correction of 70 percent, CF corrected 58 percent, and UF gave a percentage of 45.16. These results of corrections obtained with DC might be related to the refined direct feedback in which specific and additional explanation was given by the teacher for each type of errors. Therefore, the learner achieved not only correct items but also the linguistic knowledge to apply in different communicative contexts.

DC is more effective related to semantic errors of direct translation from L1 with 80 percent; syntactic error of phrase structure with 80 percent and prepositions with 90 percent; morphological errors of misselection with 83 percent. It means that DC might be complemented with supportive reinforcement about the English language features, sharpening in that way the strategy of DC. Additionally, this type of feedback influences the whole writing task since most of the errors were corrected. Thus, it not only contributed to accuracy but also to fluency.

CF gave excellent results for the errors of omission, over inclusion, spelling, and capitalization. All of them reached 100% of correction. This type of feedback led the learner to focus more on those errors in which he had to work by himself, analyzing and stating correct options. This success must respond to the learner's cognitive maturity and metalinguistic awareness, which has helped the learner keep uptake toward the process, facilitating the development of the capacity needed to understand the process of feedback.

UF provided remarkable results related to the substantial spelling and capitalization errors, reaching 100%. It might be related to the significant learning that the learner accomplished with this type of feedback regarding specific errors. Consequently, the learner's engagement altogether with UF promoted not only the development of writing skill but also to grasp of independence, discrimination, and analysis that permitted him to be confident in making language choices. For instance, internal factors such as motivation, attitude, and commitment joined with the learner's cognitive maturity and metalinguistic awareness might influence the effectiveness of the different types of feedback.

It can be concluded that the incorporation of direct, indirect coded, and indirect uncoded feedback effectively empowered the writing process of the learner. Each type of feedback shows achievement for the different types of errors.

References

1. Srinivas, R.P.: The significance of writing skills in ell environment. ACADEMICIA: Int. Multi. Res. J.**9**(3), 5–17 (2019)
2. Teo, T.W., Choy, B.H.: in. In: Tan, O.S., Low, E.L., Tay, E.G., Yan, Y.K. (eds.) Singapore Math and Science Education Innovation. ETLPPSIP, vol. 1, pp. 43–59. Springer, Singapore (2021). https://doi.org/10.1007/978-981-16-1357-9_3
3. Abbas, M.A., Hogar, M.T.: The effects of direct and indirect corrective feedback on accuracy in second language writin. Engl. Lang. Teach. **11**(6), 33–37 (2018)
4. Hossein, N., Eva, K.: The Cambridge handbook of corrective feedback in second language learning and teaching, Cambridge University Press (2021)
5. Allman, B.: Effective and appropriate feedback for English learners: Principles of language acquisition, EdTech Books (2019)
6. Khaled, K., Hossein, N.: The effects of written corrective feedback: a critical synthesis of past and present research. Equinox Publish. **3**(1), 28–52 (2019)
7. Hyland, K., Hyland, F.: Feedback in second language writing: Contexts and issues, K. Hyland and F. Hyland, Eds., Cambridge university press (2019)
8. Bitchener, J., Knoch, U.: The contribution of written corrective feedback to language development: A ten month investigation. Appl. Linguis. **31**(2), 193–214 (2010)
9. Xialong, C., Lawrance, J.Z.: Teacher written feedback on English as a foreign language learners' writing: examining native and non-native English –speaking teachers' practices in feedback provision. Front. Psychol. **12**(1), 1–16 (2021)
10. Abbas, M.A., Tawfeeq, H.M.: The effects of direct and indirective corrective feedback on accuracy in second language writing. Canadian Center Sci. Educ. **11**(6), 33–40 (2018)

11. Nina, V.: The effectiveness of written corrective feedback in teaching beginning German. Foreign Lang. Ann. **43**, 671–689 (2010)
12. La Pham, A.: The effects of indirect feedback on grammatical errors in EFL learner writing. Europ. J. Eng. Lang. Teach. **6**(6), 153–167 (2021)
13. Eslami, E.: The effects of direct and indirect corrective feedback techniques on EFL students' writing. Procedia Soc. Behav. Sci. **98**, 445–452 (2014)
14. Westmacott, A.: Direct vs. indirect written corrective feedback: student perceptions. Íkala, revista de lenguaje y cultura **22**(1), 17–32 (2017)
15. M. Wahlström, "Effects of direct and indirect feedback on ESL/EFL writing. A literature review focusing on form," 2016
16. English, C.: About the Common European Framework of Reference for Languages (CEFR), Cambridge (2016)
17. James, C.: Errors in Language Learning and Use: Exploring error Analysis. Routledge, London (2013)
18. Rajab, A.S., Darus, S., Aladdin, A.: An investigation of semantic interlingual errors in the writing of Libyan English as Foreign Language learners. Arab World Eng. J. (AWEJ) **7**(4), 277–296 (2016)
19. Chen, W.: The Effects of Corrective Feedback Strategies on English Majors' Writing. Engl. Lang. Teach. **11**(11), 55–64 (2018)
20. Hedgcock, J., Lefkowitz, N.: Some input on input: two analyses of student response to expert feedback in L2 writing. Mod. Lang. J. **80**(3), 287–308 (1996)
21. Lalande, J.F.: The Modern Language Journal. Reducing Comp. Errors Exp. **66**(2), 140–149 (1982)
22. Erel, S.a.B.D.: Error treatment in L2 writing: a comparative study of direct and indirect coded feedback in Turkish EFL context. Sosyal Bilimler Enstitüsü Dergisi Sayı, **22**(1), 397–415 (2007)

Is It Possible to Do Early Stimulation in Virtuality? An Educational Experience for Child Cognitive Development

Jhojana Rosales-Ramos, Martha Rodriguez-Uzategui, and Ivan Iraola-Real(✉) (iD)

Universidad de Ciencias y Humanidades, 15314 Lima, Perú
ivanir701@hotmail.com

Abstract. Early stimulation is a means by which the infant receives external and internal stimuli with different techniques and activities, allowing its cognitive and motor development. Therefore, the purpose of this research was to analyze early stimulation in cognitive development in the infant stage. This research objective was oriented through the qualitative approach of biographical method in which the sample was non-probabilistic by convenience, selecting a specialist teacher of early stimulation; to whom a semi-structured interview was applied, whose answers were codified and categorized. The results show that adequate stimulation at an early age will allow for participatory, active, competent and social children capable of solving different situations. In addition, the interviewee referred to modeling the stimulation strategies using a doll and a video or Zoom session, and the parents subsequently imitated the stimulation exercises with their children.

Keywords: Cognitive Development · Early Childhood Education · Early Childhood Child

1 Introduction

Early stimulation allows the development of several areas of a child's body, even more if it is given from an early age through exercises and different activities (L'Ecuyer, L'Ecuyer, 2015). There are studies that show that stimulation can develop the cognitive level, which benefits the child's learning (Santi, 2019). In this way, early stimulation allows parents to develop a communication link with their child; according to the effectiveness of this practice, the child achieves enrichment by developing their skills, turning their home into a source of development (Mercado et al., 2015). Early stimulation has the function of helping to prevent and rehabilitate whoever needs it (Cifuentes, 2016). To perform a good stimulation, we must respect the age of the infant, since learning is not equal because several aspects are involved such as health development (healthy child control), socio-cultural environment and family environment (Martínez and Matamoros, 2010). The process of receiving early stimulation develops in the child skills that help him/her in his/her cognitive progress, preoperational, concrete operations, sensory-motor, etc. (Zambrano et al., 2018). Knowing this is not simply to stimulate, but to provide adequate stimulation, which favors the comprehensive development of the infant (Segretin et al., 2016).

M. Botto-Tobar et al. (Eds.): ICAT 2022, CCIS 1757, pp. 237–245, 2023.
https://doi.org/10.1007/978-3-031-24978-5_21

1.1 Contributions of Psychology and Neuropsychology for Early Stimulation

Likewise, the cognitive process starts from the maternal fetus until the full maturation of the human being is achieved, it does not depend on genetic patterns, but on psychosocial influences according to the environment where the individual develops (Hauser & Labin, 2018). From birth and the first months of life outside the mother's womb they will receive different stimuli that will be able to be captured as the sounds of the city, the warm voice of the mother, that is where the child will begin to recognize the phonetic sounds allowing a learning (Irisarri & Villegas, 2021). Cognitive development influences the lived experience that the individual has (Mercado, Jiménez & Palacios 2015). In the intellectual development of a child, one should always take into account both the evolutionary stage through which he/she went through and the stimulation he/she receives in the family environment (Paolini, Oiberman, & Mansilla, 2017). Through the experiences that the child has in its process of fertilization, birth and growth is necessary motivation such as the manipulation of objects among other aspects that will allow a timely development of all its learning capabilities (Irisarri & Villegas, 2021).

In this way, if the child experiences, observes and manipulates the different objects that can be provided to him or herself through curiosity about things, he or she will learn to form his or her own knowledge (Segura, García & Farje, 2021). Likewise, the importance of cognitive development will allow the child to develop integrally in the process of his life, enhancing skills and abilities that he will experience in the environment, which is why in the age of 0 to 2 years the child will have a process of teaching and learning (Santi, 2019). In this way, cognitive development is a process through which learning is born from socialization, interaction with the environment and the world around him, in this way the child perceives, organizes and acquires learning that allows him to grow both intellectually and maturely (Agudelo et al., 2017).

Early intervention is fundamental for the development of children, as it focuses on the mediation of cognitive abilities and stimulation of all areas of development by receiving different techniques (Corral, 2021). For example, the brain is an important organ because it is the one that will receive all the stimuli to form neural connections that allow it to respond to its needs (Albornoz & Guzmán, 2016). In this sense, skills express a series of energy, called intelligence, which allows solving problems satisfactorily, these skills are multiple and derive from the way in which the child encodes and processes (López, 2005).

The contributions of child neuropsychology are crucial for the comprehensive approach to complex disorders such as autism, Asperger syndrome or Rett syndrome, where their evaluation instruments have been widely used in the evaluation and diagnosis of psychomotor, language and cognitive impairment disorders, among others (Martínez & Matamoros, 2010). Knowing this, it is very important that a child is properly stimulated so that he/she can develop in society and school (Romero, Romero & Barboza, 2021). That is why the stimulation centers should always be training and updating themselves, they should carry out learning strategies in different aspects such as communication, affective and values so that they can form their own critical thinking and skills (Hauser & Labin, 2018). The child needs freedom to explore and practice the skills learned, without neglecting their safety (Ríos, Coral, Carrasco & Espinoza, 2021).

1.2 Importance of Early Stimulation

Numerous studies show that the lack of affective experiences in children can influence their development (L'Ecuyer, 2015). For healthy development to take place, stimuli must be present in quality and quantity (Segretin et al., 2016). Therefore, it can be said that the more stimulating the environment, the greater the possibility of achieving optimal behaviors (Hauser & Labin, 2018). Similarly, the implementation of the environment for stimulation must have a safe structure as well as materials and instruments that benefit the development of intellectual activities (Pérez, 2013). In addition, each child learns at his or her own pace and must have effective tools and strategies that motivate his or her learning (San Andrés et al., 2021).

The importance of stimulation is that the child achieves timely motor and cognitive development by creating situations so that he/she can find a solution and at the same time motivating him/her to comply with the curricular aspects according to his/her age (Ríos, Coral, Carrasco & Espinoza, 2021). Likewise, an early stimulation specialist should be empathetic, so that the child feels confident and is able to develop his or her potential (Albarracín, Paula & Moreno, 2021). It is considered that the stimulation professional should develop all skills by proposing games that allow the child to experiment and observe in order to find a solution (Andrade, 2020). As well as working the following techniques Shantal that has as a reference the mother's caresses on the face, neck, chest, abdomen, arms, hands, legs, feet and back. In second place; the Vojta method that is the locomotion technique that are stimuli that are given through pressures in the child's body scheme where the motor activity is going to be potentiated. Thirdly; the technique of gymnastics for babies which are simple movements performed by the child. In fourth place; the aquatic stimulation technique where it allows the child to increase the IQ by strengthening affective relationships (Gonzales, 2016). Likewise, the visual technique, where the gaze and gestures will be performed (Roselló et al., 2013). As well as the language technique; where exercises with the mouth muscles are worked. Finally, the music therapy technique; where music and different musical instruments are used (Flores, 2013). On the other hand, we can also use as techniques fine motor, gross motor, for socio-affective development cognition and language development (Fajardo, Pazmiño & Dávalos, 2018). Stimulation techniques favor the sensory, motor and even social development of the child since the child grows inside the mother's body (Peña, 2014). Likewise, the stimulation exercises that can be worked with infants are massages, caresses as well as reflex and language stimulation (Fajardo, Pazmiño & Dávalos, 2018).

1.3 Research Objectives

According to the above, the objective of this research is to analyze early stimulation in cognitive development in the infant stage and as specific objectives; it is expected to identify the importance of good stimulation in the first years of life. Finally, to identify the early stimulation techniques that influence cognitive development in the infant stage.

After explaining these objectives, the methodology to be used will be explained.

2   Methodology

This article is conducted under a qualitative approach (Leavy, 2017), and corresponds to the biographical method (Cornejo, 2006).

2.1   Participants

A non-probabilistic convenience sampling (Stratton, 2021) will be used, with a sample of one teacher specialized in early stimulation and two parents. The selected teacher has been developing early stimulation in the virtual modality; likewise, the parents have been following the instructions through different means of communication.

2.2   Instruments

For this research, the semi-structured interview was used as an instrument because it offers an acceptable degree of flexibility, while maintaining sufficient uniformity to achieve interpretations in accordance with the purposes of the study (Díaz, et al., 2013). In the semi-structured interview, eight open-ended questions were considered, in relation to the two categories extracted from the two specific objectives. For the first category, identify the importance of good stimulation in the first years of life, where the following question was asked: What do you mean by early stimulation, and could you elaborate on that? For the second category, Identify early stimulation techniques that influence cognitive development in the infant stage, the following questions were posed: Argument, Could you mention some of the techniques you use for the child's cognitive development? To validate our scientific article we consider the judgment of experts (Robles & Rojas, 2015). Thus, we will proceed with the discussion and results analysis.

3   Discussion Analysis and Results

After the instrument, the methodology and the identification of the participant, the results were interpreted according to the order of the categories.

3.1   The Importance of Stimulation in the First Years of Life

It is considered that stimulation in the first years of life is important, as it helps the child to improve the progress of their emotions and strengthen their body, promoting different activities, to improve the areas that need strengthening (Corral, 2021). Taking this into account, the teacher specialist in early stimulation referred to the following emerging categories.

A. What is Meant by Early Stimulation
Early stimulation involves a set of exercises and activities that contribute to the child's body development being more efficient in the first years of life (L'Ecuyer, 2015). However, in the present study, it was decided to ask the teacher what she understands by early stimulation, and she responded as follows:

[...]Early stimulation is a method that has a group of techniques with the objective of developing capacities and abilities in early childhood and also allows for the timely correction of problems identified in the development and growth of the child (DE-1).

Thus, early stimulation is an important method, since it seeks the development of skills and abilities through stimuli to awaken and maintain the child's interest (Irisarri & Villegas, 2021). As can be seen in the following category.

B. The Importance of Stimulation in the First years of Life
While it is true that stimulation in the first years of life will be fundamental, because it will allow a timely development and follow up on their cognitive development in the process of growth (Corral, 2021), as the stimulation teacher points out.

[...] early stimulation is very important, since it has been scientifically proven that it helps and supports the optimal development of the baby's brain, since it reinforces and strengthens the brain functions of the different areas [...] that is why the conditions in which the child grows are important, since through parental care and affection the child can develop a good stimulation (DE-1).

A fundamental part of this category is that the child is correctly stimulated, since with good stimulation in the first years of life and parental care he/she will grow strong and will be able to develop in society (Romero, et al., 2021). Demonstrating that stimulation is beneficial having as a link to the family as analyzed in the following subcategory.

C. Early Stimulation and Bonding
Early stimulation involves the affective and social bond of the infant, because it will depend on their family environment, so that their learning is more favorable (Hauser & Labin, 2018). For this reason, the following question was asked to the early stimulation specialist teacher.

[...] early stimulation is a space where the bond between parents and children is created and strengthened, since they are their guides to develop each technique [...] therefore, from the first moment the baby is born, the expressions of affection from the caregiver and parents flow, such as: words, caresses and looks [...] the child reads the signs of affection and learns to respond to them. Therefore, it is through these exchanges that the first affective bonds are formed (DE-1).

Regarding the above, in the previous paragraphs it can be said that stimulation in the first years of life is very important, thanks to this it allows parents to develop a bond of interaction with their child, obtaining achievements in their development of their potentials and skills (Mercado, et al., 2015). Finally, we will reflect on the last general category.

3.2 Stimulation Techniques in the Cognitive Development of the Child

It is considered that stimulation techniques will influence the child's basic learning functions, strengthening their abilities for their future development (Peña; 2014). Taking this into account, the teacher specialist in stimulation referred to the following emerging categories.

A. Techniques for the Cognitive Development of the Child

The techniques for the cognitive development of the child can be used in different ways; one of them is the Shantal method technique, referring to the mother's caresses, as well as the Vojta method, which is the stimulus locomotion technique; likewise, the gymnastics technique, as well as the aquatic stimulation technique (Gonzales, 2016). The visual technique (Roselló, et al., 2013). Language technique and music therapy technique (Flores, 2013). In this regard, the teacher interviewed mentioned the following:

> The techniques I use are varied and depend on the age and the area to be developed [...]. One of the most recurrent techniques for girls is the visual and auditory technique in the first years of life. In the visual area, the stimuli are very important, since they receive the invitation to explore the space, for example, to move the toy and smile at their mother. While the auditory stimulation is the opposite, where we work mostly on sounds such as the sound of the bell, rattles, papers, key chains, songs and words as I mentioned at the beginning [...] these techniques are important, since they will allow them to develop socially, emotionally and cognitively (DE-1).

Knowing the stimulation techniques, it is considered that the trained person should be prepared to assist different difficulties presented by the child in its development (Andrade, 2020). As can be seen in the second category.

B. Types of Children Who Should Receive Professional Cognitive Stimulation Techniques

The children to receive professional techniques are those who present some alterations in their development, these methods will determine what type of disability or disorder present to make an assessment with the appropriate instruments and strategies allowing early prevention (Martínez and Matamoros, 2010). A situation that has generated that many children receive good stimulation, as mentioned by the specialist in the following commentary.

> Early stimulation should be developed in all children in early childhood, to consolidate and reinforce the child's development as well as to correct in time any identified either risk or deficit [...] personally, as a professional if you have identified children with developmental deficits especially in the area of language and motor skills, which is the referral for specialized care (DE-1).

Through the affirmed testimony, it can be evidenced that children should receive appropriate techniques where they reinforce fine and gross psychomotor skills as well as the language area (Fajardo, et al., 2018). Although these will be represented in different exercises, as can be evidenced in the following subcategory.

C. Exercises to Stimulate the CHILD'S Cognitive Development

The stimulation exercises provided to the infant of body contact are very important, as this helps the child to develop different areas. (Fajardo, et al. 2018). Accordingly, the teacher specialist in early childhood children made the following comment.

> The stimulation exercises vary according to the age of the child, from birth we start with words, songs, massages, using toys and different sounds. For example, now in the virtual world it has been a little complicated to provide stimulation, first we started with videos sending the parent where we used a doll as an instrument as a guide, gradually it was used through the zoom platform being hard work (DE-1).

It is considered that in order to perform the exercises, a safe space should be available that allows children to complete their activities in a peaceful and safe manner (Meléndez, 2019). As can be evidenced in the following emerging category.

D. The Early Stimulation Environment and Recommended Materials

The stimulation environment must have a good infrastructure, it must be clean, illuminated with adequate ventilation, and it must have all the appropriate instruments and materials according to the age of the child (Pérez, 2013). As pointed out by the teacher interviewed.

> [...] The environment has to be a ventilated and quiet area; the more colors the better to attract the baby's attention [...]. The materials that I can recommend and that are easily accessible are: construction materials, musical instruments, sounds, sponges, pens, primers with large images, glue, flour, plasticine, tempera [...]. Remember that all materials are used as a stimulation tool to reinforce and strengthen the areas that the child requires (DE-1).

Finally, early stimulation techniques, exercises and environment are aimed at preventing different disabilities in early childhood. That is why the only way to avoid difficulties in the future is to use different instruments to achieve a good cognitive development (Herrero, 2000).

4   Conclusions and Future Works

It is concluded that early stimulation promotes the child's physical and social abilities. In addition, it prevents cognitive and psychological alterations. It also detects learning problemsand developmental disorders, and favors family bonding. In this sense, stimulation in the first years of life for the specialist teacher is fundamental because it prevents different difficulties or disabilities. For future research work we intend to develop the interviews in person, with a greater number of people such as parents, children and specialists, we can work with quantitative or mixed methodology since they will provide us with more information in our research to be developed.

Acknowledgment. We thank God for giving us one more day of life, to carry out this research work that has been achieved under the constant advice of the research teacher. Likewise, to our families who were our engine and motive, as they motivate us every day to fulfill our dreams.

References

Agudelo, L., Pulgarin, L., Tabares, C.: La Estimulación Sensorial en el Desarrollo Cognitivo de la Primera Infancia. Revista Fuentes. **19**(1), 73–83 (2017)

Andrade, A.: El Juego y su Importancia Cultural en el Aprendizaje de los niños en Educación Inicial. Revista Ciencia e Investigación **5**(2), 132–149 (2020)

Albarracín, A., Paula, L., Moreno, J.: Recursos Pedagógicos en la Actividad Acuática. (1 ed.). Sb AIDEA. (2021)

Albornoz, E., Guzmán, M.: Desarrollo cognitivo mediante estimulación en niños de 3 años. Centro desarrollo infantil nuevos horizontes. Quito, Ecuador. Revista Universidad y sociedad, **8**(4), 184–190 (2016)

Cifuentes, E.: Estimulación temprana y desarrollo cognitivo. [tesis de licenciatura, Universidad Rafael Landívar]. (2016). Homepage, http://recursosbiblio.url.edu.gt/tesisjcem/2016/05/22/Velasquez-Yeritza.pdf, Last Accessed 21 Nov 2021

Cornejo, M.: El Enfoque Biográfico: Trayectorias. Desarrollos Teóricos y Perspectivas. Psykhe Santiago **15**(1), 95–106 (2006)

Corral, P.: La estimulación temprana como técnica creativa para el desarrollo psicomotor en niños y niñas de 1 a 3 años en la comunidad urbana Cerro Guayabal. [tesis de maestría, Universidad San Gregorio de Portoviejo] (2021). Homepage, http://repositorio.sangregorio.edu.ec/handle/123456789/1915, Last Accessed 1 Oct 2021

Díaz, L., Torruco, U., Martínez, M., Varela, M.: La entrevista, recurso flexible y dinámico. Investigación en educación médica **2**(7), 162–167 (2013)

Fajardo, E., Pazmiño, A., Dávalos, M.: La estimulación temprana como factor fundamental en el desarrollo infantil. Espirales Revista Multidisciplinaria de Investigación **2**(14), 25–37 (2018)

Flores, J.: Efectividad del programa de Estimulación temprana en el desarrollo psicomotor de un niño de 0 a 3 años. Revista Ciencia y Tecnología **3**(9), 38–49 (2013)

Gonzales, E.: Método de Estimulación Psicomotriz temprana en los infantes de 0 a 2 años. Revista Virtual Perspectivas en la Primera Infancia. **1**(4), 1–25 (2016)

Hauser, M., Labin, A.: Evaluación cognitiva de niños: un estudio comparativo en San Luis. Argentina. Revista Costarricense de Psicología **37**(1), 27–40 (2018)

Herrero, A.: Intervención psicomotriz en el Primer Ciclo de Educación Infantil: estimulación de situaciones sensoriomotores. Revista Interuniversitaria de Formación del Profesorado 37, 87–102 (2000)

Irisarri, N., Villegas, G.: Aportaciones de la Neurociencia Cognitiva y revista: El Enfoque Multisensorial a la adquisición de segundas lenguas en la etapa escolar marco ELE. Revista de Didáctica Español Lengua Extranjera **5**(32), 1–20 (2021)

Leavy, P.: Research Design: Quantitative, Qualitative, Mixed Methods, Arts-Based, and Community-Based Participatory Research Approaches. The Guilford Press, London (2017)

L'Ecuyer, C.: La estimulación temprana fundamentada en el método doma en la educación infantil en España: bases teóricas, legado y futuro. Revista de la Facultad de Educación de Albacete. **30**(2), 137–153 (2015)

López, E.: La educación emocional en la educación infantil. Revista interuniversitaria de Formación del Profesorado **19**(3), 153–167 (2005). https://www.redalyc.org/articulo.oa?id=274119 27009

Martínez, Á., Matamoros, Á.: Neuropsicología infantil del desarrollo: Detección e intervención de trastornos en la infancia. Revista Iberoamericana de Psicología 3(2), 59–68 (2010)

Mercado, U., Jiménez, G., Palacios, P.: Estimulación temprana en niños de desarrollo típico. Investigación y Práctica en Psicología del desarrollo 1, 269–274 (2015)

Paolini, C., Oiberman, A., Mansilla, M.: Desarrollo cognitivo en la primera infancia: influencia de los factores de riesgo biológicos y ambientales. Subjetividad y Procesos Cognitivos 21(2), 162–183 (2017)

Pérez, X.: Implementación de un ambiente para la estimulación temprana que ayude a desarrollar la pre-escritura en niños/as de 3 a 5 años del Centro Infantil del Buen Vivir la Casa de los Pequeños Traviesos Ubicado en la Parroquia El Corazón Canton Pangua provincia de Cotopaxi periodo 2011 - 2012. [tesis de licenciatura, Universidad Técnica de Cotopaxi] (2013). Homepage, http://repositorio.utc.edu.ec/jspui/bitstream/27000/1694/1/T-UTC-1568.pdf, Last Accessed 3 Aug 2022

Peña, L.: La Estimulación temprana como técnica influyente de la adquisición de las funciones básicas de los niños de 12 a 18 meses del CIBV " Carolina Terán" MIES". [tesis de licenciatura, Universidad Central del Ecuador] (2014). Homepage, http://www.dspace.uce.edu.ec/bitstream/25000/7670/1/T-UCE-0007-72pi.pdf, Last Accessed 9 Aug 2021

Pérez, M.: Formación profesional docente y calidad del servicio educativo en instituciones educativas de educación inicial, Distrito Ciudad Nueva de Tacna, 2018. Qualitas Investigaciones. 7(1), 12–18 (2021)

Ríos, R., Coral, S., Carrasco, O., Espinoza, C.: La Estimulación Temprana como base para los procesos de Enseñanza-Aprendizaje en la Educación Infantil. Revista Ciencia Digital. 1(5), 252–271 (2021)

Romero, J., Romero, R., Barboza, L.: Programa instruccional basado en la neurociencia para mejorar el aprendizaje en los estudiantes universitarios. Revista San Gregorio. 1(46), 16–29 (2021)

Robles, P., Rojas, M.: La validación por juicio de expertos: dos investigaciones cualitativas en Lingüística aplicada. Revista Nebrija de Lingüística (2015). Homepage, https://revistas.nebrija.com/revista-linguistica/article/view/259/227, last accessed 2021/11/21

Roselló, A., Baute, B., Ríos, M., Rodriguez, S., Quintero, M., Lázaro, Y.: Estimulación temprana en niños de baja visión. Revista Habanera de Ciencias Médicas. 12(4), 659–670 (2013)

Santi, F.: Educación: La importancia del desarrollo infantil y la educación inicial en un país en el cual no son obligatorios. Revista Ciencia Unem. 12(30), 143–159 (2019)

San Andrés, E., Macías, F., Mieles, G.: La retroalimentación como estrategia para mejorar el proceso de enseñanza-aprendizaje. Revista Científica Dominio de las ciencias. 7(4), 57–69 (2021)

Segretin, M., Hermida, M., Prats, L., Fracchia, C., Colombo, J., Lipina, S.: Estimulación de procesos cognitivos en niños de 4 años: comparaciones entre formatos individual y grupal de intervención. Revista Argentina de Ciencias del Comportamiento. 8(3), 48–61 (2016)

Segura, I., García, J., Farje, J.: Nivel de desarrollo de las nociones de seriación y clasificación de los estudiantes, Amazonas, Perú. Revista de Investigación Científica UNTRM: Ciencias Sociales y Humanidades. 4(1), 24–31 (2021)

Stratton, S.: Population research: convenience sampling strategies. Prehosp. Disaster Med. 36(4), 373–374 (2021). https://doi.org/10.1017/S1049023X21000649

Zambrano, D., Mendoza, E. & Camacho, M.: Estrategias pedagógicas en el desarrollo cognitivo. [Ponencia] In Memorias del IV Congreso Internacional de Ciencias Pedagógicas de Ecuador: La formación y superación del docente:" desafíos para el cambio de la educación en el siglo XXI" 2018, Bolivia, Quito (2018). Homepage, https://dialnet.unirioja.es/servlet/articulo?codigo=7220658, Last Accessed 2 Oct 2021

Teacher Digital Literacy and Its Influence on Learning Sessions at the Initial Level in Schools in the Context of Covid-19

Estefani Agüero Montes, Paola Badillo Acuña, Jherly Torres Pinedo, and Ivan Iraola-Real[(⊠)] ⓘ

Universidad de Ciencias y Humanidades, 15314 Lima, Perú
{paobadilloa,jhetorresp}@uch.pe, ivanir701@hotmail.com

Abstract. The objective of this study was to determine the influence of teachers' digital literacy on the development of learning sessions at the early education level in a public school in northern Lima (Peru) in the context of Covid-19. Using a qualitative case study approach, a semi-structured interview was applied to teachers with experience in teaching early childhood education. The results show that digital literacy influences the development and methodology of visual, auditory and kinesthetic learning sessions, since it is known that infants are in the digital era where many of them know how to use a variety of tools and applications. Finally, digital resources are crucial in the performance of teachers and in the cognitive process of children.

Keywords: Information literacy · Teaching method · Learning sessions · Technology tools

1 Introduction

Currently, digital literacy is necessary because it involves the knowledge of the use of different technological tools for people to perform productively at the work level (Cam & Kiyci, 2017). This digital literacy originates in people in the family environment mainly in the infant stage, however, when interacting with technology, an adequate management must be presented by their parents and teachers who are main actors in the child's learning (Sergeevna, 2020). Children at this stage tend to observe and soak up every piece of information presented to them in their social environment since through these experiences they can be guided in case of risk or doubts they have when making use of these technological tools (Enemark, 2020).

The ability to know the digital tools is not only to be able to choose the one that suits the needs, it is also to know the purpose it has and how it can help in the educational field; it is for this reason that the teacher must be able to know the technological tools and how to develop them taking into account the context of their students (Aslan, 2020). It is known that technology is something that is used on a daily basis; that is why, the digital divide is defined as individuals, families, businesses and geographical areas with different socioeconomic levels have access to opportunities and use of information and

M. Botto-Tobar et al. (Eds.): ICAT 2022, CCIS 1757, pp. 246–253, 2023.
https://doi.org/10.1007/978-3-031-24978-5_22

communication technologies either for work, leisure and learning of children (Quaicoe & Pata, 2020).

1.1 VAK Model and the Types of Learning Sessions

With respect to the perception of human learning, better ways of acquiring information are recognized through the VAK model which details perception conduits: auditory, visual and kinesthetic.

First, visual sessions help individuals to capture information through graphic, physical or virtual representations that attract the attention of observers (Reyes, Céspedes & Molina, 2017). For example, the dramatization of stories is a dynamic strategy that helps in the learning of younger children as they can imagine and create abstract thoughts (Rahiem, 2021). In the application of a learning session for preschool children, augmented reality images are projected, allowing them to observe and become familiar with the alphabet and then make strokes that allow them to identify what has been instructed (Pan et al., 2021).

Secondly, auditory sessions are perceived in a successive and structured way in which each human being can obtain information orally where a sender and receiver are located to capture the message (Reyes, et al., 2017). For example, the experiences acquired in their social context are shared with their peers and teachers, which makes it easier for them to recreate and fantasize their own stories giving a more fun sense to their early childhood education since it is known that early childhood children are like little sponges that absorb everything they can experience from home (Rahiem, 2021). Music is a resource that provides preschool children with the stimulation of active listening that influences social skills. That is, infants pay daily attention to the sounds caused by TV, Radio, and Internet among others (Koops & Wendt, 2019).

Finally, we have the kinesthetic learning sessions that refer to the ability to dominate the whole body in a physical action because it requires a lot of concentration, combination, energy and ability of the child to achieve some exercise. For the improvement of a kinesthetic learning session, a system called EXERGAME has been developed, which is used as an instrument to perform movement that can intervene in this program and this would facilitate the development of kinesthetics in children, as it will help their body balance and coordination. In today's world everything is now technology and children are more related to it, that is why schools are using it to perform physical activities (Abdurrahman & Manolya, 2020). What can also be used would be dance as it is already an aesthetic activity and contains different exercises that requires performing and reinforcing movements with the body; besides being able to perfect their coordination in a wide space and it also helps in improving their imagination as they can elaborate their steps (Gulsum, 2018).

1.2 Research Objectives

Based on the above, the following objective is proposed in this research: to determine the influence of teachers' digital literacy on the development of learning sessions at the early education level in public schools in northern Lima (Peru) in the context of Covid-19. Additionally, we propose to identify the influence of teachers' digital literacy on the development of auditory, visual and kinesthetic learning sessions at the early education level.

The following methodology is proposed for this study:

2 Methodology

The present article is a qualitative approach study in which data is collected for a definition and perception of something in particular that emphasizes the research analysis (Iño, 2018). Therefore, the case study is based on being able to define a particular event or fact that promotes some conflict that is related to an individual (Roell, 2019).

2.1 Participants

The participants were 2 early childhood education teachers who work in a public school located in northern Lima and belong to the regular basic education system (EBR). One of the teachers is 46 years old; she has specializations in early stimulation and intervention and speech therapy; her professional degree is in early education with 21 years of teaching experience applying visual, auditory and kinesthetic learning sessions. On the other hand, the second teacher is 59 years old; her professional degree is a doctor of early education with 40 years of teaching experience applying visual, auditory and kinesthetic learning sessions. The intentional sampling technique was used (Otzen and Manterola, 2017).

2.2 Instruments

Semi-Structured interview: this interview is a technique that gathers personal information from the interviewees where open and closed questions arise to know the criteria and positions of the topic to be developed (batista, lourenço & nascimento, 2017). In the present study, a semi-structured interview guide was designed with 6 open questions distributed in 3 categories extracted from the 3 specific objectives. For the first category digital literacy of teachers in the development of visual learning sessions, the following example item was posed "how did digital literacy influence you to develop visual learning sessions? Could you explain it?". For the second category of teachers' digital literacy in the development of auditory learning sessions, the following example item was proposed "how did digital literacy influence your ability to develop auditory learning sessions, could you explain?". For the third category digital literacy of teachers in the development of kinesthetic learning sessions, the following example item was posed "how did digital literacy influence you to be able to develop kinesthetic learning sessions-could you explain?".

3 Analysis and Discussion of Results

Once the methodology, participants and instruments have been described, we proceed to analyze and discuss the results through coding and triangulation procedures. This process will be guided through the categories, sub-categories, emerging categories, etc.

3.1   Teachers Digital Literacy in the Development of Visual Learning Sessions

Teacher literacy is important because it allows them to have the knowledge of the use of technological tools, thus being able to exercise their work adapting to the students (Aslan, 2020). In this way, the development of visual learning sessions in early education could be facilitated, which would consist of the projection of digital images that contribute to their learning (Pan, et al., 2021). Considering this, the subcategories related to the development and methodology of the visual learning sessions are analyzed as follows.

A. Influence of digital literacy on the development of visual learning sessions
Visual sessions require the use of graphic, physical and visual representations to have the attention of learners (Reyes, et al., 2017), for these reasons, teachers are required to handle digital tools as discussed below in the testimony of the interviewees.

It has forced almost all of us teachers to acquire a new digital culture I think this has always been the Achilles heel of education in our country [...] and it has influenced my way of teaching, now I have discovered that I like to teach by Zoom [...] new techniques, new methodologies [...] we have learned to coexist, above all, it has cost us adults more because children are digital natives (Teacher 1: 4–23).

Facilitating different tools to make them more important, interactive, fun and innovative by bringing together work with zoom, PPT and DRIVE (Docent 5: 32–33).

B. Digital literacy influence of visual sessions methodology
The importance of the imagination of children in early education attributes to the interpretation of characters they hear in oral texts such as fables or stories (Rahiem, 2021), for these reasons it is required that teachers handle digital methodologies as discussed below in the testimony of interviewees.

The platforms that the government has tried to install as I learn at home on the radio, television and on the web [...] new strategies even to my way of teaching many of us are on platforms like Google Meet, Zoom some have trained us we have had to update ourselves [...] the updates handle different programs like Classroom [...] they know how to handle even better than moms sometimes the phones the Smartphones; therefore, they connect by themselves they edit their videos their audios [...] we have learned from YouTube videos, we have learned to use tutorials, to use virtual games, the alphabet soup of so many games and so many applications [...] now it is something normal, you have to communicate with the parents through a video call, a call, a Zoom [...] this emotional support through virtual means has been something that we teachers have achieved (Teacher 1: 40–86).

It allowed me to adapt some methodologies for virtual use helping in a greater participation of children; they enjoy music and virtual games (Teacher 5: 96–97).

According to the testimonies, it can be concluded that for the teachers, becoming digitally literate has been essential to develop visual learning sessions in which they, students and parents have had to adapt to technologies using various tools, Classroom (Google., 2021.a), Google Meet (Google., 2021.b), Zoom (2021), YouTube, etc., in which students participated with great autonomy. Similar results are expected to be identified in the following category.

3.2 Teachers Digital Literacy in the Development of Auditory Learning Sessions

The origin of digital literacy in teachers is shown in relation to the management of these new technologies as it forms a fundamental part in the child's learning as a guide to their processes in technology (Sergeevna, 2020). Oral communication in auditory sessions is captured through information emitted from one to another person (Reyes, et al., 2017). Considering this, the subcategories related to the development and methodology of auditory learning sessions are analyzed below.

A. Influence of digital literacy on the development of auditory learning sessions
In early childhood children achieve habits of their social environment where they often include the creation and imagination of events spontaneously which facilitates and facilitates an entertaining education (Rahiem, 2021), for these reasons it is required that teachers handle digital tools as discussed below in the testimony of the interviewees.

> Developing auditory sessions via Zoom is a bit complicated, not everyone has the equipment, the internet band, the areas where I work, which is Carabayllo, 70% of my children do not have a computer [...] teaching this child through a cell phone where they can watch videos or listen well, singing is very difficult, but we are struggling [...] the platform involves many sessions, often with puppetry, tambourine and active listening [...] We send audios but there is no contact as before, but we have to adapt (Teacher 1: 103–110).

> Employing sound videos and audios of nature beings using Zoom, Google Meet, videos, screen recordings and audios via WhatsApp (Docent 5: 115–116).

B. Digital literacy influence of listening session methodology
The sound of music is a tool that helps active listening in the early childhood stage, which benefits the development in its context. On the other hand, we know that the media transmit sound waves that reach the auditory sense in an informative, descriptive or recreational way (Koops & Wendt, 2019), for these reasons it is required that teachers handle digital methodologies as discussed below in the testimony of the interviewees.

> I use videos, applications where I download stories, poems where I have learned to look for stories that go according to the theme that have music, rhythm and an audio with an appropriate tone of voice [...] The zoom application and WhatsApp groups [...] audios, photos, videos that are not too big since everyone does not have the capacity to see everything [...] searching Google for information [...]

we have learned and improved our teaching practice [...] downloading videos from YouTube and converting them to send them by WhatsApp has helped me to facilitate materials for my children (Teacher 1: 116–125).

In a certain aspect, it limits the close affective work and interaction with peers in this synchronous and asynchronous teaching, the use of technological resources such as class recording was possible (Teacher 5: 133–134).

According to the testimonies, it can be concluded that for the teachers, teaching digitally was demanding but not impossible. So they can develop auditory learning sessions in which they use materials that go according to the topics of each class, looking for clear audios and that are of short duration so that their students can listen to them. So teachers improve their performance in learning activities provided by various resources such as YouTube (2021) and WhatsApp (2021), which are very entertaining for children. Similar results are expected to be identified in the following category.

3.3 Teachers Digital Literacy in the Development of Kinesthetic Learning Sessions

Digital literacy covers many areas, but centrally it is required in some way or another to know the digital tools that we can use so that we can identify each purpose that we must achieve with students (Aslan, 2020). To this end, it is known that kinesthetic learning sessions are understood to work together with the whole body strengthening concentration and coordination (Abdurrahman & Manolya, 2020). Based on this, the following subcategories are analyzed in relation to the development, as well as the methodology of kinesthetic learning sessions.

A. Influence of digital literacy on the development of kinesthetic learning sessions. In the kinesthetic learning sessions the use of different activities can be done, but one of them could be what would be the dance since in this activity the whole movement of the body is used (Gulsum, 2018). That is why teachers should be well trained to be able to strengthen these sessions as analyzed below in the testimony of the interviewees.

Kinesthetic learning has been very difficult because the child needs games, not competitive games, but cooperative games [...] the dances, the relationships with psychomotor activities, that is a work that has been well detailed in inicia [...] even in Aprendo en Casa there is a guide called "lectura y movimiento" which is on Tuesdays and Thursdays where the platform tries to involve reading with psychomotor activities [...] they dramatize songs, they try to dance, sing, move, play games with the family, we have tried to reinforce that side [...] learning sessions where we have developed how to have fun with the family [...] send videos, audios, dramatize songs as a family [...] knowing space, time and space notions is basic for them to achieve good reading, writing and mathematical notions can be acquired [...] explores with their bodies [...] through zoom, videos, video calls [...] sessions that are important [...] through zoom we also do gymkhanas at Zoom level, building towers, building little glasses, dancing, jumping (Teacher 1: 135–159).

Conduct research on programs, spaces to implement, recording, editing videos using rhythm to motivate movement (Docent 5: 187–188).

B. Digital literacy influence of kinesthetic session methodology.
For the help of the kinesthetic sessions, the use of a video game called EXERGAME could be used, since this game is carried out by following the steps that we can observe on the screen (Abdurrahman & Manolya, 2020), so that the child can develop and the teacher can take advantage of this tool in her class, as analyzed below in the testimony of the interviewees.

Carrying out activities with common materials from home made it easier for me to do the kinesthetic classes synchronously and to see the children in real time to be able to give feedback (Teacher 5: 194–195).

Finally, for the teachers, distance learning digitally was complicated because they wanted the infants to be in movement for the process of their kinesthetic learning sessions. So they made use of the platform I learn at home that involves reading and movement in their weekly schedule. Also, the help of the Zoom application (2021) where the teacher will have to use the strategies that capture the attention of their students by editing videos, looking for an appropriate space and playful activities for the good development of the learning process.

4   Conclusions and Future Works

In conclusion, digital literacy in early childhood teachers influences the visual, auditory and kinesthetic learning sessions favoring in them a teaching that achieves the integral development of their students through new technological resources that at the beginning was a little complicated to adapt to this new learning modality. That is to say that these resources achieve in the child an interaction similar to those that were made in person knowing that for them it has been easy to be digital natives and meanwhile for teachers it was the opposite because they had to train continuously in the use of digital tools such as Zoom, Google Meet, Whatsapp, Classroom, YouTube, among others that facilitate and accommodate their learning activities, their social, economic and emotional context by parents who are important for the fulfillment of their academic responsibilities. It is recommended for future research to conduct live interviews as it is enriching to hear the experiences of the interviewee and to provide relevant information for the use of research to be developed.

Acknowledgment. This research has been developed thanks to the teachers who participated in the interviews and to our families, who with a lot of effort encourage us in our professional training as future teachers.

References

Abdurrahman, D., Manolya, A.: The effect of exergame education on balance in children. Malays. Online J. Educ. Technol. **8**(3), 100–107 (2020)

Aslan, S.: Analysis of digital literacy self-efficacy levels of pre-service teachers. Int. J. Technol. Educ. **4**(1), 57–67 (2020)

Batista, E., Lourenço, L., Nascimento, A.: A entrevista como técnica de investigação na pesquisa qualitativa. Revista Interdisciplinar Científica Aplicada. **11**(3), 23–38 (2017). Homepage, https://rica.unibes.com.br/rica/article/view/768/666, Last Accessed 8 Dec 2021

Cam, E., Kiyci, M.: Perceptions of prospective teachers on digital literacy. Malays. Online J. Educ. Technol. **5**(4), 29–44 (2017). Homepage, https://files.eric.ed.gov/fulltext/EJ1156711.pdf, Last Accessed 30 Aug 2021

Enemark, T.: Young children's tablet computer play, american journal of play, **12**(2), 216–232 (2020). https://files.eric.ed.gov/fulltext/EJ1255237.pdf, Last Accessed 22 Aug 2021

Google. Obtén más tiempo para enseñar e inspirar a los alumnos con Classroom (2021a). https://edu.google.com/intl/es-419/products/classroom/, Last Accessed 14 Sep 2021

Google. Videoconferencias seguras para todos (2021b). Homepage, https://meet.google.com/, Last Accessed 30 Aug 2021

Gulsum, B.: Examination of body composition, flexibility, balance, and concentration related to dance exercise. Asian J. Educ. Training. **4**(3), 210–215 (2018). https://doi.org/10.20448/journal.522.2018.43.210.215

Iño, W. Investigación educativa desde un enfoque cualitativo. Voces de la Educación. **3**(6) 93–110 (2018). https://dialnet.unirioja.es/servlet/articulo?codigo=6521971, Last Accessed 23 Sep 2021

Koops, L., Wendt, K.: Listening lessons in the early childhood music classroom. General Music Today **32**(3), 1–3 (2019)

Quaicoe, J.S., Pata, K.: Teachers' digital literacy and digital activity as digital divide components among basic schools in Ghana. Educ. Inf. Technol. **25**(5), 4077–4095 (2020). https://doi.org/10.1007/s10639-020-10158-8

Otzen, T., Manterola, C.: Técnicas de Muestreo sobre una Población a Estudio. Int. J. Morphol. **35**(1), 227–232 (2017)

Pan, Z., López, M., Li, C., Liu, M.: Introducing augmented reality in early childhood literacy learning. Research in Learning Technology, 29 (2021). Homepage, doi.https://doi.org/10.25304/rlt.v29.2539, Last Accessed 21 Nov 2021

Rahiem, M.D.H.: Storytelling in early childhood education: Time to go digital. Int. J. Child Care Educ. Policy **15**(1), 1–20 (2021). https://doi.org/10.1186/s40723-021-00081-x

Reyes, L., Céspedes, G., Molina, J.: Tipos de Aprendizaje y Tendencias según modelo VAK. TIA , **5**(2), 237–242 (2017)

Roell, C.: Using a Case Study in the EFL Classroom. In English Teaching Forum, **57**(4), 24–33 (2019). https://files.eric.ed.gov/fulltext/EJ1236098.pdf, Last Accessed 2 Oct 2021

Sergeevna, E.: Digital literacy of future preschool teachers. J. Soc. Stud. Educ. Res. **11**(1), 230–253 (2020)

WhatsApp. (2021). Mensajería confiable. https://www.whatsapp.com/ Last Accessed 11 Nov 2021

YouTube. (2021). Descubre, reproduce y comparte tus vídeos y música favoritos. https://www.youtube.com/, Last Accessed 30 Oct 2021

Zoom. (2021). Comprehensive Guide to Educating Through Zoom. https://www.zoom.us/docs/en-us/childrens-privacy.html, Last Accessed 2 Oct 2021

Consumer's Representation of Short Food Supply Chains: The Case of a Peruvian Government Program

Rosmery Ramos-Sandoval[1]([⊠]) [iD] and Jano Ramos-Diaz[2] [iD]

[1] Universidad Tecnológica del Perú, Lima, Peru
rramoss@utp.edu.pe
[2] Universidad Privada del Norte, Lima, Peru

Abstract. The quality of agri-food products is of interest because new food supply chains play a critical role in farmers, agricultural markets and society. Social media is fast becoming a key instrument to gather users' perceptions on food choices and consumption. Therefore, the present study aimed to explore consumer´s representation of short food supply chains in the context of "De la Chacra a la Olla" program ("From the Farm to the Pot, for its translation in English). By using thematic analysis, this study found three themes: "food wellbeing", "local valorization" and "food intermediaries." This study provides new insights and possibilities between producers and consumers communication via social media.

Keywords: Social media · Twitter · Short food supply chains · Thematic analysis

1 Introduction

The quality of agri-food products has shown an increased interest in the last thirty years. For example, Marsden and Arce [1] noticed that agricultural markets and local farming systems were driven by food retailers from a competitive perspective. However, a major problem of this is the overconsumption and unhealthy food choices [1, 2]. Therefore, there is a necessity to develop an alternative food chain paradigm in order to understand the importance of nearby and healthy food networks.

The term short food supply chains (SFSCs) refers to "a form of trade which is based on the direct sale of fresh or seasonal products without intermediaries -or with a minimum of intermediaries between producers and consumers" [3, p. 7]. For Rabanoldo and Arosio [4], there are three characteristics in SFSCs: low or non-existent intermediation; geographical proximity; and strengthening of social capital and trust. These definitions highlight consumers as key actors because of their demand for authentic, healthy, and seasonal products. It also describes a closer proximity between producers-consumers, direct supply chain treatment and equity in trading.

M. Botto-Tobar et al. (Eds.): ICAT 2022, CCIS 1757, pp. 254–264, 2023.
https://doi.org/10.1007/978-3-031-24978-5_23

1.1 Short Food Supply Chains

SFSCs are a major area of interest in the field of the agricultural market. For instance, recent evidence suggests that SFSCs may have the potential to achieve more sustainable food chains [5–7], improve food distribution [8, 9] and enhance consumers and producers communication channels [10–13]. However, questions have been raised about alternative consumption patterns in SFSCs such as social media.

New food supply chains play a critical role in agriculture and society. It has previously been observed that new food supply chains may have the potential to strengthen the relationship between producers and consumers [2, 14, 15]. Overall, these studies highlight the relationship between SFSCs, local food systems and the dynamics between urban and rural consumption.

In the same way, a large growing body of literature has investigated the advantages of SFSCs. Previous studies have found that SFSCs create jobs in rural communities and improve farmers and smallholder's incomes [5, 6, 16]. This is particularly useful for producers because the scheme may reduce economic uncertainty in long chains. However, there has been little agreement on what is "fair" in SFSCs [7, 13] and perceptions may vary on the actor's perspective.

In this regard, the consumer's perspective has a key role in unconventional agri-food supply chains in SFSCs. Elghannam et al. [17] pointed out that consumers were dissatisfied and concerned with the environmental effects of traditional SFSCs. In addition to this, it has been demonstrated that consumers of SFSCs preferred healthy food and products that improve local development [6, 18]. Together, these studies highlight that consumers demand alternative commercialization channels for their needs. Furthermore, face to face communication between consumers and producers may change by specific platforms such as social media.

1.2 Social Media User'S Perspectives on SFSCs

More recent attention has focused on producers and consumer's communication through social media. For example, Elghannam et al. [17] noticed that there are types of "short chains of communication" in the agri-food sector through the internet. Other studies have found that social media may strengthen communication between consumers and producers [12, 19, 20] and that it may open opportunities for SFSCs in comparison to traditional food chains [10, 17]. Considering all of this evidence, social media is a valuable source of information between between consumers and producers relationship.

Twitter is one of the most widely used social media platforms. García-León [13] reported that producers used Twitter as a food socialization tool. Previous studies have found that Twitter is vital source of information for consumer marketing research [21] and that it can innovate positioning strategies for coffee products [20]. Therefore, Twitter content such as hashtags, tweets and conversations may reveal consumers and producer's experiences and trends in agrifood industry.

Although there has been an increasing interest in alternative consumption paradigms such as SFSCs through social media, there are still few case studies in Latin American countries. Furthermore, few studies have investigated the information posted by users on social media in food consumption paradigms. Therefore, the primary goal of the present study was to explore how *"De la Chacra a la Olla"* is represented on Twitter. More specifically, we explored the meanings and understanding of SFSCs in the context of a Peruvian government support program for small-scale farmers. This preliminary work will generate fresh insight into the role of social media in understanding new alternative consumption paradigms. Similarly, this study provided an important opportunity to bridge the gap between producers and consumers in Peru.

2   Methods

2.1   Case Study

A case study approach was used to explore consumer's perceptions related to SFSCs. The case study approach is particularly adequate for diverse in social media. To ensure tweets concerning SFSCs, we selected a Peruvian national program that promoted agricultural producers' industry. *"De la Chacra a la Olla"* (From the farm to the Pot, for its translation in English) is a Peruvian government program that allows producers or agricultural organizations to sell their products directly to the population in different geographic locations. This program was implemented in 2014 in Lima, Peru and is organized according to a schedule in different geographic locations in a determined period. This program allows producers or agricultural organizations to sell their products directly to the population [22]. Currently, this program articulate local consumer markets, support the development of rural productive chains and fits in SFSCs [15, 17].

2.2   Ethics

Ethical approval was obtained from *Universidad Tecnológica del Perú* in Lima, Perú. According to ethics guidelines for internet-mediated research [23], additional care is needed for participants in virtual environments such as social media. After careful examination, we considered that the nature of the conversation #delachacraalaolla was harmless and that the consent form was not necessary because Twitter is in the public domain. However, the anonymization of participants was maximized by changing tweeter accounts names and by paraphrasing tweets without changing the original content.

2.3   Twitter Data Collection

Using web scraping with Python 3 [24], data were gathered from Twitter with the hashtag #delachacraalaolla (see Fig. 1). Tweets were searched with Python's package "GetOldTweets[1]". A major advantage of this package is that it allows retrieving tweets that are one week old. Additionally, tweets were retrieved by considering the start date of the program. A total of 1,223 Spanish tweets between January 2014 and July 2020 were obtained. Since the geographical location was not specified in the scraping command, any tweet that presented the keyword could be retrieved from any country. Because *"De la Chacra a la Olla"* program was implemented by the Peruvian government in Peruvian territory, it was expected that Twitter messages were posted by Peruvians.

---

[1] https://github.com/Jefferson-Henrique/GetOldTweets-python.

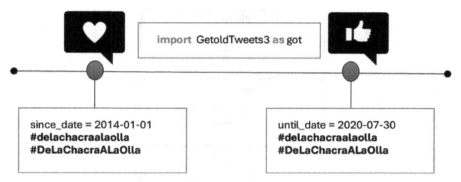

Fig. 1. *#DeLaChacraALaOlla* tag results executing GetOldTweets Python's package.

2.4   Data Analysis

To compare participants representations of *"De la Chacra a la Olla"* program, a thematic analysis was performed [25, 26]. This method is divided into six phases (see Figure 2) and is particularly useful for systematic and comprehensive data analysis [26, 27]. Another advantage of using thematic analysis is that it is theoretically flexible and it allows to identify thematic patterns in different types of data (e.g. conversations). Using NVivo for qualitative data analysis, it was possible to conduct complex and flexible iterations in all the phases (version 11, QSR International Pty Ltd, Doncaster, Victoria, Australia).

In line with Braun and Clarke´s [25, 26] recommendation, the aim was to provide rigorous descriptions of themes rather than providing a general overview of the data. Furthermore, participant's tweets were analyzed using an inductive approach where codes and themes emerged from the data rather than pre-defined concepts or theories. According to thematic analysis principles, the entire data corpus (N = 1 223 tweets) was coded, capturing the semantic and latent meanings provided by tweets. Some tweets were excluded from the analysis because they were not related to the research question.

For the purpose of data familiarization (phase 1), the first author took notes, read and re-read each tweet from the whole data with the hashtag #delachacraalaolla in order to examine the text and identify potential codes. These preliminary codes were reviewed before the data were imported into NVivo. After data input, the information was coded (phase 2) in a systematic, semantic and latent level. These codes were organized into groups with the same meaning and key analytic ideas related to the research question. Moreover, the coding was conducted inductively and the final list was double-checked to avoid coding drift. On completion of the final list of codes, these were grouped into candidate themes that were related to the research question and were visible across the data (phase 3). Once the candidate themes were identified, we started to review and check them against all codes and the whole data (phase 4). In addition to this, we developed a thematic map for candidate themes and all members of the research team examined, recoded and established the boundaries between them. After several discussions, meetings and a more focused analysis with the research team, we defined, named and approved the final themes (phase 5). Finally, the construction of an analytic

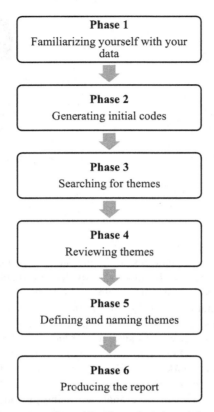

Fig. 2. Thematic analysis process adopted in this study (adapted from Braun and Clarke 2006).

narrative (phase 6) was done in relation to the research question and the understanding and interpretation of Tweets associated with the SFSCs.

3   Results

The purpose of this study was to explore how "*De la chacra a la olla*" program is represented on Twitter. After searching the data, a total of 1,223 Spanish tweets between January 2014 and July 2020 were obtained. A total of three themes related to SFSCs were identified after data analysis: "food well-being", "local valorization" and "without intermediaries". Proportions and frequencies of themes are shown in Table 1.

The thematic analysis from Twitter messages under the #*delachacraalaolla* context, was performed with the aim to identify key themes across Twitter users' perspectives regarding SFSCs. Therefore, the capture of relevant ideas regarding the research question: What is the consumer's representation of SFSCs in tweets about the #*DeLaChacraALaOlla* programme?

The purpose of this study was to explore how "From the Farm to the Pot" program is represented on twitter. After searching the data, a total of 1,223 Spanish tweets

Table 1. Frequency of citation according to main themes associated with SFSCs.

Themes	Codes	Citation (N = 544)
Food well-being (31%)	Healthy food	13% (n = 71)
	Quality food	2% (n = 10)
	Seasonal products	1% (n = 4)
	Food security	15% (n = 82)
Local valorization (28%)	Local fisheries and aquaculture	4% (n = 24)
	Local agriculture and livestock production	8% (n = 45)
	Native products	6% (n = 34)
	Value-added products	2% (n = 13)
	Regional products	8% (n = 42)
Without intermediaries (40%)	New-market access	6% (n = 35)
	Food directly from the field	8% (n = 41)
	Fair prices	4% (n = 23)
	Direct food selling	22% (n = 120)

% = The percentage n% means n citations out of 100%.

between January 2014 and July 2020 were obtained. A total of three themes related to SFSCs were identified after data analysis: "food well-being", "local valorization" and "without intermediaries". Proportions and frequencies of themes are shown in Table 1. Table 2 summarizes quotes extracted from the data that reflect Twitter user's messages regarding SFSC's. Similarly, "Without intermediaries" was the most extended theme identified in the data, which is one of the main characteristics frequently associated with SFSCs. "Food well-being" and "Local valorization" as themes had the same proportion of identification frequency.

Table 2. Table of themes (N = 1 167 tweets).

Themes	Codes	Quotes
Food well-being	Healthy food	*"..this program is in La Victoria city with the goal to promote healthy diets.";* *"...this program contains delicious and healthy products."*

(*continued*)

Table 2. (*continued*)

Themes	Codes	Quotes
	Quality food	"...they are continually offering quality food products in different parts of Peru"; "...Over 20 local agricultural producers are offering quality products for communities and families in the region."
	Seasonal products	"...ice creams, frozen and beverages are made from traditional and seasonal products."; "...I found that there are over 200 seasonal products."
	Food security	"...they are back in Carabayllo and are committed to provide food for residents and feed a large number of families."; "...approximately 33 farmers and livestock producers attended today's meeting to provide essential products."
Local valorization	Local fisheries and aquaculture	"...45 aquaculture producers from the city of San Martin were promoted by a non-profit organization against drugs and were successful in selling 800 kilos of fish meat"; "...healthy, tasty and accessible food, from the effort of our artisanal fishermen and aquaculture workers"
	Local agriculture and livestock production	"...Our farmers and peasants deserve all the support from local government agencies because of their effort and dedication"; "...people from the mountains support our community. Thanks to them we can eat everyday"
	Native products	"...let's eat out different types of Peruvian potatoes such as Canchan and Yungay"; "...There are different types of corn at the agricultural fair"
	Value-added products	"...it has value-added and creative food for Peruvian families"; "...The innovations presented at this fair included products like corn purple, panettone, cacao with maras salt, fresh fruit, olives, and olive oil in a variety of presentations"

(continued)

Table 2. (*continued*)

Themes	Codes	Quotes
	Regional products	"...Healthy and fresh products from 14 regions of the country will be present"; "...food is produced by small-scale farmers in different regions from Peru"
Without intermediaries	New-market access	"...This program allows decentralization of places where essential food products can be sold"; "...the Ministry of Agrarian Development and Irrigation continues to encourage participation of small and medium producers in agricultural markets"
	Food directly from the field	"...families across the country are safe and are able to afford agricultural products provided by farming families"; "...We will have local and national products this weekend at the fair..."
	Fair prices	"...quality food products and fair prices are reaching your home"; "this program has fair prices and no intermediaries"
	Direct food selling	"..I'm happy to continuing offering this place to our rural community so they can sell their products"; "Over 42 farmers are working with the Ministry of Agrarian Development and Irrigation to sell their products safely to hundreds of people"

4 Discussion

Several reports have shown that social media is a useful tool for discussing and analyze different issues in social sciences. The present preliminary study was designed to explore how SFSCs were represented under "*De la Chacra a la Olla*" program by Twitter users.

One interesting finding was the *without intermediaries* theme. This was the most common pattern in the data. These results reflect those of Chiffoleau and Dourian [5] who pointed out that consumer critics have a key role in the emergence of SFSCs as an alternative food consumption paradigm. A possible explanation for this might be that visitors and consumers of "*De la Chacra a la Olla*" program were in favour of an alternative agri-food supply chain rather than the conventional one. An implication of this is the direct interaction between consumers and producers as a key feature of SFSCs.

The most interesting finding was the theme "*food wellbeing*" which is a topic of discussion among Twitter users. Users highlighted the value of security, healthy and quality food. This study confirms that Twitter users focused on food well-being in relation to the SFSCs consumption model [13]. Moreover, it has been suggested that young people should be informed about the benefits of the food in these alternative markets [17]. An implication of this is the possibility to promote health benefits and reach new users between the interaction of producers and consumers. In addition to this, messages about food wellbeing among users is remarkable by considering that *De la Chacra a la Olla* program is located in urban areas of the main cities.

The current study found that *"local valorization"* promoted alternative supply chains as SFSCs as a tool for local producers. This also accords with the increasing interest in revaluing and positioning local and regional territories [28]. This result further supports the idea of how the local food system benefits when they bring producers, consumers and how local movements may promote alternative consumer paradigms [29]. It seems possible that these results are due to the expressions of the territory and the value of local food products. Similarly, other contextual factors may be involved such as the reduction of intermediaries and trust relationships between producers and consumers. These findings may help us to understand SFSCs and the value of local food products in specific territories.

Overall, it is interesting to note the role of social media platforms in SFSCs because of spontaneous user opinions that may become an important communication channel between customers and sellers in the future. Elghannam et al. [10] pointed out that social media allow producers to minimize disconnection with consumers and increase an interactive supply chain. Similarly, Samoggia et al. [20], pointed out that social media could be used to establish a dialogue with consumers. This finding, while preliminary, suggests that social media could be used to improve market access without physical proximity and that different communication channels can be used to improve producers and consumers.

The major limitation of this study is the interpretation of information collected on Twitter. According to Vidal et al. [12], social media data may have unclear results. Secondly, this study is preliminary and represents research in progress. Further analysis of the data will reveal new insights between the interaction of producers and consumers. Finally, an additional uncontrolled factor is the possibility that some of the tweets that were extracted in July 2020 may have partially influenced the results because of the onset of COVID-19. In spite of these limitations, this study adds our understanding of the interaction between consumers and producers. Moreover, to our knowledge, this is the first study to explore under a qualitative research approach consumer's representation of *"De la chacra a la olla"* program in Peru.

These findings will be of interest to government agencies that are in the agricultural sector. For instance, it would be fruitful to develop further strategies in other social media platforms such as Instagram, Facebook, Twitter, LinkedIn and YouTube in order to reach a wide number of consumers and producers that could foster SFSCs. According to Elghannam et al. [10, 17] social media represents a significant opportunity between consumers and producers. For this reason, other aspects between consumers and producers could be explored such as the financial inclusion of smallholder farmers through trading on social media.

5 Conclusions

This study aimed to explore how *"De la Chacra a la Olla"* is represented on Twitter with a qualitative perspective. This study identified three themes: "Food wellbeing", "Local valorization" and "Without intermediaries". Our research has found opportunities for success in social media as a SFSCs. More specifically, our study has shown that social media may have the possibility to establish real communication with trust between producers and consumers. Additionally, social media may be adopted by young consumers and boost their confidence to collect key customers information and receive real-time feedback. It has also been proven that these SFSCs can offer a wide range of food products and adapt to new habits. For example, it can be helpful to understand that in some parts of Peru, people are more interested about the origins of products they consume. In general, consumers must receive sufficient information about products, their benefits and certifications so that they can make reliable purchasing decisions.

References

1. Marsden, T.K., Arce, A.: Constructing quality: emerging food networks in the rural transition. Environ. Plan. A **27**(8), 1261–1279 (1995). https://doi.org/10.1068/a271261
2. Renting, H., Marsden, T.K., Banks, J.: Understanding alternative food networks: exploring the role of short food supply chains in rural development. Environ. Plan. A **35**(3), 393–411 (2003). https://doi.org/10.1068/a3510
3. CEPAL: Agricultura familiar y circuitos cortos: Nuevos esquemas de producción, comercialización y nutrición (2014)
4. Ranaboldo, C., Arosio, M.: Rural-Urban Linkages. Short Food Chains and Local Food Systems. Santiago, Chile, Paper series No. 129 (2014)
5. Chiffoleau, Y., Dourian, T.: Sustainable food supply chains: Is shortening the answer? A literature review for a research and innovation agenda. Sustain. **12**(23), 1–21 (2020). https://doi.org/10.3390/su12239831
6. Mancini, M., Menozzi, D., Donati, M., Biasini, B., Veneziani, M., Arfini, F.: Producers' and consumers' perception of the sustainability of short food supply chains: the case of Parmigiano Reggiano PDO. Sustainability **11**(3), 721 (2019). https://doi.org/10.3390/su11030721
7. Vittersø, Gunnar, et al.: Short food supply chains and their contributions to sustainability: participants' views and perceptions from 12 European cases. Sustainability **11**(17), 4800 (2019). https://doi.org/10.3390/su11174800
8. Reina-Usuga, L., de Haro-Giménez, T., Parra-López, C.: Food governance in territorial short food supply chains: different narratives and strategies from Colombia and Spain. J. Rural Stud. **75**(January), 237–247 (2020). https://doi.org/10.1016/j.jrurstud.2020.02.005
9. Paciarotti, C., Torregiani, F.: The logistics of the short food supply chain: a literature review. Sustain. Prod. Consum. **26**, 428–442 (2021). https://doi.org/10.1016/j.spc.2020.10.002
10. Elghannam, A., Escribano, M., Mesias, F.: Can social networks contribute to the development of short supply chains in the Spanish agri-food sector? New Medit **16**(1), 36–42 (2017)
11. Michel-Villarreal, R., Vilalta-Perdomo, E.L., Canavari, M., Hingley, M.: Resilience and digitalization in short food supply chains: a case study approach. Sustain. **13**(11), 1–23 (2021). https://doi.org/10.3390/su13115913
12. Vidal, L., Ares, G., Machín, L., Jaeger, S.R.: Using Twitter data for food-related consumer research: a case study on 'what people say when tweeting about different eating situations.' Food Qual. Prefer. **45**, 58–69 (2015). https://doi.org/10.1016/j.foodqual.2015.05.006

13. García-León, R.A.: Twitter and food well-being : analysis of # SlowFood postings reflecting the food well- being of consumers, pp. 1–13 (2021)
14. Belletti, G., Marescotti, A.: Short Food Supply Chains for Promoting Local Food on Local Markets (2020)
15. Marsden, T., Banks, J., Bristow, G.: Food supply chain approaches: exploring their role in rural development. Sociol. Ruralis **40**(4), 424–438 (2000). https://doi.org/10.1111/1467-9523.00158
16. Augère-Granier, M.-L.: Short food supply chains and local food systems in the EU (2016)
17. Elghannam, A., Mesias, F.J., Escribano, M., Fouad, L., Horrillo, A., Escribano, A.J.: Consumers' perspectives on alternative short food supply chains based on social media: a focus group study in Spain. Foods **9**(1), 22 (2019). https://doi.org/10.3390/foods9010022
18. Giampietri, E., Finco, A., Del Giudice, T.: Exploring consumers' attitude towards purchasing in short food supply chains. Qual. Access Success **16**, 135–141 (2015)
19. Tang, J., Zhang, P., Wu, P.F.: Categorizing consumer behavioral responses and artifact design features: the case of online advertising. Inf. Syst. Front. **17**(3), 513–532 (2014). https://doi.org/10.1007/s10796-014-9508-3
20. Samoggia, A., Riedel, B., Ruggeri, A.: Social media exploration for understanding food product attributes perception: the case of coffee and health with Twitter data. Br. Food J. **122**(12), 3815–3835 (2020). https://doi.org/10.1108/BFJ-03-2019-0172
21. Borrero, J.D., Zabalo, A.: Identification and analysis of strawberries' consumer opinions on twitter for marketing purposes. Agronomy **11**(4), 1–19 (2021). https://doi.org/10.3390/AGRONOMY11040809
22. Diario Oficial El Peruano: Ley No. 29676: Ley de Promoción del desarrollo de los Mercados de Productores Agropecuarios. Lima, Peru, pp. 441050–441057 (2011)
23. British Psychological Society: Ethics guidelines for internet-mediated research. Leicester, UK (2013)
24. VanRossum, G., Drake, F.L.: Python 3 Reference Manual. CreateSpace, Scotts Valley, CA (2009)
25. Braun, V., Clarke, V.: Using thematic analysis in psychology. Qual. Res. Psychol. **3**(2), 77–101 (2006). https://doi.org/10.1191/1478088706qp063oa
26. Braun, V., Clarke, V.: Successful Qualitative Research: A Practical Guide for Beginners, May 2014 (2013). https://books.google.com/books?id=EV_Q06CUsXsC&pgis=1
27. Gil, J., Perera, V.: Análisis informatizado de datos cualitativos (2001)
28. Marsden, T.: Governing for agri-food security and rural sustainability: antecedents and transitions. In: Marsden, T. (ed.) Agri-Food and Rural Development: Sustainable Place-Making, pp. 1–18. Bloomsbury Publishing Plc (2017). https://doi.org/10.5040/9781474203937.0007 http://www.bloomsburycollections.com/book/agri-food-and-rural-development-sustainable-place-making/ch1-governing-for-agri-food-security-and-rural-sustainability-antecedents-and-transitions/
29. Brinkley, C.: Visualizing the social and geographical embeddedness of local food systems. J. Rural Stud. **54**, 314–325 (2017). https://doi.org/10.1016/j.jrurstud.2017.06.023

Musculoskeletal Ailments and Working Conditions in Teachers Who Telework: A Case Study from a Private Institution in the City of Guayaquil

Dayana Zúñiga-Miranda[1] ⓘ, Katherine Moran-Alava[1] ⓘ,
Kenny Escobar-Segovia[2](✉) ⓘ, and Daniela Guzmán-Cadena[2] ⓘ

[1] Universidad Espíritu Santo, Guayaquil, Ecuador
[2] Escuela Superior Politécnica del Litoral, Guayaquil, Ecuador
kescobar@espol.edu.ec

Abstract. Education has suffered changes during the outbreak of the novel Coronavirus COVID-19 forcing our teachers to implement new strategies to teach online. With this new working format, we must consider that one of the most common health problems affecting our teleworkers are musculoskeletal ailments. These types of alterations constitute the pathology that generates a large number of cases of disability. The objective of this research was to determine the prevalence of musculoskeletal ailments through the use of the ERGOPAR questionnaire, the working conditions through the use of the PVD (DSE) questionnaire in teachers that perform online teaching. It's a descriptive study with a transversal approach performed with 104 teachers from an education institution in the city of Guayaquil-Ecuador in the year 2021. ERGOPAR and PVD (DSE) questionnaires were applied. The prevalence was high, finding discomfort, pain, or both in "neck, shoulders, and thoracic back pain" 77.77% in males and 81.82% in females; discomfort or pain in the "lumbar zone" 70.37% in males and 79.22% in females. It's demonstrated that there is no predisposition to a higher affection on a particular sex. Characteristically, the exposure to DSE causes discomfort due to the reflection from the screen affecting 51.85% of males and 66.23% of females. This research contributes significantly to ergonomics, it could demonstrate a negative relationship in the health of teachers linking musculoskeletal ailments and the characteristics of online teaching.

Keywords: Musculoskeletal ailments · Teleworking · COVID-19 · Online Education · Teachers

1 Introduction

With the Discovery of the novel coronavirus COVID-19 in Wuhan-China in December 2019, and in the face of the imminent spread of the infection at international levels, the World Health Organization (WHO), on January 30, 2020, declared that the outbreak was a public health emergency of international interest. Due to this, the affected countries, in order to prevent the risk of contagion and to reinforce surveillance activities of suspected cases, decided to place the population in social isolation [1].

The COVID-19 pandemic is one of the biggest challenges that society and companies have faced. With this threat to public health, the working environment has been deeply affected at an economic and social level. To ensure the safety of people and the sustainability of companies and jobs, many companies worldwide have opted for teleworking as a work alternative [2].

In Ecuador, the health alert begins in February 29th, 2020 when the MSP reports the first case of COVID-19. From that date on, society enters a new way of living due to the consequences of a mortal virus [3]. The Ministerial Agreement No. MDT-2020–076 from March 12th, 2020 establishes the guidelines for the implementation of teleworking during the sanitary emergency declared in Ecuador. Article 3 states that, "in order to guarantee the health of workers in the public and private sectors, it will be the power of the highest institutional authority of the public sector and the employer of the private sector, to implement emerging teleworking" [4].

As the pandemic progresses, education has suffered changes forcing our teachers to innovate by creating adjustments and implementing new strategies to provide online education, or in a blended manner. Thus, guaranteeing the daily learning of students, and the wellbeing of the members of the educational community of the country [5]. Take into account that during the yellow coding of the emergency, in public institutions, it's the highest authority of each institution that regulates work activity, highlighting teleworking as a priority. Additionally, they can return to face-to-face work with up to 50% of their staff at a time, the organization of shifts is empowered to avoid crowding, alternating teleworking with face-to-face work [4].

Given what is indicated in the previous paragraphs, we must take into account that wone of the most common health problems that affect our teleworkers are musculoskeletal ailments. This type of alterations that constitute the pathology that generate a large number of cases of disability. According to the CENEA (for its Spanish name, Centro de Ergonomía Aplicada de España) publication, the "ergonomic risk is a characteristic of work that may increase the probability of developing musculoskeletal ailments either because it is present in an unfavorable way, or because it is present simultaneously with other risk factors" [6].

Musculoskeletal ailments are injuries associated with the musculoskeletal system that generate physical and functional alterations of the joints or other tissues (muscles, tendons, ligaments, nerves and other structures). The symptoms range from mild aches and pains related to inflammation, decrease or loss of muscle strength, to functional limitation of the affected segment. Musculoskeletal ailments afflict the health of the staff of organizations and their productivity, and bring as a consequence a large number of cases of disability [2].

For this reason, the objective is to determine the prevalence of musculoskeletal ailments through the ERGOPAR questionnaire, and its relation with working conditions through the PVD (DSE) questionnaire in teachers who carry out online education for the prevention of occupational diseases.

1.1 Literature Review

With the COVID-19 pandemic, people have had to carry out their working activities from their homes due to restrictions and/or quarantine periods. Since they have had to balance their intensive work schedules with their daily life activities in an unfamiliar and non-ergonomic environment, problems with the musculoskeletal system have surfaced. Online education is a training system that takes place in a completely virtual environment through the use of existing computer technologies without the obligation of the student and teacher to go to an educational establishment, completely independent of time and space. In the distance education system, the use of online education tools such as computers is greater than in the traditional education system [7].

Many studies involving office workers who use computers have demonstrated that prolonged work in a sitting position and the use of computers have created musculoskeletal problems, and have exacerbated existing problems. It is known that the main reason for this is the frequent repetitive movements of the upper limbs, as well as the long computer work times, and thus, the increased loads on the musculoskeletal system [7].

Faced with this problem, the ERGOPAR Method, which is a participatory procedure for the prevention of ergonomic risk in the company, indicates that the workers are ones who best know their job, have the information and the experience necessary to address the problems from the perspective of real activity at work. This is why their participation in the different stages of the process of identification, analysis, proposal and implementation of solutions is considered to be essential for the effectiveness of preventive action on ergonomic risks [8].

A display screen equipment is any alphanumeric or graphic display screen regardless of the display process involved. These include the old screens of cathode-rays, plasma, liquid crystal (LCD), etc. that cover up to the latest technologies in three-dimensional display screens, or multi-screen technologies, which allow applications to be displayed on multiple panels [9].

The work on display screen equipment is defined as «the one performed by every worker who habitually and during a relevant part of his normal work, uses an equipment with a data display screen». Workers considered to be DSE users are:

a) Those who exceed 4 h per day, or 20 h per week of effective work with said equipment.
b) Those who perform 2.4 h per day, or 10 to 20 h a week of effective work, provided that they meet least 5 of the following requirements"

1. Depend on the equipment to do their job not being able to easily access alternative means to achieve the same results.
2. Not being able to voluntarily decide whether or not to use the equipment to do their job.
3. Need specific training or experience in the use of the equipment required by the company to do their job.
4. Regularly use display screen equipment for continuous periods of one hour or more.
5. Use display screen equipment daily, or almost daily in the manner described in the previous point.

6. That the quick access to information by the user through the screen constitutes an important requirement for the job.
7. That the necessities of the task demand a high level of attention by the user. For example, because the consequences of an error can be critical [9].

2 Research Methodology

The research was descriptive with a transversal approach. It counts with the participation of 104 teachers from an education institution from Guayaquil-Ecuador in 2021. The data was collected on October 14th, 2021 and was done in stages. The first stage consisted of the voluntary participation of the teachers answering an existing questionnaire based on online questions. This was carried out using the Google Forms platform.

Social media campaigns were used to keep the questionnaire link available for teachers in the educational unit. These campaigns were adjusted weekly during 14 days. They were also contacted through institutional and personal emails. Finally, each participant involved in this survey shared the access link with their peers. As inclusion criteria for the study, we took professional males and females who work as teachers in the educational unit in the online mode who voluntarily accepted to participate in this research whether or not they were previously diagnosed with any musculoskeletal ailment. This was done through the application of the online survey to the voluntary teachers.

The tool used was the ERGOPAR questionnaire (for its name in Spanish: Cuestionario de factores de riesgo ergonómicos y Daños) with 15 items [8] along with the PVD (DSE) questionnaire with 10 items [10] which considered DSE users to be those workers who exceed 4 h per day, or 20 h per week of effective work with said equipment. Additionally, sociodemographic data such as age, gender, workday, type of contract, job, amount of time working that job, number of hours per day in the job were added to the questionnaire.

The second stage consisted in the analysis of the date using the statistical software SPSS version 22 (IBM Corp). On the one hand, the descriptive analysis of the data was carried out using data frequency/percentage tables taking the categorical variables, and on the other hand, the correlation between them. Thus, establishing the level of significance in $\alpha = 0.05$ through the application of the Chi-squared test from Pearson (X^2).

3 Results

The general characteristics of the surveyed staff that are shown in Table 1 indicates that 104 male and female teachers participated with a reply rate of 100%. In regards to the gender of the participants, 25.96% were male, and 74.03% were female. They carry out their activities in diverse schooling areas such as high school, middle school and elementary school. Most of the teachers have more than 5 years in the job which is equivalent to 67.30%, followed by the staff who has been there between 1 and 5 years with 29.80%, and the staff who have less than a year with 2.88%. 99% of the surveyed staff works more than 4 h a day.

Table 1. Sociodemographic data

Age	Gender			
	Male n = 27	%	Female n = 77	%
18 to 25 years old	0	0.0	3	3.90
26 to 32 years old	6	22.22	24	31.17
33 to 39 years old	4	14.81	16	20.78
40 to 47 years old	4	14.81	17	22.08
48 to 54 years old	6	22.22	10	12.99
Above 55 years old	7	25.93	7	9.09
Working schedule	Male n = 27	%	Female n = 77	%
Morning shift	2	7.41	4	5.19
Afternoon shift	1	3.70	5	6.49
Both shifts	24	88.89	68	88.31
Job position	Male n = 27	%	Female n = 77	%
High School (Grades 10–12)	15	55,56	18	23.38
Primary School (Grades 1–3)	6	22.22	15	19.48
Primary School (Grades 4–6)	2	7.41	16	20.78
Middle School (Grades 7–9)	4	14.81	16	20.78
Kindergarten	0	0.0	12	15.58
Time working in the job	Male n = 27	%	Female n = 77	%
Less than 1 year	0	0.00	3	3.90
Between 1 and 5 years	6	22.22	25	32.47
More than 5 years	21	77.78	49	63.64
Working hours per day in the job	Male n = 27	%	Female n = 77	%
4 h or less	0	0.00	1	1.30
More than 4 h	27	100.0	76	98.70

The results of the ERGOPAR questionnaire that are shown in Table 2 belong to ailments and/or discomfort in different sections of the body. This sample shows a notable prevalence of discomfort and/or pain in the surveyed teachers. There is no significant difference between the surveyed genders demonstrated through the Chi-squared test. The results obtained in the neck, shoulder, and thoracic back section stand out in which the percentage of discomfort is equivalent to 44.44% in males, and 50.65% in females, and the percentage of pain decreases by half corresponding to 22.22% in males, and 23.38% in females. Both genders indicate "sometimes" as the response to the frequency at which they present these manifestations, exceeding 50.00% in both. They also indicate that in more than 80.00% of the cases, it has not prevented them from carrying out their work activity.

Table 2. Results of the ERGOPAR questionnaire, work-related health damage

Neck, shoulders and/or thoracic back		Gender				
		Male n = 27	%	Female n = 77	%	p-value
Discomfort or pain	Pain	6	22.22	18	23.38	0.898
	Discomfort	12	44.44	39	50.65	
	Discomfort, Pain	3	11.11	6	7.79	
	None	6	22.22	14	18.18	
Frequency	Sometimes	14	51.85	46	59.74	0.692
	Many times	7	25.93	19	24.68	
	Never	6	22.22	12	15.58	
Work impediment	No	22	81.48	62	80.52	0.913
	Yes	5	18.52	15	19.48	
Consequence	No	12	44.44	35	45.45	0.928
	Yes	15	55.56	42	54.55	
Back – lumbar zone		Male n = 27	%	Female n = 77	%	p-value
Discomfort or pain	Pain	10	37.04	20	25.97	0.204
	Discomfort	9	33.33	41	53.25	
	None	8	29.63	16	20.78	
Frequency	Sometimes	15	55.56	45	58.44	0.584
	Many times	4	14.81	16	20.78	
	Never	8	29.63	16	20.78	
Work impediment	No	22	81.48	58	75.32	0.514
	Yes	5	18.52	19	24.68	
Consequence	No	15	55.56	35	45.45	0.366
	Yes	12	44.44	42	54.55	
Elbow joints		Male n = 27	%	Female n = 77	%	p-value
Discomfort or pain	Pain	1	3.70	2	2.60%	0.390
	Discomfort	5	18.52	7	9.09%	
	None	21	77.78	68	88.31%	
Frequency	Sometimes	6	22.22	7	9.09%	0.150
	Many times	0	0.00	2	2.60%	
	Never	21	77.78	68	88.31%	

(*continued*)

Table 2. (*continued*)

Neck, shoulders and/or thoracic back		Gender				
		Male n = 27	%	Female n = 77	%	p-value
Work impediment	No	26	96.30	75	97.40%	0.950
	Yes	1	3.70	2	2.60%	
Consequence	No	24	88.89	71	92.21%	0.598
	Yes	3	11.11	6	7.79%	
Hands and/or wrists		Male n = 27	%	Female n = 77	%	p-value
Discomfort or pain	Pain	3	11.11	10	12.99	0.086
	Discomfort	8	29.63	18	23.38	
	None	16	59.26	49	63.64	
Frequency	Sometimes	8	29.63	19	24.68	0.880
	Many times	3	11.11	9	11.69	
	Never	16	59.26	49	63.64	
Work impediment	No	22	81.48	69	89.61	0.272
	Yes	5	18.52	8	10.39	
Consequence	No	18	66.67	58	75.32	0.383
	Yes	9	33.33	19	24.68	
Legs and knees		Male n = 27	%	Female n = 77	%	p-value
Discomfort or pain	Pain	1	3.70	10	12.99	0.304
	Discomfort	11	40.74	34	44.16	
	None	15	55.56	33	42.86	
Frequency	Sometimes	11	40.74	30	38.96	0.468
	Many times	2	7.41	13	16.88	
	Never	14	51.85	34	44.16	
Work impediment	No	25	92.59	68	88.31	0.534
	Yes	2	7.41	9	11.69	
Consequence	No	18	66.67	55	71.43	0.642
	Yes	9	33.33	22	28.57	
Feet		Male n = 27	%	Female n = 77	%	p-value
Discomfort or pain	Pain	1	3.70	9	11.69	0.480
	Discomfort	11	40.74	29	37.66	
	None	15	55.56	39	50.65	

(*continued*)

Table 2. (*continued*)

Neck, shoulders and/or thoracic back		Gender				
		Male n = 27	%	Female n = 77	%	p-value
Frequency	Sometimes	7	25.93	30	38.96	0.455
	Many times	4	14.81	8	10.39	
	Never	16	59.26	39	50.65	
Work impediment	No	25	92.59	68	88.31	0.534
	Yes	2	7.41	9	11.69	
Consequence	No	19	70.37	58	75.32	0.613
	Yes	8	29.63	19	24.68	

There are significant differences for p-values less than 0.05 (Pearson's Chi-squared test).

Regarding the postures or actions typical of the job that are shown in Table 3, the posture with the highest degree of presentation is sitting for more than 4 h, giving a percentage of 44.44% in males and 45.45% in females. In this position, there is no significance difference in both genders surveyed. The posture that follows by frequency and that is maintained for more than 4 h is "walking," which occurs in 18.52% of of males and 10.39% of females. The only posture in which there is a significant difference is "walking up or down stairs" which is demonstrated by Pearson's Chi-squared test obtaining 0.010.

Table 3. Results of the ERGOPAR Questionnaire, Postures and Actions Typical of the Job, According to Certain Postures: Legs

Work time adopting or performing these postures:		Gender				p-value
		Male n = 27	%	Female n = 77	%	
Sitting (chair, stool, vehicle, lumbar support, etc.)	Between 2 and 4 h	6	22.22	19	24.68	0.912
	Between 30 min and 2 h	4	14.81	13	16.88	
	More than 4 h	12	44.44	35	45.45	
	Never/Less than 30 min	5	18.52	10	12.99	
Standing without walking	Between 2 and 4 h	5	18.52	16	20.78	0.111
	Between 30 min and 2 h	3	11.11	22	28.57	

(*continued*)

Table 3. (*continued*)

Work time adopting or performing these postures:		Gender				p-value
		Male n = 27	%	Female n = 77	%	
	More than 4 h	2	7.41	10	12.99	
	Never/Less than 30 min	17	62.96	29	37.66	
Walking	Between 2 and 4 h	6	22.22	10	12.99	0.365
	Between 30 min and 2 h	5	18.52	22	28.57	
	More than 4 h	5	18.52	8	10.39	
	Never/Less than 30 min	11	40.74	37	48.05	
Walking while going up or down different levels (steps, ladder, ramp, etc.)	Between 2 and 4 h	5	18.52	6	7.79	**0.010**
	Between 30 min and 2 h	4	14.81	19	24.68	
	More than 4 h	4	14.81	1	1.30	
	Never/Less than 30 min	14	51.85	51	66.23	
Kneeling/ squatting	Between 2 and 4 h	2	7.41	1	1.30	0.236
	Between 30 min and 2 h	1	3.70	5	6.49	
	Never/Less than 30 min	24	88.89	71	92.21	
Lying on the back or on one side	Between 2 and 4 h	1	3.70	6	7.79	0.163
	Between 30 min and 2 h	3	11.11	6	7.79	
	More than 4 h	1	3.70	0	0.0	
	Never/Less than 30 min	22	81.48	65	84.42	

There are significant differences for p-values less than 0.05 (Pearson's Chi-squared test).

Table 4 corresponding to the ERGOPAR questionnaire shows the postures or actions taken at cervical level highlighting that keeping the neck/head forward is the position that is maintained for more than four hours with 37.04% in males and a 27.27% in females. Also, they tend to repeat it several times. Another posture that is very frequently adopted is keeping the neck to one side and turning the neck/head, which tend to be performed between 30 minutes and two hours repeating these actions. The results obtained have great significance in that a job layout design must be carried out in order to avoid ailments at this level.

Table 4. Results of the ERGOPAR questionnaire, postures and actions typical of the job, according to certain postures: neck and head

Work time adopting or performing these postures:		Gender				p-value
		Male n = 27	%	Female n = 77	%	
Neck/head leaning forward	Between 2 and 4 h	3	11.11	16	20.78	0.644
	Between 30 min and 2 h	4	14.81	11	14.29	
	More than 4 h	10	37.04	21	27.27	
	Never/Less than 30 min	10	37.04	29	37.66	
Repeating it every few seconds, or keeping it fixed	I keep it fixed	6	22.22	7	9.09	0.185
	None	6	22.22	24	31.17	
	I repeat it	15	55.56	46	59.74	
Neck/head leaning backward	Between 2 and 4 h	1	3.70	1	1.30	0.615
	Between 30 min and 2 h	3	11.11	9	11.69	
	More than 4 h	3	11.11	4	5.19	
	Never/Less than 30 min	20	74.07	63	81.82	
Repeating it every few seconds, or keeping it fixed	I keep it fixed	1	3.70	1	1.30	0.682
	I repeat it	10	37.04	26	33.77	
	None	16	59.26	50	64.94	
Neck/head to one side or both	Between 2 and 4 h	0	0.0	4	5.19	0.640
	Between 30 min and 2 h	6	22.22	14	18.18	
	More than 4 h	1	3.7	4	5.19	
	Never/Less than 30 min	20	74.07	55	71.43	

(continued)

Table 4. (*continued*)

Work time adopting or performing these postures:		Gender				p-value
		Male n = 27	%	Female n = 77	%	
Repeating it every few seconds, or keeping it fixed	I keep it fixed	2	7.41	3	3.9	0.762
	I repeat it	11	40.74	32	41.56	
	None	14	51.85	42	54.55	
Turning the neck/head	Between 2 and 4 h	0	0.0	3	3.9	0.747
	Between 30 min and 2 h	6	22.22	14	18,18	
	More than 4 h	1	3.7	3	3.9	
	Never/Less than 30 min	20	74.07	57	74.03	
Repeating it every few seconds, or keeping it fixed	I keep it fixed	2	7.41	1	1.3	0.244
	I repeat it	13	48.15	36	46.75	
	None	12	44.44	40	51.95	

There are significant differences for p-values less than 0.05 (Pearson's Chi-squared test).

Regarding the exposure to DSE and the factors of the computer that tend to cause discomfort in teachers, the reflection of the screen outstands causing discomfort in 51.85% of males, and 66.23% of females. In both cases, there is no significant difference demonstrated by Pearson's Chi-squared test. However, there is a notable difference between both genders in the artificial lighting factor in which 62.34% of women indicate that this fact bothers them when teaching online classes. This can be seen represented in Table 5.

Regarding to the exposure to DSE and the visual discomfort caused in the teachers, we can observe in Table 6 that a very similar prevalence is maintained in symptoms such as itchy eyes and sensation of blurred vision with an occurrence of "very often," and there are no significant differences between genders. However, this changes significantly in the occurrence of headaches being more prevalent in women. Regarding active breaks, we have obtained a high frequency of staff who do carry out this action during their working hours which demonstrates an adequate adherence to this good practice. Regarding the physical demands of the job, they are classified as "moderate" obtaining 59.26% in males and 62.34% in females.

Table 5. Exposure to display screen equipment during work

During work, you feel discomforted by:		Gender				p-value
		Male n = 27	%	Female n = 77	%	
Lack of character sharpness	No	17	62.96	58	75.32	0,218
	Yes	10	37.04	19	24.68	
Character or background flicker	No	21	77.78	50	64.94	0,217
	Yes	6	22.22	27	35.06	
Screen reflections	No	13	48.15	26	33.77	0,184
	Yes	14	51.85	51	66.23	
Artificial lighting	No	21	77.78	29	37.66	**0,000**
	Yes	6	22.22	48	62.34	
Natural lighting	No	24	88.89	71	92.21	0,598
	Yes	3	11.11	6	7.79	

There are significant differences for p-values less than 0.05 (Pearson's Chi-squared test).

Table 6. Exposure to display screen equipment during or after work

During or after work, do you feel:		Gender				p-value
		Male n = 27	%	Female n = 77	%	
Ithcy eyes	Sometimes	10	37.04	42	54.55	0.061
	Very often	6	22.22	20	25.97	
	Never	4	14.81	2	2.60	
	Rarely	7	25.93	13	16.88	
Burning eyes	Sometimes	7	25.93	35	45.45	0.105
	Very often	4	14.81	15	19.48	
	Never	9	33.33	11	14.29	
	Rarely	7	25.93	16	20.78	
Sensation of seeing worse throughout the day	Sometimes	6	22.22	23	29.87	0.358
	Very often	4	14.81	18	23.38	
	Never	10	37.04	16	20.78	
	Rarely	7	25.93	20	25.97	

(*continued*)

Table 6. (*continued*)

During or after work, do you feel:		Gender					p-value
		Male n = 27	%	Female n = 77	%		
Sensation of blurred vision	Sometimes	7	25.93	29	37.66		0.323
	Very often	6	22.22	20	25.97		
	Never	8	29.63	11	14.29		
	Rarely	6	22.22	17	22.08		
Headaches	Sometimes	9	33.33	36	46.75		**0.019**
	Very often	4	14.81	23	29.87		
	Never	7	25.93	5	6.49		
	Rarely	7	25.93	13	16.88		
Glares, stars or lights	Sometimes	7	25.93	23	29.87		0.588
	Very often	4	14.81	14	18.18		
	Never	10	37.04	18	23.38		
	Rarely	6	22.22	22	28.57		
Active breaks		Male n = 27	%	Female n = 77	%		p-value
No		4	14.81	24	31.17		0.099
Yes		23	85.19	53	68.83		
Physical demands of the job		Male n = 27	%	Female n = 77	%		p-value
Low		3	11.11	6	7.79		0.867
Moderate		16	59.26	48	62.34		
High		8	29.63	23	29.87		

There are significant differences for p-values less than 0.05 (Pearson's Chi-Squared Test).

4 Discussion

This study allowed the evaluation of the prevalence of musculoskeletal ailments in different body segments, and its findings returned values similar to those observed in other studies. We found that the main effects on the health of teachers that can be associated with work activity are linked to the organization of teleworking [11].

In general, workers were not prepared to carry out teleworking and online education, having to quickly adapt to this new context without having the appropriate conditions due to the pandemic, presenting a series of problems such as discomfort and pain, which may have limited the development of their job. This is affecting males and females in similar proportions. It is important to consider the nature of the work activity. The current condition is maintained and other factors are added such as prolonged exposure to computer screens, use of a keyboard and mouse, static sitting work, among others. Thus, generating musculoskeletal symptoms [12].

The prevalence of this study was high, finding discomfort, pain or both in different sections of the body highlighting the "neck, shoulders, and thoracis back" with the greatest occurrence of alteration, with 77.77% male prevalence and 81.82% in females. Continuing the order of frequency, the ailment or discomfort in the lumbar zone is present in 70.37% of males and 79.22% in females. We can compare these results with a study carried out in Chile where, in terms of musculoskeletal ailments by sections, males presented 69% and females 78% of this condition located in the neck. In the lumbar area, Chilean teachers indicate presenting this type of discomfort in 69% of males and 79.2% of females [12–14].

It was possible to determine that there is a similarity with other studies such as the one carried out with teachers from a high school in Saudi Arabia, where the prevalence of musculoskeletal ailments was of 87.3%. The study carried out in Abha during 2020 indicated that there is a percentage of occurrence of musculoskeletal ailment of 62.5% in the teachers of that study [15]. While in Turkey and China, their study also indicated similar values standing at 60.3% and 66.7% prevalence of this type of alterations [16].

5   Conclusion

A prevalence of musculoskeletal ailments and discomfort caused by exposure to DSE was found in the teachers studied. This means that a lot of work must be done in the development of ergonomic preventive measures, educational programs about the posture that the head should adopt when working with DSEs, and the appropriate design of the institutional and home workplace. Currently, there are very few educational institutions that have a department in charge of monitoring, preventing and modifying this type of risks.

Among the strengths of our study, the number of teachers who participated in it stands out. This represents a good sample of the universe of the study of the educational institution. The results obtained indicate that there could be a relationship between the musculoskeletal ailments and the characteristics of working from home with its association with the lack of useful tools, the lack of preparation for this little-known modality in our country and the general characteristics of their environment. However, its limitation was the application of the survey in an online format with which we expected to obtain a higher percentage of participation of our teachers, and the lack of studies in which the two survey instruments: ERGOPAR and PVD (DSE) are related. With this, a better comparison could be made.

This study allows to be a basis for future investigations in which it is not only required to determine the prevalence of musculoskeletal ailments such as ergonomic risks, but also other types of risks such as stress caused by the lack of balance between productive activity and daily life and its relationship with these physical discomforts. In addition, it is worth emphasizing that it can be taken as a basis for the study of anthropometric measurements, and the implementation of an ergonomic plan for the design of workstations for teachers. Intervention plans must be included in order to prevent the prevalence of musculoskeletal ailments and future diseases related to this risk.

References

1. World Health Organization WHO (2020). https://www.who.int/es/news/item/30-01-2020-sta tement-on-the-second-meeting-of-the-international-health-regulations-(2005)-emergency-committee-regarding-the-outbreak-of-novel-coronavirus-(2019-ncov). Accessed 22 Sep 2021
2. García-Salirrosas, E., Sánchez-Poma, R.: Prevalencia de trastornos musculoesqueléticos en docentes universitarios que realizan teletrabajo en tiempos de COVID-19. Anales de la Facultad de Medicina. **81**(3) (2020)
3. Secretaria General de Comunicación de la Presidencia. www.comunicacion.gob.ec. (2020). https://www.comunicacion.gob.ec/se-registra-el-primer-caso-de-coronavirus-en-ecuador/
4. del Trabajo, M.: Acuerdo Ministerial MDT-2020-076, Quito: Ministerio del Trabajo, 2020 12 de marzo
5. Ministerio de Educación. www.educacion.gob.ec (2020). https://educacion.gob.ec/seguim iento-teletrabajo/
6. CENEA. www.cenea.eu (2021). https://www.cenea.eu/riesgos-ergonomicos/
7. Kayabınar, E., Kayabınar, B., Önal, B., Zengin, H.Y., Köse, N.: The musculoskeletal problems and psychosocial status of teachers giving online education during the COVID-19 pandemic and preventive telerehabilitation for musculoskeletal problems. In: Work, pp. 33–43 (2020)
8. Gadea, R., Sevilla, M.J., García, A.M.: Manual del método ERGOPAR Versión 2.0. ISTAS, Madrid (2014)
9. Cabello, E.V.: Instituto Nacional de Seguridad y Salud en el Trabajo (2021). https://www. insst.es/documents/94886/509319/DTE_PVD-guiaTecnica.pdf/09375e8b-1de6-4793-9d07-c06f0dc16f1c
10. Ministerio de Salud Pública: Pantalla de Visualización de Datos Solana e Hijos Artes Gráficas. S.A Madrid (1999)
11. C.S. Souza, J. P. Cardoso, A. P. Aguiar, M. M. S. R. Macêdo y J. d. S. Oliveira, «Work-related musculoskeletal disorders among school teachers. In: Revista Brasileira de Medicina do Trabalho, pp. 140–150 (2020)
12. Astudillo, P., Ibarra, C.: Working conditions in educational establishments: research on ergonomics and gender among teachers in pandemic context. In: Black, N.L., Patrick Neumann, W., Noy, I. (eds.) Proceedings of the 21st Congress of the International Ergonomics Association (IEA 2021). LNNS, vol. 220, pp. 403–412. Springer, Cham (2021). https://doi.org/10.1007/978-3-030-74605-6_50
13. Chang-Camacho, L., et al.: Síntomas músculo esqueléticos y su relación con el síndrome de burnout en las actividades laborales del personal administrativo de una universidad en Ecuador. In: Proceedings of the LACCEI International Multi-Conference for Engineering, Education and Technology, Boca Ratón, EEUU (2022). http://dx.doi.org/10.18687/LACCEI 2022.1.1.552
14. Cabrera-Abad, K., Pinos-Úrgiles, P., Jara-Diaz, O., Duque-Córdova, L., Escobar-Segovia, K.: Ergonomic working conditions in workers under the modality of "homeoffice" due to a Covid-19 pandemic, in a bottling company in Ecuador. In: Garcia, M.V., Fernández-Peña, F., Gordón-Gallegos, C. (eds.) Advances and Applications in Computer Science, Electronics, and Industrial Engineering. CSEI 2021. LNNS, vol. 433, pp. 41–56. Springer, Cham (2022). https://doi.org/10.1007/978-3-030-97719-1_2
15. Althomali, O.W., Amin, J., Alghamdi, W., Shaik, D.H.: Prevalence and factors associated with musculoskeletal disorders among secondary schoolteachers in Hail, Saudi Arabia: a cross-sectional survey. Int. J. Environ. Res. Public Health. **18**(12) (2021)
16. Tami, A.M., et al.: Epidemiology of musculoskeletal disorders among the teaching staff of the university of Douala, Cameroon: association with physical activity practice. Int. J. Environ. Res. Public Health **18**(11), 6004 (2021). https://doi.org/10.3390/ijerph18116004

IT Financial and Business Management

Analysis of the Impact of the Ethical Training of Public Accounting Students at Uniminuto UVD and Their Competence About Ethical Dilemmas in the Professional Field

Efrén Danilo Ariza Ruiz⬥, María del Pilar Corredor García(✉) ⬥,
and Eduard Ferney Quintero Rengifo⬥

Corporación Universitaria Minuto de Dios - UNIMINUTO, Bogotá, Colombia
{efren.ariza,maria.corredor-g}@uniminuto.edu.co,
edward.quintero@uniminuto.edu

Abstract. This article focuses on contributing to the curricular transformation for the teaching of ethics, diagnosing the ethical position of students enrolled in the public accounting program of the Corporación Universitaria Minuto de Dios virtual and distance learning mode, facing ethical dilemmas in the professional field. This objective is developed from a correlational study, with probabilistic sampling, and analyzing a group of 375 participants who have completed more than 75% of the study plan, with a reliability of 95% and a margin of error of 5% adapting the Giving Voice to Values (GVV) method. The results are a possible modification in the ethical postures of the students due to the implementation of a change in the study plan and the adoption of case studies and simulations in the subjects of the core of professional training. However, a relativism and a relaxation of the ethical posture of students and graduates in the personal and professional lives has been identified, a situation that is framed in what Kant denounces as the double standard characteristic of modernity, based on the hypothetical imperative. Finally, a high degree of maturity is shown in the Kohlberg moral development scale, where the respondents evaluate the action based on justice, value, and the equality of all human beings.

Keywords: Professional ethics · Selfishness · Utilitarianism · Relativism · Contractualism · Moral equity · Ethical teaching in accounting · Giving Voice to Values · IES

1 Introduction

Ethical training in professionals has frequently been a topic of discussion and analysis, because as Guiñez and Vásquez (2015) affirm, citing Adela Cortina, comprehensive education contains not only purely scientific or accounting knowledge, but also requires a social contribution.

In other words, one of the main challenges that higher education institutions now face, more than ever, is to offer a solid theoretical and conceptual training, together

M. Botto-Tobar et al. (Eds.): ICAT 2022, CCIS 1757, pp. 283–292, 2023.
https://doi.org/10.1007/978-3-031-24978-5_25

with learning values that later become life values. This is why, in the educational field, the question remains, what can be done to improve the ethical training of students, so as to strengthen their criteria and life values, in order to act freely, but with a greater responsibility and awareness of the impact of their acts?

This issue has been addressed by accounting faculties and programs by incorporating specific courses on professional ethics, some of which include them in the beginning of their education while others wait until the end. They have also considered the application of hypothetical ethical dilemmas to see how the students respond.

In this way, The Minuto de Dios University Corporation, in its public accounting program, virtual and distance modality, has foreseen spaces in which the teaching of ethics is the fundamental axis, however, this occurs in times in which the role of the public accountant, due to well-known scandals at the national level such as Odebrecht, SaludCoop, Reficar, and of course Interbolsa, which do not show a favorable social evaluation of the accountants involved.

Since 2018, the Public Accounting program virtual and distance mode of the Minuto de Dios University Corporation has been articulating its investigative work into the current curriculum; understanding that the curriculum is an ongoing research project. From two of the research projects which have been developed by themselves and also a self-assessment from the Renewal of the Qualified Registry before the Ministry of National Education (MEN), it was identified that the program has been internationalized regarding the concerns of the presentation of financial statements and its students know the IFRS, NIC, and IFRS for SMEs, however, the existence of the IES by the IFAC for teaching in public accounting programs is unknown by the majority of the academic community.

The phenomenon described is not exclusive to Corporación Universitaria Minuto de Dios, as Ruíz and Ariza (2019) point out, when analyzing 15 Public Accounting study plans in Colombia "there is no unity in the contents and purposes of the subjects" (Ruiz and Ariza 2019; p. 107). In addition, through the review of the literature, the scarce application that has been given to IES 4 worldwide is evident. Several exercises carried out and some critical calls against IES 4 developed by IFAC; Bampton and Cowton (2012) cited by Ariza Ruiz and Barón Pinto (2020) point out that little research has been carried out on the teaching of business and accounting ethics; even though the information previously stated shows the importance the teaching of ethics.

Based on this diagnosis, the program has implemented a series of reforms in the micro-curriculum by using pedagogical activities that focus on the direction suggested by the IFAC (International Federation of Public Accountants), by using case studies and simulations while teaching ethics in accounting; it is time to measure the impact of these reforms on students, Corredor, Quintero, Ariza, and Piñeros (2021).

So it is essential to measure the impact of these modifications in the training of the students of the program, this constitutes the main objective of the present investigation. For this purpose, based on the information obtained with the previous application of an instrument inspired by the multidimensional scale used by Riemenschneider, Manly amd Leonard (2016), the GVV method and the six stages of moral development proposed by the North American psychologist Laurence Kohlberg (1981), in his "Theory on Moral Development" to 291 students of the Uniminuto program.

Subsequently, a new instrument was applied to students of the Public Accounting program of the Minuto de Dios University Corporation, virtual and distance mode, who have completed more than 75% of the curriculum, in this sense the population is 400 students, a random sampling of 197 students is determined, with a reliability of 95% with a margin of error of 5%. The new instrument consists of 19 sociodemographic items and 32 items corresponding to ethical dilemmas. Data analysis is carried out using SPSS software.

Finally, a discussion is proposed about the results found to promote in students a greater knowledge and application of the values and ethical principles promoted in the accounting profession and in UNIMINUTO UVD, which represents a contribution in the integral formation of future public accountants.

2 Background

A State of the art is documentary research which itself, is documentary research, which seeks to accurately identify what other authors have said about the subject to which their research belongs, that is, the methodologies applied for the ethical training of accountants following the recommendations of IFAC standard 4. This allows us to approach the problem from unprecedented angles that increase our knowledge in our field of training, which gives relevance to our research. The systematic review is carried out in academic databases such as Google Scholar, Proquest, Dialnet, ScienceDirect, and Scopus with the keywords IES 4, IFAC, Pedagogical Strategies, Accounting Ethics and Ethical Dilemmas including the inclusion of criteria methodological contributions in terms of the design of curricular strategies and practical simulation exercises and case studies; to systematize the information, bibliographic files, and worksheets are created, and the information is systematized through RAES.

Among the works identified, Ruiz Urquijo and Ariza Ruiz (2019) investigate the compliance of the requirement of IFAC's IES 4, in the sense of outlining a model of moral progress from actions that are not good or bad, oriented towards reflective processes continuously. For this, it is necessary to provoke conflicts and give the future professional the opportunity to adopt arguments and roles of the stage or level in which they are using real or very probable dilemmas, in the environment of professional practice, seeking those students and teachers adopt reasons, ways of seeing, postures to identify action criteria.

Likewise, several exercises and some critical calls are identified against IES 4 developed by IFAC; Bampton and Cowton (2012) cited by Ariza Ruiz and Barón Pinto (2020) draw attention to the fact that few investigations are carried out on teaching business and accounting ethics, on the other hand, they point out that the instruments applied in the studies from existing data contain elements that lead the researcher to confuse attitude and behavior.Within the practical exercises carried out in the classroom following the IFAC recommendations, it is worth highlighting O'Leary (2009); Dellaportas (2006); the Ignatian pedagogical paradigm proposed by Van Hise and Massey (2010).

Christensen et al. (2016) make methodological recommendations by taking into account that ethical challenges should be normalized by simulating common and repetitive events of possible ethical dilemmas which therefore prepares the future professional to respond correctly when real a event occurs that compromises your behavior.

Des Jardins and Diedrich (2003) include the environmental dimension when designing pedagogical strategies for teaching ethics, putting on the table the economic, ethical, and ecological implications of the development, marketing, use and disposal of a product specifically with which they are familiar. This methodology can be complemented with the one proposed by McWilliams and Nahavandi (2006); where students choose a single case study for the class, so that it is analyzed from all sides, including the aforementioned environmental dimension.

Along the same lines, Loeb (Loeb 2013) is the methodology of "active learning"; He however recognizes that there are difficulties such as: discomfort in the students, grading, lack of harmony in a group of students, deficiencies in realism and confidentiality problems; therefore, the author points out that it is important to take these aspects into account before applying the active learning methodology.

Mintz (2016) proposes the pedagogical method of "Giving Voice to Values" (GVV) launched by Mary Gentile in 2010. GVV seeks to develop the ability to express their opinions in a way that positively influences others.

Finally, Ariza Ruiz and Barón Pinto (2020) identifies two experiences in Colombia; the first at the University of Antioquia where Amézquita Toro et al. (2014), propose concrete reflective analysis of how the decisions of accounting professionals affect the Colombian reality, for example, in auditing and statutory auditing subjects; the ethical implications of the act of disclosing information are debated. Ovallos Gazabon et al. (2017), suggest a change in the teaching of professional accounting ethics, through a participatory experiential model that allows the student to incorporate ethical reasoning from the early stages of their education.

3   Method

The research developed is applied based on its objectives and mixed based on its sources of information, that is, it has a documentary component and a field component, the scope is exploratory and correlational, and the approach is qualitative. The field component is a correlational study, with probabilistic sampling, applying a structured survey to a representative sample of students, adapting the "Giving Voice to Values" method, Gentile (2017).

There is information corresponding to the application of previous instruments to 291 students of the program who have not been trained with the new curriculum, Corredor et al. (2021). It starts with the adaptation of the multidimensional scale used by Riemenschneider, Manly & Leonard (2016) to analyze the ethical behavior of students in information technology contexts, resorting to the GVV pedagogy that is supported by five philosophies to predict posture ethics: 1) egoism, 2) utilitarianism, 3) relativism, 4) contractualism, and 5) moral equity Riemenschneider, Manly & Leonard (2019), it is worth noting that these "philosophies" are inspired by the six stages of moral development proposed by the American psychologist Laurence Kohlberg (1981),

A new instrument is applied to students of the Public Accounting program of the Corporación Universitaria Minuto de Dios virtual and distance modality who have completed more than 75% of the curriculum, in this sense the population is 400 students, a random sampling is applied simple and a sample size of 197 students is determined, with a reliability of 95% and a margin of error of 5%. This new instrument consists of 19 sociodemographic items and 32 items corresponding to ethical dilemmas.

4 Results

The number of participants was 375 graduates and students, belonging to the Traditional Distance modality, of which 78 (21%) are men and 297 women (79%). 23% of the participants (86) are in the age range of 18 to 24 years, 44% (166) are between 25 and 35 years old, and 33% (123) are over 36 years old. Regarding the relationship with the institution, there are 331 students, and 44 graduates and degree candidates. It is noted that about 74% of the students have entered as of the year 2020, 16% enrolled during the year 2019 and 10% before 2018 and for their part, all the graduates indicated that their completion date is from before the second period of 2019.

Additionally, table number 1 is presented immediately with a description of the monthly income received, according to gender and considering that most of the sample are students, it is understood that about 58% (46 men and 171 women) of the participants earn income from US$267 to US$534. It is also noteworthy that 32% (19 men and 100 women) of the participants between men and women receive less than 1 (Table 1).

Table 1. Income of the participants in study (UBVD UNIMINUTO)

Gender/ Income	US$267 and US$534	US$534 and US$1068	More of US$1068	Less of US$267	Total
Man	12,27%	3,47%	0,00%	5,07%	20,80%
Woman	45,60%	6,40%	0,53%	26,67%	79,20%
Total	**57,87%**	**9,87%**	**0,53%**	**31,73%**	**100,00%**

Source: Own elaboration.

As for the cases that questioned the ethical positions of the students, the first, referring to a personal situation, showed the reaction of a young student when checking the cell phone of one of their classmates without their permission and discovering that they were making fun of them on social media, about very personal aspects, and decisions, in turn, to publish the intimate life of said partner on the same social networks, this will be case 1. On the other hand, case 2 addresses the decision of an auditor accepting a gift from the manager of the company they are auditing and having previously found serious findings that should be notified to the Board of Partners, and that after having received the aforementioned gift, intends to hide the findings.

Applying the aforementioned GVV method and considering Kohlberg's moral scale, students and graduates have been asked about the probability of committing the same actions as the protagonists of the cases described. Regarding the first situation, it was found that both students (68.3%) and graduates (67.7%) agree that "Publishing the intimate life of people on social networks without their authorization is a crime and could result in a legal and/or disciplinary action from the university." In addition, on average

8.45% of the participants also consider that in addition to the disciplinary sanction, the young woman would have to experience an uncomfortable situation, when everyone finds out about her decision to publish the intimate life of her partner. Finally, a significant piece of data: 7.3% of the students indicate that "Beginning the habit of using social networks to harm people now, could result in doing it more frequently in the future", compared to 2.94% of the graduates who chose this option, which shows that for the students there is not only a concern about the sanction but also that this fact is not repeated in the future.

Regarding the professional situation, 46% of the students and 38% of the graduates stated that "Hiding findings in an audit report is a professional crime and could receive a sanction or lose the professional certification", and 18% of students, as well as 26.5% of graduates, express concern that the auditor's response leads to the habit of hiding information in the future. Finally, 13.3% of the students and 14.71% of the graduates also worry that "Lina would not feel comfortable if her colleagues found out that hiding information was how she obtained additional income". The foregoing shows that, in both groups, a situation in which the professional ethics of the accountant is violated causes a deep concern about the disciplinary sanction (Table 2).

Table 2. Correlation and analysis for ethical positions

Percentage of the participants rating cases with the following moral categories			Correlation coefficient between case 1 and case 2 by moral category
Categoria moral	Case 1 personal situation	Case 2 profesional situation	
Not ethical	97,1%	97,9%	0,40287156
Unfair	91,2%	94,9%	0,32351682
Bad	96,0%	95,2%	0,5620838
Incorrect	96,8%	94,9%	0,49139794
Not acceptable for the family	96,5%	94,1%	0,57818616
Culturally unacceptable	89,3%	88,3%	0,47728495
Not acceptable according traditions	89,6%	89,1%	0,48785373
Not for gain personal	35,7%	73,1%	0,30065771
Not satisfactory	31,7%	30,4%	0,42873156
Not useful	74,4%	47,5%	0,36574856
Maximize damage	88,0%	80,3%	0,39569393
Violates rules	89,3%	89,9%	0,44839096
Breaches a promise	69,1%	90,9%	0,29123169

Source: Own elaboration

In the previous table, it is evident that when qualifying the situations described with respect to the young woman who publishes on social networks the intimate life of her partner as retaliation for making fun of her and the professional case, in which an accountant dedicated to the audit of a company fails to present the findings to the shareholders, after accepting a bonus from the manager; especially in the framework of the moral categories, the majority of participants consider that these actions were unethical, unfair, bad, incorrect, not family-acceptable, not culturally or traditionally acceptable. As evidenced, both in the first case and in the second, on average 94% of the participants indicated the aforementioned categories as their ethical positions.

On the other hand, in terms of whether it is an action for personal benefit and is satisfactory for the protagonists of the case, what is evident is that about 31% do not classify it that way, that is, 69% perceive that the actions help to personal interest and will also give them satisfaction. The foregoing would mean that most of the study participants associate an unethical or unjust action with a selfish and utilitarian posture, within the framework of the already mentioned scale, of Kohlberg's morality. Likewise, 85% of graduates and students consider that collateral damage is maximized, with an unfair or incorrect response to the situations raised in the study.

In addition, it is striking that asking about the usefulness of the decisions made in the cases, there is a variation between the personal situation and the professional situation, since in the first, 74.4% consider that it is not useful, but they make their position more flexible, in the professional situation, since the percentage is reduced to 47%. This shows that, for a professional action, utility is valued differently, and even if it is not ethical, it is attributed greater utility than on a personal level.

Thus, when investigating the possible violation of a promise, by violating ethical principles, in each case, the staff has an indication of 69.1% compared to 90.9% of the professional case. That is, when thinking about the personal treatment and the disclosure of intimate information of an acquaintance, it is considered in a greater proportion that a promise is violated, not so in the professional case. This would reinforce the idea that knowing the code of professional ethics is very relevant in public accounting curricula, since any infraction of said code violates the promise of responding to the public interest and faith, deposited in accounting professionals.

Finally, when calculating the correlations between the answers given in case 1 versus those obtained in case 2, in the same moral category, all the coefficients are positive, and the one closest to 1 stands out, with 0.58, which corresponds to the fact that it is not acceptable to the family, and immediately with 0.56 that they were "bad" actions. Then with 0.49, the "incorrect" category is found. The foregoing allows us to see that the family value has a high recognition, when the ethical positions are determined, in front of the reported cases, and then what would be considered "bad or good", which should be superior to the mere weighting of the legal or illegal, in principle.

5 Discussion and Conclusions

The implications of the results obtained with the application of the instrument can be summarized in the following elements:

Both students and graduates agree that "Publishing the intimate life of people on social networks without their authorization is a crime and could result in legal and/or disciplinary action from the university". The reflection is attached to the norm, which would indicate acting guided by the Kantian hypothetical imperative.

The concern expressed by the students not only for the sanctions but also because this fact is not repeated in the future, shows a change in the ethical position towards the graduates, that is, a possible modification due to the implementation of a change in the study plan and the adoption of case studies and simulations in the core subjects of vocational training.

This situation becomes more evident when evidencing that while 46% of the students stated that "Hiding findings in an audit report is a professional crime and could receive a sanction or lose the professional card", only 38% of the graduates stated such concern.

The opposite occurs when verifying that only 18% of the students express concern that the auditor's response leads to the habit of hiding information in the future; while 26.5% of graduates express such concern.

Students and graduates agree in expressing that a situation in which the professional ethics of the accountant is violated causes a deep concern for the disciplinary sanction, but also because it is not repeated and for the way in which this fact will be seen socially, especially by fellow accountants. That is, when the respondent is faced with evaluating actions related to his professional practice, he advances in terms of moral action.

Most of the participants consider that the actions in both cases were unethical, unfair, bad, incorrect, not family-acceptable, not culturally or traditionally acceptable.

Most of the study participants associate an unethical or unfair action with a selfish and utilitarian posture, within the framework of the already mentioned scale of Kohlberg's morality. Likewise, 85% of graduates and students consider that collateral damage is maximized, with an unfair or incorrect response to the situations raised in the study. That is, there is a proclivity to serve their own interests and instrumentalize other members of the community by pointing out that a non-strict norm is being violated.

However, a variation is evident, the posture becomes more flexible, in the professional situation, usefulness is valued differently, and although it is not ethical, it is attributed greater utility than on a personal level. This relativism will be equated to the fourth stage of Kohlberg's social system and consciousness, which in turn belongs to the conventional level and is located within what Kant denounces as the double standard characteristic of modernity, based on the hypothetical imperative.

When thinking about the personal treatment and the revelation of intimate information of an acquaintance, it is considered in a greater proportion that a promise is violated, not so in the professional case. This would reinforce the idea that knowing the code of professional ethics is very relevant in public accounting curricula, since any infraction of said code violates the promise to respond to the public interest and faith, deposited in accounting professionals.

The correlation analysis between the answers given in case 1 compared to those obtained in case 2, shows that the family value has a high recognition, when ethical positions are determined, compared to the reported cases, and then what would be considered "bad or good", which should be superior to the mere weighing of what is legal or illegal, in principle. In this sense, a high degree of maturity is identified in the Kholberg moral development scale, where the respondents evaluate the action based on justice, value, and the equality of all human beings.

References

Amézquita Toro, G.M., Díaz Montoya, J., Gutiérrez Bustamante, E.A.: Formación ética profesional del estudiante de contaduría pública de la universidad de antioquia tomando como referente el codigo de ética propuesto por la ifac. Trabajos de Grado Contaduría UdeA, **8**(1) (2014)

Ariza Ruiz, E.D., Barón Pinto, C.A.: Una propuesta metodológica para la enseñanza de la ética profesional contable en consonancia con ies 4. En m. Perez-fuentes, innovación docente e investigación en educación y ciencias sociales, pp. 409–419. Editorial Dykinson, Madrid (2020)

Bampton, R., Cowton, C.J.: Taking stock of accounting ethics scholarship: a review of the journal literature. J. Bus. Ethics. **114**, 549–563 (2012)

Christensen, A., Cote, J., Latham, C.K.: Developing ethical confidence: the impact of action-oriented ethics instruction in an accounting curriculum. J. Bus. Ethics **153**(4), 1157–1175 (2018). https://doi.org/10.1007/s10551-016-3411-4

CorredorGarcía, M.D.P., QuinteroRengifo, E.F., ArizaRuiz, E.D., Piñeros, M.I.A.: Methodological tools design to teach ethics in accounting according to IFAC IES 4. An approximation to the giving voice to values (GVV) methodology. In: BottoTobar, M., Cruz, H., DíazCadena, A. (eds.) Artificial Intelligence, Computer and Software Engineering Advances. AISC, vol. 1327, pp. 17–28. Springer, Cham (2021). https://doi.org/10.1007/978-3-030-68083-1_2

Dellaportas, S.: Making a difference with a discrete course on accounting ethics. J. Bus. Ethics **65**(4), 391–404 (2006)

Dellaportas, S., Leung, P., Cooper, B., Jackling, B.: IES 4 - ethics education revisited. Aust. Account. Rev. **16**(38), 4–12 (2006)

Des Jardins, J.R., Diedrich, E.: Learning what it really costs: teaching business ethics with life-cycle case studies. J. Bus. Ethics **48**(1), 33–42 (2003)

Gentile, M.C.: Giving voice to values: a pedagogy for behavioral ethics. J. Manage. Educ. **41**(4), 469–479 (2017). https://doi.org/10.1177/1052562917700188

GuiñezCabrera, N., VásquezPárraga, A.Z.: Orientación Ética de los estudiantes de contabilidad: evidencia en una universidad estatal de chile. Capic Rev. **13**, 51–58 (2015)

Kohlberg, L.: The Philosophy of Moral Development. Moral Stages and the Idea of Justice. Harper & Row Pubs, San Francisco (1981)

Loeb, S.E.: Active learning: an advantageous yet challenging approach to accounting ethics instruction. J. Bus. Ethics **127**(1), 221–230 (2013). https://doi.org/10.1007/s10551-013-2027-1

McWilliams, V., Nahavandi, A.: Using live cases to teach ethics. J. Bus. Ethics **67**(4), 421–433 (2006)

Mintz, S.: Giving voice to values: a new approach to accounting ethics education. Global Perspect. Account. Educ. **13**, 37–50 (2016)

O'Leary, C.: An empirical analysis of the positive impact of ethics teaching on accounting students. Taylor Francis J. **18**(4–5), 505–520 (2009)

OvallosGazabon, D., AlvarezCantillo, A., MirandaAlvarez, A.: Ética y Responsabilidad Social del Contador frente a las Normas Internacionales de Información Financiera (NIIF) en Colombia. Un Análisis Prospectivo. Espacios **38**(37), 14–33 (2017)

Quintero, E., Rodriguez, B.: Relación entre las actitudes, las normas subjetivas y el control del comportamiento percibido que tiene el estudiante frente a la decisión de matricularse en el programa de contaduría pública de uniminuto virtual y a distancia en Colombia. Revista CIDU **I**, 15 (2018)

Riemenschneider, C.K., Manly, T.S., Leonard, L.N.: Using giving voice to values to improve student academic integrity in information technology contexts. J. Inf. Syst. Educ. **27**(3), 183–196 (2016).

Ruiz Urquijo, J.C., Ariza Ruiz, E.D.: Enseñanza de la ética profesional en Contaduría Pública. Análisis de 15 syllabus en Colombia. Boletin Redipe. 8(4), 106–118 (2019). https://revista.red ipe.org/index.php

Van Hise, J., Massey, D.W.: Applying the Ignatian pedagogical paradigm to the creation of an accounting ethics course. J. Bus. Ethics 96(3), 453–465 (2010). https://doi.org/10.1007/s10 551-010-0477-2

Leadership Styles and Organizational Culture in a Real Estate Company

Carla Beatriz Vásquez Reyes[(✉)] [iD] and Julia Otilia Sagástegui Cruz[iD]

Universidad Privada del Norte, Trujillo, Peru
N00157138@upn.pe

Abstract. This study aims, this contribution considers 2 points: the conceptual one, through the systematic review of the main definitions of this construct, and the operational one, by inspecting the dimensions that have been included by the main authors to evaluate it. The objective was to determine the relationship between leadership styles and organizational culture in the company Marka Group, Trujillo 2021. The design was correlational, with a population of 132 workers. Two instruments were then applied: Multifactor Leadership Questionnaire (MLQ-5X) for the leadership styles variable, which has an approach with different dimensions according to the style of the leader; and, for the second variable, the OCAI scale-type questionnaire by Cameron and Quinn was applied, measuring the perception that employees have regarding their culture, both through google forms. The results show that 81.8% of the respondents believe that they have transformational leadership and perceive a Clan-type culture.

Keywords: Leadership styles · Organizational culture · Human behavior

1 Introduction

In the global world we live in, there are challenges such as the development of a leadership that promotes the development of companies, as well as provides better working conditions for workers, thus improving their quality of life. A topic widely discussed and analyzed was the most successful leadership style to apply, since the time of Platon (Ivancevich 2003); leadership is the basis of the living being of universal and primordial order.

In this sense, Alvear et al. (2019) propose in their research an analysis of the leadership styles developed by senior executives in the companies that export from Barranquilla. The results indicate that transformational leadership is the most used, transactional leadership is in second place followed by laissez-faire leadership, from which various theories indicate which points should be considered to maximize its applicability. In conclusion, it can be seen that by combining transactional and transformational leadership, a series of competitive advantages are generated for workers.

Serveleon (2017), the existence of the relationship between leadership and organizational culture was analyzed, which opened a knowledge horizon where there is a moderate positive correlation, which can be used as a starting point for future plans of

M. Botto-Tobar et al. (Eds.): ICAT 2022, CCIS 1757, pp. 293–302, 2023.
https://doi.org/10.1007/978-3-031-24978-5_26

continuous and sustained improvement. Finally, it is concluded that there is a relationship between leadership and organizational culture.

Leadership results from the leader's direct influence on subordinates leading them to achieve group goals (Bass 1995). Burns looks at transactional leadership as an exchange between the leader and his/her followers, in which they obtain some value from the work they do; it is a cost-benefit relationship (Bass 1999).

Fischman (2017) states the following definition: "culture includes values and beliefs and assumptions that are not always conscious but reflect a behavior in the members of a company" (p. 21).

Hellriegel et al. (2017) indicate regarding organizational culture: it plays a primary role in institutional life, given that, it contributes to learning and has a new effect on new opportunities and challenges that may be generated. By influencing situations where there are challenges and the culture generated allows overcoming these challenges, it will help to achieve the objectives that top management wants to achieve with the help of its staff.

This research aims to help solve a real problem, such as organizational culture, which is one of the most important factors for the development of a company in all its areas: productive, administrative, structural, and evolutionary. It is a key element to explain human behavior at work. For this reason, the research question formulated was: What is the relationship between leadership styles and organizational culture in the company Marka Group, Trujillo 2021? The general objective was to determine the relationship between leadership styles and organizational culture in the company Marka Group, in the city of Trujillo-Peru. It also has two specific objectives: To analyze the leadership styles identified and the organizational culture in the company Marka Group. Organizations with a weak organizational culture can hardly aspire to be better. That is why, instruments were developed and applied, whose purpose was to determine the relationship between the study variables, such as leadership styles and organizational culture. Likewise, the hypothesis shows that there is a significant relationship between leadership styles and organizational culture in the company Marka Group.

Likewise, Picurelli (2019) cited by Romero (2019) states about leadership, that it is a disadvantage not to have an adequate organizational culture that influences people to work properly and achieve the desired success.

According to Bass y Avolio (1996), the existing models were delimited into two large groups, by using as a point of view the type of interaction between the leader and the members of his/her team, calling them transformational leadership and transactional leadership. The first category describes the form of interaction between the leader and the followers. Followers allow the leader's influence if they receive resources or a transaction for meeting objectives that were initially assigned to them. Therefore, transactional leadership is based on conditional reward. Followers are motivated by promises made by leaders, providing rewards and/or possible punishments (Bass 1996). The other category is that of transformational models, where the leader moves forward without the need for any exchange. Leaders encourage followers to put the interests and benefits of the group before the particular benefit of each follower.

2   Materials and Methods

Due to the nature of the objective, a quantitative, basic, prospective, cross-sectional, correlational, and observational study was chosen, because it was possible to determine the relationship between the variables: leadership style and organizational culture. In addition, a simple, non-experimental, correlational design was used. The study was carried out in the company Marka Group, in the city of Trujillo-Peru during the period 2021.

Two questionnaires were used, one for each variable. The Multifactorial Leadership questionnaire MLQ-5X short version, adapted to Spanish, measured the Leadership Styles variable, comprising 45 Likert-type questions distributed in 3 dimensions: Transformational leadership, transactional leadership, laissez-faire. The instrument was validated and reliable with an internal consistency Alpha coefficient of 0.93 which points to high reliability for the instrument, indicating that it is a reliable instrument (Fong 2018).

For the organizational culture variable, the OCAI scale-type questionnaire by Cameron and Quinn was used, translated into Spanish, with a total of 24 questions divided into 6 dimensions: dominant characteristics, leadership in my organization, management style, organizational unity, strategic emphasis, and criteria for success, referring to 4 dominant types of culture: clan, adhocracy, market, and hierarchy.

The data collection was done through Google forms compiled in a MICROSOFT EXCEL database. The data analysis was done through SPSS statistical software, with a population of 132 workers corresponding to the commercial, administration and finance, marketing, projects, and branches areas, in order to make the analysis and obtain reliable results in this research (Table 1).

3   Results

Table 1. Leadership Styles in the company Marka Group, Trujillo 2021

Levels	Counts	% of total
Transformational leadership	108	81.8%
Transactional leadership	14	10.6%
Laissez Faire leadership	10	7.6%
	132	100%

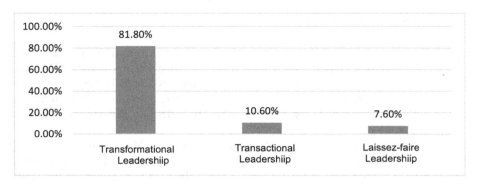

Fig. 1. Leadership Styles in the company Marka Group

In the figure it can be seen that 81.8% of respondents believe that they have transformational leadership, 10.6% of workers believe that they have transactional leadership and 7.60% believe that they have Laissez-Faire leadership (Figs. 1, 2 and Table 2).

Table 2. Perception of the Organizational Culture according to the company Marka Group, Trujillo, 2021

	Quant	%	Average	Std Dev	Min	Max
CLAN	56	42%	29.4	10.8	10	67.5
ADHOCRACY	6	5%	21.7	7.54	9.17	61.7
MARKET	60	45%	31.1	11.5	9.17	59.2
HIERARCHY	10	8%	17.7	8.25	2.5	35
	132	100%				

In the analysis of Organizational Culture, it is observed that 42% of workers perceive a Clan-type culture, i.e., it is perceived as a big family, where beliefs and values are shared. They perceive that leadership is based on consensus and the participation of all workers in the company. They perceive that the team is loyal, united, and cohesive.

45% perceive the organizational culture as a market-type culture, i.e., they believe that the company promotes competitiveness and profit orientation. The company is focused on the achievement of results and encourages all workers to be competitive, promoting competition, aggressiveness, goals to achieve the objectives.

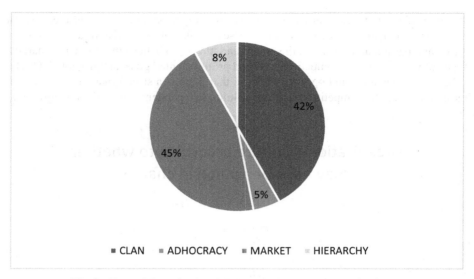

Fig. 2. Type of Organizational Culture in the company Marka Group

Fig. 3. Type of organizational culture in the company Marka Group, according to the job position.

Figure 3 shows that the Assistants perceive a clan-type organizational culture, where a family environment is perceived, and the bosses are like tutors. Decisions are consensus-based and participatory. But, on the other hand, they also believe that there is a market-type culture, i.e., where competitiveness and profit-oriented goals are promoted. On the other hand, managers and operators believe that there is a strong market-type culture, based on demands, competitiveness, and valuing independence more than integration.

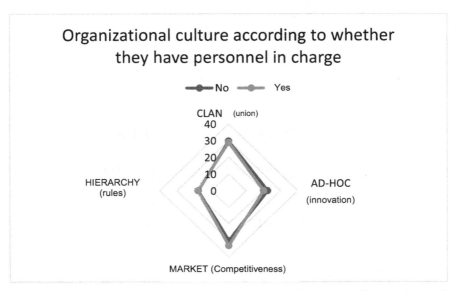

Fig. 4. Type of organizational culture in the company Marka Group, according to whether they have personnel in charge.

Figure 4 shows that employees with and without personnel in charge perceive that the predominant organizational culture in the company is market-type, i.e., it is oriented to the company's goals and profits, promoting competitiveness and aggressiveness in the achievement of goals (Table 3).

It can be observed that the p-value of X2 is $0.006 < 0.05$, so we reject Ho, and conclude that there is a significant relationship between leadership styles and Organizational Culture. Likewise, the contingency coefficient of 0.509 indicates that there is a moderate relationship between them.

Table 3. Contingency chart between leadership type and organizational culture

	Adhocracy	Clan	Hierarchy	Market	Total
Transformational Leadership	4	52	8	44	108
Transactional Leadership	2	8	2	2	14
Laissez-faire Leadership				10	10
General Total	6	60	10	56	132

Nominal	Value
Contingency coefficient	0.509
Phi-coefficient	NaN
Cramer's V	0.342

χ^2 Tests

	Value	Df	P
χ^2	23.1	9	0.006
N	66		

4 Discussion

The skills and experiences of managers have different challenges on the objectives and strategies to improve the development of the organization. Our main objective is to determine the relationship between leadership styles and organizational culture in the company Marka Group, Trujillo 2021. Definitely, the leadership style that prevails in the organization defines the motivation or discouragement of employees. It is important to highlight the Bass Transformational Leadership theory that considers leadership as the contingent leverage of the beneficiaries (transactional), the engine that enables followers to develop (transformational) (Bass 1997). The transformational model cites the type of leadership that transcends the exchange and motivates followers to an evolution of their beliefs and values. A transformer-type leader motivates a company to develop its work because of a higher-order need (Crawford 1995). An inspired transformational leader helps in the growth of a follower of Burns (1978), citing Ames' thesis (2014).

In the analysis of results, we can conclude that 81.8% of respondents believe that they have transformational leadership. This type of leadership bases its scheme on making the group interests their own, having an attitude of group commitment that leads them to try to promote the growth of the group, according to Nichols (1998). 10.6% of workers think that they have transactional leadership, and 7.60% think that they have Laissez-Faire leadership. The former is an activity of the leader who determines a transaction between the leader and the members of the group; the members accept his/her authority so that the leader contributes resources of different value for all or part of the group. Laissez-Faire leadership is the lack or inexistence of leadership, being the most inefficient and inactive style (Ames 2014).

Regarding the dimensions of the Leadership variable, all of them are at regular level, being C1 the ones with the lowest average: management by passive exception, i.e. the leaders usually leave things as they are and, in any case, they only intervene when the problems become serious, and also C2: Letting extra effort where they are not able to get the extra effort from their collaborators to achieve the optimal levels of performance. This influences the performance that the employees have. In the real estate sector, there is high competition so the organization tries to achieve optimal performance and interaction between employees and employers.

Regarding the organizational culture variable, the objective is to analyze the organizational culture in the company Marka Group, Trujillo 2021. According to our results, we can conclude that in the organizational culture, it is observed that 42% of workers perceive a clan-type culture, i.e. it is perceived as a big family, where beliefs and values are shared. They perceive that leadership is based on consensus and the participation of all workers in the company. They perceive that the team is loyal, united, and cohesive. According to Hellriegel et al. (2017), loyalty, personal commitment, tradition, high socialization, and teamwork are characteristics of this type of culture. In addition, culture is felt and can be perceived in the activities or actions that are developed daily.

Furthermore, Chura (2018), in his research: Leadership and organizational culture in the Instituto de Educación Superior Tecnológico Público El Descanso-Filial Túpac Amaru, Canas, Cusco-2018. Universidad César Vallejo, Peru. The publication sought to determine the relationship between the organizational culture of the institution under study. The specific objectives were: the relationships between the organizational culture with all the dimensions that make up the leadership. The study was carried out with a non-experimental design since none of the variables were manipulated; only the correlation between them was determined. The study was descriptive and correlational since the phenomenon studied is described with the data collected. As for the population, it was made up of 35 students and 5 teachers, from which 26 students and 4 teachers were used as the sample, with a total of 30 people from the institution. Two questionnaires were designed as instruments to learn about leadership and organizational culture. Expert judgment was used to validate the surveys. The conclusion reached is that there is no significant relationship, and there is a very low negative correlation between the variables studied.

According to the analysis of our results, 45% perceive a market-type organizational culture, i.e., they believe that competitiveness and profit orientation stand out in the company. The company is focused on the achievement of results and encourages all workers to be competitive, promoting competition, aggressiveness, goals, in order to achieve the company's objectives.

According to Hellriegel et al. (2017):

The market culture that focuses on achieving a series of financial goals highlights the competition that may exist among workers in order to achieve the financial objectives that have been projected and that incorporate rewards in exchange for the effort achieved. This implies that there is a kind of exchange between the demand for the achievement of a financial goal in exchange for some reward that the staff may receive.

The employees with and without personnel in charge perceive that the predominant organizational culture in the company is market-type, i.e., it is oriented to the company's goals and profits, promoting competitiveness and aggressiveness in the achievement of goals. Just as men and women perceive the predominant organizational culture in the company as a market-type, i.e., it is perceived in the focus on business goals, and levels of demand for achieving them timely, this leadership promotes competitiveness and aggressiveness of the winning spirit.

It is important to highlight that Calagua (2019), in his research: "Leadership style and organizational culture in an associative company: A case study on COOPERATIVA DE SERVICIOS MÚLTIPLES SOL&CAFÉ". Pontificia Universidad Católica del Perú, Lima. This study was carried out to analyze the relationship between organizational culture and leadership styles, based on the collaborators of a Cooperative dedicated to the exploitation of coffee beans in our country. It mentions the progress of the studies that relate organizational culture and leadership over time in an organization. The research conducted by the author is oriented under a mixed approach, which includes both quantitative and qualitative approaches.

5   Conclusions

According to the analysis of results, it is determined that there is a significant relationship between leadership styles and organizational culture. Likewise, the contingency coefficient of 0.509 indicates that there is a moderate relationship between them.

81.8% of respondents believe that they have transformational leadership, being this the predominant style, on which they base their scheme making group interests their own, having an attitude of group commitment; and, 10.6% of workers believe that they have transactional leadership.

42% of workers perceive a Clan-type culture, i.e., it is perceived as a big family, where beliefs and values are shared. Leadership is based on consensus and the participation of all the company's workers. They perceive that the team is loyal, united, and cohesive.

References

Bass, B.M.: Theory of transformational leadership redux (1995)
Bass, B.M.: Theory of transformational leadership redux (1999)

Ivancevich, J.M.: Comportamiento Organizacional [Organizational Behavior]. McGraw-Hill, Madrid (2003)

Alvear Montoya, L., Luna Monterrosa, O., Navarro Lobo, S., Salas Muñoz, B.: Estilos de liderazgo de la alta dirección en industrias exportadoras de Barranquilla [Leadership styles of the top management in export industries of Barranquilla]. Redalyc (2019)

Fong, M.: Adaptación del Cuestionario Multifactorial de Liderazgo (MLQ -5X) en una empresa de Call Center, Lima Metropolitana, 2018 [Adaptation of the Multifactor Leadership Questionnaire (MLQ -5X) in a Call Center company, Lima Metropolitana, 2018]. (Undergraduate thesis). Universidad César Vallejo, Lima (2018)

Bass, B.: Does the transactional-transformational leadership paradigm trascended organizational and national boundaries? Am. Psychol. **52**, 2 (1997)

Crawford, C.: Socially Supportive Transformational Leaders: Paradigm and Prescription for Organizational Stress (1995)

Ames Sora, L.H.: Estilo de liderazgo en relación de la autopercepción del desempeño laboral en la dirección de control y supervisión de comunicaciones del Ministerior de transporte y comunicaciones del Perú [Leadership style in relation to the self-perception of job performance in the direction of control and supervision of communications of the Ministry of Transport and Communications of Peru]. Repositorio UCV Lima-Norte, Lima-Péru (2014)

Nicholls, J.: Congruent leadership. Organ. Dev. J. **7**(1) (1998)

Hellriegel, D., Jackson, S.E., Slocum, J.W.: Administración. Un enfoque basado en competencias [Management: A Competency-Based Approach], 12th edn. Cengage Learning, Mexico (2017)

Romero Romero, J.W.: Relación entre los estilos de liderazgo y la cultura organizacional en nueve Startup de línea tecnológica que ganaron en el Concurso de Startup Perú, Lima 2019 [Relationship between leadership styles and organizational culture in nine Startup of technological line that won in the Startup Peru Competition, Lima 2019]. San Ignacio de Loyola, Lima (2019)

Fischman, D.: Cuando el liderazgo no es suficiente [When leadership is not enough], 1st edn. Planeta, Péru (2017)

Inclusive Policies and Teaching Practices in Educational Institutions, in Pandemic

Anita Erliz Valderrama Rios(✉) [iD], Gian Christian Orlando Orbegoso Reyes [iD],
Julia Otilia Sagástegui Cruz [iD], and Carlos Luis Pérez Urrutia [iD]

Universidad Privada del Norte, Trujillo, Perú
N00154068@upn.pe

Abstract. Currently, educational inclusion is generating more expectations in Latin American educational institutions. As an example of this, there is greater interest in providing attention to groups of students with special needs and attention, particularly in the context of the health crisis. The main objective of the study was to determine the relationship between inclusive policies and good teaching practices in private educational institutions of the primary level. Under a quantitative approach, we worked with a non-experimental, cross-sectional design and applied the validated questionnaire "Inclusion Index", a Likert-type scale, to 50 primary school teachers in the city of Trujillo. The results show a high and significant correlation (.835**) between the two variables under study, suggesting the importance of establishing adequate policies to improve inclusion practices. Likewise, from the teachers' perspective, the need to improve inclusive policies with the commitment to encourage and promote inclusive practice within their educational institutions is also noted. Finally, it is concluded that educational inclusion is a process and a strategy that helps to overcome barriers to learning. However, the critical global situation hinders the goal of implementing this system effectively.

Keywords: Educational inclusion · Inclusive policy · Inclusive practice · Teaching practice · Educational institutions

1 Introduction

Currently, educational inclusion has received greater attention in the Latin American context. This has been generating expectation in the possibilities of attention to human groups with special needs and constitutes a major step in the aspiration to build more equitable and democratic societies. All this implies a commitment to quality teaching for the entire student population, regardless of personal or social conditions. However, the task is not easy because, as Peralta Ortega (2017) argues, educational equity is still considered a deep and delicate principle to apply in Latin America.

Inclusive education emerges within the framework of special education, in relation to this, the United Nations Educational, Scientific and Cultural Organization [UNESCO] (2017) states that: "all the students count, and they count equally"; therefore, teachers and managers are required to change both in theory and in practice at all levels of the educational system.

M. Botto-Tobar et al. (Eds.): ICAT 2022, CCIS 1757, pp. 303–313, 2023.
https://doi.org/10.1007/978-3-031-24978-5_27

In the Peruvian context, educational inclusion practices have faced limitations and difficulties in their implementation and execution, because there is still an erroneous concept of the term "inclusive education". This situation becomes a barrier to learning and participation, limits lifelong learning opportunities for everyone, and hinders or reduces teachers' outreach to students. Given this, the teacher is in charge of significantly facilitating learning and developing the social skills that allow inclusive students to integrate into society (Magnússon et al. 2019).

The problem addressed in this research refers to the lack of adequate inclusive policies, which hinders the implementation of educational inclusion in particular institutions. An expression of this is the low receptivity of students and the undervaluation of teachers' work by the educational community. In the same way, the transformation of traditional teaching towards an inclusive one has been distorted, which leads to complications that directly affect the teacher-student relationship, causing uncertainties between what the government dictates and the reality that is experienced. (Espinoza et al. 2021). In this sense, it is necessary to determine the difference between school integration and inclusive education, because school integration aims to "correct" the difference and inclusion is enriched by it in such a way that integration seeks to normalize people through social and educational dynamics and inclusion aims to help each one according to their needs and abilities (Tovar 2021).

Given this scenario and the variables that arise from it, this study posed the following question: How do inclusive policies relate to good teaching practices in private educational institutions, in times of pandemic, in Trujillo? The purpose of this question was to determine the relationship between the two study variables, guided by the hypothesis of the existence of a high and significant correlation between inclusive policies and good teaching practices. In order to develop the research, the following specific objectives were formulated: a) to evaluate the perspective of teachers from private educational institutions regarding the development of a school for all and the attention to diversity; b) to evaluate the perspective of teachers from private educational institutions of primary level regarding the learning process and the mobilization of resources.

Under these parameters, different international studies that provide relevance and contribute to the research topic were identified. Campa et al. (2020) have conducted a study to examine the inclusive practices and culture of primary school teachers for the attention of neglected groups in Hermosillo, Sonora, Mexico. In this study with a quantitative, non-experimental-descriptive approach, it is shown as a result that vulnerability in the class comes from low economic conditions, dysfunctional family, and disability. And, it is concluded that education and the training of students is still a great challenge in a diverse society as well as for the educational community.

Angenscheidt and Navarrete (2017) conducted another research to describe the attitudes of early childhood and primary school educators in a private school in Montevideo, concerning inclusive education. The research design was cross-sectional and descriptive. Thanks to this study, they determined that teachers with more experience have a more favorable attitude regarding inclusive measures and practices. In conclusion, they argue that teachers' attitudes are very important nowadays, even more in a context such as Uruguay, where educational and legislative policies are being implemented and where an increase of students with some type of disability in regular classes starts to be reflected.

In the national context (Peru), there have also been studies that address the importance of the topic under investigation. Luna Andrade (2020) managed to find a relationship between inclusive practice and teaching attitude in a particular educational institution. A quantitative study, with a correlational and cross-sectional design, was applied, taking a sample of 20 teachers from that institution. The main finding was a considerably high correlation between both variables. It was also determined that all the dimensions considered in the instrument reaffirm the relationship between the variables under study.

At the local level, Alfaro Asto (2018) conducted a study on perceptions, which are interpreted as a set of ideas, policies, postures, and resources used by inclusive teachers to attend regular classes in the city of Trujillo. By using a non-experimental design and a non-probabilistic sampling, a sample of 85 teachers from the primary level was selected. As a result, it describes the main characteristics of the population studied and concludes that a large percentage of teachers express a positive attitude towards inclusive education in the social context, but that the institutions do not have adequate conditions for the inclusion of students with special educational needs.

Nomberto Guerra (2020), for his part, addressed the topic of inclusive education as an important point within his study, with the main objective of establishing the relationship between inclusive education and teaching performance in an educational institution in Trujillo, 2020. Within the framework of a quantitative, non-experimental, cross-sectional research, a descriptive correlational design was used, through the application of questionnaires with a Likert-type scale. The main finding of this research was the direct, high, and significant relationship between these two variables: the greater the importance given to inclusive education, the higher and better the teacher performance. In addition, it was concluded that between the variables of inclusive education certain normality is reflected.

Besides these findings and the results of the studies cited above, it is important to take into account what is pointed out by Booth and Ainscow (2002). They state that inclusive education comprises a process consisting of three dimensions: cultural, political, and practical. The cultural dimension is focused on creating a safe, collaborative, and inviting community in which values and beliefs are established and shared. In the political dimension, inclusion is the basis for the development of the educational institution and determines the modalities of support to face the reality; and in the dimension of inclusive practice, actions and strategies are promoted in accordance with the inclusive culture and policies.

Within this context, in order to meet the objective, this study is structured based on background information referring to the problematic reality and the theoretical framework that addresses the main concepts related to the variables studied. Secondly, the research methodology is described, from the approach and type of study, the participants, and the data collection and processing techniques used. The third section describes the results and the validity of the instrument. Finally, the discussions and conclusions of the research are shown.

1.1 Inclusive Policy

Currently, the purpose of inclusive education policies is to eliminate inequality among the student society and to faithfully support the idea of generating opportunities equally, leaving aside any type of discrimination. Therefore, it should be seen as an opportunity to face and reduce the inequalities currently existing within society. This will be possible if each of the authorities of each country promotes inclusive education within their educational institutions, whether private or public, showing respect and empathy as the main values (Ledesma et al. 2019).

1.2 Teaching Practice

Teachers play a fundamental role and are considered an irreplaceable pillar in the development of an educational system (Campa et al. 2020). For this reason, and given the current situation, teachers need to have training that allows them to build and develop their professional competencies, in order to work together to achieve progress (Campa and Contreras 2018).

1.3 Inclusive Education in Times of Pandemic

In this context of a health emergency, the education system is going through an extremely delicate and transcendental moment: not only has there been a total disruption, but this paralysis is directly affecting millions of students around the world. Education is considered a right with a direct impact on the formation of people as a society, and to avoid generating a crisis in the academic field, governments and institutions involved in this area have been encouraged to follow the new parameters and standards that promote inclusive education (United Nations [UN] 2020).

The decision to use remote education has become a major concern for authorities, parents, and teachers. It is the responsibility of educational authorities and teachers to pay more attention to inclusive practices, with the corresponding commitment to implement monitoring and control actions on all processes and students, without exception. However, at present, there are still vulnerable areas with precarious technological development. Therefore, UNESCO (2020) commits its support to all countries, especially those with educational institutions with limited resources, to mitigate the negative impact of the pandemic. This, in some way, guarantees equitable and inclusive quality education, through innovative solutions appropriate to the current context (Camacho et al. 2020).

According to the literature analyzed, the various authors address definitions and qualities about inclusive policy and teaching practice, which are hampered by the current emergency situation; Although there is an idea of what is to be achieved, the actors of the educational process and the student body have not yet effectively achieved the development of inclusive education, despite the existence of parameters to develop.

Based on these findings, this research aims to determine the relationship between the two study variables, because they are decisive factors in the construction of equal opportunities to insert themselves in society, and in the same way, they help reduce student learning barriers; This fact is intended to be achieved by applying a validated questionnaire to teachers of private educational institutions.

2 Materials and Methods

A quantitative approach to the study was used, whereby the data collected were subjected to numerical measurement and statistical analysis in order to test the existing theoretical assumptions about the study variables without being manipulated (Espinoza et al. 2021). In this research, the non-experimental, cross-sectional design oriented the collection of information in a single moment, within the framework of a descriptive-correlational study (Ñaupas et al. 2018) that allowed us to determine the type of relationship between teaching practice and inclusive policy, based on the characterization of good inclusive teaching practices in private educational institutions in the city of Trujillo, in times of pandemic.

2.1 Sample

The information was collected through non-probabilistic purposive sampling. The sample consisted of 50 primary school teachers from private educational institutions in the city of Trujillo, with 80% of them being female and 20% male. In another aspect, 42% of the sample members have obtained a bachelor's degree, 32% have a professional degree, 25% have a master's degree and 2% have a doctorate.

The inclusion criteria for the selection and composition of the sample were as follows: teachers currently working in private educational institutions in the district of Trujillo and the consideration of teaching any grade of primary school (from first to sixth grade).

2.2 Instrument

The Index for Inclusion questionnaire, which has been previously validated, was used. Originally, this instrument was organized into three dimensions: inclusive culture, inclusive policies, and inclusive practices (Booth and Ainscow 2002). However, in order to collect information to determine the relationship between inclusive policy and good teaching practices in private educational institutions during the pandemic in Trujillo, the questionnaire had to be adapted. For this purpose, a Likert-type evaluation scale was used, organized into two dimensions: inclusive policies and inclusive practices. A Cronbach's alpha reliability analysis of 0.969 was performed for the 33 items. Once all the necessary adjustments had been made, the instrument was ready for the collection of pertinent information, following the research objective.

2.3 Fieldwork and Data Analysis

For the application of the questionnaire, the support of the directors of the selected educational institutions was requested. They informed their teaching staff of the purpose of the research and, under the principle of informed consent, mediated the application of the instrument and the collection of information. This action was carried out between June 14 and 18, 2021. The virtual method was used, due to the current health emergency. Total anonymity was guaranteed to achieve the greatest possible veracity in the teachers' answers. The recording or marking of responses lasted approximately 10 to 15 min. Once the information had been collected, the SPSS (v.26) statistical program was used to carry out a reliable, descriptive, and correlational analysis; Microsoft Excel software was also used to structure the descriptive table.

3 Results

Based on the main results obtained in the research, an analysis has been made of the frequency with which primary school teachers from private educational institutions value the position they assume about the "Elaboration of inclusive policies", whose dimensions are to develop a school for all and organize the support to attend to the diversity; and its relationship with the "Development of inclusive practices", which is composed to orchestrate the learning process and resource mobilization.

Table 1. Frequencies according to the scales of inclusive policies and inclusive practices

Variable/Scale	Completely agree (4)		Agree (3)		Disagree (2)		Completely disagree (1)	
	fi	%	fi	%	fi	%	fi	%
Inclusive Policies (A)	14.5	29	30	60	5.5	11	0	0
School for all (A1)	15	30	29	58	6	12	0	0
Attend to the diversity (A2)	14	28	31	62	5	10	0	0
Inclusive Practices (B)	18.5	37	27	54	4.5	9	0	0
Learning Process (B1)	20	40	26	52	4	8	0	0
Resource Mobilization (B2)	17	34	28	56	5	10	0	0

Source: Own Elaboration

Table 1 shows that 89% of teachers agree with the improvement of inclusive policies that a) promote a school for all (88%), and b) organize the support to attend to the diversity (90%). As it is evident, they are the ones who are directly involved with the formative process of their students and, therefore, the main interested parties in the improvement of the attention conditions.

Taking advantage of their knowledge and experience, they willingly try to balance the teaching-learning process to attend to the diversity of students they have within a section or group. If this was already a complicated task in the classroom, in times of pandemic it is necessary to make a greater effort to provide special attention and not to neglect their students with different abilities. This is why they agree with the development of inclusive practices (91%), starting with structuring the learning process (92%) and a necessary mobilization of resources (90%) since the optimal functioning of these factors will allow students to receive classes within the necessary conditions of equity and quality, as it is an earned right that the political and social class usually neglects. The work begins with adequate management so that the expected results can be obtained, not only to meet a goal but also because it is crucial to respect the right that every person should have to quality education (Table 2).

Table 2. Correlations of inclusive policies and inclusive practices including their dimensions

Variable	Statistic	A	A1	A2	B	B1	B2
Inclusive Policies (A)	Correlation coefficient	1	,909**	,944**	,835**	,843**	,767**
	Sig. (bilateral)		0	0	0	0	0
School for all	Correlation coefficient		1	,740**	,772**	,778**	,734**
(A1)	Sig. (bilateral)			0	0	0	0
Attend to the diversity	Correlation coefficient			1	,780**	,797**	,686**
(A2)	Sig. (bilateral)				0	0	0
Inclusive Practices (B)	Correlation coefficient				1	,987**	,945**
	Sig. (bilateral)					0	0
Learning Process	Correlation coefficient					1	,894**
(B1)	Sig. (bilateral)						0
Resource Mobilization	Correlation coefficient						1
(B2)	Sig. (bilateral)						

Note: **. The correlation is significant at the 0.01 level (bilateral)
Source: Own elaboration

From the correlations carried out, it was found that there are direct and highly significant relationships between inclusive policy and the development of inclusive practices (.835**). This shows the importance of establishing adequate policies in favor of improving inclusive practices. This is the only way for students with different abilities or disabilities to achieve their competencies in times of pandemics.

When correlating the dimensions of the inclusive policies variable (school for all and attention to the diversity) with the dimensions of inclusive practices (teaching-learning process and mobilization of resources), a strong and relevant correlation was found, which allows us to affirm that aspects such as the attention to the diversity and the mobilization of resources are essential in any inclusive education process. Otherwise, not much can be done or expected to provide the long-awaited quality education that is sought.

According to the theoretical model, previously defined, it is understood that the dimension of "inclusive policies" in its sections encompasses the development of the educational center, to improve the learning of the student population. Regarding the dimension of the development of "inclusive practices," it aims to ensure that extracurricular activities are a reason for students to gain more experience and knowledge through the efforts and reinforcement of teachers (Fig. 1).

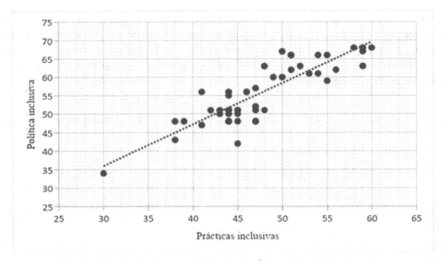

Fig. 1. Correlation between Inclusive Policy and Inclusive Practices

The analysis of the two variables under study reveals a direct and highly significant relationship between inclusive policies and teaching practices. One depends on the other to develop. According to the appreciation of the teachers of these private institutions in Trujillo, the better the application or management of the policies, the better the results in the application of inclusive practices. The determination coefficient ($R^2 = 0.7324$) explains the proportion of the total variance of the variables present in the regression and allows us to determine the goodness of fit of this model.

4 Discussion

The information collected and analyzed allows us to understand that there is a positive perspective on educational inclusion. Therefore, if teachers assume a full commitment with dynamism towards all members without exception, inclusive policies and pedagogical practices will improve, obtaining greater academic and social benefits, creating stronger links through interpersonal relationships between teachers. The students (Quintero 2020).

Inclusive education is also considered a necessary asset to improve not only the educational model but also to contribute with favorable actions and results for society. The main contribution of inclusive education lies in understanding the disadvantages faced by schoolchildren and in revealing the barriers that hinder learning. This is fundamental when designing and undertaking actions that make it possible to enrich the knowledge and enhance the skills of students (Jiménez et al. 2017), in a context of diversity. Unfortunately, the Peruvian educational system has made very little progress in this regard; and, in the case of private educational institutions, teachers feel that they are far from these considerations and that their contributions are not valued to the extent of their real importance.

In the city of Trujillo (Peru), for example, the teaching staff of private primary schools assumes that it is a source of valuable initiatives to optimize inclusive education. This was determined in the dimensions and the respective sections of the instrument used. The correlation between the variables yields a value of 0.835, which is sufficient to say that there is determination and that an improvement is possible. In the same line, the results of the research conducted by Nomberto Guerra (2020), who finds a moderately significant relationship between the study variables (inclusive education and teacher performance), obtaining a correlation of 0.05, so that if the correlation value is higher between the two variables, a better teaching effect is obtained.

Based on the analysis carried out, it is possible to affirm that teachers from private educational institutions are challenged to improve the inclusive policy, from a practical point of view. They are motivated by the desire to achieve better learning for their students and to contribute to generating greater and diverse educational opportunities in a context of equity. They aim to build a school for all through the attention to diversity and intend to contribute to the development of an inclusive practice based on the learning process and the adequate mobilization of resources. For this reason, it is essential to work on an improvement plan in educational institutions. This plan should be developed collaboratively, taking into account the reality and perspectives of teachers. Likewise, it is necessary to promote and encourage educational inclusion as outlined by the Ministry of Education [MINEDU] (2021): every institution of Regular Basic Education and Alternative Basic Education must consider at least two vacancies in each classroom for students with some type of mild or moderate disability.

4.1 Conclusions

At present, there is still a need to promote improvements in inclusive educational policies. These policies must promote and guide the practice of inclusive actions in all areas of the educational system, beyond the current situation due to the Covid 19 crisis. For this reason, in the current context and in the post-coronavirus stage, educational inclusion is a challenge and a political and socio-educational commitment. The school not only needs to assume diversity within the framework of a school for all but fundamentally needs to attend to diversity as a human right, respecting the conditions of the learner, the different ways of life; and to achieve learning, mobilizing all the resources that make real access to quality education possible.

For this study, educational inclusion is a strategy to fight against exclusion and the barriers that limit learning and training. It is a factor of mobilization of all educational actors to respond appropriately to the diverse educational needs of students. It is a tool for pedagogical transformation that fosters more open and tolerant attitudes, and positively energizes participatory and inclusive methodologies. This way of perceiving it is fundamental, especially in these times of global crisis in which not only have its advances been halted, but even setbacks have been evidenced. As it is well known, the different disability situations also require different forms of care (specialized and personalized). The critical health situation during the years 2020–2021 has seriously affected the care, and management in many institutions has failed to meet the goal of effective educational inclusion.

Therefore, the demand is implicit and the commitment too, especially in educational institutions that serve children in vulnerable situations. The results of this research show a considerable and significant correlation between the variables: inclusive policy and inclusive practice. Since there is a high correlation value, it is necessary to design well-conceived guidelines and implement actions that respond pertinently and effectively to these guidelines. It is, therefore, necessary to improve and diversify the practices of attention to students, but above all to develop an attitude of tolerance and respect towards the other, without exclusions. This will be reflected in a greater willingness by authorities, teachers, and support personnel, as well as in a growing openness to forms of participation and involvement, and in the diversification of work techniques. In short, the unity and correspondence between policy guidelines and actions will make it possible a greater scope of attention, a better quality of educational service, and, mainly, the materialization of a human right.

Acknowledgements. To God for granting us the best of our weapons:

To our parents, for forging us into the people we are today. We owe many of our achievements to them, and one of these is the completion of this research paper. They instilled values in us, such as responsibility and the desire to succeed. To our sisters, for allowing us to gain self-confidence since they were a pillar to forge our paths as leaders.

References

Alfaro, M.: Percepción de los docentes que atienden aulas inclusivas, respecto a la educación inclusiva del nivel primaria en la ciudad de Trujillo, 2017 [Perception of teachers who attend inclusive classrooms, regarding inclusive education at the primary level in the city of Trujillo, 2017]. [Degree Thesis, Universidad Nacional de Trujillo]. Digital file (2018). https://dspace.unitru.edu.pe/handle/UNITRU/10876

Angenscheidt, L., Navarrete, I.: Actitudes de los docentes acerca de la educación inclusiva [Teachers' attitudes about inclusive education]. Ciencias Psicológicas 11(2), 233–243. (2017). https://www.redalyc.org/articulo.oa?id=459553539013

Booth, T., Ainscow, M.: Guía para la evaluación y mejora de la educación inclusiva [Guide for the evaluation and improvement of inclusive education] (2002). http://www.daemcopiapo.cl/Biblioteca/Archivos/INDICE_INCLUSION.pdf

Camacho, R., Rivas, C., Gaspar, M., Quiñonez, C.: Innovación y tecnología educativa en el contexto actual latinoamericano [Innovation and educational technology in the current Latin American context]. Revista de Ciencias Sociales 26, 460–472. (2020). https://www.redalyc.org/jatsRepo/280/28064146030/html/index.html

Campa, R., Valenzuela, B., Guillén, M.: Prácticas docentes y cultura inclusiva para colectivos vulnerables de primarias en Sonora, México [Teaching practices and inclusive culture for vulnerable primary school groups in Sonora, Mexico]. Revista Latinoamericana de Ciencias Sociales Niñez y Juventud 18(2), 1–17. (2020). https://doi.org/10.11600/1692715x.18211

Espinoza, L., Lagos, N., Hernández, K., Ledezma, D.: Cultura y políticas inclusivas en profesorado chileno de educación primaria y secundaria [Culture and inclusive policies in Chilean teachers of primary and secondary education]. Revista CS (34), 17–42 (2021). https://doi.org/10.18046/recs.i34.4211

Jiménez, F., Lalueza, J., Fardella, C.: Aprendizajes, inclusión y justicia social en entornos educativos multiculturales [Learning, inclusion and social justice in multicultural educational environments]. Revista Electrónica de Investigación Educativa **19**(3), 10–23 (2017). https://doi.org/10.24320/redie.2017.19.3.830

Luna, K.: Actitud docente y práctica inclusiva de los docentes en la Institución Educativa Particular Euroamerican College, Pachacamac, 2020 [Teaching attitude and inclusive practice of teachers at the Euroamerican College Private Educational Institution, Pachacamac, 2020]. [Master's thesis, Universidad César Vallejo]. Digital file (2020). https://repositorio.ucv.edu.pe/handle/20.500.12692/52001

Ministerio de Educación [MINEDU]: Educación Básica Especial [Basic Special Education] (2021). https://www.minedu.gob.pe/educacionbasicaespecial/

Nomberto, J.: Desempeño docente y educación inclusiva en una institución educativa de Trujillo, 2020 [Teaching performance and inclusive education in an educational institution in Trujillo, 2020]. [Master's thesis, Universidad César Vallejo]. Digital file (2020). https://repositorio.ucv.edu.pe/handle/20.500.12692/48948

Ñaupas, H., Valdivia, M., Palacios, J., Romero, H.: Metodología de la investigación Cuantitativa - Cualitativa y Redacción de la Tesis [Quantitative - Qualitative Research Methods and Thesis Writing], 6th edn. Ediciones de la U (2018). https://corladancash.com/wp-content/uploads/2020/01/Metodologia-de-la-inv-cuanti-y-cuali-Humberto-Naupas-Paitan.pdf

United Nations [UN]: Informe de políticas: Educación durante COVID-19 y más allá. [Policy brief: Education during COVID-19 and beyond] (2020). https://unsdg.un.org/es/resources/informe-de-politicas-educacion-durante-covid-19-y-mas-alla

United Nations Educational, Scientific and Cultural Organization [UNESCO]: Guía para asegurar la inclusión y la equidad en la educación [Guide to ensure inclusion and equity in education] (2017). https://unesdoc.unesco.org/ark:/48223/pf0000259592

United Nations Educational, Scientific and Cultural Organization [UNESCO]: Educación: de la interrupción a la recuperación [Education: from interruption to recovery] (2020). https://en.unesco.org/covid19/educationresponse

Peralta, Y.: Análisis sobre las políticas en el proceso de inclusión de los estudiantes con necesidades educativas especiales en las instituciones educativas en la ciudad de Camaná, Arequipa, 2017 [Analysis on policies in the process of inclusion of students with special educational needs in educational institutions in the city of Camaná, Arequipa, 2017]. [Master's thesis, Pontificia Universidad Católica del Perú]. Digital file (2018). http://tesis.pucp.edu.pe/repositorio/handle/20.500.12404/12383

Quintero, L.: Educación inclusiva: tendencias y perspectivas. Educación Y Ciencia [Inclusive education: trends and perspectives]. Educ. Sci. (24), 58–74 (2020). https://doi.org/10.19053/0120-7105.eyc.2020.24.e11423

Tovar, M.: Educación en Derechos Humanos y Educación Inclusiva: Una Mirada Desde un Colegio de la Ciudad de Bogotá. Inclusión & Desarrollo [Education in Human Rights and Inclusive Education: A View from a School in the City of Bogotá]. Inclusion y Desarrollo **8**(1), 48–68 (2021). https://revistas.uniminuto.edu/index.php/IYD/article/view/2464/2082

Covid 19 Pandemic Assessment of the Employment Status of Home-Based Workers

Camilo J. Peña Lapeira$^{(\boxtimes)}$ (ID) and Liliana Vargas Puentes (ID)

Corporación Universitaria Minuto de Dios, Tansv. 73 A # 81I-19. Edificio Arturo Echeverri, Oficina 303, Bogotá D.C., Colombia

{cjpena,lilina.vargas}@uniminuto.edu

Abstract. At the arrival of Covid 19 and under the isolation measures, business-men have implemented protocols to mitigate the contagion and the advance of the disease. Thus, for activities within the organization that do not require transformation processes and where the employee's physical presence is not required, new forms of work were established, such as the implementation of temporary work from home or permanent teleworking. According to the above, the present research proposal arises, which under a mixed methodology, of a descriptive-transversal type, focuses on the analysis of the different business scenarios from the technical, technological, economic and human variables that allow evaluating the effectiveness of the implementation and adequacy of the aforementioned modalities as a contingency in the face of the Covid 19 pandemic and that in the same way they allow contributing to the economic reactivation processes.

Keywords: Work at home · Telework · Work status · Business scenario

1 Introduction

The declaration of a pandemic by Coronavirus (COVID-19) by the World Health Organization (WHO), has turned the world to transform its daily life. Different governments have had to take measures to mitigate the spread of the virus in order to protect health and life. In Colombia, as in other countries around the world, many companies, due to the restrictive measures associated with mandatory preventive isolation, had at some point to close their facilities partially or totally and send employees home in order to preserve its integrity and accept the measures established by the Government.

In relation to the study of the changes that the business scenarios have had as a result of the COVID-19 virus, it is important to highlight that the modifications can be analyzed from two points of view. The first, at the level of physical facilities, such as enabling workstations to achieve social distancing of 2 m, hand washing and the use of respiratory masks [1]. The second is based on workers who were transferred to their homes in order to carry out remote work through the work-at-home or telecommuting modality. These modalities are different, since the first is a transitory measure and the second can be permanent or in combination with an alternation model [2]. The Ministry of Labor proposed the above alternatives in Circular No. 021 of 2020, and encouraged the use of flexible hours in order to avoid crowds [3].

Being an unexpected situation, the "spontaneity" that occurred in the implementation of this type of work modality and the lack of prior structuring, led to recommendations only being made on the fly, omitting some technical, technological and humans.

Due to lack of planning, in many cases they could not have delivered the expected results under the conditions that are required, and worse still, they could have added factors that, in addition to those already existing due to the pandemic condition, could have affected the health and well-being of the collaborators, and the continuity of the business by not knowing for sure how this affected the economy of each business.

By proposing the modality of working at home and remote work to accompany the already existing teleworking, several options were given in order to protect the worker from contracting the virus. The impact that has occurred when implementing these strategies in organizations is analyzed. This study is carried out to establish the possible economic effects, the evaluation of psycho-social, occupational factors and the evaluation of technical and technological factors that participate in the process. The results obtained will contribute to the future development of a methodological guide for the implementation of work at home, and for MSMEs, this will allow the implementation of these processes permanently, taking advantage of the strengths and opportunities that it presents from formal work.

The Andean Community of Nations - CAN, Decision 584 of 2004 and Resolution 957 of 2005, seek protection for all workers. Colombia joins this commitment through Law 1562 of 2012, although technical studies are still needed from the different fields to carry out the transition to working from home and teleworking.

Employees are generally linked to companies that generate a good, service or product in a production chain. Some establishments and enterprises will be affected by the decrease in human personnel due to the pandemic and that is why they must be restructured and adapted to current working conditions [4]. It must be taken into account, getting out of complex situations such as the economic crisis due to the pandemic is not only solved with investment but also with the care of human capital, improvement of business policies and constant monitoring of the innovation process that could improve the process [5].

It is important to highlight that a large part of the work operation under the aforementioned modalities is supported mainly by the use of ICTs and as part of the contribution to the new business dynamics, the country began to strengthen Internet channels and connections in homes and access from telephony. For example, Colombia closed the year 2021 with more than 33 million mobile internet accesses according to a report from the ICT Ministry, of which more than 77% was carried out mainly through 4G technology, where the average cost associated with 1 GB of navigation per month is approximately US$1 [6]. According to other data revealed in terms of fixed connections [7], Bogotá continues to lead the country with the highest number of fixed internet accesses, with 25.3 connections per 100 inhabitants.

It is necessary to know the importance of constituting in these new companies that emerged during the pandemic, a solid legal part and a stable internal organization, depending on the needs of each organization. The foregoing so that there is greater economic development in Colombia, so that there is more productivity and thus generate more jobs in this phase that the country finds itself in "economic activation". ICTs are important in this phase, since they constitute an incident factor within companies in terms of managing internal processes, recognition in the market and economic indicators that transcend their uses [8].

With the implementation of teleworking and working at home as part of the strategies for economic reactivation at the end of 2021, unemployment has decreased. This is due to the high rate of new organizations that have been created with these modalities, since in the increase of new job opportunities all the necessary legal and analytical requirements are being applied so that these new companies continue their correct development [9].

As background to this work, it was found that the modality of teleworking and work from home or remote is not new in Colombia. Since Law 1221 of 2008 and Regulatory Decree 0884 of 2012, work began on the formalization, partially guaranteeing the equality of the rights of these workers with the rights of face-to-face workers [10].

It is important to highlight that it is the responsibility of the employer to identify all those risks to which teleworkers and those who work from home are exposed. As well as, to guarantee the necessary and sufficient physical conditions for the good performance of the work, identifying in his study as a source of important risk, the psychosocial risk, which can occur around the excessive workloads that are acquired when one does not have a forecast [11].

In relation to the treatment of occupational risks that may occur in Teleworking [12], tools such as: taking active breaks, using adjustable chairs, footrests, correct lighting in workstations, among others, can be used. The ergonomic elements are used in order to avoid injuries or musculoskeletal disorders at the level of the back. In this same study, it is stated that workers can develop job stress due to having to extend the working day, for example, as in the case of having to make calls to clients or answer emails and calls from their organization.

Through the Study Requested by the EMPL committee the impact of teleworking and digital Work on workers and society (special focus on surveillance and monitoring, as well as on mental health of worker in EU, Finland, Germany, Ireland, Italy and Romania), it concludes that The implications for health and safety in ICT are not as clear as assumed [13], this is due to the fact that the use of ICT can have both positive and negative effects. The negative effects depending on the intensity Telecommuting compared to employees who work only at the employer's premises [14].

2 Material and Method

The research proposal is part of an investigation of Mixed approach, of a descriptive-transversal type supported by [15, 16], who affirm that this type of investigation is based on three elements; first, the conceptualization and operationalization of the variables; second, the degree of intervention or application by the researcher and third, the nature of the objectives starting from contrasting, describing, evaluating and improving. That is why this research is based on the use of quantitative and qualitative variables, hence the rationality of its mixed approach.

The analysis of the information is descriptive. Because [17] investigations in a descriptive way study the possibility after collecting information: describe, narrate, review facts and situations characteristic of a population group under study, which will allow reaching general or partial conclusions of the study explored. However, although the project will be developed from a descriptive investigative approach, categorical schemes of concepts are used. In other words, the theories are formulated from the data itself once collected and analyzed [18, 19].

The initial information starts from the analysis of work environments, to determine the applicability with respect to the legal requirements that must be met for the safety and health conditions at work of those who work from home. The data for the econometric study will start from the economic figures that are published by the different official organizations and governing bodies in the matter through databases.

The research population is the workers and businessmen from the south of the city of Bogotá who are reactivating their businesses and who have exploited the potential of developing work from home during the economic reactivation due to Covid 19; having part or all of its personnel working under this modality, whose estimated figure for the city of Bogotá is 160,000 workers and in the south of about 65,000 according to figures from the Ministry of Technology and Information [20]. The sample for this investigative exercise is 400 people, through a Stratified Random Sampling, locating company personnel from each of the economic sectors.

The information is obtained from the application of a virtual survey sent to 700 people, which was answered by 465 of these and validated to take into account and of which 402 were answered correctly, 87% of these were employees. And 13% independent, understanding that the latter correspond to entrepreneurs and people who manage their own work dynamics (see Fig. 1).

Ten interviews were also conducted with businessmen in the area where the study was carried out. The analysis variables were determined in the diagnosis according to the fields in which the project was developed, such as: economic, social, labor, technical and technological aspects. Among the qualitative data collection techniques and instruments are: documentary review matrix and structured analytical summaries and information triangulation matrix.

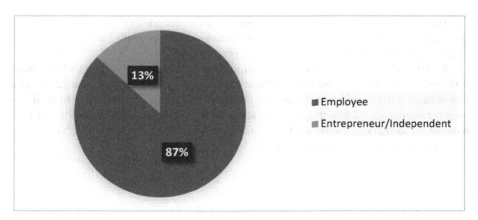

Fig. 1. Current employment situation

3   Results and Discussions

As described in the methodology, the instrument was applied in a representative manner in each of the sectors that make up the local economy and that can carry out their work at a given time from home. The sector that stands out the most is education with 22%, followed by services and consultancies with 19% and the health sector with 12%. The field of other sectors groups all those small sectors that were not initially categorized. To a very small degree, people from the restaurant and hotel sector participated because the vast majority of employees in this sector carry out their work in person, only positions such as administrative level could do it from home (see Fig. 2).

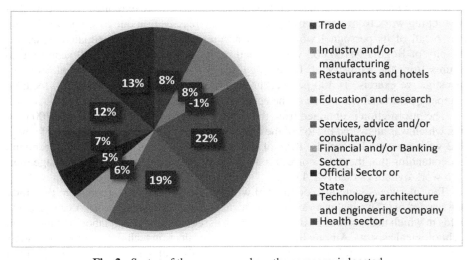

Fig. 2. Sector of the economy where the company is located

The majority is observed for companies that are of the Simplified Joint Stock Company type (see Fig. 3), followed by Official Entities and Non-profit Entities, also trying to have a presence within the study of all types of company.

Reality of those who during this pandemic have had to move their job to their home, it is observed that more than 53% of these have had to do so for more than 12 months, this being a fairly significant figure. If it is added with those who have had to do it in a time between 6 and 12 months, the value is higher than 66%, which indicates that at least 6 out of 10 workers had to be working from home for a fairly long time. With respect to what was traditionally done (see Fig. 4).

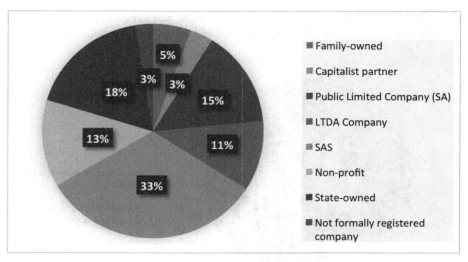

Fig. 3. Type of company

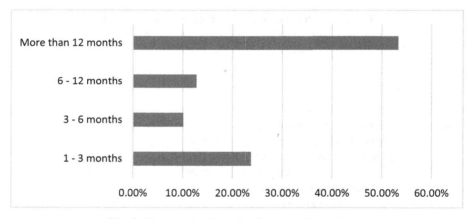

Fig. 4. Time worked from home during the pandemic

The 87% of people stated that their work depended on the use of computer equipment, the other 13% stated that its use was sporadic or not necessary due to the type of activity they performed. To the people who worked with a computer, when asked about its origin or ownership, only 38% stated that it had been supplied by the company where they worked (see Fig. 5); which indicates that many employees were sent to work from home without providing them with basic work tools and that they were the ones who had to solve the continuity of their work using their own resources. It can be highlighted that the computer equipment was not the only thing they had to provide to be able to work, but other elements such as: desk, adjustable chair, headband, keyboard, mouse, among others as the most outstanding (see Fig. 6). Others did not even have a physical space in which to work, such as a study or home office, which had to be adequate and in some cases required electrical conditioning, network and adequate furniture.

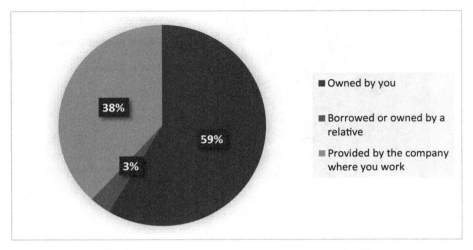

Fig. 5. Origin of the computer equipment you work with

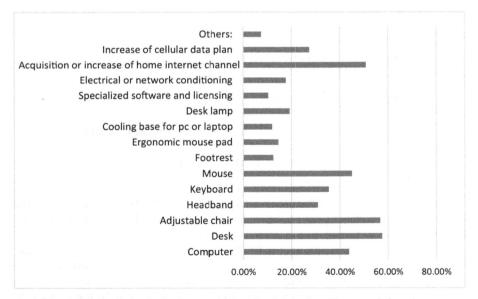

Fig. 6. Elements that had to be acquired or fitted out to be able to work from home

It is worth noting that another important economic effort that employees had to make was the acquisition or increase of the home internet channel, as well as the increase of the cellular line data plan (see Fig. 6). The foregoing, mainly due to the fact that by working from home, the demand and transit of information through these means not only increased but also became congested. Most activities moved to the home such as: study, work, meetings and conferences, e-commerce activities, personal communications, among others that were more common in person.

Only 4% of the employees consulted stated that they had received complementary elements from their company other than their computer equipment to adapt a work space in optimal conditions at home (see Fig. 7). The investment made by the employees was quite significant, being the ranges between 1–80 US$ (22.5%) and 80 US$–190 US$ (21.1%) in which more coincidences were presented, finally representing an expense for the household economy. Many of the employers associate the expense with a small expense that is balanced by not having to spend money on transportation to the workplace and part of the emotional salary represented in being able to spend more time with the family at home.

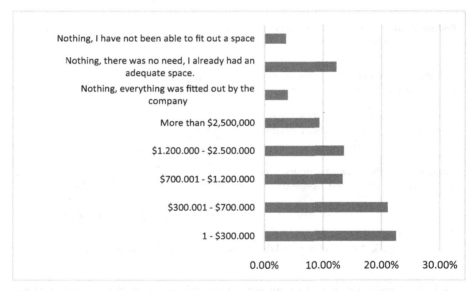

Fig. 7. Money invested to be able to adapt a space at home and to be able to work from this

Similarly, when workers were asked if they were receiving or received at any time from their company any economic subsidy for working from home after said adjustments and economic efforts, 27.3% said they received a subsidy for connectivity (internet plan), 2.7% subsidy for home energy expenditure, 0.5% received subsidy for the use of computer equipment owned by them and 2.9% subsidy for the acquisition or improvement of their cell phone data plan. These are quite low figures, considering that 70.9% of the workers did not receive any type of subsidy during this time, although these expenses were saved by the company.

As for working conditions, in some companies while the process of conditioning and rethinking working conditions from home or remotely and in order to be able to keep their job, the workers were raised with the possibility of temporary suspension of the employment contract while they proposed alternative solutions such as: salary reduction of voluntarily, mandatory salary reduction, among other options. A figure close to 28% agreed to take pending, postponed or early vacations, 9% of these during the economic reactivation process were relocated to other areas of the company and/or had to assume new or more functions in order to maintain their cargo.

In relation to the length of the working day, the perception of the workers is that during the period of work at home (see Fig. 8), there was an increase in work beyond the usual daily hours. People even work at night and in many cases on weekends, which contrasts with the increase in psychosocial risk (see Fig. 9), where it is evident that during this period, due to the increased workload, episodes of stress or anxiety arose that many of the cases contributed to the deterioration of the state of health by having to manage situations of work and personal environment in the same space.

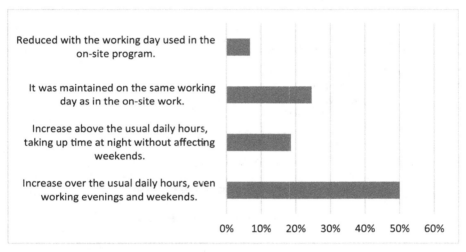

Fig. 8. Length of the workday during the period of working at home

All these inconveniences of implementation and operation of these modalities of telework, remote work and work at home show that there is great difficulty for the reorganization of the work system by organizations due in large part to the lack of experience in this model labor and the emergency situation itself due to the pandemic [21].

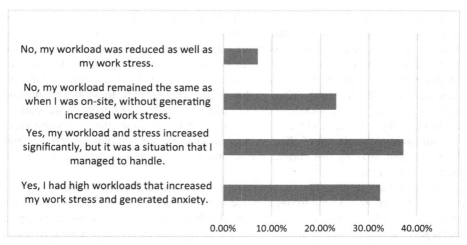

Fig. 9. You had situations of increased workload that triggered episodes of stress or anxiety that worsened your health condition.

4 Conclusions

MSMEs are implementing work at home as one of the solutions to the problems of possible contagion within organizations and due to the need to continue operating to give continuity to business. This serves as an applied model, which allows companies and workers to improve their productive efficiency within the current health emergency conditions and that results in customer satisfaction in each of the markets. However, the employee who works under these conditions must be guaranteed the minimum conditions of infrastructure and technological resources and be recognized in an economic part when he does not have the support of the company, since there is a perception of neglect on the part of the employer, regardless of whether they belong to the public or private sector alike.

It can be evidenced in figures that during the process of economic reactivation, unemployment has decreased mainly due to the high rate of organizations that have been created and that have welcomed work structures that consider work from home and telework as a functional alternative applying all legal requirements and analysis necessary for these new companies to continue their proper development [22]. Additionally, coinciding with the global trend that has been taking place, where teleworking and work-at-home activities have contributed to it, reporting an increase in the contribution to the national GDP [23].

According to the Law that regulates work at home, the employer is the first responsible for supplying the necessary equipment for the development of activities, fulfillment of functions and provision of the service under the authorization of work at home [2]; however, as stated by the respondents, in many cases this responsibility was wrongfully transferred to the worker, who ended up preparing the elements and tools necessary for their performance and without even receiving any type of remuneration or recognition cheap for it.

Despite the fact that it is stated that this type of work does not affect the worker on a large scale due to the fact that the work schedules are a little more flexible, the delivery times and the amount of work are adjusted to the worker's capacities, so that the working from home becomes a good option, with a set schedule, so that it does not interfere with housework and private life [21]. This study evidenced a significant increase in working hours at home as well as the perception of greater work pressure and stress, which produced episodes of anxiety and deterioration of health in the workers according to their concept and that in some way could have affected the job performance, without the implementation of effective measures to mitigate said risk, since the greater the time spent working from home, the greater the perception of deterioration in the working condition.

All of the above demonstrates the need to propose and implement adequate plans of action that allow not only to improve the working conditions of workers around the physical and technological infrastructure, work schedules, but also psychosocial support and organizational culture, in order to empower companies and increase productivity and competitiveness in companies.

References

1. de Salud, M.: Lineamiento de condiciones de bioseguridad para el regreso a la presencial-idad en entorno educativo en el marco de la pandemia por covid-19. Ministerio de Salud y Protección Social. Bogotá (2021)
2. Ley 2088 de 2021. Por la cual se regula el trabajo en casa y se dictan otras disposiciones. 12 de mayo de 2021. https://www.mintrabajo.gov.co/documents/20147/0/Ley+No+2088+Por+la+cual+se+regula+el+Trabajo+en+Casa+y+se+Dictan+otras+Disposiciones.pdf/887 1b87c-28cc-d6e7-757b-c369c78d51c6?t=1620914979769
3. de Trabajo, M.: Circular No. 021 de 2020. Medidas de protección al empleo con ocasión de la fase de contención de COVID-19 y de la declaración de emergencia sanitaria (2020). https://www.mintrabajo.gov.co/documents/20147/0/Circular+0021.pdf/804 9a852-e8b0-b5e7-05d3-8da3943c0879?t=1584464523596
4. Torres, A.T., Álava, Á.F.B., Moncayo, R.P.: La afectación de los emprendedores en época de pandemia. Revista Publicando 8(32), 51–60 (2021). https://revistapublicando.org/revista/index.php/crv/article/view/2267/2488
5. Peña Lapeira, C.J., Vargas Puentes, L.: Economía creativa: influencia de la inversión extranjera en el crecimiento de Bogotá-Colombia. Revista Venezolana De Gerencia 26(6), 301–317 (2021). https://doi.org/10.52080/rvgluz.26.e6.18
6. Semana: Colombia cerró el segundo trimestre de 2021 con más de 33 millones de accesos móviles a internet. Revista Semana Digital (2021). https://www.semana.com/tecnologia/articulo/colombia-cerro-el-segundo-trimestre-de-2021-con-mas-de-33-millones-de-accesos-moviles-a-internet/202110/
7. MinTIC: ¿Cómo está el país en conexiones de internet? (2020). https://mintic.gov.co/portal/inicio/Sala-de-prensa/MinTIC-en-los-medios/151654:Como-esta-el-pais-en-conexiones-de-internet#:~:text=Seg%C3%BAn%20los%20datos%20revelados%20correspondientes,acc esos%20por%20cada%20100%20pobladores
8. Serrano, C.L., Lapeira, C.J.P., Guzmán, M.Y.L.: Influencia de las TIC en el Desarrollo Económico de Colombia. Ciencias de la Informacion 49(3), 3–10 (2020). http://cinfo.idict.cu/index.php/cinfo/article/view/854

9. DANE: Mercado laboral. Obtenido de Empleo y Desempleo (2022). https://www.dane.gov. co/index.php/estadisticas-por-tema/mercado-laboral/empleo-y-desempleo
10. Ley 1221 de 2008. por la cual se establecen normas para promover y regular el Teletrabajo y se dictan otras disposiciones (2008). http://www.desarrolloeconomico.gov.co/sites/default/ files/marco-legal/Ley-1221-2008.pdf
11. Aristizábal, J.: La responsabilidad patronal derivada de los riesgos laborales en el Teletrabajo (2016). https://repository.usta.edu.co/bitstream/handle/11634/1945/Aristizabalj ulia2016.pdf?sequence=1&isAllowed=y
12. Palacio, A., Cardona, D.: Tratamiento de los Riesgos Laborales en el Teletrabajo en Colombia: Realidad y Legalidad (2016). http://repository.unaula.edu.co:8080/bitstream/123456789/ 530/1/unaula_rep_pre_der_2016_riesgos_laborales.pdf
13. Samek, M.: The impact of teleworking and digital work on workers and society. European Parliament (2021). https://www.aceb.cat/images/The_impact_of_teleworking.pdf
14. OCDE. Implicaciones del trabajo en remoto en las políticas basadas en el lugar, Una mirada a los países del G7 (2021). https://www.oecd.org/regional/PH-Remote-working-G7-SP.pdf
15. Rodríguez Gómez, D., Valldeoriola Roquet, J.: Metodología de la investigación. Universitat Oberta de Catalunya (2009). http://openaccess.uoc.edu/webapps/o2/bitstream/10609/77608/ 1/Metodolog%C3%ADa%20de%20la%20investigaci%C3%B3n_Portada.pdf
16. Rodríguez, M.C.M., Cabrera, I.P.: Tipos de estudio en el enfoque de investigación cuantitativa. Enfermería Universitaria 4(1), 35–38 (2007). https://www.redalyc.org/pdf/3587/358741821 004.pdf
17. Bernal, C.: Metodología de la investigación. Tercera edición Pearson Educación. Colombia ISBN 978-958 (2010)
18. Strauss, A., Corbin, J.: Bases de la investigación cualitativa. Técnicas y procedimientos para desarrollar la Teoría Fundamentada. Medellín: Universidad de Antioquia (2002)
19. Hernández, R., Fernández, C., Baptista, P.: Metodologia de la Investigacion Hernandez Sampieri 6a Edicion. McGrawHill, México (2014)
20. MinTIC: Colombia superó los 209.000 teletrabajadores en 2020: Ministerio de las TIC (2021). https://mintic.gov.co/portal/inicio/Sala-de-prensa/179742:Colombia-supero-los-209-000-teletrabajadores-en-2020-Ministerio-de-las-TIC
21. Pizà Bonilla, M.Á.: Factores para la eficacia del teletrabajo (2021). https://dspace.uib.es/ xmlui/bitstream/handle/11201/156218/Piz%c3%a0_Bonilla_Miguel_%c3%81ngel.pdf?seq uence=1&isAllowed=y
22. Cámara de comercio de Bogotá. Reporte del mercado laboral para bogota y Colombia, diciembre 2021 (2021). https://www.ccb.org.co/observatorio/Analisis-Economico/Analisis-Economico/Mercado-laboral/Reporte-del-mercado-laboral-para-Bogota-y-Colombia-dic iembre-20212
23. Peña Lapeira, C.J., Vargas Puentes, L.: Ict and creative economy: an analysis from technology and industry enterprises 4.0, Bogota-Colombia case. In: Botto-Tobar, M., Montes León, S., Camacho, O., Chávez, D., Torres-Carrión, P., Zambrano Vizuete, M. (eds.) ICAT 2020. CCIS, vol. 1388, pp. 69–79. Springer, Cham (2021). https://doi.org/10.1007/978-3-030-71503-8_6

Public Spending and Profitability: Analysis in Ecuadorian Public Companies

Roberto Carlos Zabala Navarrete[1] (ID), Angie Fernández Lorenzo[2](✉) (ID), and Sandra Patricia Galarza Torres[2] (ID)

[1] Ecuadorian Army, Quito, Ecuador
[2] Department of Economic, Administrative and Commercial Sciences, Universidad de Las Fuerzas Armadas-ESPE, Quito, Ecuador
aafernandez2@espe.edu.ec

Abstract. The General State Budget in Ecuador contemplates an allocation for public spending in the different entities, including the public companies studied, which operate in various sectors that, due to their competitiveness, are significant for the socioeconomic development of the country. In the investigation, an analysis was carried out between the relationship of public spending in the profitability of seven public companies in Ecuador during the period 2014–2017. To determine the relationship between variables, the Pearson, Spearman correlation coefficient was calculated and the regression analysis was performed based on the linear, logarithmic, inverse, quadratic and cubic model. Statistical processing was performed using STATA v.12 and SPSS v.23, to determine relationships between budget allocation and profitability indicators in companies during the study period. Low levels of profitability were identified in the companies during the period studied, which are not influenced by the state budget allocation. The above evidences the need for companies to focus on internal measures that generate sources of profitability, and in the same way the State promotes policies that tend to it, and not only consider budget allocation as the way to support public business development.

Keywords: Public spending · Public policy · Profitability · State · Public company

1 Introduction

Under the approaches of the different economic theories that promote the interference of the State on the economy, the behavior and control of the different economic actors, one of the most used public policy actions is the allocation of direct budget or contracts, agreements or others. Instruments that turn national companies into strong public providers. Despite the fact that this type of theory has had a strong opponent with the liberal and neoliberal models, since the middle of the previous century they began to resurface, especially in the Latin American context at the hands of ECLAC and its structuralist prescriptions [1].

The Ecuadorian economy has shown in recent years an economic contraction [2], which has also been evidenced in the variation of the General State Budget, which,

M. Botto-Tobar et al. (Eds.): ICAT 2022, CCIS 1757, pp. 326–335, 2023.
https://doi.org/10.1007/978-3-031-24978-5_29

for example, from 2014 to 2016 decreased by more than four billion dollars [3]. The foregoing has had an impact on the decrease in public capacity to attend to the various economic and social needs that allow continuing to advance in the aspirations consigned in the different national development plans. This implies that, in conditions of reduced budget resources, allocation problems are faced, where the analysis to determine the effectiveness of said allocations is useful for decision-making and the corresponding definition of public policy. In Sánchez opinion [4], it is necessary to reduce the social incompetence associated with spending and public policy, which should have an impact on economic policy favoring the revitalization of the economic and social activity of the countries.

Public companies in Ecuador are one of the actors in the economic system, recognized as *"(…) legal entities of public law, with their own assets, endowed with budgetary, financial, economic, administrative and management autonomy"* [5]. *Among its main functions, according to the law, is to perform with "efficiency, rationality, profitability and social control", as well as "(…) to preserve and control state property and public business activity"* [5].

Public companies carry out their economic activity in different sectors; in the case of the companies under study, their scope of action is industry, services and insurance. These companies receive a budget allocation from the State, which are part of the General State Budget as "instrument for the determination and management of income and expenses of the State" [6].

Hence, many public companies and others linked to the State through contracts and agreements, handle the hypothesis that the instability of the state budget allocation is one of the fundamental causes of the deterioration of their financial indicators. In the present investigation, the specific indicators of ROE will be handled as "indicator that measures the return on capital, measures the profitability obtained by the company on its own funds" [7], and ROA which in turn drives the performance of the company's assets; to meet the proposed objective, which is to analyze the influence of the state budget allocation on the profitability of seven Ecuadorian public companies in the 2014–2017 period.

2 Materials and Methods

An analysis of the period 2014–2017 was carried out on the relationship between the variable (independent) public spending, represented by the percentage of budget allocation (ALLOC) to each of the seven public companies and the variable (dependent) profitability, which It was measured through economic profitability (ROA) and financial profitability (ROE).

Table 1 shows the data of the variables under analysis.

Table 1. Budget allocation and profitability data (ROA and ROE)

Enterprise	Year	ALLOC	ROA	ROE
1	2014	0,09	0,23	0,44
	2015	0,08	0,15	0,33
	2016	0,07	0,01	0,01
	2017	0,06	−0,18	−0,29
2	2014	0,08	0,01	0,02
	2015	0,07	0,01	0,01
	2016	0,04	0,00	0,01
	2017	0,01	−0,12	−0,26
3	2014	0,01	0,02	0,32
	2015	0,01	0,01	0,21
	2016	0,02	0,01	0,12
	2017	0,05	0,00	0,04
4	2014	0,01	0,41	0,65
	2015	0,01	−0,51	−3,71
	2016	0,01	0,48	0,85
	2017	0,03	0,65	1,09
5	2014	0,06	0,01	0,04
	2015	0,06	0,06	0,30
	2016	0,02	0,04	0,12
	2017	0,03	0,01	0,04
6	2014	0,01	0,24	0,33
	2015	0,04	0,22	0,29
	2016	0,02	0,16	0,21
	2017	0,03	0,14	0,19
7	2014	0,02	0,01	0,02
	2015	0.03	−0,03	−0,05
	2016	0.03	−0,26	−0,70
	2017	0.02	0,04	0,08

Source: The data for the budget allocation variable (ALLOC) were obtained from the General State Budget 2014, 2015, 2016 and 2017 [8]. The data for the ROA and ROE variables were obtained from the audited financial statements of the seven companies studied [9].

Taking into account that the database is small, the normality of the dependent variables was determined through the Kolmogorov-Smirnov test, the result of which is shown in Table 2.

Table 2. Kolmogorov-Smirnov test

	ROA	ROE
P	28	28
Normal parameters Mean	,0650	,0254
Typical deviation	,22050	,80684
More extreme differences Absolute	,206	,320
Positive	,188	,210
Negative	−,206	−,320
Kolmogorov-Smirnov (Z)	1,087	1,693
Asymptotic sig. (bilateral)	,188	,006

Source: Authors' results

According to the Kolmogorov-Smirnov test [10], only ROA follows a normal distribution.

To determine the relationship between variables, the Pearson (r) and Spearman correlation coefficients were calculated, and the regression analysis was performed based on the linear, logarithmic, inverse, quadratic and cubic model. Statistical processing was performed using STATA v.12 and SPSS v.23.

3   Results

The following histograms represent the frequency of the data of the profitability variables. In the case of the ROE variable (Fig. 1) it shows a distribution with a single tail to the left, most of the companies have a lower ROE with a tendency to low levels, given the accumulation in the middle and high and low parts. Density on the right side.

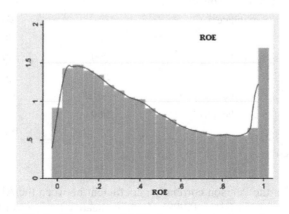

Fig. 1. Histogram of ROE. Source: Author's results.

In the case of the ROA variable, as can be seen in Fig. 2, its distribution is with a single long tail to the right, most companies have low profitability, given the concentration in the lower part and very little density in the medium and high levels.

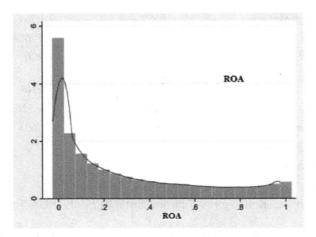

Fig. 2. Histogram of ROA. Source: Authors' results.

In order to determine whether an influencing factor in the low profitability of public companies is the budget allocation by the State, inferential statistical techniques were applied. The correlation with the ALLOC variable was calculated using the Pearson coefficient (Table 3).

Table 3. Pearson's correlation coefficient between the ROA and ALLOC variables

		ROA	ALLOC
ROA	Pearson correlation	1	−,023
	Sig. (bilateral)		,909
	P	28	28
	Sig. (bilateral)	,000	,506
	P	28	28
ALLOC	Pearson correlation	−,023	1
	Sig. (bilateral)	,909	
	P	28	28

Source: Authors' results

As can be seen, the Pearson correlation coefficient between the ALLOC and ROA variables is not significant (sig = 0.909) of a low negative type, according to the scale proposed by Suárez [11].

Additionally, to determine the relationship between ROE and ALLOC variables, the Spearman correlation coefficient was applied as shown in Table 4.

Table 4. Spearman's correlation coefficient between the ROE and ALLOC

		ROE	ALLOC
ROE	Pearson correlation	1	,131
	Sig. (bilateral)		,506
	P	28	28
ALLOC	Pearson correlation	,131	1
	Sig. (bilateral)	,506	
	P	28	28

Source: Authors' results.

It is additionally evident that in the case of the ROE variable that does not follow a normal distribution, the relationship with the independent variable ALLOC is not significant (sig $= 0.506$), of a positive average type according to the scale suggested by Mondragón [12].

Taking into account the result of the normality test, of the two variables that represent profitability, only the ROA variable will be used as a dependent variable in all the possible regression models to be applied: linear, logarithmic, inverse, quadratic and cubic, for determine if the budget allocation (ALLOC) is related to or influences the profitability levels of the companies under study. These results are shown in Table 5.

Table 5. Regression models between the variables ROA (dependent) and ALLOC (independent)

Equation	R square	F	Sig.
Linear	,001	,013	,909
Logarithmic	,001	,031	,861
Reverse	,001	,031	,862
Quadratic	,001	,143	,867
Cubic	,046	,381	,767

Source: Authors' results.

As can be seen, the values of R squared are all less than 0.01, except for the cubic model, with a value of 0.046, which is still less than 0.05. Therefore, it can be stated that in none of the cases analyzed is the return on assets (ROA) influenced by the budget allocation (ALLOC). A graphical approach allows corroborating these approaches. None of the curves analyzed allows us to describe the behavior of the ROA, as can be seen in Fig. 3.

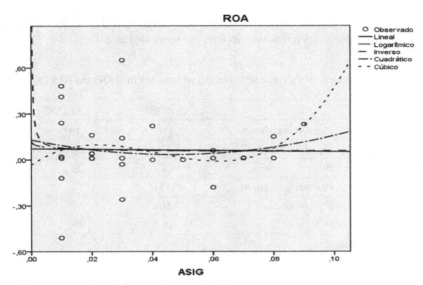

Fig. 3. Regression models. Source: Authors' results.

It can be affirmed that the alternatives framed within the ordinary least squares regression confirm the lack of relationship between ALLOC and ROA, as a variable that measures the performance of the companies. In this sense, the multilevel approach was applied, as a more powerful approach that allows evaluating the joint effect of different variables on a construct [13].

The application of this approach made it possible to determine whether some of the fixed or random effects are reflected in the return variable through ROA, through robust estimates in the presence of heteroskedasticity and dependence. Two levels were worked on: level 1, the repeated measurements during the 4 years and level 2, the company.

Multilevel, hierarchical, or random coefficient models were used in this work to describe the trajectories followed by the dependent variable ROA and the incidence that ALLOC has on this variable.

Hierarchical models were adjusted where the dependent variable or criterion was profitability measured by ROA and the independent variable ALLOC, showing the results in Tables 6 and 7.

Table 6. Estimation of fixed effects between the variables ROA and ALLOC (Estimates of fixed effects with ROA)

Parameter	Estimate	Typical error	gl	t	Sig.	Confidence interval 95%	
						Lower limit	Upper limit
Intersection	0,063248	0,079576	9,568	0,795	0,446	−0,115149	0,241644
ALLOC	0,048102	1,778691	14,155	0,027	0,979	−3,762885	3,859090

Source: Authors' results.

The table shows the average value of the intercept at the origin for all companies due to budget allocation is 0.063, which was not significant (sig = 0.446).

Table 7. Estimates of random effects for the model with the covariate ALLOC (Estimates of parameters of covariance with ROA)

Parameter		Estimate	Typical error	Wald Z	Sig	Confidence interval 95%	
						Lower limit	Upper limit
Waste		0,048053	0,015232	3,155	0,002	0,025817	0,089440
Intersection	Variance	0,002924	0,010529	0,278	0,781	2,517940E-006	3,396070

Source: Authors' results

It is observed that neither of the two estimated parameters was statistically different from zero, in both cases the significance was greater than 0.05, which means that there are no differences between the average intercepts of the companies and also the coefficient of the ALLOC variable is significantly equal to zero, that is, there is no relationship between ALLOC and ROA. On the other hand, there is no significant variability between companies (sig = 0.781). For all of the above, it is concluded that companies do not suffer an effect of public spending on their profitability.

4 Discussion

The General State Budget is an instrument used to determine and manage the income and expenses of the public sector, with the exception of those belonging to social security, public banking and decentralized autonomous governments. Budget execution is based on the policies issued by the National Government within the current macroeconomic program, as well as on the objectives and goals contemplated in the National Development Plan.

In it are the income that comes from the sale of oil, tax collection, among others. It also includes the expenses that the Government executes for the operation of its entities and the provision of its services. In addition, public financing from other governments and international organizations materialized through investment projects is included. Along the same lines, public spending represents the cost of public sector activities that include the production and supply of goods and services and income transfers.

The objective of this research is to analyze the development of a sample of seven public companies and analyze the relationship of public spending in profitability during the 2014–2017 period.

The research developed is important if the relevance of public companies for the socioeconomic development of Ecuador is considered [14], hence the results in relation to the low levels of profitability (ROA and ROE) in the seven companies studied. They warn about the need for immediate internal decision-making on the improvement of strategic and operational processes that influence their economic indicators.

For this reason, one of the main challenges that the public administration must assume is towards the modernization of its management, pointing to the need to think of a modern administration that is concerned with being more efficient, efficient and effective in the use of its resources. This paradigm shift involves the creation of management schemes characterized by facing permanent changes in the internal and external environment.

Considering the focus of State protectionist theories on companies, higher public spending should have a positive effect on the profitability of the companies that benefit from it, especially in a country like Ecuador where the management regulations of public companies are It is broad and is aimed at generating a supportive environment for public business activity. However, in Ecuador and as reflected in the data obtained from the budget allocation variable, the drop in the price of oil, the drop in remittances and other factors, have marked a crisis where the state's capacity to finance public spending has been reduced, coupled with a limited participation of private investment [15].

Thus, the main strategies implemented by the governments of the day consist of maintaining adjustments in public spending, reclassifying expenses in their objective of ordering public finances and expecting higher collections through tax revenues.

Finally, the results on the non-association between the budgetary allocation variables and profitability in the seven public companies studied are due to the fact that public companies have a role oriented towards social profitability and allow safer access to public goods and services, but not a focus on business profitability. However, the results of the profitability indicators applied indicate the need for improvement in their internal management processes, based on their own capabilities and resources, developing strategies for growth and continuous improvement, focused on the field of budget management, accounting, financial and others [16].

5 Conclusions

The analysis of the behavior of the profitability of seven public companies based on the calculation of the ROA and ROE in the period 2014–2017 determined low levels of profitability, which are not influenced by the budget allocation by the Ecuadorian State.

Due to the above, it is recommended that companies carry out a financial analysis in a systematic way so that public companies determine liquidity and solvency, measure their operating activity, the efficiency in the use of their assets, their capacity for indebtedness and cancellation. of contracted obligations, required investments, their performance and profitability through the use of financial indicators such as those used in this investigation.

The results of the research indicate the need for public policy to be directed more towards promoting management strategies that influence better results of the activity of public companies, and not only to increase budget allocations, which, as evidenced in the study done, do not always have a positive effect on business profitability.

In short, we live in an environment of low growth, slowdown and global uncertainty that is further aggravated by the effects of the COVIT-19 pandemic. Not far from this reality, Ecuadorian public companies show a drop in the allocation of their budgets derived from the decrease in public investment. This scenario does not help to return to the path of growth, so it is imperative to establish government strategies that are not only focused on protecting spending but also on revitalizing public investment.

References

1. González, A., Cruz, M.: The bases of protectionism in the economy. Universidad Autónoma del Estado de Hidalgo, Hidalgo (2018). https://www.uaeh.edu.mx/docencia/P_Presentaci ones/icea/asignatura/comercio_exterior/2018/AdrianComer.pdf
2. ECLAC. Economic study of Latin America and the Caribbean. Main determinants of fiscal and monetary policies in the post-COVID-19 pandemic era. United Nations, Santiago de Chile (2020). https://repositorio.cepal.org/bitstream/handle/11362/46070/89/S2000371_es.pdf
3. Ministry of economy and finance. General state budget. Quito: ministry of economy and Finance (2017). https://www.finanzas.gob.ec/el-presupuesto-general-del-estado/
4. Sánchez, I.: Public spending, competitiveness index and social policy in Mexico. Problemas del Desarrollo **49**(192), 1–16 (2018). http://www.scielo.org.mx/pdf/prode/v49n192/0301-7036-prode-49-192-109-en.pdf
5. Ecuador. Organic Law of Public Companies. Quito: General Assembly (2009)
6. Ecuador. Organic Code of Planning and Public Finance. Quito: General Assembly (2010)
7. Oriol, A. Economic financial analysis. Madrid: Editions Management 2000 (2008)
8. Ecuador. General state budget. Quito: Ministry of Economy and Finance (2018). https://www.finanzas.gob.ec/el-presupuesto-general-del-estado/
9. Superintendence of Companies, Securities and Insurance. Document portal (2018). https://www.supercias.gob.ec/portaldocumentos/
10. López, L., Lozano, J.: Some statistical hypothesis tests with SPSS. Ciencia y Desarrollo **11**, 51–56 (2007). https://revistas.unjbg.edu.pe/index.php/cyd/article/view/224
11. Suárez, M.: Karl Pearson correlation coefficient (2011). http://www.monografias.com/trabaj os85/coeficiente-correlacion-karl-pearson/coeficiente-correlacion-karl-pearson.shtml
12. Mondragón, M.: Use of Spearman's correlation in a physiotherapy intervention study. Movimiento científico **8**(1), 98–104 (2014)
13. Goldstein, H.: Multinivel Satatistical Models. Institute of Education, London (1999)
14. Bastidas, C.A., Robles, P.: Public companies: mechanisms of commitment to local and institutional development. Guayas: Universidad Estatal del Milagro (2020). http://repositorio.unemi.edu.ec/handle/123456789/5162
15. Saltos, CM. The impact of the public policy of productive investment in the economic growth of Ecuador in the period 2013–2017. Universidad de Guayaquil, Guayaquil (2018). http://repositorio.ug.edu.ec/bitstream/redug/34455/1/SALTOS%20SOLIS.pdf
16. Fernández, A., Rivera, C.A.: Methodology for the improvement of the business management system of the Tobacco Agricultural Production Cooperatives. Universidad de las Fuerzas Armadas – ESPE, Sangolqui (2016). http://repositorio.espe.edu.ec/xmlui/handle/21000/11693?locale-attribute=en

Intellectual Capital and Its Impact on the Financial Efficiency of Commercial and Manufacturing Companies for Pichincha Province (2017–2019)

David Andrés Chushig Tene[(✉)] [iD], Danny Iván Zambrano Vera[iD],
Vicente Rolando Merchán Rodríguez[iD], and Eddy Antonio Castillo Montesdeoca[iD]

Universidad de las Fuerzas Armadas – ESPE, Sangolquí, Ecuador
{dachushig,dizambrano,vrmerchan,eacastillo}@espe.edu.ec

Abstract. Intellectual capital is a set of capabilities, skills, knowledge, and experiences that are difficult to imitate, and which constitute the value of the intellectual knowledge that organizations have throughout the achievement of results, seen from the point of view of decision-making. The objective of this study is to analyze the impact of intellectual capital on the financial efficiency of commercial and manufacturing companies located in the Pichincha province during the period 2017–2019. To guarantee the data records, the analysis included those companies in levels C and G, known as "large companies", on which the value-added intellectual capital model (VAICTM) and the indicators of profitability, productivity, and economic value added were applied. The results show that the average return on equity (ROE) is higher than the opportunity cost offered by the market at the time; furthermore, when comparing the ROE and ROA indicators, it was found that there is greater financial leverage, that is the companies resorted to contracted debt to increase their investment. In conclusion, the empirical evidence shows that the higher the level of intellectual capital, the lower the probability of financial efficiency indicators showing a deficit.

Keywords: Intellectual capital · Return on equity · Financial efficiency · Pulic scale

1 Introduction

Today, the new business environment is dynamic and demanding, due to the fact that today's consumer is more active than passive, forcing companies to generate and maintain a competitive advantage in order to stand out in the market. Therefore, in a knowledge-based economy, business management contributes to improving internal management and promoting innovation by influencing the development of skills and competencies to achieve greater organizational value (Escorcia and Barros 2020). Two elements stand out in the process of knowledge management: *intellectual capital*, considered as the seedbed of value creation, and *information systems*, an element that provides the storage, transformation and distribution of knowledge (Panizo 2019).

M. Botto-Tobar et al. (Eds.): ICAT 2022, CCIS 1757, pp. 336–351, 2023.
https://doi.org/10.1007/978-3-031-24978-5_30

In the case of Ecuador, the economic sectors of commerce, manufacturing, and services are the main generators of sales, according to figures published in the Directory of Companies and Establishments (INEC 2020). In this sense, Ecuadorian organizations require their own capacities and resources to create competitive advantages through the management of their intellectual capital, which turns out to be a key factor in the development of their business transcendental process to establish, grow and remain in the market (Villegas et al. 2017). Therefore, this research focuses on the analysis of intellectual capital through the VAIC™ tool and how it influences the financial efficiency of the business fabric (commercial and manufacturing) in the Pichincha province.

1.1 Historical Background

Intellectual capital is one of the fundamental elements of knowledge management, which favors the creation and generation of competitive advantages, which constitutes a differentiating resource. In North American, European and Asian countries, intellectual capital is valued, transformed, and transmitted to improve resource management; however, in Latin American countries it is difficult to value and measure intellectual capital, as tangible assets predominate over intangible ones (Acosta 2020).

For Peña et al. (2019) intellectual capital identifies and values the intangible assets that contribute to improving the competitiveness, productivity, and performance of the organization. In this sense, it must be understood that, to obtain results that are not insufficient in their measurement, they must be treated as a whole (Ibarra and Hernández 2019). Measuring this element will determine the effectiveness and efficiency of organizations by determining the current state of business development in terms of relevant outcomes that satisfy stakeholder interests (Gazzera and Lombardo 2020).

Intellectual capital can be broken down into three dimensions: human capital (HCE), structural capital (SCE), and relational capital (CEE). HCE represents people's knowledge of values, attitudes, and skills that differentiate them from other organizations. SCE involves processes, innovation, infrastructure, and other intangible assets that relate to organizational culture. Finally, CEE deals with the organization's links or relationships with external and internal agents linked to the business activity.

For Gómez (2007), the valuation of companies focused its interest on the measurement of intellectual capital, a new trend that committed efforts and resources. In this sense, there are academic methods and methodologies developed by international organizations for measuring and evaluating this resource. One of the most widely used is the one developed by Ante Pulic, known as VAICTM, which employs simple and direct procedures, which are traditional financial indicators, commonly used in organizations, easily understandable and with quantifiable results.

1.2   Literature Review

Agency Theory

This theory conceives of the firm as a legal function, which through a contractual nexus links the relationships between individual economic agents, where each party seeks to maximize its utility (Ramírez and Palacín 2018). To this end, the shareholder (principal) delegates to the managers (agent) an administrative task, which is reflected in the maximization of profits (Quintero et al. 2020).

In this context, López and Gómez (2020), agree that the power and influence lies with both the principal and the agent, who have the decision-making power in negotiations to achieve their objectives effectively and efficiently, with the company's resources being the basis for the achievement of the parties' expectations. It is therefore important to examine the management to ensure that its resources are used optimally (Bueno and Santos 2012).

For Villegas et al. (2017) the main element of a company is its human capital, because knowledge is a decisive intangible asset in the production of any organization, which belongs to the workers and, being transferable, represents a strategic aspect from its production, acquisition, application, and retention (Máynez and Noriega 2015). Thus, the worker (agent) provides human and intellectual capital, while the principal (shareholder) provides financial resources.

Stakeholder Theory

In the 1980s, the theory gained strength with the studies of Edward Free-man, who initially developed strategic theory, but in later decades moved towards business ethics and a more pragmatic point of view (Quinche 2017). Here, related parties are recognized as a decisive factor, as they contribute and provide access to resources. Consequently, a positive relationship with stakeholders is recognized as an intangible asset, generating competitive advantages (Ochoa et al. 2012).

Stakeholders are groups or individuals aligned to a common goal, who benefit or are harmed by the activities of an organization (Reyes et al. 2019). To this end, it is important for the company to consider each of its stakeholders, as the focus on maximizing economic profit shifts to a multi-objective approach, where it seeks to satisfy all of the organization's agents (Gazzera and Lombardo 2020).

Resources and Capabilities Theory

The basis of the theory is that each organization develops its strategy with the resources it has available to achieve profitability (Villa et al. 2019). To this end, companies adopt an inside-out perspective, where it is specified that the creation of a competitive advantage stems from their resources and capabilities or those that they can acquire (Acosta 2019). However, the productivity and competitiveness developed will depend on the degree of efficiency in the use of physical, technological, and human resources, and their capacities such as skills, abilities, experience, and knowledge, among others (Cajigas et al. 2019).

Following Guerrero et al. (2020), the diversity of resources stands out in a company, as these factors are available or can be controlled stably, even if there are no property rights over them. However, to Ochoa et al. (2012), not all resources have a similar strategic value, some are more valuable because they sustain a greater competitive advantage, this is the case of intangibles. The above is supported by the fact that competitors find it easier to imitate physical or tangible assets than intangible ones, as the latter is valuable, scarce, and irreplaceable (Villa et al. 2019).

2   Methodology

The research has a space-temporal dimension, of longitudinal type, which implied examining more than two periods of time in order to deduce the behavior of the variables. To this end, the financial information of a fixed population or sample of commercial and manufacturing companies for the period 2017–2019 was subjected to a descriptive and correlational analysis.

2.1   Conceptual Model

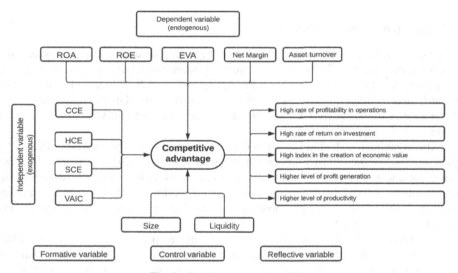

Fig. 1. Study conceptual model.

The model presented (Fig. 1) takes as its basis the proposal by Villegas et al. (2017); however, the variables Market To Book (MTB), Tobin's Q, and long-term indebtedness were excluded because they are oriented towards a market capitalization approach. In their place, based on the review of empirical studies, variables such as the "EVA" were included, based on the research of Iazzolino et al. (2013); Hatane (2019). The "net margin" and the "asset turnover" are based on the approaches of Yao (2019), for the estimation of financial efficiency. On the other hand, "liquidity" is included as a control variable, supported by the study of Pardo et al. (2018b), showing the ability of the manufacturing and trading company to honor its short-term commitments.

2.2 Research Hypotheses

Ten hypotheses were constructed involving the VAIC™ and its elements: HCE, SCE and CEE, in relation to the five indicators of the financial efficiency variable: ROA, ROE, EVA, net margin (MARN) and turnover of assets (ROTA) of commercial and manufacturing companies.

- H1: VAIC™ is related to the ROA.
- H2: VAIC™ is related to the ROE.
- H3: VAIC™ is related to the EVA.
- H4: VAIC™ is related to the MARN.
- H5. VAIC™ is related to the ROTA.
- H6. CEE, HCE y SCE is related to the ROA.
- H7. CEE, HCE y SCE is related to the ROE.
- H8. CEE, HCE y SCE is related to the EVA.
- H9. CEE, HCE y SCE is related to the MARN.
- H10. CEE, HCE y SCE is related to the ROTA.

2.3 Selection of the Population

The first step corresponds to the selection of the best-positioned companies within the Business Ranking (2017–2019) of the Superintendence of Companies, Securities, and Insurance-based on information from the 2017, 2018, and 2019 financial years. In this regard, large companies were chosen from the levels of the National Classification of Economic Activities (CIIU); C: Manufacturing industries, and G: Wholesale and retail trade.

The organizations had to belong to the stock market sector, be located in Pichincha province, and in the information for the financial year 2017, 2018, and 2019, they did not present losses in their balance sheet. In addition, the delimitation process excluded organizations that did not publish complete data and information on wages and salaries in their financial statements and notes to the financial statements, a basic item for the calculation of the VAICTM.

By Arias (2006), if the number of units that make up the population is accessible, it is possible to investigate and obtain data from the entire population, in this situation, it will not be necessary to select and extract a sample. Similarly, Tamayo and Tamayo (2003), indicates that "when the entire population is taken for a study, sampling is not necessary" (p. 176). Based on these considerations, the number of units of analysis for the study covers the entire population, consisting of 17 manufacturing industries and 20 wholesale and retail trade enterprises covering 111 observations (Table 1).

2.4 Data Collection Instrument

The research is based on two variables, intellectual capital, and financial efficiency, which are supported by empirical models. To specify the operationalization of the variables covered by the financial ratios, a measurement instrument was designed for use in this research, which consists of an observation sheet that covers a large number of figures

Table 1. Study observations.

Companies	Number
Total companies for the study Manufacturing (17) / Trade (20)	37
Number of periods	3
Total observations (37 × 3)	111

and allows analysis and measurements to be established. For this reason, the sheets were constructed in the Excel computer tool, both for the independent variable, the dependent variable, and the control variables. Also, in each instrument, the calculation procedure for each indicator was systematized using the mathematical formulas provided by the tool, to estimate the values of the variables (indicators), once the necessary information contained in the audit reports was entered.

Thus, a compilation was made of the external audit reports published in Superintendence of Companies, Securities and Insurance from 2017 to 2019 for each company subject to analysis, which provides reliability, validity, and objectivity to the data in the financial statements and the notes to the financial statements, as they are figures audited by renowned national and international firms. In this sense, once the information was available, each of the figures necessary for the calculation of the indicators was extracted, and once the file for each variable was completed, a final summary was made with the results of each ratio, to enter them into the STATA statistical program to proceed with the development of the regression models and their validation.

2.5   Regression Models

In order to test the hypotheses of the study, ten econometric linear regression models have been incorporated, based on the studies of Meles (2016); Pardo et al. (2017); Villegas et al. (2017); Pardo et al. (2018a); Hatane (2019); Yao (2019), each corresponds to the hypotheses set out in the research proposal.

- H1: $ROA = \beta_0 + \beta_1 VAIC^{TM} + \beta_2 TAM + \beta_3 LIQ + E$
- H2: $ROE = \beta_0 + \beta_1 VAIC^{TM} + \beta_2 TAM + \beta_3 LIQ + E$
- H3: $EVA = \beta_0 + \beta_1 VAIC^{TM} + \beta_2 TAM + \beta_3 LIQ + E$
- H4: $MARN = \beta_0 + \beta_1 VAIC^{TM} + \beta_2 TAM + \beta_3 LIQ + E$
- H5: $ROTA = \beta_0 + \beta_1 VAIC^{TM} + \beta_2 TAM + \beta_3 LIQ + E$
- H6: $ROA = \beta_0 + \beta_1 CEE + \beta_2 HCE + \beta_3 SCE + \beta_4 TAM + \beta_5 LIQ + E$
- H7: $ROE = \beta_0 + \beta_1 CEE + \beta_2 HCE + \beta_3 SCE + \beta_4 TAM + \beta_5 LIQ + E$
- H8: $EVA = \beta_0 + \beta_1 CEE + \beta_2 HCE + \beta_3 SCE + \beta_4 TAM + \beta_5 LIQ + E$
- H9: $MARN = \beta_0 + \beta_1 CEE + \beta_2 HCE + \beta_3 SCE + \beta_4 TAM + \beta_5 LIQ + E$
- H10: $ROTA = \beta_0 + \beta_1 CEE + \beta_2 HCE + \beta_3 SCE + \beta_4 TAM + \beta_5 LIQ + E$

The value of βn corresponds to the regression estimators of the linear coefficients of the independent variables. On the other hand, E corresponds to the estimation error.

3   Results and Discussion

3.1   Descriptive Analysis

The information was processed in the statistical program STATA version 16.0. According to the values submitted (Table 2), the analysis variables have a positive average from 2017 to 2019, indicating favorable results. However, the EVA obtained a negative response, because its profitability was generated below the cost of capital, indicating that during the period of analysis no value was produced for the organization.

Table 2. Descriptive statistics of the study.

Variable	Obs.	About media	Under media	Media	Std. dev.	Min	Max
CEE	111	40	71	0.4852491	0.3390423	0.0870278	1.96518
HCE	111	23	88	4.363984	6.14799	0.3088999	37.82857
SCE	111	77	34	0.5748131	0.4222836	−2.237.295	0.973565
VAIC™	111	22	89	5.424046	6.294366	−1.789197	39.17566
ROA	111	44	67	0.0474682	0.0406635	0.0006852	0.2006725
ROE	111	39	72	0.1663236	0.1832942	0.0018923	0.856652
EVA	111	85	26	−2.115.488	7323.537	−48795.42	10920.17
MARN	111	41	70	0.0343162	0.0286869	0.0008762	0.1371808
ROTA	111	47	64	1.364422	0.5821854	0.3643439	2.962.707
TAM	111	26	85	156762.4	367212.9	2390	3027545
LIQ	111	44	67	1.459308	0.4796116	0.8605149	3.299629

On the other hand, the EVA presented a very large deviation, which indicates high volatility, since, unlike the other ratios, its calculation includes data such as the opportunity cost of shareholders and the cost of debt, which present a high change in value over time. Similarly, the TAM variable of the company obtained a very high deviation, due to the fact that the study is being applied to a population of large companies that, due to their economic activity, have a considerable value of assets in accordance with the branch to which they belong.

The results (Table 2) of the mean ROA of 4.75% indicate that manufacturing and trading companies invest a large amount in their production of assets; however, at the same time, they earn a very low profit on the capital allocated. All these ideas are affirmed by observing that the average ROTA is 1.36 times and that the number of observations above the mean is only 47 out of 111, thus inferring the existence of underutilization of assets in firms below the mean.

As for the ROE value, its average is 16.63% higher than the reference active rate that oscillates between 7% and 9% according to data from the Central Bank of Ecuador, which is profitability higher than the minimum expected, however, when comparing

ROE and ROA, the former is higher than the latter because there is greater financial leverage, that is. Debt was used to increase the amount of investment in the production of the organizations.

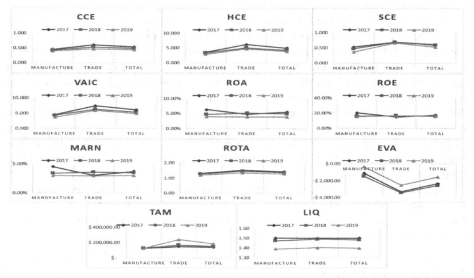

Fig. 2. Results of the variables.

The trading company has generated a higher value of CCE compared to manufacturing (Fig. 2), in the years of analysis for each unit of physical and financial capital, however, the results at a general level show a downward trend in both types of the organization over the years analyzed. As for the HCE, the manufacturing industry is relegated by the commercial industry, because its results are lower, however, the values achieved exceed the limit of 2.00 during the period of analysis, a measure that indicates a successful performance in the participation of each unit of investment in employees in the value-added.

On the other hand, the SCE of commerce companies maintains the tendency to be higher than that of manufacturing companies; however, this type of organization (manufacturing industry) in the years 2018 and 2019 presents a value below the threshold of 0.50 that the literature sets out to define whether an organization has a successful performance. This means that the amount of wages and salaries relative to value-added is higher in these entities. Considering the previous paragraphs, for the VAICTM the same trend is presented, in which the commercial enterprise obtains better results, in 2017 it presents a value of 7 450 per monetary unit invested in recourses, that is, for each dollar invested it generates 7 times more value; however, in 2018 it only reaches a value of 6 274 and in 2019 a value of 5 861, a downward trend.

The return on assets as a whole shows a downward trend, in 2017 their ROA as a whole was 5.47%, for 2018 4.89%, and in 2019 3.38%. As of 2017, the total units under analysis have an average ROE of 17.48%, by 2018 it decreases to 16.51% and in 2019 it ends with 15.91%, these results indicate that the profit decreases every year. From 2017 to 2019 the EVA value on average of the study units is negative, which indicates companies with returns lower than what it costs to generate them. Within these results, the idea of organizations seeking returns that exceed their cost of capital is evident in the fall in the value of the indicator from 2017 to 2019.

Regarding the net margin by economic activity, manufacturing predominates over trade, due to its better results in 2017 (4.52%) and 2019 (3.05%). However, in 2018, the commercial company stands out with a net margin of 3.63% compared to 3.44% for manufacturing. With reference to asset turnover in the trading company, 2017 is the period with the highest efficiency, as the asset turnover was 1.52 times. As for the manufacturing industry, the highest efficiency in asset management was achieved in 2017 with a turnover of 1.32 times, and in subsequent years productivity decreased. On the size of the company, it is observed that on average the companies have suffered an increase in the total amount of their assets for 2017 its value was USD 137 112.78 and became USD 184 953.65 in 2019, which indicates a greater amount of resources to be used by the organizations.

Regarding the average liquidity of the units of analysis, the results show that commercial and manufacturing companies are able to meet their short-term obligations, as their overall result is greater than 1, which denotes that the organizations have control over their liquidity.

3.2 Correlation Analysis

In the correlation analysis (Table 3), the correlations between CEE and the ROA, ROE, EVA and ROTA indicators stand out, due to the fact that this variable is within the models and is also one of the elements of the VAIC™. In addition, VAIC™ stands out for its inverse relationship with ROA (-0.0319), ROE (-0.0094), ROTA (-0.0994) because it maintains a weak negative correlation, which indicates that as the value of one variable increases, the value of the other decreases. Around the variables MARN (0.0109) and EVA (0.0492) the relationship is weak but positive, so when one variable increases in value the other will also follow the same trend.

In relation to ROA with the indicators TAM (0.1028) and LIQ (0.2278*) there is a weak positive correlation degree; however, ROE with TAM (-0.0599) and LIQ (-0.1835) presented a weak, but negative correlation. The results for EVA show a considerable negative correlation with TAM (-0.6735**) and a weak correlation with LIQ (-0.0643). Likewise, a weak association was identified between MARN with TAM (0.1552) and LIQ (0.2628**). Finally, ROTA is positively related to LIQ (0.0425) and negatively related to TAM (-0.0752).

3.3 Regression Analysis

The results of the regression models (Table 4) helped us to explain the impact of the independent variable and the control variables on the dependent variable. In addition, the validation of each of the models and thus the research hypotheses were included. Therefore, to check the degree of independence between the residuals, and that there is

Table 3. Correlation análisis.

Variable	CEE	HCE	SCE	VAIC^TM	ROA	ROE	EVA	MARN	ROTA	TAM	LIQ
CCE	1.0000										
HCE	−0.0612	1.0000									
SCE	0.1976*	0.3325**	1.0000								
VAIC^TM	0.0073	0.9958**	0.4025**	1.0000							
ROA	0.2912**	−0.0601	0.1660	−0.0319	1.0000						
ROE	0.4987**	−0.0496	0.1808	−0.0094	0.6795**	1.0000					
EVA	−0.1312	0.0626	−0.0730	0.0492	−0.4279**	−0.3415**	1.0000				
MARN	0.0600	−0.0032	0.1610	0.0109	0.8790**	0.4535**	−0.3829**	1.0000			
ROTA	0.5175**	−0.1359	0.0820	−0.0994	0.4590**	0.5571**	−0.1705	0.0391	1.0000		
TAM	−0.1315	−0.0696	−0.0102	−0.0758	0.1028	−0.0599	−0.6735**	0.1552	−0.0752	1.0000	
LIQ	−0.1518	−0.2102*	−0.1628	−0.2244*	0.2278*	−0.1835	−0.0643	0.2628**	0.0425	0.1356	1.0000

*Correlation is significant at the 0.05 level (2-tailed).
**Correlation is significant at the 0.01 level (2-tailed).

no autocorrelation in the models, the Durbin-Watson statistic was applied, which states that a value close to 2 indicates the non-existence of this phenomenon.

Meanwhile, White's test was used to check for homoscedasticity, whereby a value greater than 0.05 indicates that the model has no problems of heteroscedasticity. Finally, the diagnosis of non-collinearity indicates if the independent variables do not have an exact linear relationship; if the FIV test of a variable exceeds the limit of 10, it is eliminated.

The main results after analyzing the 10 linear regression models are to accept hypotheses 1, 2, and 5, while the remaining hypotheses are rejected. Thus, to validate them, the "p" value associated with the F statistic was used, the null hypothesis being validated when Prob > F is greater than 0.05 and the alternative hypothesis accepted when Prob > F is less than 0.05.

The correlation of the variables in hypothesis 1 is inverse, so that the higher the coefficient of intellectual value-added, the lower the possibility that commercial and manufacturing companies will obtain a lower return on assets. In this respect, the linear regression analysis of model 1 showed that the three indicators VAICTM (0.25), TAM (0.78), and LIQ (2.30) have a positive impact on ROA, that is the higher the value of these indicators, the higher the ROA. In this sense, when the intellectual value-added increases its value by one unit, the return on assets will increase by 0.0001535, whereas if total assets increase by one dollar, the effect on ROA will be 8.23e−09 more, and if liquidity increases its value by one unit, 0.0189134 will be added to ROA.

As for hypothesis 2, the variables VAICTM and ROE present an inverse correlation, which indicates that the higher the coefficient of intellectual value-added, the lower the possibility that both the trading company and the manufacturing industry will obtain a higher return on equity. The above evidence is supported by the results of the linear regression analysis of model 2, which shows that the VAICTM (−0.57), TAM (−0.40) and LIQ (−1.95) indicators have a negative impact on ROE. Consequently, for each unit increase in the value of VAICTM this will affect the value of financial performance by −0.001605, the same tendency is presented for the size of the company and liquidity, which by increasing their value by one unit will reduce the value of ROE by 1.91e−08 and −0.0728839 respectively.

In the case of hypothesis 5, the variables of asset turnover and the coefficient of intellectual value-added have an inverse correlation, with a high VAICTM not allowing for a higher ROTA value. Therefore, according to the linear regression analysis applied to model 5 only one variable obtained a positive relationship with asset turnover, being liquidity (0.32), while VAICTM (−1.00) and TAM (−0.90) have a negative relationship. On the other hand, the VAICTM (−1.00) and TAM (−0.90) have a negative relationship. The effect of increasing the value of each variable by one unit must be considered, which in the case of liquidity would increase the ROTA by 0.0390673. Within this framework, VAICTM and firm size will decrease the value of ROTA by 1 −0.009132 and 1.38e−07 respectively.

On the other hand, the most relevant results on the unaccepted hypotheses indicate that VAICTM and EVA are not related (hypothesis 3), the same result is presented by the net margin (hypothesis 4). As for the remaining hypotheses, the models do not explain

Table 4. Regression analysis.

Research hypotheses	R² corrected	Durbin-Watson	Test White	FIV	F	Prob > F	Coef	t	Conclusion
H1:El VAICTM está relacionado con el ROA	0.0313	2.3527	0.8106	TAM:1.07 VAIC^{TM}:1.06 LIQ:1.02	2.18	0.0941	TAM:8.23e−09 VAIC^{TM}:0.0001535 LIQ:0.0189134	TAM:0.78 VAIC^{TM}:0.25 LIQ:2.30	Accepted
H2:El VAICTM está relacionado con el ROE	0.0108	2.1766	0.0882	TAM:1.07 VAIC^{TM}:1.06 LIQ:1.02	1.40	0.2464	TAM:−1.91e−08 VAIC^{TM}:−0.001605 LIQ:−0.0728839	TAM:−0.40 VAIC^{TM}:−0.57 LIQ:−1.95	Accepted
H3:El VAICTM está relacionado con el EVA	0.4319	1.9605	0.0000	TAM:1.07 VAIC^{TM}:1.06 LIQ:1.02	29.71	0.0000	TAM:−0.0135032 VAIC^{TM}:4.978947 LIQ:434.4359	TAM:−9.38 VAIC^{TM}:0.06 LIQ:0.39	Rejected
H4:El VAICTM está relacionado con el MARN	0.0641	2.3946	0.4328	TAM:1.07 VAIC^{TM}:1.06 LIQ:1.02	3.51	0.0178	TAM:9.80e−09 VAIC^{TM}:0.0003626 LIQ:−0.0157686	TAM:1.35 VAIC^{TM}:0.84 LIQ:2.76	Rejected
H5:El VAICTM está relacionado con la ROTA	−0.0098	1.9948	0.6507	TAM:1.07 VAIC^{TM}:1.06 LIQ:1.02	0.64	0.5887	TAM:−1.38e−07 VAIC^{TM}:−0.009132 LIQ:0.0390673	TAM:−0.90 VAIC^{TM}:−1.00 LIQ:0.32	Accepted

(continued)

Table 4. (*continued*)

Research hypotheses	R^2 corrected	Durbin-Watson	Test White	FIV	F	Prob > F	Coef	t	Conclusion
H6:El CEE, HCE y SCE está relacionado con el ROA	0.1565	2.400	0.3038	CEE:1.20 HCE:1.19 SCE:1.10 TAM:109 LIQ:1.04	5.08	0.0003	CEE:0.0377256 HCE:−0.0001822 SCE:0.0153985 TAM:1.17e−08 LIQ:0.0238663	CEE:3.42 HCE:−0.29 SCE:1.67 TAM:1.19 LIQ:3.07	Rejected
H7:El CEE, HCE y SCE está relacionado con el ROE	0.2360	2.3047	0.0072	CEE:1.20 HCE:1.19 SCE:1.10 TAM:109 LIQ:1.04	7.79	0.0000	CEE:0.2479876 HCE:−0.0023043 SCE:0.0421228 TAM:5.87e−09 LIQ:−0.0443028	CEE:5.24 HCE:−0.85 SCE:1.06 TAM:0.14 LIQ:−1.33	Rejected
H8:El CEE, HCE y SCE está relacionado con el EVA	0.4808	1.9931	0.0000	CEE:1.20 HCE:1.19 SCE:1.10 TAM:109 LIQ:1.04	21.37	0.0000	CEE:−4640.278 HCE:16.46008 SCE:−750.8765 TAM:−0.0319694 LIQ:−93.14557	CEE:−2.98 HCE:0.18 SCE:−0.58 TAM:10.01 LIQ:−0.08	Rejected
H9:El CEE, HCE y SCE está relacionado con el MARN	0.0908	2.4345	0.2447	CEE:1.20 HCE:1.19 SCE:1.10 TAM:109 LIQ:1.04	3.20	0.0100	CEE:0.0071181 HCE:0.0000412 SCE:0.0129175 TAM:1.01e−08 LIQ:0.017396	CEE:0.88 HCE:0.09 SCE:1.91 TAM:1.40 LIQ:3.06	Rejected
H10:El CEE, HCE y SCE está relacionado con la ROTA	0.2566	2.1936	0.0146	CEE:1.20 HCE:1.19 SCE:1.10 TAM:109 LIQ:1.04	8.59	0.0000	CEE:0.8920174 HCE:−0.0087175 SCE:0.0381468 TAM:−4.43e−08 LIQ:0.1339543	CEE:6.02 HCE:−1.03 SCE:0.31 TAM:−0.33 LIQ:−1.28	Rejected

the relationship of the separate components of the coefficient of intellectual value-added with the indicators of the dependent variable.

3.4 Discussion

Empirical studies confirm the results of this research, according to Sumedrea (2013) VAICTM is the variable that explains ROA and ROE better than its components, a conclusion that is shared with the literature, because within the research all hypotheses on the relationship between intellectual capital variables (CEE, HCE and SCE) with financial efficiency were rejected, while hypotheses 1 and 2 comparing ROA and ROE with VAICTM as the only element of intellectual capital were accepted.

In accordance with Meles (2016), the intellectual value-added ratio plays an important role in financial performance, measured through ROA and ROE. In terms of Pardo et al. (2017), Villegas et al. (2017), and Pardo et al. (2018a); conclude in their research that VAICTM has a positive impact on ROA and ROE, while VAICTM has a positive impact on ROA and ROE while Yao (2019), indicates the existence of a relationship between intellectual capital with ROA and turnover on assets. Thus, the above statements were verified in the study, because the only accepted hypotheses are linked to the mentioned indicators ROA, ROE, and ROTA. However, the study differs from the idea that the coefficient of intellectual value-added has a positive impact on ROE because the linear regression model applied on the basis of the information provided by the commercial companies and manufacturing industries showed that the VAICTM indicator has a negative impact on ROE.

Also, Iazzolino et al. (2013), analysis of his research shows that there is no relationship between the economic value-added and the VAICTM, a criterion he shares with the study by Hatane (2019), where it is shown that the VAICTM has no effect on the economic value of the company. Consequently, the literature is confirmed by practice, as it is a rejected hypothesis that there is a relationship between the coefficient of intellectual value-added and economic value-added.

4 Conclusions

In examining financial efficiency from three different perspectives, namely financial performance (ROA, ROE, and net margin), productivity (asset turnover), and economic value added (EVA), it was identified from the literature that the theories underpinning this research highlight the role of human capital, which recognizes the unique skills, experience, knowledge, and value, all of which are valuable resources that are difficult for competitors to easily copy.

On the other hand, during the period of analysis 2017–2019, a higher financial return than a return on assets was evidenced in commercial companies and manufacturing industries, indicating positive financial leverage, was resorting to debt served to have a positive and multiplier effect on profitability, however, being the average value of negative EVA, most of the companies analyzed did not generate value to cover the costs generated by own or external resources, also leave in evidence the decisions taken by managers of these organizations to increase the value-added business.

According to the results of the linear regression models, the relationship of VAICTM with the ROA, ROE, and ROTA indicators has been identified, in addition to the control variables LIQ and TAM, being important to highlight that this index has presented a decline in recent years; however, this trend has only affected the ROA indicator because it has a direct relationship unlike ROE and ROTA that present an inverse, so the lower the coefficient of intellectual added value, the higher the results of financial performance and asset turnover will be.

Finally, intellectual capital in commercial and manufacturing companies is on a scale of successful performance according to Pulic's scale, but produces favorable results up to a certain point, so its development to higher levels would have unfavorable consequences on ROE and ROTA indicators, this provides a warning to the managers of each organization by placing a limit on the investment in assets and on their management in a strategic way.

References

Acosta, J.: Influencia de los recursos y capacidades en los resultados financieros y en la competitividad empresarial: una revisión de la literatura. I+D Revista de Investigaciones 13(1), 147–157 (2019)

Acosta, M.: Medición y Valoración del capital intelectual en la empresa Vehicentro S.A. (2020). Pontifica Universidad Católica del Ecuador: https://repositorio.pucesa.edu.ec/bitstream/123 456789/3031/1/77203.pdf

Arias, F.: El proyecto de investigación: Introducción a la metodología científica, Quinta Edición. Venezuela: Episteme (2006)

Bueno, J., Santos, D.: Teoría de la agencia en la determinación de la estructura de capital. Casos sectores económicos del departamento del Valle del Cauca. Prolegómenos. Derechos y Valores XV(30), 161–176 (2012)

Cajigas, M., Ramirez, E., Ramirez, D.: Capacidad de producción y sostenibilidad en empresas nuevas. Espacios 40(43), 15 (2019)

Escorcia, J., Barros, D.: Gestión del conocimiento en Instituciones de Educación Superior: Caracterización desde una reflexión teórica. Revista de Ciencias Sociales (Ve) XXVI(3), 83–97 (2020)

Gazzera, M., Lombardo, L.: El Capital Intelectual Dinámico en el Sector Alojamiento de la Ciudad de San Martín de los Andes (Patagonia – Argentina). Estudios y Perspectivas en Turismo -30° Aniversario 29, 501–518 (2020)

Gómez, J.: El capital intelectual (2007). Gestiopolis: https://www.gestiopolis.com/capital-intele ctual-que-es-importancia-y-como-medirlo/

Guerrero, C., Rodales, H., Chávez, M.: Análisis de los recursos y capacidades de las empresas hoteleras de ciudades de playa en la República Mexicana. In: Global Conference on Business and Finance Proceedings, vol. 15, no. 1, pp. 187–197 (2020)

Hatane, S.: Do value added intellectual coefficient and corporate governance contribute do value added intellectual coefficient and corporate governance contribute. Petra Int. J. Bus. Stud. 2, 96–108 (2019)

Iazzolino, G., Laise, D., Migliano, G.: Measures of value creation: a comparison between VAIC and EVA. ResearchGate 501–514 (2013)

Ibarra, M., Hernández, F.: La influencia del capital intelectual en el desempeño de las pequeñas y medianas empresas manufactureras de México: el caso de Baja California. Innovar 29(71), 79–95 (2019)

INEC. Directorio de Empresas y Establecimientos (2020). INEC https://www.ecuadorencifras. gob.ec/documentos/web-inec/Estadisticas_Economicas/DirectorioEmpresas/Directorio_Empr esas_2018/Boletin_Tecnico_DIEE_2018.pdf

López, M., Gómez, A.S.: Gestión de las PyME en México. Ante los nuevos escenarios de negocios y la teoría de la agencia. Estudios de Administración 27, 69–91 (2020)

Máynez, I., Noriega, S.: Transferencia de conocimiento dentro de la empresa: Beneficios y riesgos individuales percibidos. Frontera Norte 27(54), 29–52 (2015)

Meles, A.: The impact of the intellectual capital efficiency on commercial banks performance: evidence from the US. J. Multinational Financ. (2016)

Ochoa, M., Prieto, M., Santidrían: Una revisión de las principales teorías aplicables al Capital Intelectual. Revista Nacional de administración 3(2), 35–48 (2012)

Panizo, M.: Caracterización de la Gestión del Conocimiento en Organizaciones Orientadas a la Producción de Bienes y Servicios como área de investigación. Revista Tekhné 22(2), 1–29 (2019)

Pardo, M., Armas, R., Chamba, L.: Valoración del capital intelectual y su impacto en la rentabilidad financiera en empresas del sector industrial del Ecuador. Revista Publicando 193–206 (2017)

Pardo, M., Armas, R., Higuerey, Á.: La influencia del capital intelectual sobre la rentabilidad de las empresas manufactureras ecuatorianas. Revista Espacios 39, 14 (2018a)

Pardo, M., Reinaldo, A., Higuerey, Á.: El capital intelectual y su influencia en la rentabilidad de las empresas de comunicación ecuatorianas. Revista Ibérica de Sistemas e Tecnologias de Informação 335–347 (2018b)

Peña, C., Arias, B., Da Silva, S.: Incubadoras de negocios en red: Capital intelectual de incubadoras de negocios de Latinoamérica y la relación con su éxito. Revista Electronica de Administración 96–118 (2019)

Quinche, F.: Una mirada crítica a las teorías predominantes de la responsabilidad social corporativa. Revista de la Facultad de Ciencias Económica: Investigación y Reflexión XXV(2), 159–178 (2017)

Quintero, W., Peñaranda, M., Rodriguez, M.: Naturaleza de las organizaciones y sus costos de transacción: Análisis de la teoría de agencia, teoría de la organización y teoría de la firma. Revista Espacios 90–101 (2020)

Ramírez, L., Palacín, M.: El estado del arte sobre la teoría de la estructura de capital de la empresa. Cuadernos de Economía 37(73), 143–165 (2018)

Reyes, J., Bonales, J., Ortiz, C.: Responsabilidad Social de las Empresas Exportadoras de Brócoli. CIMEXUS XIV(2), 47–66 (2019)

Sumedrea, S.: Intellectual capital and firm performance: a dynamic relationship in crisis time. Procedia Econ. Financ. 6, 137–144 (2013)

Tamayo, Tamayo, M.: El proceso de la investigación científica, Cuarta edición. México: Limusa S.A (2003)

Villa, Y., Hernández, V., Ávalos, J.: El Capital Intelectual En Las Pymes. Revista de la Facultad de Contaduría y Ciencias Administrativas 4(7), 32–40 (2019)

Villegas, E., Hernández, M., Salazar, B.: La medición del capital intelectual y su impacto en el rendimiento financiero en empresas del sector industrial en México. Contaduría y Administración 62, 184–206 (2017)

Yao, H.: Intellectual capital, profitability, and productivity: evidence from Pakistani financial institutions. Sustainability 2019, 11 (2019)

Influence of Technological Capabilities on Business Innovation in Ecuador

Maribel Maya Carrillo[1,2(✉)] [iD], Carla Suntaxi Imbaquingo[1] [iD], Valentina Ramos[2] [iD], and Edgar Ramiro Guerrón[3,4] [iD]

[1] Departamento de Ciencias Económicas, Administrativas y de Comercio, Universidad de las Fuerzas Armadas "ESPE", Av. General Rumiñahui s/n, Sangolquí, Ecuador
ammaya@espe.edu.ec

[2] Facultad de Ciencias Administrativas, Doctorado en Gestión Tecnológica, Escuela Politécnica Nacional, Av. Ladrón de Guevara 253, Quito, Ecuador

[3] Departamento de Ciencias Exactas, Universidad de las Fuerzas Armadas "ESPE", Av. General Rumiñahui s/n, Sangolquí, Ecuador

[4] Facultad de Geología, Minas, Petróleos y Ambiental, Universidad Central del Ecuador, Av. Universitaria, Quito, Ecuador

Abstract. Technological capabilities are a determinant for innovation in companies since they permeate different aspects of the development of the organization. The research objective was to determine the influence that technological capacity has on innovation results, for this 50 metalworking SMEs from the Metropolitan District of Quito participated, which were identified as innovative and potentially innovative, due to the efforts and innovation results obtained in products and processes. The level of technological capabilities is medium, and its most relevant components are investment and learning, and technological relationships. Through the correlation analysis of Spearman, it was determined that there is a positive correlation significant between technological capacity and innovation in both product and process, therefore, the more developed this technological skill, there is a greater likelihood of innovation impact that enables SMEs to gain a more competitive business.

Keywords: Technological capacity · Innovation · Management

1 Introduction

The transformational changes in the world economy and the current requirements demanded by globalization have forced companies in emerging economies to assimilate, use, adapt, change, create and improve technologies to face the current demands imposed by the markets [1]. Several studies mention that exist disadvantages in emerging countries due to their lack of technological capabilities because this condition limits the possibilities of innovation compared to mature economies [2]. Based on this reality, Figueiredo [3] proposes that companies should resort to technological learning to create technological capabilities, that is, to propose technological development and innovation based on the successful experiences of mature economies.

© The Author(s), under exclusive license to Springer Nature Switzerland AG 2023
M. Botto-Tobar et al. (Eds.): ICAT 2022, CCIS 1757, pp. 352–367, 2023.
https://doi.org/10.1007/978-3-031-24978-5_31

In emerging economies, small and medium-sized enterprises (SMEs) have become an essential pillar in the development of a country, due to their important representation in the economy and their contribution to the generation of employment sources [4]. In recent years, in this business sector, it has been proven that technology is one of the main engines of sustainable economic growth; therefore, there is an increase in efforts to invest in obtaining technological knowledge, as well as the development of technological capabilities, where these actions become the set of knowledge typical of the industrial field that facilitates the creation of innovative products or processes [5].

Technology constitutes the knowledge and the use that is given to it, as an essential asset of companies in the practical application to obtain benefits [6]. This application is based on the ability to manage technology as a social learning process from which new possibilities for business growth are derived from the perspective of innovation [7].

From the approach of the theory of resources and capabilities, organizations are unique because of their differences in terms of resources and capabilities. Technological capabilities constitute the faculty to make use of scientific and technological resources that facilitate the integration of new knowledge with existing knowledge for its subsequent exploitation [8, 9]. Two approaches are derived from this theory. The first is based on the knowledge exposed by Nonaka and Takeuchi [8] who highlight the importance of intangible resources. The second is the dynamic capabilities approach based on the development of resources and capacities, as well as their renewal according to the changes in the environment [10].

The knowledge-based approach suggests that the latter is the main input of innovation processes on the basis that resources are heterogeneous, non-imitable, substitutable, and transferable, so they generate a sustainable competitive advantage [11]. On the other hand, the theory of dynamic capabilities emerged at the end of the 90s as a response to the need for companies to adapt and innovate according to the dynamism of the environment [12]. In this context, SMEs need to develop competencies in the global era, strengthening the ability to absorb new knowledge and assimilate it to achieve business purposes, this is called technological capacity [13].

Exist various definitions of technological capacity from a general context, it is defined as the ability to make effective use of knowledge that allows assimilating, using, and modifying available technologies [14]. From the business perspective, it is stated that technological capability is the ability of the company to perform technical functions, develop new products and processes, and operate the company's facilities effectively [15].

Technological capacity is related to technological management factors that lead to sustained growth and development, as well as knowledge, techniques, and skills to acquire, use, absorb, adapt, improve and generate new technologies that contribute to business growth [16]. Among the most relevant benefits of technological capabilities are the design of appropriate strategies, openness to innovation in products and processes, and the ability to efficiently allocate available resources [1, 17].

Several studies affirm that technological capacity plays an important role in innovation [13]. The determinants of technological capacity, such as exploring and exploiting technological opportunities, core technological capacity, and R&D autonomy are important elements for innovation in the company [18]. In this regard, Hsieh and Tsai [19] revealed that technological capability is the driving force of a company's innovation.

These revelations align with the neoclassical approach to innovation, considering that innovation comes from a rational decision of companies when investing resources in Research and Development (R&D) activities as the main element of competitive advantage [20]. However, in contrast to this, the neo-Schumpeterian approach highlights the importance of those inputs other than R&D, such as design, development and experimental engineering, learning, the exploitation of new products and markets, and marketing for the development of innovations [21]. In this sense, innovation represents a knowledge-based change that requires a high degree of imagination and represents a significant break in the way of doing things integrally based on knowledge [22].

Innovation is related to dynamic economic and social environments, responsible for the production and transformation of scientific and technological knowledge that translates into economic wealth, social well-being, and human development [5]. Therefore, it is important to understand the management of technology in SMEs, since it makes science and technology instruments of innovation, well-being, and development [5].

In this context, innovation is the action and effect that allow significant improvements in things by changing novel and is the key to success for companies being the technological capability, the main factor in obtaining these results [23]. However, authors such as Berry and Taggart [24] suggest distinguishing between innovation and technological innovation, in this sense posit that innovation is the introduction and diffusion of new products and processes and/or improvements, while technological innovation goes beyond that, due to its relationship with the advances in knowledge and technology, as well as the exploitation of these.

Therefore, the technological capacity has an important influence on the results of innovation at the enterprise level, due to which the innovation is comprised of two processes of technological learning, the first of the ability of technology development, which can be seen in technological innovations that include changes in the products and services, as well as in the technology of production processes, therefore, may be subdivided into product innovations and process, these are characterized by developing or adopt technologies for its implementation. The second process is the changes in management routines, which can be called administrative innovations, which involve the organizational structure, administrative processes, and management systems [25, 26].

The objective of this research is to analyze the technological capabilities and their impact on the innovation of SMEs in the metalworking sector of the Metropolitan District of Quito, through a quantitative, cross-sectional, and correlational study. The metalworking sector is one of the economic sectors with the greatest possibilities for generating development, well-being, and employment, due to the assimilation of technologies, design features, quality, and differentiation in its products and processes, in addition to its interrelation with other sectors [27].

2   Materials and Methods

2.1   Participants

The sample is composed of 50 metalworking SMEs from the Metropolitan District of Quito affiliated with the Chamber of Small and Medium Industry (CAPEIPI). Of these, 62% are small businesses and 38% are medium-sized enterprises. Its activity is 28% the manufacture of metal accessories, 22% the assembly of metal structures, 18% providing metalworking services, and 8% carrying out electrical and electronic related activities.

2.2   Instrument

The instrument consists of 7 sections, which respond to the characteristics of companies, technological capabilities, and innovation. Section 1, describes the company's data, and Sects. 2 and 3 to innovation activities and innovation results in products and processes (technological innovation). In the measurement of innovative activity and innovation results, an adaptation of the National Survey of Applied Science, Technology and Innovation Activities in the period 2012–2014 was carried out; and the Oslo Manual 2018. These measurement systems respond to international parameters and represent a guide for the measurement, analysis, and interpretation of innovation data.

Sections 4, 5, and 6 evaluate technological management [28] and technological capabilities based on the proposal of Domínguez and Brown [29] based on Lall's taxonomy [30], which distinguishes between investment, production, and linkage capabilities, with the proposal to assimilate, adapt and improve the acquired technology.

2.3   Process

2.3.1   Validation of the Measuring Instrument

The questionnaire was evaluated by experts who judged the instrument's ability to evaluate the dimensions of interest and the content of the questions [31]. According to Clemen and Winkler [32], the judgment can be given by between 3 and 5 experts. The research convened a committee of 5 experts, 2 professionals with experience in technology management and innovation, and 2 university professors from the Management area. Each of the experts evaluated the instrument according to four criteria proposed by Escobar and Cuervo [33]: i) clarity, ii) coherence, iii) relevance, and iv) sufficiency; according to a Likert scale of 1 to 4 points.

2.3.2   Application of Questionnaire

The application of the instrument was made through an online request to the general managers, and heads of departments or R& D & I managers of the companies in March, April, and May of the year 2021. The instrument contains questions of order scales, multiple-choice, and 5-point Likert that includes a midpoint as proposed by the literature [34].

2.3.3 The Internal Consistency

The instrument was evaluated by the Cronbach's Alpha coefficient whose values range from 0 to 1 [31]. To this end, the elements of each of the different dimensions proposed were evaluated: innovative activity, technological innovation, investment and learning, technological management, production, and technological relationship.

The internal consistency of the sections measuring the innovative activity and technological innovation (Sects. 2 and 3) has a Cronbach's alpha of 0.9 each. The sections measuring technological capabilities (Sects. 4, 6, 7) have a Cronbach's alpha greater than 0.85. Whereas, the section evaluating technology management (Sect. 5) has a Cronbach's alpha of 0.93. In all cases, Cronbach's alpha exceeds the value of 0.7, corroborating an acceptable level of reliability.

2.3.4 Data Processing and Analysis

It was carried out using the statistical software SPSS Statistics since it allows to execution of descriptive and inferential analysis of a large volume of data [34]. The statistical correlation analysis and the graphs were performed using the R software, where the normality tests were executed, and the correlation with the Spearman coefficient to determine the relationship between technological capacity and innovation results in product and process.

3 Results and Discussion

The results analyze the data to verify the hypothesis through the collection of fundamentals based on the numerical measurement and statistical analysis [34]. The study observes the phenomena in their natural context and the data collection is carried out in a single period between March and May 2021.

3.1 Innovation Activities

The innovative activity was evaluated concerning all the development, financial and commercial actions carried out by a company that gives rise to innovation [35].

The results of innovation, from the typology of product innovation and process innovation [36]. Product innovation is highlighted by new or significantly improved features, this includes the significant improvement of technical features, components, and materials, change of functional parts, and other utilitarian distinctive. For its part, process innovation adopts methods that may involve significant changes in techniques, materials, and computer programs in the equipment or the organization of production and may result from the use of new knowledge [36, 37].

The systematic mechanism that evaluates the innovative potential of a company is defined through characteristics that represent the innovative effort, activities that create a favorable environment, and the type of innovation implemented by SMEs [37] (see Table 1).

Among the main innovation activities, the research and development processes that are carried out in the company's areas stand out, where the creation of R& D projects and actions is promoted to apply them in production processes, another important effort is the industrial engineering and design activities, to create product design requirements, generate prototypes, determine manufacturing processes and finally evaluate the results that are implemented through new products and processes.

Table 1. Activities for innovation

Activities for innovation	Percentage
In-house research and development	56%
Engineering and industrial design activities	50%
Acquisition of software	44%
Staff training	40%
Hardware acquisition	38%
Market research	28%
External research and development	20%
The hiring of consulting and technical assistance	20%
Acquisition of disincorporated technology	20%
Type of innovation	Percentage
Product technological innovation	70%
Process technological innovation	58%

The implementation of technological innovation in products is the one that stands out about innovation in processes in the metalworking company's object of the research (see Table 1). The technological innovation of the product emphasizes the significant improvement of existing products, through the incorporation of new materials and technological components, however, a smaller proportion has implemented new functional features and has introduced radically new technologies, which may indicate that due to this, companies don't stand out in the creation of new products recognized by the company or the industry (see Table 2).

Table 2. Product innovation and technical features

Product innovation	Percentage
Significantly improved product	42%
New product	30%
None	16%
New product and significantly improved product	12%
Technical characteristics	Percentage
New materials	76,8%
New technological components	75,2%
New functional parts	70,4%
New functional features	69,2%
Radically new technology	52,0%

Otherwise, the percentage of companies that don't conduct innovation in processes exceeds 40%. However, of the companies that have implemented technological innovation in processes, most of them opt for the significant improvement in their processes, from the incorporation of new tools or technology, equipment, and new methods of logistics to improve the productivity, efficiency, and control of their products, to a lesser extent, the adoption of new or significantly improved technology of information and communication (see Table 3).

Table 3. Process innovation and its features

Process innovation	Percentage
None	42%
Significantly improved process	30%
New process	16%
New and significantly improved process	12%
Technical characteristics	Percentage
New technological tools or equipment	85,2%
New logistics methods to improve productivity, efficiency, and control of your processes	69,2%
New or improved computer programs for the management of the administrative system	66,0%
New or significantly improved Information and Communication Technology (ICT)	63,6%

SMEs in the metalworking sector have developed innovative processes in recent years through the improvement of their technical characteristics that, even in some cases, have led to product innovations. However, few companies have introduced innovations characterized by a high degree of novelty to the market, considered new [37].

In this context, Carvache and others [38] point out that Ecuadorian SMEs have since medium to a low level in terms of innovation and technology, showing a high concentration in primary products and a low technological level [38]. SMEs in the industrial sector, despite investing in technology, mainly the acquisition of software and hardware, and automating some administrative activities, still show poor technological capacity and there is no significant improvement in the development of new production processes [39].

Based on the results of technological innovation in product and process and the innovative effort, SMEs can be grouped into three categories: innovative, potentially innovative, and non-innovative (see Table 4).

Table 4. Companies according to their innovative activity

Categorization	Activities for innovation	Technological innovation
Innovative company	1 or more	1 o más
Potentially innovative company	1 or more	None
Non-innovative company	None	None

Innovative companies are those whose innovation activities or efforts have resulted in technological innovations. Potentially innovative companies are those that have carried out innovation activities but abandoned efforts before achieving results, or in turn continue to carry out innovation activities that have not yet led to concrete results. And non-innovative companies are those that have not managed to introduce some kind of technological innovation, nor have they developed innovation activities [37].

In this context, SMEs investigated mostly located as innovative companies and potentially innovative, due to efforts for the development of innovations and the results of innovation mainly in the improvement of the products, however, are still deficient in efforts to give way to the improvement of technical processes within the industry. In the reality of emerging economies, it is stated that there are companies considered potentially innovative, where the role played by market forces as stimulants of innovative activity are highlighted [40].

SMEs identified as "innovative" and "potentially innovative" are mainly engaged in the manufacture of metal accessories and the assembly of metal structures. Meanwhile, "non-innovative" SMEs manufacture machinery and equipment, parts and pieces, and there are those that offer services for the industry in general.

At present, SMEs make efforts to create favorable scenarios for innovation, however, it has not been enough to realize disruptive technological innovations, this may be due to the inadequate capacity for knowledge acquisition or the lack of integration of disincorporated technology. In this sense, the importance of technology transfer as a mechanism to promote the culture of innovation in companies is highlighted [41]. Where knowledge-generating entities such as research centers and universities play a fundamental role in strengthening innovation.

Collaboration between the business sector, the state, and knowledge-generating entities is a vital process to promote innovation, however, in countries such as Ecuador and Colombia, the number of innovative companies is really low, due to this lack of integration and an innovative culture [41].

3.2 Technological Capabilities

The level of technical skills is determined through the evaluation of its components: investment and learning, production, and technological relationship [13]. The study by Domínguez and Brown [29] identified that technological capability, due to its effect on the innovation behavior of companies, positively influences business performance and helps to understand the differences between companies in a heterogeneous situation that characterizes developing economies.

Technological capacity was transformed into a categorical variable for descriptive analysis. Considering the minimum and maximum values exposed in the research of Moreno et al. [28], three levels were established: high, medium, and low (see Table 5).

Table 5. Categorization of the variable: technological capabilities

Level	Average range
Low	1,0–2.5
Medium	2,6–3,75
High	3,76–5

In this sense, SMEs in the Ecuadorian metalworking sector has managed to develop an average level of technological capabilities, since more than half of the companies have developed investment and learning skills and technological relationship. However, it is necessary to improve production capacities (see Table 6).

Table 6. Level of capabilities in companies

Components technological capacity	Punctuation	Level
Investment and learning	2,92	Medium
Production capacity	1,98	Low
Technological relationship	2,83	Medium
Technological capabilities	2,58	Medium

Concerning investment and learning capabilities, investment in the acquisition of machinery and equipment, technological R& D, acquisition of administrative technology, technical advice, and, to a lesser extent, the acquisition of trademarks and patents stands out. Although investment in these areas favors an innovative environment, these are not decisive actions to obtain innovative results [28]. Therefore, SMEs accompany their investments with organizational learning activities, such as feedback on the operation of the operating system, the implementation of technical changes in processes, and, to a lesser extent, the development of attraction plans and training of human resources.

The results of production capacities, concerning the implementation of "just time" production systems, safety benefits, occupational health, training for human resources, and statistical control of the production process, reveal deficiencies in the production processes carried out by SMEs. However, the processes are improving, due to the interest of these companies in the development of R& D activities, and the establishment of formal rules and procedures, for the quality control of production processes.

Finally, the technological relationship capacities in SMEs are strengthened by the association with the national and international sectors, where they maintain formal links thanks to the different technology transfer mechanisms through institutions such as universities and government institutions. However, deficiencies in participation in R&D projects with other institutions, as well as the lack of rules regulating technological interrelationships, still limit the strengthening of technological relationship capacities.

Studies on technological capabilities have increased in recent years, different variables are postulated that through a joint analysis explain the level of this type of capabilities. For example, technological innovation, efficiency in processes, the design of industrial plants, the execution of projects, and technological learning [42]. This last is related to the theoretical basis that is part of the taxonomy proposed by Lall [30]: investment & learning, production, and relationship-building technology, which together enable the development and strengthening of technological capabilities, which affect the development of innovations, and in the performance of an organization [29]. Therefore, it is relevant to differentiate between the activities that contribute to capacity development and what gives rise to technological innovation, as a result of a set of efforts and skills.

3.3 Relationship Between Technological Capabilities and Innovation

To analyze the statistic to be used, the Kolmogorov-Smirnov normality test is performed, which yields a value lower than the considered significance level of 0.05 (see Table 7), so the null hypothesis is rejected, that is, the innovation data in product and process, don't have normal behavior.

To analyze the relationship between technological capacity and the results of innovation in product and process, the Spearman correlation is performed, which is a nonparametric statistical method, which aims to examine the intensity of association between two quantitative variables [34].

The first relationship analysis makes it possible to check the following hypotheses:

H0: Technological capabilities influence the results of technological innovation in the products of SMEs.

Table 7. Data normality test

Product innovation		
Statistical	D =	0.20291
P	p-value	2.094e−05
Innovation in process		
Statistical	D =	0.26572
P	p-value	1.525e−09

H1: Technological capabilities don't influence the results of technological innovation in the products of SMEs.

The Spearman coefficient analysis is one of the most widely used non-parametric statistical tests that is applied to nominal and ordinal data with non-normal distributions to determine the level of correlation [34]. The results obtained by the Spearman coefficient in the relationship between technological capacity and product innovation (see Table 8).

Table 8. Degree of the relationship between components of technological capacity and product innovation

Components technological capacity vs product innovation	Spearman's Rho
Investment and Learning (IL)	0.5218094
Production Capacity (PC)	0.4378678
Technological Relationship (TR)	0.2408939
Technological capabilities (TC)	0.5420385

With a significance value of less than 0.05, a positive correlation between product innovation and technological capabilities is evidenced. On the other hand, the component of the technological capacity that is called investment and learning is the one that shows a positive correlation significant (rho 0.52) with the innovation of the product, as well as the sum of the components of what is called the technological capacity (rho 0.54), indicating that the technological capacity influences the outcomes of innovation in product, on the other hand, the production capacity and the relationship between technology have a positive relationship average, which confirms that there is an association between the variables accepting the null hypothesis.

The correlation does not become very strong or perfect positive, this may be due to the influence of elements that have not been measured, such as other internal resources of the company or macroeconomic agents. These results contrast with the study carried out by Lestari and Ardianti [13], who points out that technological capacity not only has a direct but also an indirect effect on the performance of SMEs, through innovation. Like the postulates made by García, Blázquez, and López [43], who indicate that technological capabilities are a determining factor of innovation, which is subject to the level of development of countries.

Table 9. Degree of the relationship between components of technological capacity and innovation in the process

Components technological capacity vs process innovation	Spearman's Rho
Investment and Learning (IL)	0.7286373
Production Capacity (PC)	0.4436800
Technological Relationship (TR)	0.3065876
Technological capabilities (TC)	0.6621186

Likewise, the level of correlation between technological innovation and each of the components of technological capabilities was determined to identify the deficient components that require efforts by Ecuadorian SMEs (see Table 9). In this context, investment and learning is the component that has the greatest positive correlation it has on the results of innovation in processes, that is, the more this capacity is strengthened, the better the results will be innovation in processes, this is corroborated with a significance value < 0.05.

H0: Technological capabilities influence the results of technological innovation in SME processes.
H1: Technological capabilities don't influence the results of technological innovation in SME processes.

Therefore, the null hypothesis is approved, technological capabilities influence the results of technological innovation in processes of SMEs, this means that, as the metalworking SMEs increase their level of technological capabilities, the greater the number of companies that introduce technological innovations in processes.

Thus, in the quantitative analysis by García, Pineda, and Andrade [1] it was found that technological capabilities are a determining factor of innovation, which depends on different elements, such as the type and size of the company, the sector, technological requirements and the type of manufacturing processes implemented in the integration of all its activities, and mainly the level of economic development of the countries.

In this context, a confirmatory analysis is carried out among the categories that make up each of the variables to characterize the situation of SMEs. It was found that the metalworking SMEs that don't carry out technological product innovation, for the most part, have a low level of technological capacity. In contrast, SMEs that have medium to high levels of technological capacity essentially carry out technological process innovations (see Table 10).

Table 10. Confirmation analysis between the level of technological capacity and technological innovation

Technological innovation		Level of technological capability		
		Low	Medium	High
In product	Yes	40,5	51,4	8,1
	No	92,3	7,7	0,0
In process	Yes	34,4	56,3	9,4
	No	88,9	11,1	0,0

Finally, corroborating the results are presented in the scatter diagrams of each of the correlations of the data, which confirm that there is an influence of the technological capacity and each of its components with the results of innovation in products and processes within SMEs. However, ensuring a perfect correlation requires a deepening of the analysis with new macroeconomic variables and the business environment (Fig. 1).

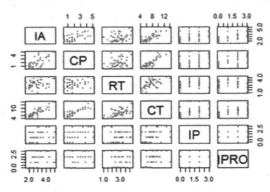

Fig. 1. Data dispersion diagram

4 Conclusions

In Ecuador, the SMEs have an important influence on the development of the country, therefore, enhancing its technological capabilities will allow more and better innovation performance, due to its effective application of knowledge in the context in which they unfold, and in this way contribute to the social and economic growth.

The investigated metalworking SMEs are mostly located in innovative and potentially innovative companies, because they make innovation efforts that lead to obtaining innovative results, however the products and processes that are implemented lack novelty before the company and the market, and this may be because they still need to strengthen their technological learning capacity.

In terms of technological capacity, the SMEs in the engineering sector is located at a medium level, since more than half of them have developed their skills of investment and learning, where not only buy equipment and technologies, but it makes effective use of that capital; the relationship between technology each time is better in terms of partnerships with internal and external stakeholders, however, it is necessary to strengthen and expand the actors in support of knowledge, and this can be a trigger in the low production capacity.

Finally, there is evidence of a positive correlation significant between technological capabilities and innovation in products and processes, it denotes that the greater the development of technological literacy in the company, there is the possibility of more and better innovation performance, and this in turn will allow for greater competitiveness and growth in the industry.

Acknowledgments. We are especially grateful to the companies that were part of this investigation, for their openness and commitment to providing the information.

References

1. García, A., Pineda, D., Andrade, M.: Las capacidades tecnológicas para la innovación en empresas de manufactura. Universidad Empresa **17**(29), 257–278 (2015)
2. Dutrénit, G., Vera, A., Arias, A.: Diferencias en el perfil de acumulación de capacidades tecnológicas en tres empresas mexicanas. El Trimestre Económico **70**(277), 109–165 (2003)
3. Figueiredo, P.: Aprendizagem tecnológica e inovação industrial em economias emergentes: uma breve contribuição para o desenho e implementação de estudos empíricos e estratégias no Brasil. Revista Brasileira de Inovação **2**(3), 323–361 (2004)
4. Peña, M., Vega, N.: Estructura de las pymes en la economía ecuatoriana. Revistas de la Universidad Nacional de Loja 30–34 (2017)
5. Robledo, J.: Introducción a la gestión de la tecnología y la innovación empresarial (Primera ed.). Universidad Nacional de Colombia, Medellín (2020)
6. Ahmed, P., Shepherd, C., Ramos, L., Ramos, C.: Administración de la innovación. Pearson Educación (2012)
7. Rincón, É., Rincón, J., Coromoto, C.: La innovación y el cambio tecnológico desde la perspectiva de la mesoeconomía. Económicas CUC 89–108 (2014)
8. Nonaka, I., Takeuchi, H.: The Knowledge-Creating Company. Oxford University, Oxford (1995)
9. Grant, R.: Prospering in dynamically-competitive environments: organizational capability as knowledge integration. Organ. Sci. 375–387 (1996)
10. Teece, D., Pisano, G., Shuen, A.: Dynamic capabilities and strategic management. Strateg. Manag. 509–533 (1997)
11. Urgal, B., Quintás, M., Arévalo, R.: Conocimiento tecnológico, capacidad de innovación y desempeño innovador: el rol moderador del ambiente interno de la empresa. Cuadernos de Economía y Dirección de la Empresa 53–66 (2011)
12. González, C., Hurtado, A.: Propuesta de un Indicador de Capacidad de Absorción del Conocimiento: evidencia empírica para el sector servicios en Colombia. Facultad de Ciencias Económicas 29–46 (2014)
13. Lestari, E., Ardianti, F.: Technological capability and business success: the mediating role of innovation. In: IOP Conference Series: Earth and Environmental Science, vol. 1, no. 250, p. 012039 (2019)

14. Kim, L.: Imitation to Innovation. The Dynamics of Korea's Technological Learning. Harvard Business Review Press (1997)
15. Ruiz, M.: Competitive strategies and firm performance: technological capabilities' moderating roles. J. Bus. Res. **63**(12), 1273–1281 (2010)
16. Lugones, G., Gutti, P., Le Clech, N.: Indicadores de capacidades tecnológicas en América Latina. Naciones Unidas, México D.F. (2007)
17. Zhou, K.Z., Wu, F.: Technological capability, strategic flexibility, and product innovation. Strateg. Manag. J. **31**(5), 547–561 (2010)
18. Huang, K.F.: Technology competencies in competitive environment. J. Bus. Res. **64**(2), 172–179 (2011)
19. Hsieh, M.H., Tsai, K.H.: Technological capability, social capital and the launch strategy for innovative products. Ind. Mark. Manag. **36**(4), 493–502 (2007)
20. Nelson, R.: Why do firms differ and how does it matter? Strateg. Manag. J. 61–74 (1991)
21. Smith, K.: Measuring innovation. Oxford Handb. Innov. 148–177 (2005)
22. Nelson, R., Winter, S.: An Evolutionaty Theory of Economic Change. Belknap Press, Cambridge (1982)
23. Mendizábal, G.: Estrategias para la innovación tecnológica en Castillas y León. Tesis doctoral, Universidad de Valladolid, Valladolid (2002)
24. Berry, M., Taggart, J.: Managing technology and innovation. R & D Manag. 341–353 (1994)
25. Zawislak, P.A., Alves, A.C., Tello-Gamarra, J.: Innovation capability: from technology development to transaction capability. J. Technol. Manag. Innov. **7**(2), 14–26 (2012)
26. Damanpour, F.: Innovation type, radicalness, and the adoption process. Commun. Res. **15**(5), 545–567 (1988)
27. Ovalle, A., Ocampo, O., Acevedo, M.: Identificación de brechas tecnológicas en automatización industrial de las empresas del sector metalmecánico de Caldas, Colombia. Ingeniería y Competitividad. Revista Científica y Tecnológica 171–182 (2013)
28. Moreno, S., García, A.: Sistema para la evaluación de capacidades de innovación en PYMES de países en desarrollo: Caso Panamá. Facultad de Ciencias Económicas: Investigación y Reflexión 109–122 (2014)
29. Domínguez, L., Brown, F.: Measuring technological capabilities in the Mexican industry. CEPAL Rev. 129–144 (2004)
30. Lall, S.: Technological capabilities and industrialization. World Dev. **20**(2), 165–186 (1992)
31. Arribas, M.: Diseño y validación de cuestionarios. Matronas Profesión 23–29 (2004)
32. Clemen, R., Winkler, R.: Limits for the precision and value of information from dependent sources. Oper. Res. 427–442 (1985)
33. Escobar, J., Cuervo, A.: Validez de contenido y juicio de expertos: una aproximación a su utilización. Avances en Medición 27–36 (2008)
34. Hernández, R., Fernández, C., Baptista, M.: Metodología de investigación. McGraw Hill, México D.F. (2010)
35. OCDE. Manual de Oslo (Tercera ed.). OCDE, Madrid (2005)
36. OECD. Proposed Guidelines for Collecting and Interpreting Technological Innovation Data. OECD, París (2018)
37. Instituto Ecuatoriano de Estadística y Censos. Principales Indicadores de Actividades de Ciencia, Tecnología e Innovación. Ecuador (2015)
38. Carvache, O., Gutiérrez, G., Frías, C.: Incidencia de la innovación y la tecnología en el desarrollo competitivo de las pequeñas y medianas empresas (PYMES) exportadoras de Guayas-Ecuador. Revista Espacios **39**(47) (2018)
39. Leal, M., Labarca, N., Bracho, O., Vargas, V.: Gestión Tecnológica en pymes del sector textil del municipio Maracaibo-estado Zulia- Venezuela. Revista Venezolana de Gerencia 314–331 (2018)

40. Ortiz, F.: Medición de la Capacidad de Innovación Tecnológica (Caso de Estudio: Industria Papelera Venezolana). In: II International Conference on Industrial Engineering and Industrial Management. XII Congreso de Ingeniería de Organización, Burgos, Spain, 3–5 Septiembre (2008)

41. Velásquez, S., Pino, A., Restrepo, E., Vaina, N.: Innovación en empresas: estado del arte considerando tendencias para su implementación. Revista Espacios, **39**(48) (2018)

42. López, A., Molina, R., Gómez, D.: Enfoque estratégico, orientación emprendedora y experiencia: factores que impulsan el desarrollo de capacidades tecnológicas en el sector automotriz. Revista SBIR 43–57 (2018)

43. García, M., Blázquez, M., López, J.: Uso y aplicación de la técnica de análisis estadístico multivariante de cluster sobre la capacidad de innovación tecnológica en Latinoamérica y España. INNOVAR. Revista de Ciencias Administrativas y Sociales 21–39 (2012)

Culture and Job Satisfaction in an Agroindustrial Company Chepén, 2021

Marko Rodrigo Ramos Gamarra[1] , Julia Otilia Sagástegui Cruz[2]([✉]) ,
and Ricardo Martín Gómez Arce[3]

[1] Universidad Nacional de Trujillo, Av. Juan Pablo II, Trujillo, Peru
[2] Universidad Privada del Norte, Av. El Ejercito 920 – Urb. El Molino, Trujillo, Peru
julia.sagastegui@upn.edu.pe
[3] Universidad Nacional de Trujillo, Av. Juan Pablo II, Trujillo, Peru

Abstract. The organizational culture is always related to the job satisfaction of the collaborators and Agroindustrias José & Luis S.A.C. is no stranger to this premise, always striving for rapid growth since its foundation, as well as for its efforts to consolidate its organizational culture and achieve a feeling of acceptance in their collaborators, to feel their satisfaction. Therefore, the main objective of this research was to analyze the relationship between organizational culture and job satisfaction in the organization's employees, Chepén, 2021. The design of this research was non-experimental, cross-sectional and correlational design, the sample population It was composed of all field collaborators (110) and the questionnaire was used as an instrument to collect data, which were validated through validity coefficients of 0.707 and 0.750 for organizational culture and job satisfaction, respectively, demonstrating that they were valid. For its application, the main result was the correlation coefficient and its significance between organizational culture and job satisfaction (0.233; 0.037), indicating that there is a positive and significant relationship. Being able to establish in the investigation that the organizational culture impacts on the job satisfaction that each employee of the company manifests, making it necessary to manage their own culture, to obtain employees with a sense of belonging and job satisfaction individually and collectively.

Keywords: Culture · Job satisfaction · Norms · Interpersonal relations · Relationship

1 Introduction

History is not distant from the "organizational culture"; on the contrary, it was and is present in each of the different stages of it, and just as the universal history has been evolving and changing, this term, its meaning, nature, and approaches have also presented diverse modifications, due to the continuous attempts of mankind to find "the secret factor" to increase productivity, going from a purely economic approach, known as the "Homo Economicus", given and established by Taylor's scientific management to the valuation and importance given to the multiple knowledge of the factors that can influence the interaction within an organization today. Thus, the various representatives of companies or organizations have found it necessary to resort to different schools, which, with a different approach proper to their discipline, have sought to find the answer to that determining factor.

Currently, organizational culture, which can be defined according to Díaz et al. (2021) as: "basic assumptions about the world and the values that guide life in organizations" (p. 1643), is a competitive advantage for large companies and has an impact on continuous growth and high profits. According to Expansion magazine and Top Companies, through a ranking prepared in 2019, the three companies that best manage their culture are Mars, McDonald's, and Nestlé. According to reports from specialized sites, these companies generated revenues of 30 billion dollars, 6,760 million dollars, and 38,786 million dollars, respectively, demonstrating that good practices in organizational culture are not an "expense" but rather an investment. An adequate culture guides the company to obtain great economic results through the effort of its employees.

All of the above is directly related to a second term in this research, which is entirely linked to the feelings and well-being of workers in an organization, thus giving rise to "job satisfaction", which can be defined, according to Bazalar and Choquehuanca (as cited in Garbuglia 2013), as: "the attitude of workers, which has an emotional and a cognitive basis, depending on their experience which can be positive or negative for them".

Likewise, according to Bazalar and Choquehuanca (2020), valuing the importance of keeping their employees satisfied allows managers of the best companies to understand: "that the human resource of the organization allows for a different management style, which can decentralize decisions, delegate responsibilities, design more dynamic and flexible jobs that motivate people, involve everyone, and consult them about the tasks they have to perform, which generates a more democratic and participatory business environment, where the workers feel an important part and are motivated to give their best effort so that they can meet the objectives set by the organization at all times". Among the companies with a high level of job satisfaction are the ones highlighted in a Love Monday's study conducted in 2019, which revealed that the three organizations that best encourage the job satisfaction of their staff through their culture, in the world, are American. The first one is Costco, the largest chain in price club format in the world with annual revenues of 62.675 million euros, followed by the multinational company with worldwide expansion in the automotive sector, Ford, with revenues of $136.34 billion; and, finally, the multinational corporation of information technology and consulting IBM with revenues of US$17.6 million.

Within the national territory, the consolidation of both terms by Peruvian companies has positive and negative results - negative results in a study conducted by "Trabajando. com", which sought to know the percentage of company employees who were satisfied with their work and with the environment surrounding them, obtaining that 76% were not happy since 22% considered that their work was not challenging; 20% indicated that there was not a good work environment, 19% stated that their boss was not a good leader, 12% stated that their remuneration was very low, 10% did not feel that their achievements were recognized, 10% felt unable to contribute ideas, and the last 10% had no options for professional growth or promotion, thus showing that at the national level there is still much to work on if the goal is to grow successfully and sustainably, generating a positive impact on all stakeholders related to the organization.

After having known the negative results, we must also mention positive findings such as those obtained by the research and organizational consulting firm Great Place to Work (GPTW) which during a study in 2020 sought to know the importance that Peruvian organizations gave to organizational culture and how they turned it into a management tool for the success and satisfaction of their employees, achieving to be considered as "the best place to work". In addition to showing that the first places in this research were occupied by companies in the commercial sector, they also showed that agro-exporting companies are beginning to gain a place on this list, due to the great progress and growth they have been experiencing at the national level.

Due to the great relevance that was exposed lines above, in the province of Chepén, a great growth and boost of entrepreneurship in the agro-export sector are also evidenced, outstanding in it the company "Agroindustrias José & Luis S.A.C." which, besides taking advantage of its privileged location in a fertile and productive area such as Huaca Blanca Baja, since its founding in 2004, has been demonstrating a remarkable interest in providing not only quality products (grapes, blueberries, etc..) but also in achieving growth, conformity and sense of belonging in each of its employees, an effort that is evident from the top management to field employees, who, in a joint effort, allow the company to continue improving and achieving the objectives set every year. Under the following situation and context, the question that motivates this research is: What is the relationship between Organizational Culture and Job Satisfaction among the employees of Agroindustrias José & Luis S.A.C., Chepén, 2021? In this sense, the main objective of the study is to analyze the relationship between organizational culture and job satisfaction among the employees of Agroindustrias José & Luis S.A.C., Chepén, 2021. According to the research objective, different authors through their studies have sought to understand the importance of developing an adequate organizational culture and how it relates to job satisfaction, all this to understand which factors have an impact on the feelings of an employee and lead him/her to develop a high degree of conformity and acceptance towards the company, as in the case of Córdoba (2020), whose main objective through her research was to find out the relationship between organizational culture and job satisfaction from the perception of medical and nursing workers in the NICU of a public maternity hospital in the city of Rosario - 2020. Its design is descriptive and correlational. This study concluded that there is a relationship between organizational culture and job satisfaction from the point of view of the NICU workers since they affirm that the more limitations are established in their work and the more unfavorable factors appear, the more their dissatisfaction increases. Likewise, it was concluded that although human and material resources are increasingly available, the dissatisfaction curve does not decrease, but rather increases, which leads to a higher level of dissatisfaction. The level of commitment in the NICU does not depend on the quantity and quality of resources, but on the individual's knowledge about the objectives pursued by the organization according to the current public health policies. Likewise, the objective of Loayza (2018) was to determine the influence of organizational culture on the job satisfaction of the workers of the Provincial Municipality of Puno - 2018. Its design was non-experimental, cross-sectional, qualitative, and correlational. The study sample consisted of 234 workers from the Municipality. The results of this research showed that the dimension Values of the Workers has a low level of influence, representing 33.7%. This allowed affirming that values are not frequently practiced in the culture that is currently in force. It is followed by the dimension Norms Shared by the Workers, where a low influence was obtained, represented by 35.7%, showing that the workers do not make a commitment to the current norms. Likewise, when studying the Institutional Identity dimension, a result of 49.6% was obtained, considered moderate and indicating that among the workers of the public entity there is no adequate confidence to reinforce the identity of the Municipality. Then, in the Communication dimension, a value of 50.9% was obtained categorized as moderate, indicating that interpersonal relationships among workers are bad. Continuing with Acevedo (2018), who in his research aimed to determine the relationship between organizational culture and job satisfaction of the operational staff of the company SGS del Perú SAC, Chimbote - 2018. The design used was non-experimental, descriptive, correlational, and cross-sectional. The study sample consisted of 60 operational workers. The results indicated that there is a relationship between organizational culture and the job satisfaction of the company's operational personnel, through a Spearman's Rho with a value of 0.724, also affirming that the organization has aspects to be taken into account for improvement, such as labor stability, because the workers do not feel a degree of stability since the work is only for hours, causing uncertainty in them. On the contrary, it showed a relationship between the following dimensions of organizational culture, such as values and beliefs with a Spearman's rho of 0.451 and 0.770, respectively. Finally, Tamayo (2017) conducted a research study that aimed to determine the correlation between organizational culture and job satisfaction among the workers of the Mining Company Poderosa S.A., Trujillo - 2017. The design used was descriptive, correlational, and cross-sectional. The study sample consisted of 493 male employees of the company, aged between 25 and 55 years old. The results indicated that organizational culture showed a clear dominance in specific scores, starting with those located in the lower levels with 34.9%, contrasting with the value of 33.9% that was located in the upper part. This result is explained in the low identification the employees show with the organization, due to the short time they have been in their job. Finally, it was concluded that there is a direct and highly significant relationship ($p < .01$) between the variables organizational culture and job satisfaction, supported by a median Spearman's Rho correlation coefficient (rho $= .522$).

1.1 Organizational Culture

- Definition
  Organizational culture can be defined according to Schein (1988) as: "the group's learned responses to its problems of subsistence in its external environment and its problems of internal integration".

  In the same line, according to the author, we can affirm that organizational culture is oriented to satisfy the needs and desires of the staff, because, whether individually or collectively, they are the most important component of each of the organizations. In addition, we must add that human talent plays a fundamental role in the achievement of objectives. The most successful and recognized organizations worldwide achieve their goals not only with the economic factor but also through the ability, skill, and intelligence of each of their employees. This explains the need to not only be satisfied with having the best employees but with providing them with a pleasant and positive culture to find the so-called "synergy".

Likewise, after a thorough study of the different definitions and concepts assigned to the organizational culture, it can be affirmed that it is usually described by taking into account common and repetitive terms used by the authors such as values, principles, traditions, and how it is decided to do each thing, while it is shared by all the members of the organization, being influenced to a great extent by the use it is given as well as the customs previously established by the society or the external environment of the organization.

That is why organizational culture has implications in most situations with three aspects since, first, we should mention that culture is perceptible, because, as it has been stated, even though it is an invisible and intangible term, the company's employees are capable of experiencing it. Second, it is descriptive, since all those who are part of the organization are capable of perceiving and describing it, although it does not guarantee that they will like it. And, finally, it is said that it is shared because although collaborators, workers, or employees indeed come from different societies with their own customs that become background, they perform their work in different areas and levels of the organization; and when they are immersed in the same work environment, they tend to describe the organizational culture in common and similar terms.

- Importance of organizational culture:
  According to Guerrero and Silva (2017), "it transmits a sense of identity to the employees of an organization, helps to generate employee commitment, increases the stability of the organization as a social system, and provides a frame of reference for understanding organizational activities and a guide for behavior."
- Dimensions of organizational culture:
  Taking Schein (1988) as a reference, Olmos and Socha (2006) categorize and classify the dimensions of organizational culture as follows: values, "understood as the set of principles or qualities considered by the members of an organization, such as customer service, innovation, among others"; beliefs, "defined as the hypotheses or considerations held about the business model in the organization which may be true or false"; climate, "understood as the atmosphere or feelings in the organizational environment which is visible in the physical part of the place, how employees work, among others"; norms, "known as the standards or rules that surround the organization including how workers should behave"; symbols: "defined as the set of icons, rituals, and traditions essential to the company, such as the ceremonies held annually"; and, philosophy, "understood as the established policies and ideologies guiding organizational actions".

1.2   Job Satisfaction

According to Palma (2006), job satisfaction is defined as "the relatively stable disposition or tendency towards work, based on beliefs and values developed from occupational experience".

The author's theory is supported since job satisfaction is a broad term that goes even from a deeper perspective and analysis than just the physical facilities or the environment that can be observed since it also seeks to understand, study and evaluate how the non-perceptible aspects impact the mood and predisposition to work of the employees.

- Importance of job satisfaction:
  According to Duran et al. (2021), "organizations with more satisfied employees tend to be more effective, focus their work on achieving defined goals, assume a positive attitude towards life, and integrate into society more healthily. In contrast, when an employee is dissatisfied with his or her job, he or she shows a negative attitude in his or her family environment, demonstrating rejection towards activities, responsibilities at home and with society in general."
- Dimensions of job satisfaction:
  Following Palma (2006), who uses the theory of motivation, discrepancy, and dynamics as a basis, the dimensions of job satisfaction are classified as follows: physical and/or material conditions, defined as the means that make it easier to carry out daily activities, also functioning as an indicator of efficiency and performance; labor benefits and/or remuneration, bonus and/or compensation that employees receive in exchange for performing their work; administrative policies, degree to which agreements are made following organizational guidelines or norms, which are oriented to regulate the interpersonal relationships among employees, thus constituting means to achieve goals or objectives; interpersonal relationships, which respond to the interaction between employees, but in a company or organization, since when the relationships are positive, they influence trust and credibility; personal development, a completely healthy person is motivated mainly by all the needs that must be satisfied and all the activities that allow him/her to fully develop his/her potential and capacity; task performance, related to the value and importance that the employee assigns to the daily activities that he/she carries out in the organization for which he/she works; The relationship with the authority is the appreciation and value that the employee confers to the relationship that he/she establishes with his/her direct boss for his/her daily activities.

Different authors through their studies have sought to understand the importance of developing an adequate organizational culture and how it relates to job satisfaction. The main objective of this article is to analyze the relationship between organizational culture and job satisfaction among the employees of Agroindustrias José & Luis S.A.C., Chepén, 2021. Besides identifying the level of organizational culture and job satisfaction of employees, it also determines the relationship between the dimensions of organizational culture and the dimensions of job satisfaction of employees in the company Agroindustrial José & Luis S.A.C., Chepén, 2021.

2 Materials and Methods

This study was non-experimental because the variables were not manipulated; cross-sectional because the data were taken at a certain time; and, descriptive-correlational - non-causal, because the study variables were described with their respective relationship between them. The research was developed following the inductive, analytical, and statistical methods. The population consisted of all employees (10 in administrative areas,

80 in the field, and 20 in packaging) of the Agroindustrial company, working with a con-venience (non-random) sample since only the field area was accessible. Therefore, the sample consisted of 80 employees; the data were collected from July 2021 to February 2022. The face-to-face survey technique was used, and the instruments used were: the questionnaire to measure the organizational culture, which was designed and created by Olmos and Socha (2006), consisting of 18 items, which seek to measure organizational culture by classifying it into six dimensions (values, beliefs, climate, norms, symbols, and philosophy); a questionnaire created by Sonia Palma Carillo (2008) to measure job satisfaction, which consists of 36 indicators, classifying it into seven dimensions: physical and/or material conditions, labor and/or remuneration benefits, administrative policies, interpersonal relationships, personal development, task performance, and rela-tionship with the authority. The data processing was carried out by using a statistical program Statistical Package for Social Sciences, starting with the construction of the database, initially generated in the Excel 2019 spreadsheet. After being analyzed and debugged, it was exported to the SPSS – version 26; the procedures were executed so that the information could be shown and ordered through tables and statistical figures, cre-ating the univariate frequency tables, with their respective statistical figures. Likewise, bivariate frequency tables were created, considering both study variables, as well as their respective dimensions, in order to calculate the Spearman's Rho correlation coefficient and determine the significance of the statistical hypothesis tests.

3 Results and Discussion

Table 1. Level of organizational culture among the employees of the company Agroindustrias José & Luis S.A.C

Organizational culture	Employees	% employees
High	11	14%
Medium	67	84%
Low	2	3%
Total	80	100%

Note. Own Elaboration

Table 1 shows that 67 employees perceive an organizational culture at a medium level, representing 84% of the total. When analyzing in detail, the employees have medium levels in four of the six dimensions, except for Symbols, because the organization lacks the celebration of institutional rites and ceremonies which, in the current competitive environment and with a notable valuation of people, are vital to developing a sense of belonging in the employees, as well as to allow them to know the origins and beliefs that the founders established and the reasons and/or motives that led them to create the company; as well as the Philosophy dimension, based on the lack of knowledge of the mission and vision pursued by the company (being also necessary to take into account that dimension).

Table 2. Job satisfaction level among the employees of the company Agroindustrias José & Luis S.A.C.

Job satisfaction	Employees	% employees
High	11	14%
Medium	69	86%
Low	0	0%
Total	80	100%

Note. Own Elaboration

Regarding the level of job satisfaction, 69 employees perceive a medium level of job satisfaction accounting for 86% of the total. These results are explained by the uneven levels of each of the dimensions of job satisfaction, being found dimensions with high levels such as Physical and Material Conditions, since the company has an extensive area to carry out its activities, providing each employee with their own space where they can keep their belongings and have the necessary privacy to put on their work uniforms. But, at the same time, there are low levels in Administrative Policies, explained by the lack of knowledge, on the part of field employees, of the decisions made by the management and how they could be affected or benefited, having a strong perception that their opinion is not important and that they are there only to obey orders. Finally, there are medium-level dimensions such as Labor Benefits and/or remuneration, explained by the uneven level at which employees are rewarded since even when the company pays its employees correctly, including the overtime they work, they express a desire to receive a higher remuneration, equivalent to the heavy work they perform during their entire working hours in the company. Thus, all the aforementioned factors and /or dimensions cause the level of job satisfaction to be expressed and defined as medium.

Before finding the correlation degree between both variables, it was necessary to apply the Kolmogorov Smirnov normality test, to identify whether the data had a normal or non-normal distribution, using SPSS software version 26, indicating that both variables had a significance greater than 5%. Thus, it was stated that they followed a normal distribution and the application of Spearman's Rho coefficient was appropriate.

Finally, the hypothesis test was performed, obtaining the following values:

This table shows the crossing of the research variables; therefore, it is observed that out of the group of 69 employees who feel medium job satisfaction, 84.1% perceive a mid-level organizational culture and 13.0% perceive a high-level organizational culture. Then, out of the remaining employees who feel high job satisfaction, 81.8% perceive a mid-level organizational culture, and 18.2% perceive a high organizational culture. Spearman's Rho correlation coefficient, which measures the relationship between organizational culture and job satisfaction, was also calculated with a value of 0.233 and indicates a low and positive relationship between both variables globally. Then, after observing the p-value of the test (0.037) and less than 0.05, it is determined that the relationship between both variables is significant. Therefore, it is affirmed that there is a significant relationship between organizational culture and job satisfaction among the employees of the company Agroindustrias José & Luis S.A.C., in the year 2021.

Table 3. Level of organizational culture and job satisfaction among employees of the company Agroindustrias José & Luis S.A.C.

Organizational culture		Level of Job satisfaction		Total
		High	Medium	
Low	Employees	2	0	2
	%	2.9%	0.0%	2.5%
Medium	Employees	58	9	67
	%	84.1%	81.8%	83.8%
High	Employees	9	2	11
	%	13.0%	18.2%	13.8%
Total	Employees	69	11	80
	%	100.0%	100.0%	100.0%

Spearman's Correlation Coefficient (Rho) = 0.233 p-sig. = 0.037 < 0.05

Note. Own Elaboration

After obtaining the results corresponding to the research, we compared them with the results obtained by various authors in previous research studies to discuss the similarities or differences between them. Thus:

Regarding the specific objective of identifying the level of organizational culture among the employees of the company Agroindustrias José & Luis S.A.C., Chepén, 2021, Table 1 shows that 67 employees perceive a mid-level organizational culture, representing 84% of the total. This is because the company has medium levels of culture in four of its six dimensions, except for the symbols dimension, which is explained by the lack of institutional ceremonies that are vital for each of the employees to feel part of the company, and the philosophy dimension, based on the lack of knowledge of the company's mission and vision. These results agree, among many aspects, with the research conducted by Tamayo (2017), who managed to determine that organizational culture showed a clear dominance in specific scores, starting with those located in the lower levels with 34.9%, contrasting with the value of 33.9% that was located in the upper part. This result is explained by the low identification that the employees show with the organization, due to the short time that they have been in their job, and is supported by the theory of Ambrossi and Marconi (2017), who state that "organizational culture is a set of homogeneous values and behaviors, defined by the organization and that must be lived intensely by all its members". It is also stated that "the organizational culture plays a fundamental role in the motivational processes, from the moment the employee begins his or her activities in the administrative process he or she performs until he or she finishes his or her duties" according to Ortiz et al. (2021).

Regarding another specific objective, i.e., to identify the level of Job Satisfaction among the employees of the company Agroindustrias José & Luis S.A.C., Chepén, 2021, Table 2 shows that 69 employees perceive a medium level of job satisfaction, representing 86% of the total. These results are explained by the uneven levels of each of the dimensions of Job Satisfaction, finding dimensions with high levels such as Physical and material conditions, but, at the same time, finding dimensions with low levels such as administrative policies; and dimensions with medium levels such as Labor benefits and/or remuneration, causing job satisfaction to be categorized as médium. These results agree, among many aspects, with the results evidenced by Córdoba (2020), since the author points out that among the respondents, although human and material resources are increasingly available, the dissatisfaction curve does not decrease but rather increases, which leads to a higher level of dissatisfaction. These results may be due to the fact that employees show a notorious dissatisfaction regarding their relationship with their closest bosses, which is much more noticeable in extractive and/or mining companies. This is supported by the theory of Duran et al. (2021), which states: "organizations with more satisfied employees tend to be more effective, focus their work on achieving defined goals, assume a positive attitude towards life, and integrate into society more healthily. In contrast, when an employee is dissatisfied with his or her job, he or she shows a negative attitude in his or her family environment, demonstrating rejection towards activities, responsibilities at home and with society in general." According to the results described above, we can state that for the managers and those in charge of leading an organization such as Agroindustrias José & Luis S.A.C., it is not only important to have fertile and extensive land as well as an adequate physical environment, but it is much more important to achieve an optimal level of job satisfaction in each of its employees. Only in this way, the human talent of the company will be able to give one hundred percent of their capacity to the service of the company, enhancing the results obtained, allowing the personal and collective growth of its employees, as well as the fulfillment of the goals set by the company.

Finally, the general objective was: to analyze the relationship between Organizational Culture and Job Satisfaction among employees of the company Agroindustrias José & Luis S.A.C., Chepén, 2021. Then, Table 3 shows that out of the group of 69 employees who perceive a medium job satisfaction, 84.1% perceive a medium-level organizational culture, and out of the remaining employees who feel high job satisfaction, 81.8% also perceive a medium-level organizational culture. Spearman's Rho correlation coefficient, which measures the relationship between organizational culture and job satisfaction, was also calculated, showing a value of 0.233 and indicating a low and positive relationship between both variables overall. Likewise, the significance value of the test (p-sig. = 0.037) is less than 0.05, which determines that there is a significant relationship between both variables. Therefore, it is stated that there is a significant relationship between organizational culture and job satisfaction among the employees of the company Agroindustrias José & Luis S.A.C., in the year 2021. These results agree, among many aspects, with Loayza (2018) who states that there is indeed an impact of organizational culture on job satisfaction at a moderate and positive level (0.515) with a significance level of 0.000, which meets the condition of being less than 5%, according to Spearman's scale and demonstrated in the Hypothesis test, under the application of Kendall's Tau B statistical method on workers belonging to the Municipality of the province of Puno. In the same sense, Acevedo (2018) through his research concluded that organizational culture does have a relationship with the job satisfaction of the company's operating staff, evidenced by the correlation degree between the variables determined by Spearman's Rho with a value of 0.724, also adding that there is a high positive relationship, and highlighting aspects such as job stability, which, since it was only for hours, did not generate a feeling of full job stability for the worker, as he/she would like it to be, leading to a certain degree of indecision in them.

4 Conclusion

Through the analysis carried out in this research, as well as its subsequent support by various authors and theories mentioned, it was concluded firstly that there is a significant relationship between organizational culture and job satisfaction, supported by Spearman's rho with a value of 0.233 and a p-sig. $0.037 < 0.05$ among the employees of the company Agroindustrias José & Luis S.A.C., Chepén, 2021. With this result, we can affirm that the organizational culture in the company plays a preponderant role and that the adequate management of this could lead to a high level of job satisfaction among all employees. This is due to the importance that employees assign to culture since even without knowing the term very well, they perceive it, feel it, and appreciate it in the same way, being a fundamental pillar where the company must work to improve since the more care, work, and importance are assigned to it by the area in charge of the organization such as the "Human Resources area", optimal results will be obtained in the mid-term through the implementation, development, and consolidation of personal and labor well-being, individually and collectively, for its employees. In short, a high level of job satisfaction will be obtained. We must remember that one of the first lessons that a professional in Administration receives is the valuation not only for what can be seen, but much more for what is not observed, but perceived, understanding that an internal employee of the organization is a different world, each one of them with their qualities, abilities, intelligence and different contributions, with different motivations but gathered under the same objective, i. e. to contribute to the achievement of goals and growth of the company in exchange for an adequate economic and non-economic valuation, which allows him/her to develop as a person. That is why we must remember a very important phrase within Administration, "administration is science, but at the same time, it is art", emphasizing the complexity of guiding human groups, unifying efforts, and assigning to each one of them their corresponding place, as well as the pertinent valuation, being this the fundamental role of an Administration professional.

As a second conclusion, we can affirm that the level of organizational culture among employees is medium, with a percentage of 84%, in the company Agroindustrias José & Luis S.A.C., Chepén, 2021, allowing us to affirm that there is still a lot of work to be done by the company to consolidate its own identity, the one that differentiates it from the existing competing companies in the province of Chepén since to achieve not only economic growth but also socially responsible with the community, it is necessary to have the best human talent existing in the labor market, understanding that it contributes and plays a fundamental role in the achievement of the objectives. There are many cases around the world, where the largest, most successful organizations, recognized for their extensive growth and improvement prospects, have achieved their goals not only with heavy investments of economic capital or with the acquisition of technological resources and huge facilities with great amenities, but really through the ability, skill, and intelligence of all their employees, being there a turning point and where the need to not only be satisfied with having the best employees and the most outstanding professionals in the workplace is explained, but it is necessary to provide them with a pleasant culture, that they feel like their own, to motivate them, invite them to work as a team positively, thus finding the so-called "synergy"; but above all achieving the consolidation of the culture so that it can endure over time and become considered as a "strong organizational culture", which is not influenced over time, but especially that the values and beliefs with which the company was constituted may never be forgotten over the years.

Finally, as a last conclusion, the level of Job Satisfaction among employees is medium, with a percentage of 86%, in the company Agroindustrias José & Luis S.A.C., Chepén, 2021, affirming through the results that as with the organizational culture, there is also much work to be done to obtain a notorious job satisfaction in every employee in the company. Adequate management of the "Human Resources area" is required to identify those factors that have a direct impact on the feelings and perception of employees, since the aforementioned area has the arduous task of managing the human talent of the organization, also understanding that it is not a job to be developed in isolation, but on the contrary, it must have the support of the top management in the organizational structure such as middle managers and general managers.

This joint work is necessary because it must be taken into account that to achieve sustainable, continuous, and constant growth over time, it is not only necessary to have large extensions of fertile land and/or to be located in a purely commercial area with tough competition. Because, although they are indeed factors to be taken into account for the development of daily activities, they are not everything. On the contrary, according to the different studies carried out and what was stated in the research described above, it assumes a much more primordial value if it is possible to enhance and optimize the satisfaction felt by the company's employees, ensuring that each of the people working in the company shows an adequate sense of belonging, emphasizing that, for managers and those in charge of leading an organization such as Agroindustrias José & Luis S.A.C., it is not only important to have fertile and extensive lands as well as an adequate physical environment, but it is much more important to achieve an optimal level of job satisfaction in each of its employees. Only in this way, the human talent of the company will be able to give one hundred percent of their capacity to serve the company, enhancing the results obtained, allowing the personal and collective growth of its employees as well as the fulfillment of the goals set by the company.

References

Acevedo, A.: Cultura organizacional y satisfacción laboral del personal operativo de campo de la empresa SGS del Perú SAC – Chimbote 2018. [Organizational culture and job satisfaction of field operating personnel of the company SGS del Perú SAC - Chimbote 2018] (Thesis for professional degree. Universidad de San Pedro). USANPEDRO Repository (2018). http://repositorio.usanpedro.edu.pe/handle/USANPEDRO/15338

Ambrossi, D., Marconi, L.: Diagnóstico de la cultura organizacional en el banco de Loja [Diagnosis of the organizational culture in the bank of Loja]. Revista PODIUM edición especial. pp. 7–27 (2017). https://revistas.uees.edu.ec/index.php/Podium/article/view/74

Bazalar, M., Choquehuanca, C.: Clima organizacional y satisfacción laboral de los trabajadores de Universidad Nacional del Callao [Organizational climate and job satisfaction of the workers of the National University of Callao]. Revista de investigación científica y tecnológica Llamkasun **1**(2), 35–51 (2020). https://doi.org/10.47797/llamkasun.v1i2.12

Guerrero, M., Silva, D.: La Cultura Organizacional, su importancia en el desarrollo de las empresas [The organizational culture, its importance in the development of companies]. Revista INNOVA Res. J. **2**(3), 110–115 (2017). https://doi.org/10.33890/innova.v2.n3.2017.188

Córdoba, N.: Cultura organizacional y la satisfacción laboral de los trabajadores médicos y enfermeros de UCIN de una maternidad pública de la ciudad de Rosario, Argentina Año 2018 [Organizational culture and job satisfaction of NICU medical and nursing workers of a public maternity hospital in the city of Rosario, Argentina, 2018]. (Thesis of profesional degree, Universidad Nacional de Rosario). UNR Repository (2020). http://hdl.handle.net/2133/18892

Díaz, A., Merino, A., Valderrama, O., Nuñez, L.: Satisfacción laboral y cultura organizacional en docentes universitarios en una Facultad de Ciencias de la Salud [Job satisfaction and organizational culture in university teachers in a Faculty of Health Sciences.]. Revista Investigación en Ciencias de la Educación **5**(21), 1642–1648 (2021). https://doi.org/10.33996/revistahoriz ontes.v5i21.304

Durand, S., García, J., Paz, A., Boscán, M.: Satisfacción laboral como actitud integradora de los individuos en organizaciones no gubernamentales [Job satisfaction as an integrative attitude of individuals in non-governmental organizations]. Revista Venezolana de Gerencia **26**(6), 223–244 (2021). https://doi.org/10.52080/rvgluz.26.e6.14

Loayza, M.: Cultura organizacional y su incidencia en la satisfacción laboral de los trabajadores de la municipalidad provincial de puno, 2017 [Organizational culture and its impact on the job satisfaction of workers of the Provincial Municipality of Puno, 2017]. (Thesis of profesional degree. Universidad Andina Néstor Cáceres Velásquez) UANCV Repository (2018). http://rep ositorio.uancv.edu.pe/handle/UANCV/1643

Olmos, M., Socha, K.: Diseño y validación mediante jueces expertos del instrumento para evaluar cultura organizacional [Design and validation by expert judges of the instrument to assess organizational culture]. (Doctoral thesis, Universidad de la Sabana). Repositorios LATINOAMERICANOS (2006). http://hdl.handle.net/10818/1838

Ortiz, M., Villar, E., Llanos, M.: Cultura organizacional y bienestar laboral de los trabajadores de la Red de Salud Huamalíes [Organizational culture and labor welfare of Red de Salud Huamalíes workers]. Revista Gaceta Científica **7**(1), 37–45 (2021). https://doi.org/10.46794/gacien.7.1. 1064

Palma, S.: Elaboración y validación de una escala de satisfacción laboral en trabajadores de Lima Metropolitana e Investigación en Psicología [Elaboration and validation of a job satisfaction scale in workers of Metropolitan Lima and Research in Psychology]. Revista Teoría e Investigación en Psicología **9**(1), 27–34 (2006)

Schein, E.: La cultura empresarial y el liderazgo. Una visión dinámica [Organizational Culture and Leadership: A Dynamic View]. Plaza & Janes Editores (1988)

Tamayo, M.: Cultura organizacional y satisfacción laboral en trabajadores de la compañía Minera Poderosa S.A. – 2017. [Organizational culture and job satisfaction in workers of the Mining Company Poderosa S.A. – 2017]. (Thesis of professional degree, Universidad César Vallejo). UCV Repository (2017). https://hdl.handle.net/20.500.12692/11604

Administrative Management and Labor Disputes in the Municipality of Cochorco

Kassandra Benites Polo[✉] [ID] and Julia Otilia Sagástegui Cruz[ID]

Universidad Privada Del Norte, Trujillo, Peru
n00213018@upn.pe

Abstract. This research is based on determining the relationship between the variables, administrative management, and labor disputes, in the District Municipality of Cochorco, 2021, being this one of the main issues of great importance for public and private entities. An extensive exploration of different sources has been carried out. This information has been studied and correlated to answer the objective. The methodology of this research follows a correlational type, quantitative approach, and non-experimental design. To obtain the data, instruments such as the questionnaire were used, presented to Cronbach's Alpha Statistic. To measure the reliability value for Administrative Management, a value of 0.901 was obtained and for labor disputes a value of 0.771. Among the results obtained, it was found that administrative management and labor disputes have a significance level of 0.135. This indicates that it is greater than 0.05, which means that there is no direct correlation between these two variables. This is a low-degree relationship with a coefficient of 0.241. In conclusion, the research hypothesis, that there is a low degree of direct relationship between administrative management and labor disputes in the District Municipality of Cochorco, 2021, was analyzed and proved.

Keywords: Administrative management · Labor disputes · Dimensions · Intrapersonal · And interpersonal

1 Introduction

Through observation, it can be seen that administrative management and labor disputes are key elements for public and private entities to be able to direct their work and operations through excellent administrative management, centered on rules, policies, and moral principles. Therefore, the organization must suitably manage resources to achieve the goals set.

Administrative management is a fundamental element within labor organization for the development of management, achieving a corporate strategy that is solid and profitable through the use of people and resources. It is also noted that some of the municipalities do not acquire tools that meet modern requirements (Santana Mañay 2016). On the other hand, administrative management in a company considers the connection and proper governance of the organization towards the fulfillment of the objectives set (Quintero Caicedo and Sotomayor Sellan 2018). Administrative management is defined

M. Botto-Tobar et al. (Eds.): ICAT 2022, CCIS 1757, pp. 381–390, 2023.
https://doi.org/10.1007/978-3-031-24978-5_33

as an administrative process with seven elements: research, planning, control, coordination, organization, foresight, and command (Flores Orozco 2015). To analyze the level of administrative management, dimension tools with administrative approach, management level, use of operations research, and decision making are used to determine the use of operational research (Pacheco et al. 2018). On the other hand, every organization must have adequate administrative management and obtain good competitiveness with the most efficient and effective collaborators. Good administrative management depends on the level of competitiveness of the collaborators who make the organization more competitive (Chaca Oliveros and Rivera Quispe 2018). A study determined that the better the administrative management, the better the internal control within the organization (Meneses Paucar 2019).

Regarding labor disputes, it is concluded that the cause of conflicts is poor communication, lack of recognition, and demotivation, negatively influencing the work performance level, affecting the attitudes to solve problems, separating into intrapersonal and extra-personal conflicts (Cuba Panduro 2020). Likewise, it is important to first study each situation and circumstance in which a conflict occurs or is caused, and in which strategies designed according to the type of conflict generated must be applied to manage it properly, to reach a negotiable agreement between both parties involved (Pallas Guiral 2013). On the other hand, it is concluded that alternative strategies for conflict resolution should be used, such as dialogue and appropriate negotiation that benefit both parties (Cordon Padilla 2013). It is said that having a good leadership trained and enriched in knowledge is a great useful and indispensable tool to be able to manage an organization where leaders serve to contribute to solving labor disputes and problems in a short period. That is why it is suggested to often strengthen communication and trust among collaborators to improve and obtain a good working environment (Dominguez 2015). A study evaluated the relationship between training and labor disputes in the public entity DREI, Ica, where it is indicated that training is a tool through which short-term objectives are established and applied in an organized way, benefiting collaborators and the organization. It also states that a dispute is a verbal confrontation between two or more people (Hernández Tapullima 2019). A research report shows that labor disputes are unavoidable and affect several variables, such as workers' performance, causing lower performance and making it difficult to meet objectives and goals (Avila Huancaya and Vivar Retuerto 2021).

This summarized bibliographic review informs us that labor disputes affect in some way different variables, such as the administrative management of an organization, harming or delaying the objectives and goals of that entity. That is why the following research question arises: What is the relationship between administrative management and labor disputes in the District Municipality of Cochorco, 2021? The objective of this study is to analyze the relationship between administrative management and labor disputes in the District Municipality of Cochorco, 2021. This research was carried out to understand the importance of administrative management and its relationship with labor disputes in the District Municipality of Cochorco. A thesis report showed that there is a high level of positive relationship ($r = 0.687$) between administrative management and labor productivity with the administrative collaborators of the District Municipality of José Leonardo Ortiz, Lambayeque (León Cachay, 2020). It is also said that administrative management has a significant impact on labor disputes, since the lack of strategies for the management of such disputes within the organization may affect the achievement of objectives, causing an imbalance in the labor relationship (Bullón Ingaroca 2017). Therefore, the administrative management is in the hands of the executives who are in charge of each operation of the organization, such as: elaborating training programs for the personnel and proposing and implementing improvements in personnel management policies (González Rodríguez et al. 2020). On the other hand, it is stated that a variety of labor disputes occur in different areas of the organization, so the use of conflict resolution strategies is very important for the proper management to achieve the internal and external wellbeing of the organization. (Rodriguez 2014).

In order to have a better understanding of the research, the main basic concepts were investigated and examined.

Administrative management: this is defined as a set of coordinated activities and processes to run an organization and achieve the fulfillment of its objectives (Fayol 2016). In other words, it is a model that defines the administrative act, which is made up of 4 dimensions, namely:

Planning: visualizing the future and outlining the action program that allows the organization to obtain and devote resources to achieve its objectives. There are two types of plans: one-time plans and permanent plans; the former is made up of the proposed programs and projects and the latter of the policies, procedures, and rules. In addition, it is indicated that at this stage the bases that will serve as a guide for the other activities and actions to be carried out are determined.

Organize: Building the material and social structure of the company, establishing objectives and plans. The organization process has several stages: Description of the work to be done; Division of work; Coordination of work; Departmentalization or organizational structure; Monitoring and reorganization.

Management: Guiding and orienting the personnel. It arises from management, which is related to action, to implementation, and has a lot to do with people.

Control: Verifying that everything happens according to the established rules and given orders. As an administrative function, it is a process that ensures that the purposes and policies of a company are fulfilled and that the resources available for this are being properly managed in terms of effectiveness and efficiency.

According to what has been investigated, it can be said that having good administrative management by adequately using the strategies helps the organization to maintain a good working environment since it is fundamental to work together so as to achieve the objectives of the organization.

Labor disputes: It is defined as a confrontation between members of the organization that may be generated by several factors, causing disunity and the non-compliance of the activities as a whole. (Territorial 2019) points out that there is a variety of conflicts, which can directly affect the organization, but according to the most involved parties they would include:

Intrapersonal: this type of conflict is found in the person him/herself. The cause is because it arises from a direct contradiction in the way he/she thinks or feels.

Interpersonal: this type of conflict affects several people in the organization and is caused by different values, interests, beliefs, norms, and lack of communication and empathy.

2 Materials and Methons

In order to carry out this research, a non-experimental quantitative methodological design was used, because it seeks to analyze the variables without manipulating them. It is correlational because it seeks and analyzes the relationship between the two variables studied; transversal, since the data collection will be carried out at a certain time during the development of the study.

The population of this study is made up of the administrative workers of the District Municipality of Cochorco, 2021, of which an average of 45 collaborators belong to it, with a probabilistic sampling of 40 administrative workers.

As an instrument, the questionnaire was applied to the Administrative Management variable, distributed in four dimensions: planning, organization, direction, and control, on an ordinal Likert-type scale. This instrument has already been applied to measure administrative management in companies, with a high level of validity and consistency with the professional academic school of Administration, published in Google Scholar (Martin 2018). For the labor disputes variable, a questionnaire was applied, divided into two dimensions: Intrapersonal and interpersonal, on an ordinal Likert-type scale. This instrument was applied to measure the level of labor disputes in an organization, from the School of Administration, published in Google Scholar (Bullón Ingaroca 2017).

After obtaining the information, we proceeded to prepare the collection instruments to be applied through digital media, using the Google Forms platform. The data collected were tabulated and analyzed, using Microsoft Excel and SPSS, to be included in this report.

3 Results

In the results, after collecting the information, we proceeded to determine the level of administrative management and labor conflicts in the District Municipality of Cochorco, according to the administrative personnel surveyed.

Table 1 shows that the administrative workers of the Municipality who were surveyed with respect to the variable Administrative Management is low with a percentage of 2.50%, followed by 40% who consider it a medium level and 57.50% a high level.

Table 2 it can be observed that 12.50% of the workers consider that the labor conflicts variable of the Municipality is at a low level, followed by 67.50% at a medium level and 20% at a high level.

The findings of the study and interpretation of results and the hypothesis test are described narratively. To carry out the hypothesis test, the Pearson Correlation test was used, obtaining the following results.

Table 1. Level of the variable administrative management of the District Municipality of Cochorco 2021.

Level	Frequency	Porcentaje
Low	1.0	2.5
Medium	16.0	40
High	23.0	57.5
Total	40.0	100

Source: Own elaboration.

Table 2. Level of the variable labor conflicts of the District Municipality of Cochorco 2021.

Level	Frequency	Percentage
Low	5.0	12.5
Medium	27.0	67.5
High	8.0	20
Total	40.0	100

Source: Own elaboration.

General Hypothesis Test:

HO: Administrative management has a significant impact on labor disputes according to the administrative personnel of the District Municipality of Cochorco.

H1: Administrative management does not have a significant impact on labor disputes according to the administrative personnel of the District Municipality of Cochorco.

Table 3. Correlation of the administrative management variable with the labor disputes variable

		V1 Administrative management	V2 Labor disputes
V1 Administrative management	Pearson correlation	1	0.241
	Sig. (bilateral)		0.135
	N	40	40
V2 Labor disputes	Pearson correlation	0.241	1
	Sig. (bilateral)	0.135	
	N	40	40

Source: Own elaboration.

Table 3 shows that the significance level is 0.135, which is greater than 0.05, i.e., there is no direct correlation between these two variables. This is a low-degree relationship, with a coefficient of 0.241. Subsequently, the specific hypothesis of the study, that there is a low degree of direct relationship between administrative management and labor disputes in the District Municipality of Cochorco, 2021, was analyzed and proved.

The Pearson correlation test was used to evaluate the correlation between the dimensions (planning, organization, direction, and control) of administrative management and the labor disputes variable, considering a confidence level of 95% and a significance level of 0.05.

Specific hypothesis test:

HO: The dimensions of administrative management have a significant impact on labor disputes according to the administrative personnel of the District Municipality of Cochorco.

H1: The dimensions of administrative management do not have a significant impact on labor disputes according to the administrative personnel of the District Municipality of Cochorco.

Table 4. Correlation between the planning dimension and the labor disputes variable.

		D1 Planning	V2 Labor disputes
D1 Planning	Pearson Correlation	1	0.236
	Sig. (bilateral)		0.143
	N	40	40
V2 Labor disputes	Pearson Correlation	0.236	1
	Sig. (bilateral)	0.143	
	N	40	40

Source: Own elaboration.

Table 4 shows that the significance level is 0.143, which is greater than 0.05, indicating that there is no relationship between the planning dimension and the labor disputes variable. This is a low-degree correlation because it represents a correlation of 0.236.

Table 5. Correlation of the organization dimension and the labor disputes variable.

		D2 Organization	V2 Labor disputes
D2 Organization	Pearson Correlation	1	0.195
	Sig. (bilateral)		0.227
	N	40	40
V2 Labor disputes	Pearson Correlation	0.195	1
	Sig. (bilateral)	0.227	
	N	40	40

Source: Own elaboration.

Table 5 shows that the significance level is 0.227, which is greater than 0.05, indicating that there is no relationship between the organization dimension and the labor disputes variable. This is a very low-degree correlation because it represents a correlation of 0.195.

Table 6. Correlation of the direction dimension and the labor disputes variable.

		D3 Direction	V2 Labor disputes
D3 Direction	Pearson Correlation	1	0.093
	Sig. (bilateral)		0.566
	N	40	40
V2 Labor disputes	Pearson Correlation	0.093	1
	Sig. (bilateral)	0.566	
	N	40	40

Source: Own elaboration.

Table 6 shows that the significance level is 0.556, which is greater than 0.05, indicating that there is no relationship between the direction dimension and the labor disputes variable. This is a very low-degree correlation because it represents a correlation of 0.093.

Table 7. Correlation of the control dimension and the labor disputes variable.

		D4 Control	V2 Labor disputes
D4 Control	Pearson Correlation	1	0.240
	Sig. (bilateral)		0.136
	N	40	40
V2 Labor disputes	Pearson Correlation	0.240	1
	Sig. (bilateral)	0.136	
	N	40	40

Source: Own elaboration.

Table 7 shows that the significance level is 0.136, which is greater than 0.05, indicating that there is no relationship between the control dimension and the labor disputes variable. This is a low-degree correlation because it represents a correlation of 0.240.

After analyzing the results, it can be affirmed that there is no relationship between Administrative Management and Labor Disputes. Therefore, the degree of relationship is low, rejecting the null hypothesis and accepting the alternative hypothesis in the District Municipality of Cochorco, 2021.

4 Discussion

From the studies found and the results of the analysis concerning the general objective, it was found that there is no direct correlation between the variables: administrative management and labor disputes. The level of significance is 0.135 and the correlation coefficient is 0.241, with a low degree of direct relationship between the variables mentioned, thus proving the research hypothesis, rejecting the null hypothesis and accepting the alternative hypothesis, a result that does not agree with research by Bullón Ingaroca (2017) where it is observed that the variables, administrative management and labor disputes, have a high significance value, i.e. the significance test level is less than 0.05, showing that labor disputes are associated with administrative management.

On the other hand, regarding the results obtained for the first specific objective, it was identified that the level of administrative management is high according to 57.50% of workers. Likewise, the results of the level of each dimension of administrative management were obtained: Planning 70%, organization 77.50%, direction 65%, and control 32%. Each dimension resulted in a high level of good administrative management. Therefore, Veliz Valencia (2020), in his research conducted in a municipality, concluded that good administrative management is due to good internal communication within the organization.

Second specific objective: the level of labor disputes was determined. It was identified that it is at a medium level according to 67.50% of workers. The level of each dimension of labor disputes was determined: Intrapersonal 65% and Interpersonal 57.50%. Each dimension resulted in a medium level concerning labor disputes. Bullón Ingaroca (2017) in his study concerning the incidence in labor disputes in the District Municipality Coronel Gregorio Albarracín Lanchipa, 2016, found that labor disputes have a prevalence of 50%, and points out that good and proper management such as communication leads to more positive results, avoiding problematic situations, and reaching goals more easily.

Third specific objective: the correlation between each dimension of administrative management and the labor disputes variable was evaluated. After analyzing the data, it was determined that there is no relationship between the planning dimension and the labor disputes variable, with a significance level of 0.143 and a low degree (Rho = 0.236). It was also found that there is no relationship between the organization dimension and the labor disputes variable, where the significance level is 0.227 and has a very low degree (Rho = 0.195). Likewise, it was confirmed that there is no relationship between the direction dimension and the labor disputes variable, where the significance level is 0.556 and has a very low degree (Rho = 0.093). Similarly, it was affirmed that there is no relationship between the control dimension and the labor disputes variable where the significance level is 0.136 and has a low degree (Rho = 0.240), a result that does not agree with the research conducted by Caruajulca Quispe (2019), where it was found that the dimensions studied have a significance of less than 0.05, meaning that the dimensions of administrative management have a significant influence on labor disputes in the special project Sierra Centro Sur, Ayacucho.

According to the results obtained from the administrative workers of the District Municipality of Cochorco, it became evident that administrative management and labor disputes have a low degree of relationship. Thus, it is considered that there is no direct relationship between these two variables.

5 Conclusions

This research shows that there is no direct relationship between administrative management and labor disputes in the District Municipality of Cochorco, 2021, with a significance level of 0.135 and a correlation coefficient of 0.241, as a result.

First specific objective: the level of each dimension of the Administrative Management variable was determined, according to the administrative personnel of the District Municipality of Cochorco, 2021, which showed that in each dimension a high level of administrative management was obtained: planning 70%, organization 77.50%, direction 65% and control 32%. Therefore, it was concluded that in the District Municipality of Cochorco there is a high level of administrative management.

Second specific objective: the level of each dimension of the labor disputes variable in the District Municipality of Cochorco, 2021 was determined, obtaining as a result in each dimension: intrapersonal 65% and interpersonal 57.50%. Therefore, it was determined that in the District Municipality of Cochorco, 2021, there is a medium level regarding the labor disputes variable.

Third specific objective: to establish the correlation between the dimensions (planning, organization, direction, and control) of administrative management and the labor disputes variable. According to the administrative personnel of the District Municipality of Cochorco, 2021, it was determined that in each of them there is a low degree of correlation: planning dimension (Rho = 0.236), organization dimension (Rho = 0.195), direction dimension (Rho = 0.093), control dimension (Rho = 0.240).

References

Avila, E.K., Vivar, B.P.: Conflictos laborales y desempeño de los trabajadores de la Municipalidad Provincial de Jauja 2020 [Labor disputes and performance of workers of the Provincial Municipality of Jauja 2020]. Universidad Continental, Jauja. CONTINENTAL-Institucional (2021)

Bullón Ingaroca, C.d.: Gerencia administrativa y su incidencia en los conflictos laborales Municipalidad Distrital Coronel Gregorio Albarracín Lanchipa 2016 [Administrative management and its impact on labor disputes District Municipality Coronel Gregorio Albarracín Lanchipa 2016.]. Universidad Cesar Vallejo, Tacna. UCV-Institucional, (2017)

Caruajulca Quispe, W.: La gestión administrativa y el ambiente laboral en los conflictos laborales del Proyecto Especial Sierra Centro Sur, Ayacucho 2018. [Administrative management and labor environment in labor disputes in the Sierra Centro Sur Special Project, Ayacucho 2018]. Universidad Cesar Vallejo. Lima: UCV-Institucional, (2019)

Cordon Padilla, E.M.: Métodos alternativos de resolución de conflictos aplicados a la negociación por la vía directa de pactos colectivos de condiciones de trabajo y a los conflictos laborales ya planteados [Alternative dispute resolution methods applied to the direct negotiation of collective bargaining agreements on working conditions and to labor disputes that have already arisen]. Universidad de San Carlos De Guatemala, Guatemala (2013)

Cuba Panduro, D.J.: Conflictos laborales del servidor civil en la Municipalidad Metropolitana de Lima. Lima [Labor disputes of civil employees in the Metropolitan Municipality of Lima]. Lima: UCV-Institucional (2020)

Chaca Oliveros, A.E., Rivera Quispe, L.J.: Gestión administrativa para lograr la competitividad de la empresa constructora y multiservicios Valcer S.A.C. – 2017 [Administrative management to achieve the competitiveness of the construction and multiservices company Valcer S.A.C. - 2017]. Universidad Nacional Daniel Alcides Carrión, Pasco (2018)

Dominguez, A.S.: Liderazgo Y Gestión De Conflictos Laborales [Leadership and Labor Dispute Management]. Guatemala, (2015)

Fayol, H.: La Teoría clásica de la Administración. Aprendiendo Administracion [The Classical Management Theory. Learning Management] (2016)

Flores Orozco, S.E.: Proceso administrativo y gestión empresarial en coproabas jinotega [Administrative process and business management at Coproabas Jinotega]. Universidad Nacional Autonoma de Nicaragua, Managua, Matagalpa (2015)

González Rodríguez, S.S., Viteri, D.A., Izquierdo, A.M., Verdezoto, G.O.: Modelo de Gestion Administrativa [Administrative Management Model]. Revista Científica de la Universidad de Cienfuegos, Universidad y Sociedad. Quevedo (2020)

Hernández, W.G.: Capacitación y conflictos laborales en la entidad pública DREI, Ica 2019 [Training and labor disputes in the public entity DREI, Ica 2019]. Universidad Cesar Vallejo, Ica (2019)

León, J.D.: Gestión administrativa y productividad laboral en la Municipalidad Distrital de José Leonardo Ortiz [Administrative management and labor productivity in the District Municipality of José Leonardo Ortiz]. Universidad Cesar Vallejo. Peru, UCV-Institucional (2020)

Martin, A.C.: Calidad de servicio y satisfacción del cliente de la academia preuniversitaria andreas vesalius, Nuevo Chimbote [Quality of service and customer satisfaction of the pre-university academy Andreas Vesalius, Nuevo Chimbote]. (2018)

Meneses Paucar, P.: Gestión administrativa y control interno en la Municipalidad de Independencia [Administrative management and internal control in the Municipality of Independencia]. Independencia: UNE-Institucional (2019)

Pacheco, R., Robles, C., Ospino, d.: Análisis de la Gestión Administrativa en las Instituciones Educativas de los Niveles de Básica y Media en las Zonas Rurales de Santa Marta, Colombia [Analysis of the administrative management in the educational institutions of the basic and middle levels in the rural areas of Santa Marta, Colombia]. Colombia: Informacion Tecnologica (2018)

Pallas, B.: El conflicto laboral y la negociación colectiva en épocas de recesión económica [Labor disputes and collective bargaining in times of economic recession]. Universidad de Zaragoza, Spain (2013)

Quintero Caicedo, A.K., Sotomayor Sellan, J.M.: Propuesta de mejora del proceso logístico de la empresa Tramacoexpress Cía.Ltda del cantón Durán [Proposal to improve the logistic process of the company Tramacoexpress Cía.Ltda del cantón Duran]. Universidad de Guayaquil Facultad de Ciencias Administrativas (2018)

Rodriguez, J.: La importancia del manejo de conflictos. [The importance of conflict management]. Universidad Militar Nueva GRANADA, Colombia (2014)

Santana, S.E.: La planificación estratégica y la gestión administrativa de los Gobiernos Autónomos Descentralizados Municipales (GADM) de Tungurahua [Strategic planning and administrative management of the Autonomous Decentralized Municipal Governments (GADM) of Tungurahua]. Universidad Técnica de Ambato, Ecuador (2016)

Territorial., S. d.: Resolucion de conflictos laborales [Labor Dispute Resolution]. Madrid: UGT-Madrid (2019)

Veliz, J.M.: Relación entre gestión administrativa y comunicación interna de la Municipalidad Distrital De Majes – Caylloma – Arequipa, 2020 [Relationship between administrative management and internal communication of the District Municipality of Majes - Caylloma - Arequipa, 2020]. Universidad Católica San Pablo, Arequipa. UCSP-Institucional (2020)

Job Satisfaction in Teacher Training: A Look from Burnout Syndrome

Cristina Ysabel Chumpitazi Torres⊙ and Julia Otilia Sagástegui Cruz$^{(\boxtimes)}$ ⊙

Universidad Privada del Norte, Av. El Ejercito 920 – Urb. El Molino, Trujillo, Perú
julia.sagastegui@upn.edu.pe

Abstract. The purpose of this research was to establish whether Burnout Syndrome influences the job performance of teachers of the IESPP Indoamérica (Public Higher Education Pedagogical Institute "Indoamerica"), Trujillo 2019. The population included 70 teachers and a sample of 52, obtained through a random probability sampling. The type of research was predictive because it was aimed at testing whether the ordinal logistic regression model of job performance is likely to be explained by Burnout Syndrome. The technique used was the application of the test, which collected information on Burnout Syndrome and job performance, from the perception of the teachers surveyed, through the Maslach Burnout Inventory and the Rosana Choy Vessoni Teacher Referential Inventory, both adapted. Finally, Burnout Syndrome has an inverse influence on the job performance of the teachers surveyed.

Keywords: Influence · Burnout syndrome · Job performance

1 Introduction

Burnout syndrome is a latent phenomenon in different spaces and organizations in Latin America and with more notorious manifestations in educational institutions. Thus, in Mexico, in Basic Education, a considerable number of teachers experience difficulties with their students. These interactions show stressed teachers with deficits in their job performance (Rodríguez et al. 2017). In Ecuador, Higher Education teachers with more than ten years of service show some symptoms of Burnout syndrome, which reveal frustration and that they feel forced to perform their role with their students and colleagues at the university (Rivera et al. 2018). Similarly, in Quito, teachers perceive job performance evaluation as a threat. Moreover, they are in disagreement with the way they are evaluated. This situation causes poor internal communication among the members of the educational community. Undoubtedly, this creates the scenario and conditions for Burnout Syndrome (Tenorio, 2017).

At the national level, specifically in Arequipa, Burnout syndrome impacts with a higher expansive and moderate incidence among male teachers, 93.7% (119), compared to 91.5% (97) among female teachers. However, in severity it is inverted, 7.5% (8) for female teachers, versus 6.3% (8) for male teachers (Arias and Jiménez, 2013). On the other hand, in Lima, when emotional intelligence increases or decreases, this is reflected in job performance, in the different areas of productivity: it increases production in those who have greater control, self-knowledge, self-motivation, or others; and, decreases when workers do not have these skills. This coincides with the effects caused by Burnout, regarding emotional exhaustion, depersonalization, or personal fulfillment (Orué-Arias, 2012).

In the local context, in the Unidad de Gestion Educative N° 02 (Education Management Unit N° 02) of "La Esperanza", district of Trujillo, job performance is disturbed due to workers' dissatisfaction, which is aggravated by an overload of work, job insecurity and lack of leisure activities. Consequently, Burnout Syndrome is severe in specialists, managers, and coordinators; and, moderate in office workers (Zavaleta, 2016).

In the teaching community of the Instituto de Educación Superior Pedagógico Público Indoamérica (IESPPI), there is evidence of Burnout Syndrome symptoms and an occurrence in their job performance, leaving an opportunity for cause and effect between them. In Burnout Syndrome, regarding the Emotional Exhaustion dimension, most trainers feel tired when working with their colleagues, others experience feelings of frustration and extreme situations at work. In the Depersonalization aspect, some teachers generally treat others harshly; students are in their second order and feel victimized by the academic results. To conclude this analysis with the Personal dimension, few trainers demonstrate positive influence on their colleagues and students, express energy and joy in the classroom, or assume that valuable things are achieved at work.

Concerning job performance, in terms of Academic Preparation, the explanation given by the teachers is not clear to their students and, at the same time, they receive information that is not updated. In Teaching Skills, interaction with students is not frequent; only sometimes, teachers provide feedback with a regression to fill gaps or explain them. In the Teacher-Student aspect, teachers are not very open to answering their students' questions, or sometimes they do not have self-control in response to the questions and concerns. Finally, in Pedagogical Norms, the communication of evaluation instruments, criteria, products, and results is not timely.

In this context, the following question was formulated: What is the influence of Burnout Syndrome on the job performance of the teachers of the Instituto de Educación Superior Pedagógico Público Indoamérica, Trujillo, 2019?

Likewise, the central hypothesis was the following: Burnout Syndrome has an inverse influence on the job performance of the teachers of the Instituto de Educación Superior Pedagógico Público Indoamérica, Trujillo, 2019.

On the other hand, the general objective of this study was to establish whether Burnout Syndrome influences the job performance of the teachers of the Instituto de Educación Superior Pedagógico Público Indoamérica, Trujillo, 2019.

Furthermore, the specific planned and guiding objectives were as follows: a) To determine the influence of Burnout Syndrome on the Academic Preparation dimension in the subjects surveyed; b) to determine the influence of Burnout Syndrome on the Teaching Skills dimension in the subjects surveyed; c) to determine the influence of Burnout Syndrome on the Teacher-Student Relationship dimension in the subjects surveyed; and, d) to determine the influence of Burnout Syndrome on the Pedagogical Norms dimension in the subjects surveyed.

In this research, the model of job resources and demands proposed by (Demerouti, Bakker, Nachreiner, and Schaufeli, 2001) has been assumed as a construct to interpret, explain, and potentially predict Burnout Syndrome. From this model, contexts are classified into two categories: labor resources and labor demands. Thus, if the physical, psychological, social, and organizational components involve physiological costs and sustained efforts of the worker, it becomes a labor demand. On the contrary, if they reduce them and allow the achievement of task objectives, then they become labor resources. This construct is based on four postulates: first, the construct applies to all work environments and all professions and occupations; second, the impairment of the motivational process reflects work demands and resources; third, there are interactions between work resources and demands; and, fourth, inverse causal relationships are likely to decrease or increase the distance to Burnout Syndrome.

Consequently, Burnout Syndrome is a continuous process of emotional exhaustion, hostility to others, and negative attitudes toward oneself, as a product of work overload (Al-Asadi, and others, 2018; Pinel, Pérez and Carrión, 2019 and Castillo, 2000). Similarly, in teachers, it can be perceived as emotional exhaustion, depersonalization, and a feeling of personal accomplishment. Emotional exhaustion is expressed in the absence of resources to face a situation or challenge; depersonalization, insensitive attitudes toward others; and, a feeling of personal accomplishment, a set of negative responses to oneself, as a result of work pressure. The teacher avoids interpersonal relationships.

In this study, job performance is interpreted in the theoretical line of the organizational field by Chiavenato. The organizational field is understood as the area of human knowledge; it responds to the environment and differential features of the company. From this perspective, an organization depends on its contingencies and situations, and, likewise, on the position adopted for decisions and operations. In addition, it is impacted by the environmental context: intellectual capital and core business. In this framework, job performance is defined as a set of competencies for the objectives of the company. In this sense, intellectual wealth and intrinsic value are attributed to them, a fundamental structure for the success of the organization. This situation is understood from two principles: a) Human capital is a convergence of talent, behavior, and organization; b) If internal changes are greater than external changes, the company would be successful; otherwise, obsolete (Chiavenato, 2009).

Therefore, from the above context, job performance is a complex behavior, focused on the achievement of goals and organizational human capital, and inherent to the position (Chiavenato, 2009; Vallejos, 2016; and Rodríguez, K. and Lechuga, 2019).

By extension, in the field of higher education, there are four dimensions or operational spaces for teachers: academic preparation, teaching skills, teacher-student relationship, and pedagogical norms. Academic preparation or professional teaching competence implies the possibility of activating students' knowledge to successfully face the challenges of their future professional careers (Mas, 2011). Teaching skills are specific processes aimed at generating individual and group learning (Zabalza, 2003). The teacher-student relationship is the interaction, during the teaching-learning process, in a common scenario: the classroom (Quiroz, and Franco, 2019). And, pedagogical norms, are the closing or evaluation dimension, where the teacher verifies the achievement of learning, collects information, and communicates the results, under a protocol and pedagogical norms, whose function is not to control, but to motivate learning (Moreno, 2018).

2 Materials and Methods

In this study, the population consisted of 70 teachers from the Instituto de Educación Superior Pedagógico Público Indoamérica, Trujillo, 2019, a province belonging to the La Libertad Region, in Peru, where teachers are predominantly hired over appointed. Likewise, the appointed teachers are older adults between 48 and 69 years old versus young hired teachers, with an average age of 35 years old.

In this research, the calculated sample size was 52 active teachers of the Instituto de Educación Superior Pedagógico Público Indoamérica, in 2019, which was calculated by the algorithm of finite populations. Likewise, the sampling used was simple probabilistic, because, on the one hand, the sample was calculated by finite populations, and, on the other hand, the selection of subjects was done by simple randomization, using the lottery technique.

The technique used to measure Burnout Syndrome and job performance among the teachers under study was the application of the test.

Two measurement instruments were used in this study. First, the Maslach Inventory (2004), adapted by Cristina Ysabel Chumpitazi Torres, whose purpose was to measure the level of Burnout syndrome or professional exhaustion in teachers of the IESPP Indoamérica, in 2019, in three dimensions: Emotional Exhaustion, Depersonalization, and Personal Accomplishment. The second instrument was the Rosana Choy Vessoni Teacher Referential Inventory (2017), adapted by Cristina Ysabel Chumpitazi Torres, in order to measure job performance in four dimensions: Academic Preparation, Teaching Skills, Teacher-Student Relationship, and Pedagogical Standards.

The validity of the Leiter and Maslach Inventory (Leiter and Maslach, 2004) was carried out using the expert judgment technique, with the V-Aiken test in two stages: in the first stage, items 5 and 8 were observed with values of 0.80 and 0.60, associated with a p-value of 0.156 and 0.312 (Appendix 6); however, the reliability results were 0.887 in the first stage and 0.928 in the second stage.

Likewise, the validity of the Teacher Referential Inventory (2019) was carried out through the technique of expert judgments, with the V-Aiken test in two stages: in the first stage, items 7 and 15 were observed with values of 0.80 and item 0.60, associated with a p-value of 0.156 and 0.312 (Annex 8); however, the reliability results were 0.642 in the first stage and 0.978 in the second stage.

For data analysis, simple frequency tables and graphs were used, as well as contingency tables and graphs or crosstabs. Likewise, the influence or association was established through the ordinal logistic regression model of job performance, after confirmation of the Smirnov test for normality.

The steps in this study were: a) application of both inventories to the 52 teachers considered as the study sample; b) organization of the data collected in a data matrix; c) preparation and interpretation of tables and graphs according to the objectives; d) testing the hypothesis through the ordinal logistic regression model of job performance.

The hypothesis testing was performed with the following ritual: 1) statistical hypothesis formulation; 2) test normality (Sample distribution); 3) determination of prediction (Endogenous variable: the probability of being explained); 4) model adjustment (Improve adjustment method); 5) goodness-of-fit application (Correlation discard); 6) pseudo R-squared (Percentage influence); 7) parameter estimation (Inverse influence); and, 8) testing for parallel line (Ordinal logistic regression model).

3 Results and Discussion

3.1 Results

In this research, the most significant results regarding the purposes and hypotheses are expressed in the following tables:

Table 1. Pseudo R-squared of the job performance model

Cox and Snell*	,767
Nagelkerke*	,883
McFadden*	,717

Note. * Logit link function. Developed by Cristina Isabel Chumpitazi Torres

In Table 1, the R2 values obtained are significant or respectable for the variability explained by the job performance model (> 0.7). Likewise, Nagelkerke estimates an 88.3% influence of Burnout Syndrome.

Table 2. Pseudo R-squared of the academic preparation model

Cox and Snell*	,682
Nagelkerke*	,787
McFadden*	,569

Note. * Logit link function. Developed by Cristina Isabel Chumpitazi Torres

In Table 2, the R2 values obtained are significant or respectable for the variability explained by the academic preparation model (> 0.7). Likewise, Nagelkerke estimates a 78.7% influence of Burnout Syndrome.

Table 3. Pseudo R-squared of the teaching skills model

Cox and Snell*	,697
Nagelkerke*	,806
McFadden*	,596

Note. * Logit link function. Developed By Cristina Isabel Chumpitazi Torres

In Table 3, the R2 values obtained are significant or respectable for the variability explained by the teaching skills model (> 0.7). Likewise, Nagelkerke estimates an 83.5% influence of Burnout Syndrome.

Table 4. Pseudo R-squared of the teacher-student relationship model.

Cox and Snell*	,676
Nagelkerke*	,785
McFadden*	,572

Note. * Logit link function. Developed by Cristina Isabel Chumpitazi Torres

In Table 4, the R2 values obtained are significant or respectable for the variability explained by the teacher-student relationship model (> 0.7). Likewise, Nagelkerke estimates an 80.6% influence of Burnout Syndrome.

Table 5. Pseudo R-squared of the pedagogical norms model

Cox and Snell*	,721
Nagelkerke*	,835
McFadden*	,641

In Table 5, the R2 values obtained are significant or respectable for the variability explained by the pedagogical norms model (> 0.7). Likewise, Nagelkerke estimates a 78.5% influence of Burnout syndrome.

3.2 Discussion

After performing an exhaustive analysis of the data collected on Burnout Syndrome and job performance, in the inventory of (Leiter and Maslach, 2004) and the teacher referential inventory, adapted by Chumpitazi (2019), an inverse influence was detected between Burnout Syndrome and job performance, extending to the dimensions of variable 2, endogenous or criterion, which shows significant influences in each of them, in teachers of the Instituto de Educación Superior Pedagógico Público Indoamérica.

This research is framed within a quantitative approach, as it assesses Burnout Syndrome and job performance in frequency ranges, organized in ordinal scales, which were collected in valid and reliable inventories, i. e., adapted, under the requirement of statistical quality controls (Garcia, 2017).

On the other hand, a criterion to be taken into account, when cited as background, in future studies, is to examine that this is a study sample with a non-normal distribution. In this context, conclusions will be extended to the population and the corresponding background.

A significant result consisted in confirming the inverse influence of Burnout Syndrome on the job performance of the surveyed teachers, expressed in the final adjustment model (Sig. = 0.000); where it is evident that the Job Performance model with the exogenous variable Burnout Syndrome improves the adjustment method. Likewise, it is evident that Burnout Syndrome has an inverse influence on the dimensions of Job Performance. Thus, the finding of the inverse influence of Burnout Syndrome on the Academic Preparation dimension was recorded in the final adjustment model (Sig. = 0.000); Burnout Syndrome on the Teaching Skills dimension, recorded in the final adjustment model (Sig. = 0.000); Burnout Syndrome on the Teacher-Student Relationship dimension, recorded in the final adjustment model (Sig. = 0.000); and, Burnout Syndrome on the Pedagogical Norms dimension, recorded on the final adjustment model (Sig. = 0.000).

The strongest inverse influence between Burnout Syndrome and Job Performance reaches an estimated R2 of Nagelkerke (,883). This would imply that the exogenous variable, Burnout Syndrome, used in the regression model only explains 88.3% of Job Performance. This finding is similar to that found by Rivera, Segarra, and Giler (2018), in Ecuador, where the length of service of teachers is directly proportional to Burnout Syndrome; however, it is inverse to their job performance. Likewise, it happened with Hernandez (2018), where competences and self-efficacy beliefs were considered predictors of Burnout Syndrome, matching with the reflection of an inverse influence.

The findings of Al-Asadi, Khakaf, Al-Waaly, Abed, and Shami (2018) in Iraq, where emotional exhaustion is inversely proportional to age, length of service, and self-efficacy in teachers, whose difference is highly significant ($p < .001$), only corroborates the study results: the higher the level of Burnout, the lower the job performance and vice versa. Nagelkerke estimates an 88.3% influence of Burnout Syndrome. Likewise, a second study, carried out by Rodriguez and Sanchez (2018), ratify a tendency to an inversely proportional influence between Burnout Syndrome and Job performance, as evidenced by the significant difference in the Chi-square between Burnout and Job performance (.041).

Likewise, these results are corroborated by Gonzalez and Guevara (2018) in the La Libertad Region, specifically among teachers and workers of the Universidad Privada del Norte (UPN) [Northern Private University], in which 41.9% of the teaching and administrative staff were observed to have always complied with their job performance despite 22.6% of them had stress, with a high correlation of 0.751 and a significant level of 0.000, lower than the significance level ($a = 0.05$).

The three previous events can be explained, despite referring to different geographical locations and cultural contexts, if they are perceived on the basis of the Theory of Job Demands and Resources of Demerouti, Bakker, Nacreiner, and Schaufeli (2001). The first assumption argues that environments and professions offer particular demands and resources, which require sustained efforts and psychological and physiological costs. In this framework, job demands cannot be negative; however, the worker is not recovered and suffers the impairment of job stress. Obviously, the results reflect an inverse influence between Burnout Syndrome and Job Performance.

Finally, the p-value results are less than,05 (p-value <,05); (,003 <,05). Consequently, the null hypothesis is rejected, indicating that the ordinal procedure and inversely proportional influence are correct because the equality of slopes is not accepted (Table 37).

4 Conclusion

Burnout Syndrome inversely influences the job performance of teachers of the IESPP Indoamerica, Trujillo 2019, in 88.3% (Table 1, Pseudo R-squared, Nagelkerke (,883)).

Burnout syndrome inversely influences the Academic Preparation dimension of teachers of the IESPP Indoamerica, Trujillo 2019, in 78.7% (Table 2, Pseudo R-squared, Nagelkerke (,787)).

Burnout syndrome inversely influences the Teaching skills dimension of teachers of the IESPP Indoamerica, Trujillo 2019, in 83.5% (Table 3, Pseudo R-squared, Nagelkerke (,835)).

Burnout syndrome inversely influences the Teacher-Student Relationship dimension of teachers of the IESPP Indoamerica, Trujillo 2019, in 80.6% (Table 4, Pseudo R-squared, Nagelkerke (,806)).

Burnout syndrome inversely influences the Pedagogical Norms dimension of teachers of the IESPP Indoamerica, Trujillo 2019, in 78.5% (Table 5, Pseudo R-squared, Nagelkerke (,806)).

References

Al-Asadi, J., Khakaf, S., Al-Waaly, A., Abed, A., Shami, S.: Burnout among primary school teachers in Iraq: prevalence and risk factors. EMJH **24**(3), 262–268 (2018). https://pubmed.ncbi.nlm.nih.gov/29908021/

Arias, W.L., Jiménez, N.A.: Síndrome de burnout en docentes de Arequipa [burnout syndrome in teachers of Arequipa]. Educación **12**(42), 53–76 (2013)

Castillo, S.: Las XIV Jornadas de Medicina Legal. El Síndrome "Born out" o síndrome de agotamiento profesional [The XIV Conference on Forensic Medicine. The "Born out" syndrome or professional exhaustion syndrome]. [Content presentation]. San Joaquín de Flores. Heredia. Costa Rica (2000). https://www.scielo.sa.cr/scielo.php?script=sci_arttext&pid=S1409-001520 01000100004#:~:text=El%20s%C3%ADndrome%20de%20agotamiento%20profesional,3% 2DSentimiento%20de%20Realizaci%C3%B3n%20Personal

Chiavenato, I.: Administración de Recursos Humanos [Human Resources management]. Mc. Graw Hill, New York (2009)

Choy, R.: Bournot y Desempeño Laboral en Docentes Universitarios de una Carrera en una Universidad Privada de Lima [Burnout and job Performance in University Teachers of a Career in a Private University in Lima] [Master's thesis]. Universidad Cayetano Heredia, Lima (2017)

Demerouti, E., Bakker, A.B., Nachreiner, F., Schaufeli, W.B.L.: demanda laboral y los recursos del modelo del desgaste profesional [the job demands-resources model of burnout]. Psicología Appl. **86**(1), 499–512 (2001)

García, B.: Manual de Métodos de Investigación Para la Ciencias Sociales [Handbook of Research Methods for the Social Sciences]. Modern handbook (2017)

González, Y., Guevara, C.: Relación del estrés con el desempeño laboral en el personal docente y administrativo [Relationship Between Stress and Job Performance in Teaching and Administrative Staff] [Bachelor's thesis]. Universidad Privada del Norte, Cajamarca (2018)

Orué-Arias, E.: Inteligencia emocional y desempeño laboral de los trabajadores de una empresa peruana [Emotional intelligence and job performance of workers in a Peruvian company]. San Martín Emprendedor. **3**(1), 79–95 (2012)

Quiroz, C., Franco, D.: Relación entre formación docente y rendimiento académico de los estudiantes universitarios [Relationship between teacher training and academic performance of university students]. Educación **28**(55), 166–181 (2019). https://revistas.pucp.edu.pe/index.php/educacion/article/view/21358

Leiter, M.P., Maslach, C.: Áreas de la vida laboral: un enfoque estructurado para los factores predicitivos de agotamiento, organizacionales del trabajo [Areas of worklife: a structured approach to organizational predictors of job burnout]. Perrewe. **3**, 91–134 (2004)

Mas, O.: El profesor universitario: competencias y formación [The university professor: competences and training]. Curríc. formación prof. **5**(3), 195–211 (2011). https://www.ugr.es/~recfpro/rev153COL1.pdf

Mora, J., Mariscal, Z.: Correlación entre Satisfacción laboral y desempeño laboral [Correlation between job satisfaction and job performance] **7**(100), 1–11 (2019). https://dilemascontemporaneoseducacionpoliticayvalores.com/index.php/dilemas/article/view/1307/123

Moreno, T.: Evaluación docente en la universidad [Teacher evaluation at the university]. Reice **16**(3), 87–101 (2018). https://revistas.uam.es/reice/article/view/9715

Pinel, C., Pérez, M., Carrión, J.: Investigación sobre el burnout en docentes españoles: una revisión sobre factores asociados e instrumentos de evaluación [Researching burnout in Spanish teachers: a review of the associated factors and assessment instruments]. Bordón **71**(1), 115–131 (2019). https://recyt.fecyt.es/index.php/BORDON/article/view/62122

Rodríguez, J.A., Guevara, B., Viramontes, E.: Síndrome de burnout en docentes [Burnout syndrome in teachers] [Bachelor's thesis, Universidad Pedagógica Nacional del Estado de Chihuahua] (2017). http://www.scielo.org.mx/pdf/ierediech/v8n14/2448-8550-ierediech-8-14-45.pdf

Rodríguez, E., Sánchez, M.: Síndrome de Burnout y variables sociodemográficas en docentes de una universidad privada de Lima [Burnout syndrome and sociodemographic variables in teachers from a private university in Lima]. Revisa de investigación educativa **36**(2), 401–419 (2018). https://revistas.um.es/rie/article/view/282661

Rivera, A., Segarra, P., Giler, G.: Síndrome de Burnout en docentes de instituciones de educación superior [Burnout syndrome in teachers of higher education institutions]. Revista AVTF **37**(2), 78–84 (2018). http://saber.ucv.ve/ojs/index.php/rev_aavft/article/view/15169/144814481951-1-PB-pdf

Rodríguez, K., Lechuga, J.: Desempeño laboral de los docentes de la institución universitaria ITSA [Job performance of teachers at ITSA university institution]. EAN **87**, 79–101 (2019). http://www.scielo.org.co/scielo.php?script=sci_arttext&pid=S0120-81602019000200079

Tenorio, A.: Satisfacción de docentes frente a la evaluación de desempeño laboral [Satisfaction of teachers with job performance evaluation] [Master's thesis, Universidad Andina Simón Bolívar] (2017). https://repositorio.uasb.edu.ec/bitstream/10644/5698/1/T2338-MIE-Tenorio-Satisfacc ion.pdf

Zabalza, M.: Competencias Docentes del Profesor Universitario [Teaching Competencies of University Professors]. Calidad y desarrollo professional, Narcea (2003)

Zavaleta, M.: Satisfacción y desempeño laboral en la Unidad de Gestión Educativa Local La Esperanza de Trujillo [Job satisfaction and performance at the Unidad de Gestión Educativa Local La Esperanza de Trujillo (Local Education Management Unit La Esperanza de Trujillo)]. [Bachelor's thesis, Universidad César Vallejo] (2016). https://repositorio.ucv.edu.pe/bitstream/ handle/20.500.12692/463/zelada_jm.pdf?sequence=1&isAllowed=y

Importance of Organizational Culture in the Sustainability of Paperboard Companies in the Metropolitan District of Quito (DMQ)

Juanita García Aguilar[1]([⊠]), Miguel Montenegro Amaquiña[2], and Carlos Estrella Paredes[1,2,3]

[1] Universidad de las Fuerzas Armadas – ESPE, Sangolquí, Ecuador
{jcgarcia,cmestrella}@espe.edu.ec
[2] Instituto Gulich, CONAE-Universidad Nacional de Córdoba, Córdoba, Argentina
lmmontenegro@espe.edu.ec
[3] Geospatial Research Group, Universidad de las Fuerzas Armadas – ESPE, Sangolquí, Ecuador

Abstract. The objective of this current research is to determine the influence of organizational culture in the sustainability of companies in the cardboard sector of the Metropolitan District of Quito. The methodology used has a quantitative approach, it is also a non-experimental research of trans-sectional, descriptive, and correlational type. A total of 23 companies were analyzed, obtaining a total of 96 surveys. For the analysis of the study variables, the statistical techniques exploratory factor analysis and Pearson's correlation were used. The results show that the dominant culture in this group of companies is based on the clan organization. The sustainability actions are oriented to the social dimension and with respect to the relationship between the variables, the correlation coefficient − 0.143 with a significance level $p < 0.05$ shows statistically that there is a weak and non-significant negative correlation. Therefore, it is concluded that organizational culture is not an influential variable in sustainable development.

Keywords: Organizational culture · Sustainability · Factor analysis · SMEs

1 Introduction

Organizational culture should be considered as an integral part of the sociocultural system, which allows highlighting aspects of a society and how it influences people's behavior. Having said this, Léon (2001) points out that people within the organization share experiences, forms of expression and ideologies, allowing the creation of a sense of belonging. Garcia (2006) mentions that culture can be a guide of conduct, values practices and beliefs to which employees must adapt in order to model people's behavior at work.

Likewise, in terms of sustainability, it should be considered that there is no difference between the terms sustainable and supportable. This statement is made taking into consideration the Brundtland report (1987), which is the first official article on environment and development. This report established guidelines and long-term objectives

© The Author(s), under exclusive license to Springer Nature Switzerland AG 2023
M. Botto-Tobar et al. (Eds.): ICAT 2022, CCIS 1757, pp. 401–414, 2023.
https://doi.org/10.1007/978-3-031-24978-5_35

for the benefit of future generations. Finally, the Rio Declaration on Environment and Development established principles that are still accepted today. According to Achkar (2005), sustainability should be based on four interacting dimensions: physiological, social, economic, and political. However, United Nations (2001) proposes four dimen sions of sustainability: social, economic, environmental, and institutional.

In recent years, the paper and cardboard industry worldwide has shown a decline in consumption, due to different changes that have occurred, whether cultural, consumer, or technological. The latter being the most relevant, given by the emergence of electronic mail that largely eliminated the amount of physical letters. In addition, graphic pa per not only in the press, but also in editorial works has shown a decrease in sales. Finally, in relation to photographs and airline tickets, they have been replaced by applications for smart phones, devices that currently constitute a working and usage tool for people.

However, the growth in the use of the internet provides a new possibility for the paper and board industry. Even more so with the rise of e-commerce in emerging economies, which has led to an increase in the demand for inputs to package products. By 2030, according to Poyry Management Consulting, the demand for paper and board is estimated at 290 billion tons, with the largest consumers in Asia. It should be noted that a factor of social and business interest is the absence of pollution prevention policies, which is evidenced by the lack of integration between the production processes of companies and the environment. In addition to this, there is the scarce investment made by the business community in green technology, which is considered an unnecessary expense. In the same way, Mihelcic and Zimmerman (2012) point out that the lack of objectives focused on environmental care and the use of natural resources should not affect social conditions and people's health.

The objective of this current research is to determine the influence of organizational culture on the sustainability of companies in the cardboard sector of the Metropolitan District of Quito (MDQ).

Organizational Culture

For Schein (1988), culture is a model of basic assumptions discovered or developed by a group in the face of its problems in its external environment and internal integration. Therefore, the basic beliefs of the people within an organization are shared on a daily basis and the interaction among personnel involuntarily provokes attitudes that are reflected in the identity of each organization. Pfeffer (2000) adds that culture is a set of rules and means that shape the members of an organization. This differs from Schein (2010), who points out that the basic beliefs of people within an organization are shared daily. The interaction between personnel involuntarily provokes attitudes that are reflected in the identity of each organization.

Consequently, organizational culture makes it possible to establish differences between different organizations, even if they are in the same productive sector, tak-ing into consideration the daily interaction and the set of rules. Chiavenato (2010) adds that, in order to know an organization, the first thing to do is to identify its culture and how the staff assimilates this culture and, undoubtedly, how they put it into practice.

For the purpose of understanding the concept of organizational culture, Martin, Frost and O'Neill (2006) propose four approaches that bring together the different studies of organizational culture. The first approach is called integration, according to which a strong, imitable, desirable culture predominates in organizations and its implementation leads to business success. The second one is known as differentiation, and it basically points out that the clarity of cultures only exists within subcultures. The third is fragmentation or ambiguity and its salient aspects are lack of consistency, general agreement, and ambiguity. According to the fourth approach of interdependence or diversity, to understand the culture of organizations it is necessary to understand the culture of the context in which they run, since companies are not islands Garcia (2019). In this research, the integration approach will be used since it is necessary to determine the dominant culture of the sector.

In order to diagnose this variable, the Competent Values Framework Model (CVF) developed by Cameron and Quinn (2011) will be applied. This model considers two dimensions: the first is flexibility, discretion, and dynamism versus stability, order, and control; and the second one is internal orientation, integration, and unity versus external orientation, differentiation, and rivalry. By joining these two dimensions, they form four quadrants, each representing a cultural subdomain: adhocratic, clan, hierarchical, and market. The four cultural types can be defined based on six organizational factors, or traits, which typify the foundation of their culture Garcia (2019). These elements are: dominant characteristics, organizational leadership, cohesion factors, organizational environment, success criteria, and management style.

Sustainability
Calvente (2007) points out that sustainability is the ability to achieve economic prosperity over time as long as the natural system is protected, and it can provide a better quality of life for people. For Daly (1973), there are some conditions that guarantee the existence of the human race for a prolonged period of time. To which, Mooney (1993) adds that human actions should allow interaction with the environment over time. The theoretical foundation of sustainability is based on the Brundtland report, an official article on environment and development, in which some guidelines and long-term objectives were established for the benefit of future generations. Three theories that seek the development of productive activities without affecting the environment emerge from this tracking.

The first theory deals with Sustainable Development considered as a process of social and economic improvement considering the different stakeholders. Velázquez and Vargas (2012) mention that there must be economic, social, and environmental balance in order to develop sustainability strategies. For Larrouyet (2015), sustainable development requires promoting the modernization of business management by generating awareness in the management of natural, social, and human resources. The second one refers to environmental economics, which seeks to develop solutions to different environmental problems based on economic foundations. Rothman (1998), argues that in the early stages of economic development there is a greater environmental impact, and later on to reach a peak and gradually decrease. Considering that nascent organizations do not have the necessary resources to invest in environmentally friendly technology. The third one is related to Ecodevelopment, which promotes the application of preventive measures with the care of the environment. In this same approach, Maurice (2008), points out that it is more costly to correct damages than to prevent them, considering that resources are scarce and important for the development of industries. Sachs (1981) concludes that a company should seek a socially desirable, economically viable, and ecologically prudent development. In this research, the theoretical framework of sustainable development will be used as the basis of the model and instrument to be applied for the diagnosis of this variable.

The sustainable development model of Carro, Reyes, Rosano and Garnica (2017) consider four dimensions: social, economic, environmental, and institutional. The social dimension is focused on human resources management, occupational health and safety, and the corporate social responsibility. For the authors, this dimension is oriented to the search for development and personal benefit, as well as to provide a safe environment for the fulfillment of their activities. The environmental aspect is focused on the care of the environment, taking into account the entire production process, from the purchase of raw materials to the production of the finished product. Carro, Reyes, Rosano and Garnica (2017), state that pollution prevention is based on a good management of natural resources, which allows obtaining environmental-friendly products and processes that do not generate pollution throughout their life cycle. As for the economic element, the authors propose making technological investments to reduce the consumption of non-renewable energies and thus improve the environmental quality of the processes. It should be taken into consideration that this dimension not only seeks to obtain an economic gain, but also to give something back to society. Finally, the institutional dimension refers to the implementation of a sustainability-oriented culture in companies, established in their organizational philosophy.

In addition, a documentary review of the last ten years was carried out on the most significant research works on organizational culture, sustainability, and the relationship between the two variables, among which the following can be mentioned:

García (2019), in his study analyzed the influence of leadership on organizational culture among small and medium-sized companies in the manufacturing sector in the province of Pichincha. To this end, he used a mixed quantitative and qualitative methodology, of an exploratory, descriptive, and correlational, cross-sectional nature. Two surveys were applied to a sample of 234 companies, 150 small, and 84 medium-sized, and two focus groups were carried out with a sample of directors and middle managers of small and medium-sized companies. The statistical techniques used were Confirma tory Factor Analysis (CFA) and Structural Equation Modeling (SEM). The results of the research show that the predominant leadership style in SMEs is transformational, the type of organizational culture is clan and regarding the relationship between the variables at a significance level $p < 0.05$ (0.017) the correlation coefficient is -0.159, showing that there is a weak, but significant linear correlation.

The research by Carro, Reyes, Rosano and Garnica (2017), aimed at proposing a sustainable development model for the ceramic coating industry. The methodology used was qualitative, documentary, considering sustainability factors and previous instruments to determine a new instrument, which was applied to five companies in the sector. The results show that sustainable companies are those that carry out actions in the environmental, social, economic, and institutional dimensions.

Sarmiento, Rosano and Carro (2017), studied the influence of organizational culture on the sustainability of the ceramic industry in Mexico. For the diagnosis of culture, Denison's culture model was taken into consideration and for sustainability the authors' previous study. The results show that organizational culture influences the social and institutional dimensions, concluding that strategies must be developed and implemented in each one of the dimensions of the model.

2 Methods

The methodology used has a quantitative approach and it is non-experimental research of transectional, descriptive, and correlational type. A total of 23 companies were analyzed, obtaining a total of 96 surveys. The statistical techniques used for the analysis of the study variables were exploratory factor analysis and Pearson's correlation. For the organizational culture variable, the OCAI questionnaire of Cameron and Quinn (2011) was applied, which is made up of six dimensions, with four literals in each one corresponding to each cultural type. The respondent had to distribute a total of 100 points among the four types by giving a higher score to the one that most closely resembles to the organization's reality. To obtain the results, all the scores for each of the responses are added together and then divided by six. The highest score determines the dominant culture. It should be noted that the survey makes it possible to observe both the current and the desired situation.

The reliability of the instrument has been demonstrated by some studies, among which the one carried out by Quinn and Spreitzer (1991), in which 796 executives from 86 different public utilities companies participated and rated the type of culture of their organization. The results obtained according to Cronbach's alpha coefficient are: (0.74) for clan culture, (0.79) for adhocratic culture, (0.73) for hierarchical culture and (0.71) for market culture. Likewise, Yeung, Brockbank and Ulrich (1991), conducted a study of 10,300 executives from 1,064 companies; several of these organizations were on the Fortune list. The following coefficients were obtained: (0.79) for clan culture, (0.80) for adhocratic culture, (0.76) for hierarchical culture, and (0.77) for market culture.

Regarding sustainability, a survey was designed considering the model developed by (Carro, Reyes, Rosano and Garnica, 2017). The instrument has twenty-seven questions divided into four dimensions. To rate each of the items, the following Likert scale was used: Never (1); Sometimes (2); Occasionally (3); Almost always (4); Always (5). Being a new instrument, its respective validation was performed taking into account the methodology developed by Crespo, D'Ambrosio, Racines and Castillo (2016). According to this methodology, experts rate the following criteria on a scale of 1 to 3: representativeness, comprehension, interpretation, and clarity. The validation was carried out with ten experts previously selected according to the needs of the research. Among the criteria used to select the experts were: profession, level of knowledge, professional experience, and work experience in manufacturing companies. Each of the experts evaluated the content of the instrument, obtaining a score greater than or equal to 70% in each of the questions. Huh, Delorne and Reid (2006) point out that the reliability value in an investigation must be equal or greater than 60%, which is why the questions of the instrument are considered accepted.

Additionally, the Cronbach's Alpha statistic was analyzed, obtaining a value of 0.971, which indicates a strong reliability of the instrument for implementation in this research. The Excel tool was used to process the data of the organizational culture variable. In the case of sustainability, the SPSS statistical software and the multivariate factor analysis technique were used. The following hypotheses are proposed:

- **H1:** The type of organizational culture of companies in the MDQ cardboard sector is clan.
- **H2:** The sustainability actions of companies in the MDQ cardboard sector are oriented to the environmental dimension.
- **H3:** There is a strong and significant correlation between organizational culture and business sustainability in companies in the MDQ cardboard sector.

3 Results

Typology of the Organizational Culture of the MDQ'S Cardboard Sector
Using the methodology described above, the scores for each cultural type were obtained for the companies in the cardboard sector, which made it possible to construct an idea of the organizational culture, as conceived by the members of the companies at the time the information was collected (current situation). Figure 1 shows the dominant cultural orientation of the 23 companies.

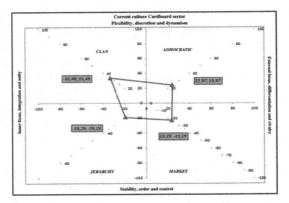

Fig. 1. Cultural orientation - current situation. Note: The graph represents the orientation culture situation. Source: Own elaboration

This dominant orientation is ratified with cultural strength, determined by the number of points awarded to a specific culture type (Cameron Quinn, 2006). The highest score obtained in one of the cultural types defines the dominant culture. Table 1 presents the results of the dominant culture, current situation.

In the current situation, it is evident that 69.57% of the companies in the Cardboard Sector of the MDQ (16) have key artifacts, values, and assumptions that are dominant in the clan culture. These companies are characterized by having a family atmosphere in which the participation and commitment of the collaborators stand out. Likewise, collaboration and teamwork prevail, which allows the achievement of objectives (Cameron Quinn, 2011). It is important to mention that this type of culture allows the development of a human work environment, being the main objective to enhance the skills of employees (Cameron Quinn, 2011).

Table 1. Dominant culture in the sector current situation

CLAN	ADHOCRATIC	JERARCHY	MARKET
16	2	4	1
69,57%	8,70%	17,39%	4,35%

Note: This table shows the dominant culture of the cardboard sector in the current situation determined by the concentration of companies in each quadrant. Source: Own elaboration

Four companies, representing 17.39%, consider it important to evolve to a hierarchical culture in order to have internal processes, structure, and formalization. 8.70% of companies (2) have an adhocratic type of culture, which is focused on innovation and development of new products or services, as well as strengthening the participation of employees in the organization, the main objective was adaptation (Cameron and Quinn 2011). In a smaller proportion 4.35%, have features of market culture, which establishes characteristics of competitiveness and productivity within its market segment; being the main characteristic the exchange with external stakeholders (Cameron and Quinn 2011). The same procedure was applied to determine the desired cultural orientation and strength, results are shown in Fig. 2 and Table 2.

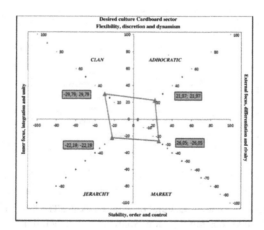

Fig. 2. Cultural orientation - current situation. Note: The graph represents the desired cultural orientation and situation. Source: Own elaboration

In the desired situation, 52.17% of the companies estimate that they will remain in the clan culture type. 21.74% are looking for a transition to the market culture, this would imply change processes, considering that the main characteristics of this type of culture are competitiveness and productivity (Cameron and Quinn 2011). Four companies representing 17.39% remain in the hierarchical culture. However, if companies intend to move to the market culture, they must operate under a structure of internal processes,

Table 2. Dominant culture in the sector desired situation

CLAN	ADHOCRATIC	JERARCHY	MERKET
12	2	4	5
52,17%	8,70%	17,39%	21,74%

Note: This table shows the dominant (desired) culture of the cardboard sector, determined by the concentration of companies in each quadrant. Source: Own elaboration.

procedures, formalization, and standardization. By considering these aspects, companies can develop management models based on four pillars: culture, strategy, execution, and structure, which will allow them to achieve a competitive advantage.

Finally, 8.70% of the companies wish to return to an adhocratic culture, which would encourage innovation, the development of new products and services, and creativity. The main objective of this type of culture is the adaptability of companies to changes that may occur in the environment (Cameron and Quinn 2011). Figure 3 shows the dominant culture in both the current and the desired situation, which makes it possible to identify the vectors of change that will give rise to the action plans to be implemented by cardboard companies.

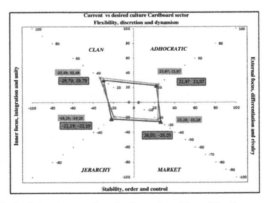

Fig. 3. Current vs. desired dominant cultural orientation. Note: The figure represents the cultural orientation of the current vs. desired situation. Source: Own elaboration

Sustainable Development in the Companies of the MDQ Cardboard Sector

The diagnosis of sustainability in cardboard companies was carried out using the exploratory factor analysis technique. For which its feasibility was measured by the KMO coefficient, Barlett, and total variance, the results of which are presented in Table 3

Table 3. KMO and BARtlett's test

Kaiser-Meyer-Olkin measure of sampling adequacy		,821
Bartlett's test for spheric-Ity	Aprox. Chi-square	266,361
	gl	6
	Sig.	0,000

Note: This table shows the KMO and Barlett test. Source: Prepared by the authors.

As for the KMO test, a value of 0.821 was obtained, indicating the feasibility of applying factor analysis. Bartlett's test of sphericity has a value of 266.361 and a degree of significance or p-value of 0.000, which is why it is assumed that the data can be treated using the factorial model. Subsequently, the number of components was determined, which in the case of the cardboard companies was one, which explains 79.40% of the total variance of the data. Using the Varimax method, whose objective is to minimize the number of variables in the model with high weights in each component, the rotated components matrix was calculated, which is shown in Table 4.

Table 4. Component Matrix

Component	
Dimensions	1
DIM2SOCI	,918
DIM3ECON	,888
DIM4AMBI	,887
DIM1INST	,871

Note: This table shows the component matrix main. Source: Own elaboration.

As shown in Table 4, the social dimension is the most important (0.918) followed by the economic dimension (0.888), then the environmental dimension (0.887) and finally the institutional dimension (0.871). These results are complemented by the descriptive analysis of each dimension, for which the percentages were obtained for each type of scale, grouping the scales into two groups: 1) always, almost always, and 2) never, rarely, occasionally; these are shown in Fig. 4.

Regarding the institutional dimension, it is observed that 59.97% (almost always and always) of the respondents indicate that the organizations foster a culture oriented to sustainability established both in the mission and vision, creating habits, values, and in turn integrating science for sustainable development within the organization. While 40.03% of the respondents mentioned that such activities are not encouraged within the organizations. Regarding the social dimension, 60.86% (almost always and always) of

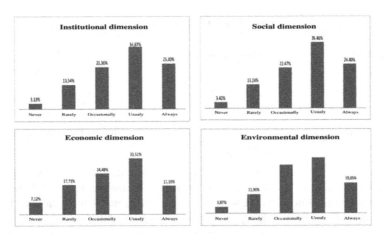

Fig. 4. Descriptive analysis by dimension. Note: The figure shows the frequency of each perception scale by dimension. Source: Own elaboration.

the respondents indicate that the companies have occupational health and safety policies, as well as corporate social responsibility actions. They seek personal development and benefit, providing a safe environment for the fulfillment of their activities. While 39.14% of the respondents mentioned that such actions are not guaranteed within the organizations.

As far the results obtained in the economic dimension, for 50.70% (almost always and always) of the respondents, the companies try to make technological investments to reduce the consumption of non-renewable energies and thus improve the environmental quality of the processes. They not only seek to obtain an economic gain, but also to give something back to society. Meanwhile, 49.30% of the respondents mentioned that there are no controls on these actions within the organization. Finally, in the environmental dimension, 53.87% (almost always and always) of the respondents indicate that the organizations carry out actions for the prevention of pollution from the procurement of raw materials, manufacturing process, and finally the product. In other words, they manage natural resources to obtain environmentally friendly products and processes. While 43.13% of the respondents mentioned that the commitment to environmental care is not promoted within the organizations.

Organizational Culture and Sustainability
The influence of organizational culture on sustainability was determined through Pearson's correlation coefficient. Table 5 shows the results obtained for the companies in the cardboard sector.

As shown in Table 5, in this case, the Pearson correlation index has a value of -0.143 with a significance level of $p < 0.05$. Statistically there is a weak and non-significant negative correlation between the study variables.

Table 5. Pearson correlation between organizational culture and sustainability

		Sustainability Index	Culture Index
Sustainability Index	Pearson correlation	1	− ,143
	Sig. (bilateral)		,516
	N	23	23
Index Culture	Pearson correlation	− ,143	1
	Sig. (bilateral)	,516	
	N	23	23

Note: This table shows the correlation between organizational culture and sustainability Source: Own elaboration

4 Discussion

With the purpose of corroborating the type of dominant culture (current/desired) in the cardboard companies, an analysis of cultural congruence was carried out. The results showed that there is indeed congruence, since in all the individual plots (dominant characteristics, organizational leadership, organizational climate, cohesion factors, success criteria, and management style), the clan culture is dominant. With the analysis of the information collected, the H1 is accepted, the dominant culture in the companies of the MDQ cardboard sector is clan; considering that 86.96% of the total are oriented to this type of culture. Since the cardboard sector belongs to the manufacturing industry, it is feasible to compare the results obtained with the findings of the study of leadership and culture conducted by Garcia (2019) in ISIC C SMEs, concluding that, indeed in manufacturing companies the clan culture predominates. By confirming this result, the clan culture profile for manufacturing companies can be constructed, which is shown in Table 6.

Regarding the second variable, the companies of the MDQ's cardboard sector are carrying out actions aimed at sustainability. The social dimension is the most important (0.918), followed by the economic dimension (0.888), then the environmental dimension (0.887) and finally the institutional dimension with a (0.871). Additionally, with the information obtained from the factor analysis, H2 is partially accepted: The sustainability actions of the companies in the MDQ cardboard sector are oriented to the environmental dimension. Considering that the dimension with the greatest participation in the model is the social dimension, the environmental dimension is placed in third place in the hierarchy of importance.

However, when analyzing the relationship between the two variables under study, based on Pearson's correlation coefficient, organizational culture is not an influential variable in sustainable development. This is since there are other factors such as technological, economic, strategic, and administrative factors that can directly influence sustainable development. Having said this and considering the p-value of Pearson's correlational analysis, the null hypothesis is rejected, and the alternative hypothesis is accepted. Although there is no correlation, organizational culture is one of the most

Table 6. Profile of the clan-type culture in manufacturing-cardboard companies

Type of culture	Dominant features	Organization al leadership	Cohesion factors	Organizatio nal climate	Success criteria	Manage ment style
Clan	- There is an affective and personal con-text	- The leader is considered as a mentor	-Promotes loyalty to the organization	- Establish a participatory environment	- Seeks the development of hu-man talent	- Promotes teamwor k
	- Establish a family atmosphere	- The leader is considered as a facilitator	-There is a high commitment of the workers with the organization	- It establishes trust between the parties.	- Has an interest in each of the collaborators	- Seek consensus with each of the parties
	- Share their own experiences	- The leader is considered a fatherfigure	-Promotes teamwork	- Establish a comfortable work environment	-Establish teamwork	-Proposes employee participatio n

Note: This table shows the profile of the clan type culture according to the 6 dimensions of organizational culture. Source: Own elaboration, based on (Cameron & Quinn, 2011).

important administrative variables in companies, since it constitutes their DNA, character, and personality. From its heart, which constitutes the values or objectives of superior order, the organizational philosophy, the management model, and the operability of the companies unfold. Therefore, it is the mainstay and cornerstone from which all strategies aimed at ensuring sustainability and sustainability can be deployed.

5   Conclusions

The dominant type of culture in the companies of the cardboard sector is clan. Therefore, the more elements that guide the behavior of the members are identified by the personnel of this group of companies, at each of the levels of appreciation of the culture, the more vigorous is the dominant culture in these organizations.

In the companies of the MDQ cardboard sector, the dominant clan culture is a constant of the actual (current) and desired culture. The identification of the actual and desired culture showed a high coincidence; therefore, the congruence between the two is greater. Given this congruence, there will be greater resistance to change towards the hierarchical and market culture.

Companies in the cardboard sector wish to maintain the profile of the clan culture; however, there is a slight tendency to formalize and structure themselves (hierarchical culture), as well as to increase their competitive position (market culture). To achieve this, they must first establish, within the framework of a hierarchical culture, principles of daily action, such as: efficiency, predictability, control, quality is the cornerstone, continuous improvement, mastery of tasks. Therefore, the operating theory that drives the success of the organization is that control promotes efficiency and consequently effectiveness.

The companies in the cardboard sector have carried out actions aimed at corporate sustainability, emphasizing the social dimension. These companies have occupational health and safety policies, as well as corporate social responsibility actions. They seek personal development and benefit, providing a safe environment for the performance of their activities. However, it is necessary for this group of companies to invest in green technology by making appropriate use of natural resources and improving value chain processes. As a result, they could market environmental-friendly products.

Organizational culture and corporate sustainability are independent variables. This means that the dominant culture (clan) does not influence the sustainability actions of companies in the cardboard sector.

References

Achkar, M.: Indicadores de sustentabilidad. Ordenamiento ambiental del territorio. DIRAC Facultad de ciencias, Montevideo (2005)

Brundtland, G.: Informe de la Comisión Mundial sobre el Medio Ambiente y el Desarrollo. Naciones Unidas, Oslo (1987)

Cameron, K., Quinn, R.: Diagnosing and Changing Organizational Culture: Based on the Competing Values Framework. Wiley, San Francisco (2011)

Carro, J., Reyes, B., Rosano, G., Garnica, J.: Modelo de desarrollo sustentable para la industria de recubrimientos cerámicos. Revista Internacional de Contaminación Ambiental **33**(1), 131–139 (2017)

Chiavenato, I.: Innovaciones de la administración. Tendencias y estrategias, los nuevos paradigmas. México DF: McGraw-Hill (2010)

Crespo, A., D'Ambrosio, G., Racines, A., Castillo, L.: Cómo medir la percepción de la responsabilidad social empresarial en la industria de gaseosas. Yura: Relaciones internacionales **8**, 1–18 (2016)

Crozier, M.: El fenómeno burocrático 1 : ensayo sobre las tendencias burocráticas de los sistemas de organización modernos y sus relaciones con el sistema social y cultural. Buenos Aires: Amorrortu (1969)

Rovenský, J., Payer, J., Herold, M.: W. In: Rovenský, J., Payer, J., Herold, M. (eds.) Dictionary of Rheumatology, pp. 347–348. Springer, Cham (2016). https://doi.org/10.1007/978-3-319-21335-4_23

García Aguilar, J.D.: Influencia del liderazgo en la cultura organizacional. Estudio comparativo en pequeñas y medianas empresas de pichincha (ecuador). Quito, Pichincha, Ecuador (16 de Diciembre de 2019)

García, C.: Una aproximación al concepto de cultura organizacional. Universitas Psychologica **5**(1), 163–174 (2006)

García, L., Hernández, R., Vargas, B., Cuevas, H.: Diagnóstico de la cultura organizacional en universidades tecnológicas bajo el Modelo de Valores en Competencia. Estudios en Ciencias Sociales y Administración de la Universidad de Celaya, **2**, 9–29 (2012)

García, M., Hernade, R., Vargas, B., Cuevas, H.: Diagnóstico de la cultura organizacional en universidades tecnológicas bajo el Modelo de Valores en Competencia. Estudios en Ciencias Sociales y Administrativas de la Universidad de Celaya **2**, 9–29 (2012)

Hernández, R., Fernández, C., Batista, P. (2014). Metodología de la investigación. México D.F.: McGraw-Hill

Hofstede, G.: Culturas y Organizaciones. El Software Mental. Alianza, Madrid (1999)

Kotter, J., Heskett, J.: Cultura de empresa y rentabilidad. Díaz de Santos S.A, Madrid (1995)

Larrouyet, M.: Desarrollo sustentable: origen, evolución y su implementación para el cuidado del planeta. RIDAA (2015)

Maurice, S.: Teoría del desarrollo. Ecovida (2008)

Pfeffer, J.: Nuevos rumbos en la teoría de la organización: problemas y posibilidades. Oxford University Press, México (2000)

Sachs, I.: Ecodesarrollo: concepto, aplicación, beneficios y riesgos. Agricultura y sociedad **18**, 9–32 (1981)

Sarmiento, S., Rosano, G., Carro, J.: La cultura organizacional y su influencia en la sustentabilidad empresarial. La importancia de la cultura en la sustentabilidad empresarial. Estudios Gerenciales **33**(145), 352–365 (2017)

Schein, E. (1988). La cultura empresarial y el liderazgo: una visión dinámica. Barcelona: Plaza y Janés

Schein, E.: Organizational Culture and Leadership, 4 th edn. Wiley, San Francisco (2010)

United Nations. Indicators of sustainable development: Framework and Methodologies. Obtenido de http://www.un.org/esa/sustdev/csd/csd/9_indi_bp3.pdf (15 de 10 de 2001)

Weick, K.: Psicología social del proceso de organización. México: Fondo Educativo Interamericano (1982)

Author Index

Printed in the United States
by Baker & Taylor Publisher Services